HERMENEUTISCHE UNTERSUCHUNGEN ZUR THEOLOGIE

Herausgegeben von

HANS DIETER BETZ · PIERRE BÜHLER
DIETZ LANGE · WALTER MOSTERT

32

The Manumission of Slaves
in Early Christianity

by

J. Albert Harrill

J. C. B. Mohr (Paul Siebeck) Tübingen

306.3620937
H297 m
1995

Die Deutsche Bibliothek – CIP-Einheitsaufnahme

Harrill, James Albert:
The manumission of slaves in early Christianity / by J. Albert Harrill. –
Tübingen: Mohr, 1995
   (Hermeneutische Untersuchungen zur Theologie; 32)
   ISBN 3-16-146285-8
NE: GT

© 1995 by J. C. B. Mohr (Paul Siebeck), P.O. Box 2040, D-72010 Tübingen

The book was typeset by Martin Fischer in Tübingen using Bembo typeface, printed by Gulde-Druck in Tübingen on acid free paper from Papierfabrik Buhl and bound by Heinr. Koch in Tübingen.

ISSN 0440-7180

James A. Harrill Jr.
Marie Cardwell Harrill

† James A. Harrill, M.D.

Not until this last separation, dear reader, had I touched those profounder depths of desolation, which it is the lot of slaves often to reach. I was solitary and alone within the walls of a stone prison, left to a fate of lifelong misery. I had hoped and expected much, for months before, but my hopes and expectations were now withered and blasted. ... The possibility of ever becoming anything but an abject slave, a mere machine in the hands of an owner, had now fled, and it seemed to me it had fled forever. A life of living death ... seemed to be my doom.

Frederick Douglass

Acknowledgements

This book is a revision of my doctoral dissertation at the University of Chicago. I would like to thank the editors of Hermeneutische Untersuchungen zur Theologie for accepting the work into this monograph series; Hans Dieter Betz, Adela Yarbro Collins, Arthur J. Droge, and Richard P. Saller for their invaluable guidance as my teachers; Elizabeth Asmis, Margaret M. Mitchell, and Carolyn Osiek for commenting on the work in whole or in part; and David Brakke for reading the entire manuscript several times and for being a dear friend. Portions of this work were delivered at the Society of Biblical Literature, the North American Patristics Society, and the Chicago Society of Biblical Research; the participants gave helpful responses. Creighton University generously provided funds for the final editing process, and Matt Jackson-McCabe helped to correct the page proofs. However, the remaining errors are my own. Additional thanks go to the publisher, Georg Siebeck, and his staff at J. C. B. Mohr (Paul Siebeck) for the book's fine production.

A portion of chapter 2 will appear as "Paul and Slavery: The Problem of 1 Cor 7:21," *Biblical Research* 39 (1994): in press; copyright 1994 by the Chicago Society of Biblical Research. Chapter 4 was first published as "Ignatius, *Ad Polycarp.* 4.3 and the Corporate Manumission of Christian Slaves," in the *Journal of Early Christian Studies* 1.2 (1993): 107–42; copyright 1993 by the Johns Hopkins University Press. Both are reprinted in revised versions with permission.

I dedicate this monograph to my family; first, to my parents, whose loving patience saw me through the many (and I am sure for them, seemingly endless) years of undergraduate and graduate education; and second, to my grandfather, who was Professor and Head of the Section of Otolaryngology at Wake Forest University's Bowman Gray School of Medicine, where he was appointed an original member of its faculty and its first Chief of Otolaryngology, serving in that position from 1941 to 1979 and as professor emeritus until his death in 1982. May his memory as a great physician, teacher, and scholar be honored by this book.

Chicago and Omaha, July 1994   J. Albert Harrill

Contents

Abbreviations

This monograph generally follows the abbreviations for periodicals, reference works, serials, and Jewish and early Christian literature listed in "Instructions for Contributors," *Journal of Biblical Literature* 107 (1988): 579–96; Everett Ferguson, ed., *Encyclopedia of Early Christianity* (New York: Garland Publishing, 1990), ix–xii; and *L'Année philologique*. References to classical and patristic literature follow the abbreviations listed in N. G. L. Hammond and H. H. Scullard, eds., *The Oxford Classical Dictionary*, 2d ed. (1970; reprint, Oxford: Clarendon Press, 1991), ix–xxii; Henry George Liddell and Robert Scott, *A Greek-English Lexicon*, rev. Henry Stuart Jones with a supplement (1968; reprint, Oxford: Clarendon Press, 1990), xvi–xlv; P. G. W. Glare, *Oxford Latin Dictionary*, combined edition (1982; reprint, Oxford: Clarendon Press, 1988), ix–xxi; G. W. H. Lampe, *A Patristic Greek Lexicon* (Oxford: Clarendon Press, 1961), 1: ix–xlvii; and Albert Blaise and Henri Chirat, *Dictionnaire latin-française des auteurs chrétiens* (Paris: Librairie des Méridiens, 1954), 9–29. In the notes, critical editions of ancient texts have been cited in parentheses, usually by abbreviation followed directly by volume, page/column, and/or line numbers.

AAWM	Abhandlungen der Akademie der Wissenschaften in Mainz, Geistes- und sozialwissenschaftliche Klasse
AB	Anchor Bible
ABD	*Anchor Bible Dictionary*, ed. David Noel Freedman, 6 vols. (New York, 1992)
ABSA	*Annual of the British School at Athens*
ACNT	Augsburg Commentary on the New Testament
ACW	Ancient Christian Writers
AGR	Akten der Gesellschaft für griechische und hellenistische Rechtsgeschichte
AHR	*American Historical Review*
AJA	*American Journal of Archaeology*
AJP	*American Journal of Philology*
AncSoc	*Ancient Society*
ANF	*The Ante-Nicene Fathers*, ed. Alexander Roberts and James Donaldson, 10 vols. (Edinburgh, 1885–97)
ANRW	*Aufstieg und Niedergang der römischen Welt*, ed. Hildegard Temporini and Wolfgang Haase (Berlin, 1972–)
APF	*Archiv für Papyrusforschung und verwandte Gebiete*
ArchClass	*Archeologia Classica*
Arctos	*Arctos: Acta philologica Fennica*
Athenaeum	*Athenaeum: Studi di Letteratura e Storia dell'Antichità*

b.	*The Babylonian Talmud*
BAGD	W. Bauer, *A Greek-English Lexicon of the New Testament and Other Early Christian Literature*, 2d ed., rev. W. F. Arndt, F. W. Gingrich, and F. W. Danker (Chicago, 1979)
BASP	*Bulletin of the American Society of Papyrologists*
B.C.E.	before the common era (equivalent to B.C.)
BIBR	*Bulletin de l'Institut historique belge de Rome*
BJS	Brown Judaic Studies
BZ	*Biblische Zeitschrift*
CAH	*The Cambridge Ancient History* (Cambridge, 1970–)
CBQ	*Catholic Biblical Quarterly*
CCSL	Corpus Christianorum, Series Latina
C.E.	of the common era (equivalent to A.D.)
CII	*Corpus Inscriptionum Iudaicarum*, ed. J.-B. Frey: vol. 1 (Europe), corr. reprint with prolegomenon by Baruch Lifshitz (1936; New York, 1975)
CIL	*Corpus Inscriptionum Latinarum* (Berlin, 1862–)
CIRB	*Corpus Inscriptionum Regni Bosporani* (Moscow & Leningrad, 1965)
CJ	*The Classical Journal*
ClAnt	*Classical Antiquity*
C & M	*Classica et Mediaevalia*
CMG	Corpus medicorum Graecorum (Leipzig, 1908–)
CNT	Commentaire du Nouveau Testament
Cod. Theod.	*Codex Theodosianus*
ConBNT	Coniectanea biblica, New Testament
Const. App.	*Apostolic Constitutions* (*Constitutiones apostolorum*)
CP	*Classical Philology*
CPJ	*Corpus papyrorum Judaicarum*, ed. Victor A. Tcherikover et al., 3 vols. (Jerusalem, 1957–64)
CQ	*Classical Quarterly*
CR	*Classical Review*
CRDAC	*Centro ricerche e documentazione sull'antichità classica*
CRINT	Compendia rerum iudaicarum ad novum testamentum
CSCO	Corpus scriptorum christianorum orientalium
CSEL	Corpus scriptorum ecclesiasticorum latinorum
CSSH	*Comparative Studies in Society and History*
DGE	*Dialectorum Graecarum exempla epigraphica potiora*, ed. E. Schwyzer (Leipzig, 1923)
Didasc. Ap.	*Didascalia apostolorum*
Digest	*The Digest of Justinian* (*Digesta Iustiniani*)
DR	*Downside Review*
Ebib	Études bibliques
EKKNT	Evangelisch-katholischer Kommentar zum Neuen Testament
EMC	*Échos du Monde classique. Classical Views*
EvK	*Evangelische Kommentare*
EvT	*Evangelische Theologie*
F	Fragmentum
fasc.	fascicle
FB	Forschung zur Bibel

FGH	*Die Fragmente der griechischen Historiker*, ed. F. Jacoby (Berlin & Leiden, 1923–)
FRLANT	Forschungen zur Religion und Literatur des Alten und Neuen Testaments
Gaius, *Inst.*	*The Institutes of Gaius*, trans. W. M. Gordon and O. F. Robinson (Ithaca, 1988)
GCS	Die griechischen christlichen Schriftsteller
GDI	*Sammlung der griechischen Dialekt-Inschriften*, ed. H. Collitz et al. (Göttingen, 1884–1915)
Gnomon	*Gnomon: Kritische Zeitschrift für die gesamte klassische Altertumswissenschaft*
GNS	Good News Studies
Goodspeed	Edgar Johnson Goodspeed, *Die ältesten Apologeten* (1914; reprint, Göttingen, 1984)
G & R	*Greece and Rome*
GRBS	*Greek, Roman, and Byzantine Studies*
GTA	Göttinger theologische Arbeiten
HDR	Harvard Dissertations in Religion
Hermeneia	Hermeneia: A Critical and Historical Commentary on the Bible
Historia	*Historia: Revue d'histoire ancienne*
HNT	Handbuch zum Neuen Testament
HR	*History of Religions*
HTKNT	Herders theologischer Kommentar zum Neuen Testament
HTR	*Harvard Theological Review*
HUTh	Hermeneutische Untersuchungen zur Theologie
HZ	*Historische Zeitschrift*
ICC	International Critical Commentary
IG	*Inscriptiones Graecae* (Berlin, 1873–)
ILS	*Inscriptiones Latinae Selectae*, ed. H. Dessau (Berlin, 1892–1916)
Inst.	*Justinian's Institutes*, trans. with an introd. by Peter Birks and Grant McLeod (Ithaca, 1987)
JAC	*Jahrbuch für Antike und Christentum*
JBL	*Journal of Biblical Literature*
JDS	Judean Desert Studies
JEH	*Journal of Ecclesiastical History*
JES	*Journal of Ecumenical Studies*
JHS	*Journal of Hellenic Studies*
JJP	*Journal of Juristic [Juridical] Papyrology*
JJS	*Journal of Jewish Studies*
JNES	*Journal of Near Eastern Studies*
JQR	*Jewish Quarterly Review*
JR	*Journal of Religion*
JRH	*Journal of Religious History*
JRS	*Journal of Roman Studies*
JSJ	*Journal for the Study of Judaism in the Persian, Hellenistic and Roman Period*
JSNTSup	Journal for the Study of the New Testament-Supplement Series
JSS	*Journal of Semitic Studies*
JTS	*Journal of Theological Studies*
Just. C.	*The Code of Justinian (Codex Iustinianus)*

JWG	_Jahrbuch für Wirtschaftsgeschichte_
LB	R. A. Lipsius and M. Bonnet, eds., _Acta Apostolorum Apocrypha_, 2 vols. (Leipzig, 1891, 1903)
LCL	Loeb Classical Library (Cambridge, Mass., 1912–)
Lieberman	Saul Lieberman, ed., _Tosefta_, 2d ed. (Jerusalem, 1992–)
LSJ	Henry George Liddell and Robert Scott, _A Greek-English Lexicon_, rev. Henry Stuart Jones (Oxford, 1968)
LXX	Septuagint
_m._	_The Mishnah_
MBAH	_Münsterische Beiträge zur antiken Handelsgeschichte_
MEFRA	_Mélanges d'Archéologie et d'Histoire de l'École Française de Rome, Antiquité_
MeyerK	H. A. W. Meyer, _Kritische-exegetischer Kommentar über das Neue Testament_
MS(S)	manuscript(s)
Musurillo	H. Musurillo, ed. and trans., _The Acts of the Christian Martyrs_ (Oxford, 1972)
NAWG	_Nachrichten der Akademie der Wissenschaften in Göttingen_
NCB	New Century Bible
NICNT	New International Commentary on the New Testament
NovTSup	Novum Testamentum, Supplements
NRSV	New Revised Standard Version Bible
NTD	Das Neue Testament Deutsche
NTS	_New Testament Studies_
NTTS	New Testament Tools and Studies
OCD	_Oxford Classical Dictionary_, 2d ed. (Oxford, 1970)
OECS	Oxford Early Christian Studies
OECT	Oxford Early Christian Texts
OGI	_Orientis Graeci Inscriptiones Selectae_, ed. W. Dittenberger (Leipzig, 1903–5)
1QS	_Serek hayyaḥad (Rule of the Community, Manual of Discipline)_
PBSR	_Papers of the British School at Rome_
PCPhS	_Proceedings of the Cambridge Philological Society_
_PG_	_Patrologia Graeca_, ed. J.-P. Migne
_PL_	_Patrologia Latina_, ed. J.-P. Migne
P. Oxy.	_Oxyrhynchus Papyri_, ed. B. P. Grenfell and A. S. Hunt (London, 1898–)
_P & P_	_Past and Present: A Journal of Historical Studies_
PW	A. Pauly and G. Wissowa, eds., _Real-Encyclopädie der classischen Altertumswissenschaft_
PWSup	Supplement to PW
QUCC	_Quaderni Urbinati di Cultura classica_
RAC	_Reallexikon für Antike und Christentum_
_RB_	_Revue biblique_
_RD_	_Revue historique de droit française et étranger_
REG	_Revue des études grecques_
RIDA	_Revue internationale des droits de l'antiquité_
RSA	_Rivista storica dell'Antichità_
RSV	Revised Standard Version Bible
SAQ	Sammlung ausgewählter kirchen- und dogmengeschichtlicher Quellenschriften
SBLDS	Society of Biblical Literature Dissertation Series

SBLMS	Society of Biblical Literature Monograph Series
SBLSP	*Society of Biblical Literature Seminar Papers*
SBLSBS	Society of Biblical Literature Sources for Biblical Study
SBS	Stuttgarter Bibelstudien
SC	Sources chrétiennes
SCO	*Studi Classici e Orientali*
ScEccl	*Sciences ecclésiastiques*
SCHNT	Studia ad corpus hellenisticum novi testamenti
SecCent	*The Second Century*
SEG	*Supplementum epigraphicum Graecum*, ed. J. J. E. Hondius (Leiden, 1923–)
SHAW	Sitzungsberichte der Heidelberger Akademie der Wissenschaften, Philos.-Hist. Klasse.
*SIG*³	*Sylloge inscriptionum Graecarum*, ed. W. Dittenberger, 3d ed. (Leipzig, 1915–24)
SJLA	Studies in Judaism in Late Antiquity
SNTSMS	Society for New Testament Studies Monograph Series
SPAW	*Sitzungsberichte der preussischen Akademie der Wissenschaften*
Stob.	*J. Stobaeus*, ed. C. Wachsmuth and O. Hense (1884–1912; reprint, Berlin, 1974)
Str-B	[H. Strack and] P. Billerbeck, *Kommentar zum Neuen Testament*, 4 vols. (Munich, 1926–28)
t.	*The Tosephta*
TAPA	*Transactions and Proceedings of the American Philological Association*
TAPhS	*Transactions of the American Philosophical Society*
TDNT	*Theological Dictionary of the New Testament*, ed. G. Kittel and G. Friedrich, English trans. G. W. Bromiley, 10 vols. (Grand Rapids, 1964–76)
TLG	*Thesaurus Linguae Graecae*
TLZ	*Theologische Literaturzeitung*
TQ	*Theologische Quartalschrift*
TRev	*Theologische Revue*
TU	Texte und Untersuchungen
UPZ	*Urkunden der Ptolemäerzeit:* I. *Papyri aus Unterägypten* (Berlin & Leipzig, 1922); II. *Papyri aus Oberägypten*, ed. U. Wilcken (Berlin & Leipzig, 1935–)
USQR	*Union Seminary Quarterly Review*
VC	*Vigiliae Christianae*
WD	*Wort und Dienst*
WS	*Wiener Studien: Zeitschrift für klassische Philologie und Patristik*
WUNT	Wissenschaftliche Untersuchungen zum Neuen Testament
YClS	*Yale Classical Studies*
ZNW	*Zeitschrift für die neutestamentliche Wissenschaft und die Kunde der älteren Kirche*
ZPE	*Zeitschrift für Papyrologie und Epigraphik*
ZRG	*Zeitschrift der Savigny-Stiftung für Rechtsgeschichte (romanistische Abteilung)*
ZTK	*Zeitschrift für Theologie und Kirche*
Zuck.	M. S. Zuckermandel, ed., *Tosephta*, 3d ed. (Jerusalem, 1970)

Introduction

Social History and Exegesis

"It is beautiful to die instead of being degraded as a slave" (*occidi est pulchrum, ignominiose ubi servias*).[1] So Publilius Syrus, a pantomimic performer who came to Rome in the first century B.C.E., is reported to have said. Publilius spoke from firsthand experience, for he was a slave who later earned manumission by his wit and dramatic talent. The apothegm reflects ancient conventional wisdom, or common sense, that slavery meant dishonor, humiliation worse than death. Ancient slaveholders regarded their slaves instrumentally, as breathing objects, equipment similar to utensils or "things," rather than as socially living beings. The personal reflection of an ancient slave on his progress through the slave system, from bondage to freedom, is quite rare. Such a firsthand account provides evidence for reconstructing how manumission operated in the ancient world. Like the appearance of a newborn baby, liberation from chattel servitude was a milestone, an occasion for public celebration and personal pride. The case of Publilius, whose dramatic ability as a Latinized mime caught the attention even of Julius Caesar, is an example of this controlled upward social mobility toward a new life, which a small yet significant number of liberated slaves enjoyed.[2] Early Christianity found its birth in this Greco-Roman slave culture that symbolized manumission with the language of "death" and "life."

Much current scholarship on Christian origins seeks to place early Christian groups in their proper social contexts. Since its goal is to provide a social description of earliest Christianity, this approach to the early Christian documents differs from other methodologies. In particular, interpretative approaches, or hermeneutics, based on historical theology – a kind of intellectual history – read the canonical texts purely for understanding the literary-philosophical development of the history of ideas. To be sure, such an approach has merits; yet it and other "history of ideas" approaches can isolate New Testa-

---

[1] Publilius Syrus, *Sententiae* 489.

[2] Macrobius, *Sat.* 2.79; *OCD*, q.v. "Publilius Syrus" and "Laberius, Decimus"; "Publilius II.B.1," *Der kleine Pauly: Lexikon der Antike* 4 (1972): 1239–40; J. Wight Duff and Arnold M. Duff, *Minor Latin Poets*, LCL (Cambridge: Harvard University Press, 1934), 3–12.

ment studies from other disciplines that seem likely to be relevant to the investigation of early Christianity, such as the historical study of the Roman Empire or the history of religions in the Greco-Roman era. From the perspective of a literary-philosophical hermeneutic, early Christian *people* disappear into early Christian *ideas.* As Wayne Meeks writes, "If we ask [New Testament scholars], 'What was it like to become and be an ordinary Christian in the first century?' we receive only vague and stammering replies."[3] But the other interpretive extreme can lead to similarly unsatisfactory results. For example, scholars investigating early Christianity from a purely sociological hermeneutic often do not aim to provide better readings of specific texts, but rather produce broad theoretical models, complete with grids and graphs that require their own exegetical decipherment. Our hermeneutical problem is how to direct social history, now enjoying something of an upsurge in interest, back to the interpretation of texts, the main function of the exegete. The present monograph attempts to contribute to this hermeneutical task.

The specific topic for this study is ancient slavery. It is the social institution that will be studied here, rather than the abstract philosophical concept of "enslavement," although philosophical understandings of what constitutes a slave do play an important role in my analysis. The texts selected for detailed exegesis are 1 Corinthians 7:21 and Ignatius, *Ad Polycarp.* 4.3, paired and analyzed here because they both treat the same topic: the manumission of Christian slaves in early congregations. Indeed, they constitute the first known pieces of Christian literature that address the liberation of slaves.

One might ask why other texts are not included, such as Paul's letter to Philemon.[4] To be sure, in Phlm 16 Paul directs Philemon to receive back his

---

[3] Wayne A. Meeks, *The First Urban Christians: The Social World of the Apostle Paul* (New Haven: Yale University Press, 1983), 2.

[4] The literature on this, the briefest of all Pauline letters, is extensive. John Knox, *Philemon among the Letters of Paul: A New View of Its Place and Importance,* rev. ed. (Nashville: Abingdon, 1959); Heinrich Greeven, "Prüfung der Thesen von J. Knox zum Philemonbrief," *TLZ* 79 (1954): 374–78; Ferdinand Hahn, "Paulus und der Sklave Onesimus: Ein beachtenswerter Kommentar zum Philemonbrief," *EvT* 37 (1977): 179–85; Peter Stuhlmacher, *Der Brief an Philemon,* 2d ed., EKKNT 18 (Zurich: Benzinger Verlag; Cologne: Neukirchener Verlag, 1981); Joachim Gnilka, *Der Philemonbrief,* HTKNT (Freiburg: Herder, 1982); Norman Petersen, *Rediscovering Paul: Paul and the Sociology of Paul's Narrative World* (Philadelphia: Fortress Press, 1985); Wolfgang Schenk, "Der Brief des Paulus an Philemon in der neueren Forschung (1945–1987)," *ANRW* 2.25.4 (1987): 3439–95; Sara C. Winter, "Paul's Letter to Philemon," *NTS* 33 (1987): 1–15; idem, "Methodological Observations on a New Interpretation of Paul's Letter to Philemon," *USQR* 39 (1984): 203–12; J. Duncan M. Derrett, "The Functions of the Epistle to Philemon," in *Studies in the New Testament,* vol. 5, *The Sea-Change of the Old Testament in the New* (Leiden: E. J. Brill, 1989), 196–224; John M. G. Barclay, "Paul, Philemon, and the Dilemma of Christian Slave-Ownership," *NTS* 37 (1991): 161–86; S. Scott Bartchy, "Philemon, Epistle to," *ABD* 5 (1992): 305–10.

newly converted slave Onesimus "no longer as a slave but more than a slave, a beloved brother – especially to me but how much more to you, both in the flesh and in the Lord." The prepositional phrase "in the flesh" (ἐν σαρκί) suggests perhaps (but not certainly) a request for the personal manumission of the Christian slave Onesimus. Yet the reference is extremely brief and imprecise, and one wonders what exactly is being described here. The prepositional phrase can be interpreted in many quite different ways, a manumission request being only one possibility. In the end, therefore, because the evidence in Phlm 16 proves too slim to support a positive conclusion on whether manumission is even at issue, I have decided to omit Paul's letter to Philemon from this discussion. But the hermeneutical investigations of the present work do not depend on this exclusion for their argument. If Philemon does in fact deal with manumission, my conclusions about how to relate social history to the interpretation of texts, exegetically based on 1 Corinthians 7:21 and Ignatius, *Ad Polycarp.* 4.3, are still valid, independent of Philemon.

Before examining the passages in detail, however, some clarification of terms is needed, and several overarching methodological concerns need to be addressed. Slavery is a good example of modern and ancient worldviews in collision. The modern interpreter approaches the study of these texts, and indeed of ancient slavery in general, from two main contexts. One context is modernity, to which the mind of the interpreter belongs. Here, the exegete ordinarily brings to the ancient text a thoroughly modern assumption that although the enslavement of (usually, other) peoples unfortunately has a long tradition in human history, it is, nonetheless, wrong. The second context is antiquity, to which the text belongs. There slavery existed as a fundamental given in daily life, and virtually nobody thought to question its morality. To be sure, some ancients considered slavery to be *contra naturam*, but as will become apparent from chapter 1, this did not mean that it was considered morally wrong. Although even the Roman jurists acknowledged that human enslavement was contrary to the law of nature (albeit in accord with the law of nations), they clearly presumed slavery to be legitimate, proper, and morally right. Because the two contexts, ancient and modern, are in conflict, modern interpreters often feel the need to exculpate slavery or downplay its significance in ancient life. We must avoid a kind of ethnocentrism that does not recognize the diversity of forms, attitudes, and circumstances surrounding human chattel bondage in ancient and modern times. It is both methodologically anachronistic and intellectually inappropriate to hold ancient people to modern standards of morality, although the modern person can and should reject certain features of ancient morality, including slavery.[5]

---

[5] M. I. Finley, *Ancient Slavery and Modern Ideology* (New York: Viking Press, 1980), 11–66.

A further confusion often arises between the *manumission* of slaves and the *emancipation* of slaves. "Manumission" means the formal and informal procedures and ceremonies performed by a master, legally recognized within a given society, to effect a slave's liberation. The freed slave then becomes a freedman/woman, who normally retains the social stigma of slavery and is still ranked in an order (*ordo*) below that of the freeborn population. "Emancipation" means the liberation of slaves done without the observance of any manumission procedures and regardless of the slaveholders' interests. The two terms will maintain these distinct meanings in this monograph. In ancient usage, a Roman householder "emancipated" (*emancipo*) a son or daughter from his *patria potestas*, but "manumitted" (*manumitto*) a slave. Ancient Christians neither emancipated slaves nor held abolitionist tendencies, but considered slavery a natural, integral part of human civilization, which was, as such, part of the fallen world. This view was not shared by non-Christian society, although some contemporary philosophical views regarded civilization as a condition of degenerated nature. At the same time, ancient Christians used slavery as a fundamental metaphor for the believer's proper relation to God.

A third term, "abolition," refers exclusively to the moral and political conviction (originating out of the Enlightenment) that slavery, both as an institution and an ideology, is repugnant to the aims of all civilized and just societies of human beings. When both Paul and Ignatius wrote, the reigning ideology of slavery was Roman, and the Romans manumitted – but did not emancipate – their urban slaves with a regularity unparalleled in the global history of slavery; they even granted most freedmen/women citizenship. This has led some biblical commentators to claim that ancient slavery was not that bad; the allegedly "humane" character of ancient slavery, then, explains why Paul did not become an abolitionist. However, the issue of manumission and its impact upon the institution and ideology of Roman slavery proves more complex. To understand the complexities behind these two pieces of early Christian literature on slavery, the interpreter must first clearly distinguish the modern and ancient contexts to understand how manumission operated in the Roman world. To be sure, no exegete can escape the intellectual influences of his or her age. Yet at the same time, he or she must take seriously the marked difference in worldview of the ancient author under study. Nowhere is it more important to clarify this difference than in the academic study of ancient slavery. Here social history can provide a means for keeping exegesis of a text in its ancient context and for keeping modern presuppositions in check.

A further clarification is required. One must distinguish between a sociology of antiquity and a social history of antiquity. Sociology (or the "social scientific" approach) and social history (or the "social historical" approach) are two distinct modes of interpretation that more often than not are collapsed as if one. The difference between the two is best understood by considering some history of their development.

"Sociological" study of early Christianity is nothing new. In the late 1890s the University of Chicago established the first graduate department of sociology in the United States, and around the same time faculty in the University's Divinity School began to read widely in this emerging field. In particular, Shirley Jackson Case and Shailer Mathews of the "Chicago School" found the new sociology useful in explaining early Christian social origins.[6] More recent American investigations into social questions began in the 1970s, when terms such as "social world" began to appear in New Testament book titles for the first time. The term "social world" reflected influence of the emerging fields of symbolic anthropology and "sociology of knowledge," particularly as developed by Peter L. Berger and Thomas Luckmann. Hermeneutically, it describes the social construction and maintenance of cognitive "worlds" within which persons make sense of the various institutions, structures, and patterns they encounter in day-to-day social interactions.[7] While some scholars see the value of talking about a person's "social world," others question the role that social scientific goals and methods ought to play in New Testament scholarship. Two distinct methods of incorporating social questions into exegesis have developed. Adherents of the "sociological" or "social scientific" approach seek to apply theoretical models, modes of analysis, and processes of explanation developed by social scientists to complement conventional historical and exegetical analyses of the Bible. Adherents of the opposing "social historical" approach object that the source material is too sparse to support use of sociological models and that such models, as mental constructs, are too modern to present a plausible explanation of the ancient data. Susan Garrett describes their scholarly position as follows: "In its most pointed form, the [social historical approach] refrains from using sociological methods, confining attention instead to more traditional historiographic questions about the social background and practices of the early Christians."[8] Cast in the language of this debate, my interpretive methodology is that of the social historical approach. By making explicit my own presuppositions, and so controlling them as much as possible, my hermeneutic aims not to impose abstractions on ancient texts, but to reconstruct as best we can the actual situations in which early Christians lived and the reality of their experiences, especially with chattel slavery.

---

[6] Shirley Jackson Case, *The Social Origins of Christianity* (Chicago: University of Chicago Press, 1923); Shailer Mathews, *Jesus on Social Institutions*, ed. Kenneth Cauthen, Lives of Jesus Series (1928; reprint, Philadelphia: Fortress Press, 1971).

[7] Peter L. Berger and Thomas Luckmann, *The Social Construction of Reality: A Treatise on the Sociology of Knowledge* (Garden City, N.Y.: Doubleday, 1966); Susan R. Garrett, "Sociology of Early Christianity," *ABD* 6 (1992): 90.

[8] Garrett, "Sociology," 90.

In this way, social history can guide interpretation of early Christian texts by suggesting more plausible social contexts against which to read the documents, and by removing false claims based on unexamined assumptions. Ignatius, *Ad Polycarp.* 4.3 and 1 Corinthians 7:21 are cases in point. One proposed social context found in the commentary literature for a phrase in Ignatius, "slaves of lust," is that liberated slaves often fell into economic destitution and were forced by their poverty to sell their bodies sexually. Social history can suggest a more plausible social context (I point to the patron-client system) against which to read the passage. Similarly, it is sometimes claimed that Paul, in 1 Corinthians 7, cannot be advising slaves on whether or not to accept manumission since slaves could not refuse an offer of manumission. Social history reveals that slaves in fact could refuse manumission, and thus suggests a more likely solution to the crux (I argue from philological and contextual grounds that Paul incorporated the Roman institutionalized exercise of urban manumission into his theology). In addition, many commentators have interpreted both of these passages in a negative sense: namely, that slaves must not expect their conversion to the Christian religion to result in their legal, social liberation from chattel slavery. In other words, Christian slaves must remain slaves. This monograph, however, argues that Paul's supposed negative exhortation on manumission is really positive, and that Ignatius's presumed ban is qualified and must be read as curtailing a specified kind of manumission, not prohibiting all kinds. While the two authors do share some common concerns, they should not be conflated as if they articulate identical messages. Paul and Ignatius do not reveal "normative" early Christian opposition against manumission as practiced in the Greco-Roman world. On the contrary, Paul and Ignatius reflect separate responses to their particular situations.

Social history must work with the actualities of people's lives. The approach of this study, therefore, is to look beyond purely juridical definitions of a slave. Unlike many standard discussions, this one does not analyze slavery solely in terms of legal property. Such a model based on law is inadequate for an investigation of the complex problems inherent in any ideology of control, since legal statutes often do not reflect social practice. Rather than describing what actually was, the laws typically reflected what ought to be, according to the ruling ideology of members of the leisured levels of society who were themselves large slaveholders. Social history, as history built from the ground up, ideally aims at recovering knowledge about those people pushed to the margins of society, those often overlooked by scholars writing the military, political, or intellectual history of antiquity. In the end, this analysis builds upon the efforts of cultural historians, historical sociologists, and modern ethicists to concentrate less on the stated rules and more on the actual modes of behavior in a given culture. The monograph is essentially a case study in the hermeneutics of early Christian literature, which has implications for the methodologies of exegesis. It deals with the problem of how to relate social history to the interpretation of texts.

The procedure is first to examine the social context of each passage under study (chapters 1 and 3), then to interpret each text within the social context established (chapters 2 and 4). The first chapter offers background material necessary for the detailed chapters that follow. The chapter specifies terms and deals with several fundamental issues: first, defining slavery and identifying a slave society; and second, evaluating the usefulness and limitations of comparing ancient and modern slaveries. The chapter outlines the kinds of primary sources available to the historian, highlighting their nature and difficulties. The chapter discusses labor in antiquity, concentrating upon the origins and sources of slaves. A consideration of the jobs that slaves held leads to the determination that, whatever their actual numbers, it is the position of slaves in particular economic and social structures that earns a society the designation "slave society." The chapter examines slaves within the context of the Greco-Roman family. Unlike slaves in modern societies, who invariably lived in quarters separated from the slaveowner's family, Roman urban domestic slaves regularly lived under the same roof with their master's family and were considered part of the *familia*. The last two sections of this chapter study the various forms of manumission and draw important conclusions regarding how manumission operated differently in the two contexts of classical Athens and classical Italy. The chapter ends by observing that very little research has been done on Jewish freedmen/women as an identifiable group in antiquity. As a first step, the chapter offers findings on the specific question of the social and economic position of Jewish freedmen/women in the city of Rome.

The second chapter investigates the philological and contextual problems of 1 Cor 7:21b. Generations of New Testament scholars have considered the ellipsis μᾶλλον χρῆσαι, which I translate as "use instead [freedom]," the *locus classicus* for assessing the Pauline position on slavery. The verse is not without difficulties. The knotty puzzle begins with how to read correctly the clause μᾶλλον χρῆσαι. Does Paul mean that slaves should use *slavery*? Or does he mean the opposite, that slaves should use *freedom*? The Greek is unclear. The ambiguity of this interpretive crux is notorious and has generated a long history of exegesis going back at least to John Chrysostom. Despite S. Scott Bartchy's attempt two decades ago to solve the crux, the problem remains today unresolved;[9] many scholars consider it insoluble. This chapter will offer a positive contribution toward a solution of the translation problem. The chapter collects seventeen texts, from authors such as Aretaeus, Ps.-Hippocrates, Aelius Theon, Vettius Valens, Galen, and Ps.-Herodianus, reflecting a wide

---

[9] S. Scott Bartchy, *ΜΑΛΛΟΝ ΧΡΗΣΑΙ: First-Century Slavery and the Interpretation of First Corinthians 7:21*, SBLDS 11 (1973; reprint, Atlanta: Scholars Press, 1985).

range of genres and periods in order to amass sources with which to compare and so to interpret the syntax of μᾶλλον χρῆσαι in 1 Cor 7:21. These texts demonstrate one major philological point. The force of the adverb μᾶλλον, when used with the deponent verb χράομαι, is normally adversative when opposition is implicit in the lexical environment. In sum, the texts used for syntactical comparison lend compelling support to the argument that in 1 Cor 7:21 Paul is contrasting two possible courses of action for Christian slaves facing two different situations. The μᾶλλον is adversative not with respect to its protasis (the premise: "if you can *indeed* become free"), but with respect to the previous apodosis (the answering clause: "do not worry about it").[10] Paul exhorts the slave facing this new situation to be concerned, and to take another option ("use *instead* [freedom]"). The result of this syntactical, philological study is that μᾶλλον + χράομαι grammatical constructions are to be considered adversative, unless strong contextual evidence supports the contrary. The exegete, therefore, confronts an accumulation of compelling arguments heavily favoring the "use freedom" side of interpretation.

While Paul addressed the individual slave who might receive a manumission offer, Ignatius wrote to a bishop on the propriety of using the church's shared funds for manumitting slaves. Thus, the third chapter studies the common chest as an institution in the classical world. After an initial discussion concerning terms relating to money deposit, coffers, and ancient banking, the chapter turns to the serious social meanings and functions of the community common chest, particularly its unitive function. The chapter studies the common fund in the various known Athenian and Hellenistic voluntary associations (*orgeōnes* and *thiasoi*). The chapter then discusses corporations in the Roman world, particularly the Roman *collegium*, and slaves both as members in and as property of *collegia*. The chapter concludes with an analysis of a recently discovered charter of a city in Roman Spain, which provides rare, detailed evidence of the specific procedures involved in municipal manumission, a model upon which corporate manumission was based. Greek and Roman voluntary associations, as corporate institutions, established a system of allegiance (on the administrative model of a municipality) that freed members from outside patronal ties. In this way, associations provided freedmen/women with alternative avenues of patronage outside the normal legal requirement of deference (*obsequium*) and work duties (*operae*) to their former masters.

The fourth chapter applies these findings to the advice given by Ignatius of Antioch to his fellow bishop, Polycarp in Smyrna, concerning the liberation of baptized slaves (Ign. *Ad Polycarp.* 4.3). In this passage, Ignatius does not

---

[10] For a good introduction into protasis-apodosis constructions (in this case, conditional sentences of simple fact), see Eric G. Jay, *New Testament Greek: An Introductory Grammar*, 12th corr. impression (London: S.P.C.K., 1987), 227–30.

prohibit private manumissions of Christian slaves by individual slaveowners in general, but seeks in particular to curb abuses of common chest (or corporate) manumissions by local house churches. The chapter then locates the passage within the context of Greco-Roman rhetorical and literary commonplaces alarming audiences to the dangers of slave recruitment. Ignatius's apprehension about the corporate manumission of Christian slaves reveals not his conservatism on slavery (by ancient standards), but his wider apologetic stratagem for social acceptability and internal unity under his own terms as bishop. I conclude that the passage addresses a clearly specified economic procedure and, therefore, cannot be used as a text proving that the early church was generally opposed to the manumission of Christian slaves.

This monograph is not an effort to explain away the horror of slavery or to mask its intrinsic brutality. The apothegm of the liberated slave Publilius Syrus, "It is beautiful to die instead of being degraded as a slave," voices the utter dishonor and humiliation that a slave faced daily in the ancient world. I believe that slavery was, is, and always will be an evil, but I cannot make Paul or Ignatius abolitionists. To understand the horror, we must see slavery not as a static institution of law, but a dynamic process of violence, alienation, and (perhaps) eventual integration. The alienation exists even in the surviving ancient evidence, the problems with which will be discussed in chapter 1.

Because I am primarily interested in the physical institution of chattel slavery, larger theological issues concerning religious language that uses slavery metaphorically to express ultimate freedom in Christ fall beyond the bounds of my present study.[11] However, investigating the relationship between the social/institutional and the theological/metaphorical language concerning slavery would be a very interesting project; these levels of language certainly interact with each other, especially in Paul's letters. I have chosen, instead, to focus upon the question of manumission in early Christianity and to exegete the two earliest passages in Christian literature that address it.

The aims and intentions of this monograph include reaching a wide audience, not just those interested in early Christian studies, but also those concerned with the social and cultural history of antiquity and with the academic study of slavery in general. New Testament exegesis is a text-based discipline that interprets, among other things, an author's arguments and beliefs. Social history cannot replace this work, only augment it. It is my hope that this study

---

[11] On the theology of metaphorical slavery to Christ, see now two recent works: Dale B. Martin, *Slavery as Salvation: The Metaphor of Slavery in Pauline Christianity* (New Haven: Yale University Press, 1990), although I do not accept his thesis that slavery as an image in Greco-Roman culture could have been heard as an honorific badge of leadership to some urbanites in Paul's audience; and Gerd Theissen, *Social Reality and the Early Christians: Theology, Ethics, and the World of the New Testament*, trans. Margaret Kohl (Minneapolis: Fortress Press, 1992), 187–201.

contributes to an understanding of how churches functioned socially within the Roman Empire. The goal is to present a concrete reconstruction of how manumission operated in the early congregations, one that will increase our understanding of how early Christian slaves sometimes moved from bondage to freedom.

Chapter 1

Slavery in the Ancient World

Scholars debate how to analyze the essential elements of classical slavery. This chapter introduces the field of slave studies for the nonspecialist and lays the groundwork for reading the following chapters. Readers already acquainted with current scholarship on ancient slavery may still profit from sections of this chapter, particularly the excursus on the social and economic position of Jewish freedmen/women in the city of Rome, which contributes to the standard studies on liberated slaves. Although not all scholars agree on the usefulness of comparative study, this chapter incorporates comparative material, particularly from American historians of slavery in the antebellum U.S. South. The reasons for its inclusion here are (1) to draw parallels necessary for the argument, (2) to clarify the problems in assuming one understands the phenomenon of slavery without knowledge of the historical specificity of its appearances, (3) to learn from the investigations of modern historians who have much larger bases of primary material upon which to draw, and (4) to encourage an informed interdisciplinary approach to slave studies. After addressing the fundamental problems of definition and the limitations of comparison, this chapter will discuss the nature and difficulties of the primary sources; how enslavement occurred; the value of calculating slave numbers as opposed to specifying the positions held by slaves in the determination of a "slave society"; how slaves lived among the Greco-Roman families that owned them; the various forms of manumission in classical Athens and Rome; and finally, the specific case of Jewish freedmen/women, which serves as a transition into the next chapter on Paul and the question of Christian freedmen/women.

The secondary literature on ancient slavery is immense, requiring entire books to provide even a basic bibliography.[1] Before beginning any new inves-

---

[1] Joseph Vogt and Heinz Bellen, eds., *Bibliographie zur antiken Sklaverei: Im Auftrag der Kommission für Geschichte des Altertums der Akademie der Wissenschaften und der Literatur*, new ed., 2 pts., rev. E. Herrmann and N. Brockmeyer (Bochum: N. Brockmeyer, 1983), lists 5,162 books and articles, and is far from complete; see now Joseph C. Miller, ed., *Slavery and Slaving in World History: A Bibliography, 1990–1991* (Milford, N.Y.: Kraus Interna-

tigation, however, a few basic terms need clarification. This monograph applies the term "slaves" exclusively in the property notion of chattels; thus, the helots of classical Spartan society, for example, do not qualify as slaves. The terms "ancient slavery" or "classical slavery" designate institutionalized human chattel bondage in two different contexts: the Greek and the Roman worlds. The expression "Greek world of classical Athens" refers exclusively to fifth- and fourth-century Athens. The term "Roman world of the Principate" designates the period of Rome's zenith from the middle Republic to the end of the early Empire (200 B.C.E.–235 C.E.).[2] It is important to keep the evidence from Athens and Rome separate, for Athenian slavery differed markedly from the institution in the Roman Principate. Although both Paul and Ignatius lived under the Roman Empire, the discussion below will occasionally include evidence from fifth- and fourth-century Athens because it is so often used by scholars in interpreting Paul. But even though some argumentation in the secondary literature on early Christianity rests upon this Athenian evidence, classical Athens in fact has little to do with Paul's Roman situation. However, the Athenian material can usually illumine the history of the development of later Hellenistic practices in the East (such as Greek manumission forms) that are directly relevant to Paul's writings.

---

tional, 1993); idem, ed., *Slavery: A Worldwide Bibliography, 1900–1982* (White Plains, N.Y.: Kraus International, 1985), esp. 249–306 (ancient slavery), 387–88 (ancient slave trade). The classic study remains M. I. Finley, *Ancient Slavery and Modern Ideology* (New York: Viking Press, 1980), esp. 11–66. See also Thomas E. J. Wiedemann, *Slavery*, Greece and Rome: New Surveys in the Classics 19 (Oxford: Clarendon Press, 1987); Joseph Vogt, *Ancient Slavery and the Ideal of Man*, trans. Thomas Wiedemann (Cambridge: Harvard University Press, 1975), 211–17; J. Deininger, "Neue Forschungen zur antiken Sklaverei (1970–1975)," *HZ* 222 (1976): 359–74; Norbert Brockmeyer, *Antike Sklaverei*, Erträge der Forschung 116 (Darmstadt: Wissenschaftliche Buchgesellschaft, 1979), 16–73; Géza Alföldy, ed., *Antike Sklaverei: Widersprüche, Sonderformen, Grundstrukturen*, Thyssen-Vorträge 7 (Bamberg: C. C. Buchners, 1988); Michael Grant, *A Social History of Greece and Rome* (New York: Charles Scribner's Sons, 1992), 85–122; Yvon Thébert, "The Slave," in *The Romans*, ed. Andrea Giardina, trans. Lydia G. Cochrane (Chicago: University of Chicago Press, 1993), 138–74; Jean Andreau, "The Freedman," in Giardina, *The Romans*, 175–98.

[2] I understand that the "Roman world" did not end in 235, but the Principate did; Peter Garnsey and Richard Saller, *The Roman Empire: Economy, Society, and Culture* (Berkeley and Los Angeles: University of California Press, 1987), 1. In the period after 235 (the late Empire), the institution of ancient slavery changed dramatically with the emergence of the colonate, and so it deserves separate treatment that cannot be done here. On how the changes in military structure of the late Empire resulted in the gradual (but not complete) replacement of slaves by *coloni*, see Finley, *Ancient Slavery and Modern Ideology*, 123–49.

Problems of Definition and Comparison

Critical investigation of ancient slavery faces two immediate obstacles. The first concerns methodology; the other, philosophy. The methodological problem is a lack of primary sources, compounded by the fact that what little survives emanates virtually exclusively from ancient slaveholders and does not express the views of the slaves themselves. The philosophical problem involves explaining cogently what one actually means by the terms "slave" and "slavery." To answer even such elementary questions as "What is a slave?" and "What is slavery?" in any historical sense, one must critically engage interpretive and speculative literature on the nature and purposes of historical inquiry. Philosophers and intellectual historians have been trying to answer these kinds of basic questions about slavery – and its antithesis, freedom – for centuries.[3] Nearly everyone agrees that we can legitimately study a particular slave for whom there is evidence such as Epictetus (ca. 55–135 C.E.) or Frederick Douglass (1817–1895). However, there is philosophical disagreement over whether we can actually study some phenomenologically perceptible entity

---

[3] Thomas Hobbs, *Leviathan*, ed. Richard Tuck, Cambridge Texts in the History of Social Thought (Cambridge: Cambridge University Press, 1991), §21; John Locke, *The Second Treatise of Government*, in *Two Treatises of Government*, 2d ed., rev. Peter Laslett, Cambridge Texts in the History of Political Thought (Cambridge: Cambridge University Press, 1988), §4.22–24; G. W. F. Hegel, *Phänomenologie des Geistes*, 5th ed., rev. J. Hoffmeister, Philosophische Bibliothek 114 (Hamburg: Felix Meiner Verlag, 1952), §178–230; Ruth Anshen, ed., *Freedom: Its Meaning* (New York: Harcourt, Brace, 1940); C. Wirszubski, *Libertas as a Political Idea at Rome during the Late Republic and Early Principate* (1950; reprint, Cambridge: Cambridge University Press, 1960); Isaiah Berlin, *Four Essays on Liberty* (Chicago: University of Chicago Press, 1960); William L. Westermann, "Slavery and the Elements of Freedom in Ancient Greece," in *Slavery in Classical Antiquity: Views and Controversies*, ed. M. I. Finley (Cambridge: W. Heffer & Sons, 1960), 17–32; H. J. Muller, *Freedom in the Ancient World* (London: Secker & Warburg, 1962); Carl J. Friedrich, ed., *Liberty*, Nomos 4 (1962; reprint, New York: Atherton Press, 1966); Dieter Nestle, "Freiheit," *RAC* 8 (1972): 269–306; C. Spicq, "La liberté selon le Nouveau Testament," *ScEccl* 12 (1960): 229–40; idem, *Charité et liberté selon le Nouveau Testament*, 2d ed. (Paris: Les Éditions de Cerf, 1964); Modestus van Straaten, "Menschliche Freiheit in der stoischen Philosophie," *Gymnasium* 84 (1977): 501–18; Hans Dieter Betz, "Paul's Concept of Freedom in the Context of Hellenistic Discussions about the Possibilities of Human Freedom," in *Paulinische Studien: Gesammelte Aufsätze III* (Tübingen: J. C. B. Mohr [Paul Siebeck], 1994), 110–25; idem, *Galatians: A Commentary on Paul's Letter to the Churches of Galatia*, Hermeneia (Philadelphia: Fortress Press, 1979), 255–81; Lawrence Crocker, *Positive Liberty: An Essay in Normative Political Philosophy*, Melbourne International Philosophy Series 7 (The Hague: Martinus Nijhoff, 1980); F. Stanley Jones, *"Freiheit" in den Briefen des Apostels Paulus: Eine historische, exegetische und religionsgeschichtliche Studie*, GTA 34 (Göttingen: Vandenhoeck & Ruprecht, 1987); Orlando Patterson, *Freedom in the Making of Western Culture* (New York: Basic Books, 1991); Samuel Vollenweider, *Freiheit als neue Schöpfung: Eine Untersuchung zur Eleutheria bei Paulus und in seiner Umwelt*, FRLANT 147 (Göttingen: Vandenhoeck & Ruprecht, 1989).

generically called "slavery." Slave studies as a field is essentially comparative social history. Yet the very existence of the field begs a larger question of legitimacy. Although these philosophical questions make an interesting study unto themselves, this monograph will not engage in this kind of speculative inquiry.

Currently there is no general theory that allows a single definition of slavery for all cultures and times. In the words of David Brion Davis, "The more we learn about slavery, the more difficulty we have defining it."[4] Earlier studies simply took the objectivity of slavery for granted as a categorical and trans-cultural concept.[5] The problem in defining a slave involves the question of whether a slave is a thing or a person. Classic definitions found in Aristotle and Roman private law declare the slave property, essentially no different than a farm implement or domesticated animal. Yet to accept uncritically these definitions, which classify a slave solely in terms of legal property, is methodologically questionable. Legal codes, at best, provide only inexact knowledge about social practice and, at worst, can build a highly misleading model of slavery. Reading law codes as descriptive rather than prescriptive overlooks the course of juridical decisions in the practice of law (jurisprudence). Most studies of slavery based on law codes have proven unsatisfactory in this regard. One of the most influential critics of the law-oriented approach is the historical sociologist Orlando Patterson, who writes:

Many modern students of slavery, in failing to see that the definition of the slave as a person without a legal personality is a fiction, have found irresistible a popular form of argument that amounts to a red herring. The argument has a standard formula. The scholar, usually not very well informed about comparative legal practice, declares as a legal fact that the slave is defined and treated by the slaveholding class as a person without legal or moral personality. He then digs into his data and comes up with "proof" that the slave is indeed treated as a person in law — for is he not punished for his crimes? and are there not laws restricting the powers of the master? Thus there is, we are told, a fundamental problem posed by slavery, the so-called conflict between the treatment of the slave as a thing and as a human being. The formula ends with some ringing piece of liberal rhetoric to the effect that human dignity is irrepressible: "You may define a person as a thing," goes the flourish, "but you cannot treat him as one" (or some such pious statement). The whole formula is, of course, a piece of irrelevance. No legal code I know of has ever attempted to treat slaves as anything other than persons in law. The irrelevance, I might add, springs from confusion of jurisprudence with law. It is unfor-

---

[4] David Brion Davis, *Slavery and Human Progress* (New York: Oxford University Press, 1984), 8.

[5] Davis, *Slavery and Human Progress*, 9. See Bernard J. Siegel, "Some Methodological Considerations for a Comparative Study of Slavery," *American Anthropologist* n.s. 47 (1945): 357–63, on how the anthropological treatment of non-Western slavery in the early part of this century was fundamentally a continuation of the positivist tradition.

tunate that most students of slavery tend to be as knowledgeable about jurisprudence as they are ignorant of law.[6]

Patterson suggests a different approach for understanding the essential nature of a slave. Exploding many popular as well as scholarly myths about slavery as a global cultural phenomenon, Patterson offers a model that has particularly useful application to the study of ancient slavery, one that envisions slavery as a process of dishonor, alienation, and "social death." Patterson argues that to define a slave solely in terms of legal property fails at definition.[7]

Yet not all scholars agree with Patterson's wholesale abandonment of legal definitions of a slave, particularly in the investigation of Greco-Roman material. M. I. Finley holds Roman legal distinctions to be crucial to understanding slavery as one form of dependent labor, but not the only form.[8] The terms δοῦλος and *servus* cover wide semantic domains that name a variety of inferiors and are often nontechnical in ancient vernacular. The language of slavery does not always refer to what we would call slaves, but (unfortunately for the historian) ranges in meaning from the metaphorical, such as senators as political or moral slaves, to the general, such as laborers.[9] Ancient authors often

---

[6] Orlando Patterson, *Slavery and Social Death: A Comparative Study* (Cambridge: Harvard University Press, 1982), 22–23. Patterson understands his monograph to be responding to, even supplanting, the classic comprehensive study of slavery as a global human phenomenon by H. J. Nieboer, *Slavery as an Industrial System: Ethnological Researches* (The Hague: Hijhoff, 1910). For the most part, slavery specialists consider Patterson quite successful in his task; see the critical reviews of Patterson by Richard Hellie, *AHR* 89 (1984): 411–12; Bertram Wayatt-Brown, *Society* 21.3 (1984): 92–94; Peter L. van den Berghe, *Ethnic and Racial Studies* 7 (1984): 301–5; Heinz Heinen, *European Sociological Review* 4 (1988): 263–68.

[7] Patterson is certainly correct to point out that legal statutes do not necessarily reflect social practice. *Pace* Paul R. Coleman-Norton, "The Apostle Paul and the Roman Law of Slavery," in *Studies in Roman Economic and Social History in Honor of Allan Chester Johnson*, ed. idem (Princeton: Princeton University Press, 1951), 155–77; Ephraim E. Urbach, "The Laws Regarding Slavery as a Source for Social History of the Period of the Second Temple, the Mishnah and Talmud," trans. R. J. Loewe, in *Papers of the Institute of Jewish Studies London*, ed. E. G. Weiss (1964; reprint, Lanham, Md.: University Press of America, 1989), 1:1–94. Because they implicitly argue that legal statutes do reflect social practice, Coleman-Norton and Urbach provide models of how *not* to study slavery. For solid criticism against Urbach's method, see Paul V. M. Flesher, *Oxen, Women, or Citizens? Slaves in the System of the Mishnah*, BJS 143 (Atlanta: Scholars Press, 1988), x–xiii.

[8] Finley, *Ancient Slavery and Modern Ideology*, 68.

[9] E. Sereni, "Recherche sur le vocabulaire des rapports de dépendance dans le monde antique," in *Actes du colloque 1973 sur l'esclavage*, Annales littéraires de l'Université de Besançon 182, Centre de recherches d'histoire ancienne 18 (Paris: Les Belles Lettres, 1976), 11–43; Fritz Gschnitzer, *Studien zur griechischen Terminologie der Sklaverei*, 2 pts., AAWM 13, Forschungen zur antiken Sklaverei 7 (Wiesbaden: Franz Steiner, 1964, 1976); G. R. Stanton, "Τέχνον, παῖς, and Related Words in Koine Greek," in *Proceedings of the XVIII International Congress of Papyrology*, ed. Basil G. Mandilaras (Athens: Greek Papyrological Society, 1988), 1:470–80.

name helots "slaves," for instance, yet helots, unlike chattel slaves, were not imported from outside but were subjected within their own native territories and could not be bought or sold.[10] Despite the linguistic overlap, chattel slavery differed from other forms of dependent labor, such as debt bondage, indentured servitude, clientship, peonage, helotage, and serfdom.[11] The semantic domain of slave vocabulary, therefore, poses a problem for the interpreter.

Patterson, however, offers a solution. In his effort to provide a universally applicable definition for all known slaveholding societies, Patterson does not limit his understanding of slavery to the Roman definitions of property in private law. Contrary to the convictions of Finley, Patterson sees the internal relations of slavery as governed not by the concept of chattel property, but by the concept of absolute power. Patterson understands slavery to be an intrinsically violent relationship of control, in which the enslaved person is functionally denied access to autonomous relations outside the master's sphere of influence. Although not biologically dead, slaves in effect are "socially" dead to the free population.[12] Removing all juridical categories, Patterson investigates the meaning of violent genealogical isolation in order to relocate discussion over slave definition. For Patterson, slavery is neither simply the loss of freedom, nor the same as coerced labor, nor equatable with loss of civil rights. As a confined outsider deprived of the ties of birth in both ascending and descending generations, the slave exists as what social anthropologists and historians of religion term "the Other." The slave had been physically, violently removed from his or her native home, stripped of previous ethnicity and all dignity, and typically forced to learn a foreign language and to obey unfamiliar customs on pain of death. Now as an outsider enslaved, he or she lived in fear, fundamentally without honor, and on the margin of the slaveholders' society.[13] With this interpretive approach, Patterson solves the problem of narrow juridical definitions and wide semantic domains. Another

---

[10] Douglas M. MacDowell, *Spartan Law*, Scottish Classical Studies 1 (Edinburgh: Scottish Academic Press, 1986), 37–42; Robert Parker, "Spartan Religion," in *Classical Sparta: Techniques Behind Her Success*, ed. Anton Powell, Oklahoma Series in Classical Culture (Norman: University of Oklahoma Press, 1988), 145; J. Ducat, *Les hilotes*, Bulletin de Correspondance Hellénique Suppl. 20 (Paris: École Française d'Athènes, 1990).

[11] Finley, *Ancient Slavery and Modern Ideology*, 68; idem, "Slavery," in *International Encyclopedia of the Social Sciences*, ed. David L. Sills, 14 (1968): 307–13. See also Peter Garnsey, ed., *Non-Slave Labour in the Greco-Roman World*, Cambridge Philological Society Suppl. 6 (Cambridge: The Society, 1980). Keith R. Bradley, *Discovering the Roman Family: Studies in Roman Social History* (New York: Oxford University Press, 1991), 103–24, discusses child labor in the Roman world.

[12] Patterson, *Slavery and Social Death*, 1–75. The concept of "dead to …" is found also in Gal 2:19 and Rom 6:10 (cf. Rom 7:4, 6), so Patterson agrees with Paul.

[13] On "otherness" as essential to slavery, Patterson and Finley agree; see Finley, "Slavery," 308–9.

scholar, Richard Hellie, helps further this approach as a global model, since he documents the exceptional case of Russian slavery, a system that enslaved (and made socially dead) its own people.[14]

Patterson's definition of a slave as socially dead appreciates the alienating dynamics of the enslavement process: "Slavery is the permanent, violent domination of natally alienated and generally dishonored persons."[15] Finley and others place greater stress on the concept of chattel property, especially when dealing with the ancient material. Finley writes:

> the property element remains essential. ... what separates the slave from the rest [of the forms of dependent labor], including the serf or peon, is the totality of his powerlessness in principle, and for that the idea of property is juristically the key – hence the term "chattel slave."[16]

In addition to emphasizing juridical classifications, however, Finley does place equal stress on the slave's otherness or "deracination."[17] Both Finley and Patterson make significant advances over previous definitions of a slave, especially in seeing the slave as the Other. Unlike Patterson, however, Finley retains the legal category of slavery as one (but not the only) form of dependent labor. I call Finley's approach the dependent labor or "chattel" hermeneutic and Patterson's the "social death" hermeneutic.

From this comparison of Patterson and Finley, we now see how complex our original questions are. Even an apparently simple one, such as "What is a slave?" draws considerable debate. Nonspecialists must appreciate the great diversity of approaches that slavery scholars take. This monograph draws upon the findings of Finley, Patterson, and others (such as Brunt, Bradley, and Hopkins) without limiting itself to one school or method.[18] Knowledge of these debates and disagreements over the philosophical problematics of slavery as a global phenomenon helps biblical exegetes develop an informed hermeneutic.

---

[14] Richard Hellie, *Slavery in Russia: 1450–1725* (Chicago: University of Chicago Press, 1982). See also van den Berghe, review of Patterson, 303.

[15] Patterson, *Slavery and Social Death*, 13.

[16] Finley, "Slavery," 307.

[17] Ibid.

[18] I am also aware of, but do not adhere to, the German "School of Mayence" (Arbeitsgruppe Sklavenforschung der Kommission für Geschichte des Altertums der Mainzer Akademie), which has taken an avowedly polemical stance against some of M. I. Finley's views of ancient slavery; e.g., Fridolf Kudlien, *Sklaven-Mentalität im Spiegel antiker Wahrsagerei*, Forschungen zur antiken Sklaverei 23 (Stuttgart: Franz Steiner, 1991), 12, 150–51 (cf. Walter Schiedel, "Slavery and the Shackled Mind: On Fortune-telling and Slave Mentality in the Graeco-Roman World," *The Ancient History Bulletin* 7 [1993]: 107–14).

The Primary Sources: Their Usefulness and Limits

Debates and disagreements occur in the secondary literature in part because the primary evidence is problematic. The first task in any historical inquiry is to determine the nature of the available primary source material, and for slavery the problem is formidable. As a response, this section has two goals: to list sources, and to comment on their usefulness and limits. Considering the ubiquity and significance of slaves in ancient daily life, there is surprisingly little discussion of them by ancient authors.[19] The significance of this absence is difficult for moderns to appreciate. Both Aristotle and Athenaeus tried to imagine a world without slaves. They could only envision a fantasy land, where tools performed their work on command (even seeing what to do in advance), utensils moved automatically, shuttles wove cloth and quills played harps without human hands to guide them, bread baked itself, and fish not only voluntarily seasoned and basted themselves, but also flipped themselves over in frying pans at the appropriate times.[20] This humorous vision was meant to illustrate how preposterous such a slaveless world would be, so integral was slavery to ancient life. But what do the primary sources tell us about this life so different from our own? The answer is frustratingly little.

The primary sources fall in the following categories:

I. Archaeology
    A. Architectural remains
    B. Skeletal remains
    C. *Realia* (chains, whips, collars, etc.)
II. Inscriptions
III. Papyrus and parchment fragments
IV. Literature
    A. Legal material
    B. Histories and biographies
    C. Personal and other letters
    D. Moral literature
    E. Advice literature on household management
        1. *Oeconomicus* handbooks for large agricultural estates
        2. Domestic codes (*Haustafeln*) for all households, large or small
    F. Imaginative literature
        1. Satires
        2. Poetry
        3. Drama
        4. Parables and myths
        5. Proto-novels

---

[19] William L. Westermann, *The Slave Systems of Greek and Roman Antiquity*, Memoirs of the American Philosophical Society 40 (Philadelphia: The Society, 1955), 1.

[20] Arist. *Pol.* 1.4 (1253b); Ath. *Deipnosophistai* 6.267.

The limitations of this evidence are the following:

I.   Virtually all ancient authors were themselves owners of slaves.
     Their literature, when it does mention slaves, reflects the views of masters, not necessarily of slaves.
II. Extant evidence is principally limited to urban slavery.
III. No quantifiable data is available.
     A. The total number of slaves is unknown (census data only from Egypt).
     B. The size of individual slave holdings can only be conjectural.
     C. The number of slaves working in manufacture or agriculture is unrecorded.
IV. The documentary evidence is inadequate.
     A. No account ledgers survive except from Egypt.
     B. No estate archives survive.
V.   No "slave literature" (e.g., autobiographies, personal letters) survives, and slave oral literature is irretrievable.

To be sure, there were writers such as Terence and Epictetus who personally experienced enslavement. Yet M. I. Finley argues that their works "show no influence of that experience, emotional or intellectual, and nothing to distinguish them from writers who lacked that experience."[21] P. A. Brunt takes a similar position:

> It has been observed that no Stoic attaches more emphasis to freedom than Epictetus, the former slave. But the freedom he had come to value has nothing to do with legal status; for him as for Seneca and Marcus Aurelius, it is a freedom from the chains of desire for what is never certainly within a man's power to attain, freedom that Diogenes enjoyed, though a slave (III 24, 66 ff.).
> Indeed the doctrine, on which no one insists more repeatedly than Epictetus (1.2.8 ff.; 2.23, 24 ff.), that every man is called to serve in the station in which he finds himself and to accept his lot contentedly, whatever it may be, in so far as it was propagated among and accepted by slaves, would have tended to reconcile them to servitude. But there is no evidence or probability that Stoicism penetrated far into the lower levels of society. Epictetus himself, who was a highly educated man, cannot of course be regarded as typical of the countless slaves employed as labourers and menials.[22]

Both Brunt and Finley are reacting against the views of other scholars, such as W. A. Oldfather and Chester Starr, who had claimed that no other Stoic spoke of freedom more frequently or passionately than Epictetus, and that this emphasis on liberty was a direct result of his personal experience with slavery.[23] Finley rightly points out that Arrian's account of Epictetus's work certainly is not a slave narrative like those from the American South, yet Finley underes-

---

[21] Finley, *Ancient Slavery and Modern Ideology*, 117.

[22] P. A. Brunt, "From Epictetus to Arrian," *Athenaeum* 55 (1977): 24. See also 23, where Brunt addresses specific passages in Epictetus that have led previous scholars to believe (to Brunt's mind, erroneously) that Epictetus, because of his experience as a slave, held a higher passion for liberty than either Seneca or other Stoics.

[23] W. A. Oldfather, *Epictetus*, LCL (1925; reprint, Cambridge: Harvard University Press, 1989), 1:xvii; Chester Starr, "Epictetus the Tyrant," *CP* 44 (1949): 23.

timates the significance of some passages in Epictetus, which do reflect some personal experience with slavery.[24]

Besides the evidence in Epictetus, another possible source for the slaves' point of view is the fable, which as a literary genre exemplified by authors like Aesop and Phaedrus may have had servile origins. With its "trickster" slave character, the fable may have functioned as a vehicle for slave protest and indirect criticism of slaveowners.[25] In the end, however, this is only a conjecture, which may lie beyond proof. Unlike those who study the modern period, ancient historians simply have no oral repository out of which to reconstruct slave life or folklore. Scholars of American slavery, for example, can turn to at least four major sources, both written and oral, of slave literature: (1) the extant black slave autobiographies, which number over one hundred; (2) the many biographic and autobiographic stories published in nineteenth-century abolitionist newspapers and church organs; (3) the folk music of "Negro spirituals"; and (4) the forty-one volume slave narrative collection. This last item, over 10,000 pages of typescript, contains over 2,000 personal interviews with ex-slaves transcribed in the 1920s and 1930s by several groups of investigators.[26] In contrast, the scholar of ancient slavery has nothing like this and

---

[24] See Arr. *Epict. diss.* 1.12; 1.13; 2.10; 2.16.42; 2.21.5; 3.24.43; 4.1.52–53. Even from reading these few pages one can learn that Epictetus's arguments indeed reflect his experiences with slavery. He often employs metaphors and images that did not come from the standard commonplaces of Greco-Roman moral exhoration literature, but were drawn from his own experience and reflect the slave's point of view. E.g., Arr. *Epict. diss.* 2.20.29–31 (here Epictetus brings a new twist to the stock *servus callidus* figure by making the slave a hero); 1.25.7–8 (on the joys of Saturnalia); 4.1.25–28 (servile sympathy with caged animals); 1.29.59–60 and 2.1.9–11 (the frightened runaway); 1.9.8–10 (the resourceful runaway); 2.18.12 and 3.25.9–10 (fear of the whip); 2.17.29–33 (athletic training and competition, perhaps as a slave); 1.8.14 and 1.12.24 (crippled leg, perhaps as a result of a sports injury while a slave, but cf. Origen, *Contra Celsum* 7.53 for another reason for Epictetus's crippled leg: Henry Chadwick, *Origen, Contra Celsum* [1953; corr. reprint, Cambridge: Cambridge University Press, 1986], 440). The best study of Epictetus's personal history remains Fergus Millar, "Epictetus and the Imperial Court," *JRS* 55 (1965): 141–48.

[25] Keith R. Bradley, *Slaves and Masters in the Roman Empire: A Study in Social Control* (1984; reprint with suppl. bibliog., New York: Oxford University Press, 1987), 151–53; Paul Cartledge, "Rebels and Sambos in Classical Greece: A Comparative View," in *Crux: Essays in Greek History Presented to G. E. M. de Ste. Croix on His 75th Birthday*, ed. P. A. Cartledge and F. D. Harvey (London: Gerald Duckworth, 1985), 25.

[26] George P. Rawick, ed., *The American Slave: A Composite Autobiography*, vol. 1, *From Sundown to Sunup: The Making of the Black Community*, Contributions in Afro-American and African Studies 11 (Westport, Conn.: Greenwood Publishing, 1972), xiii–xxi, 163–78; Michael Craton, "A Cresting Wave? Recent Trends in the Historiography of Slavery, with Special Reference to the British Caribbean," *Historical Reflexions/Réflexions historiques* 9 (1982): 413.

so faces a formidable task. The most promising sources are archaeological remains, inscriptions, papyrus/parchment fragments, and works of literature.

Some archaeological evidence provides limited insight into the physical conditions of slave life. For example, the structural remains of excavated Roman houses reveal that the Romans did not ordinarily build separate, free-standing slave quarters; slaves typically lived in rooms within the master's walls.[27] Such proximity and daily interaction between slaves and the master's nuclear family have significant implications for Greco-Roman family history.[28] Physical anthropology has also contributed to slave studies, but this evidence can be misused. For example, in their study of labor patterns in ancient Greece, some scholars use skeletal evidence to establish a decline in back problems during the archaic and classical times, which they attribute to improvements in the labor conditions of freeborn persons, and which they claim is a direct result of the rise of slavery from 700 to 300 B.C.E. Yet recent scholars in the field have undermined such conclusions.[29] Other archaeological evidence includes unearthed objects relating to slavery, such as shackles and collars.[30] An example is a collar of a slave owned by a Christian cleric, which reads, "I am the slave of archdeacon Felix: hold me so that I do not flee."[31] Sculpture and the plastic arts also provide important evidence.

---

[27] Andrew Wallace-Hadrill, "The Social Structure of the Roman House," *PBSR* 56 (1988): 78–81; Bradley, *Discovering*, 9, 90–93, 183.

[28] On Roman families (meaning related persons living under the same roof) being nuclear, see Richard P. Saller and Brent D. Shaw, "Tombstones and Roman Family Relations in the Principate: Civilians, Soldiers, and Slaves," *JRS* 74 (1984): 124–56; but see the cautionary remarks (*contra* Saller and Shaw) of Bradley, *Discovering*, 3–17, 89, 95, 125–45, 180. When the Romans spoke of their household (in the sense of our English word "family") in ordinary social discourse, they used *domus*. The Latin *familia* was, first, a legal term for the father (*pater*) and those under his authority (*potestas*), including his wife (if the marriage was with *manus*), children, and slaves. In the case of a *non-manus* marriage, the wife would have had her own property and slaves legally separated from that of her husband. Thus one household could have had two *familiae*. In daily social discourse (e.g., from the letters of Cicero), *familia* had a secondary meaning that referred to one's slaves only.

[29] On the problems of using skeletal evidence to study labor patterns, see Ian Morris, *Death-Ritual and Social Structure in Classical Antiquity*, Key Themes in Ancient History (Cambridge: Cambridge University Press, 1992), 93–94 with the material in notes.

[30] Wiedemann, *Slavery*, supplies a photograph of shackles, presumably for slaves, discovered in the Laureum silver mines of classical Athens. See Joyce Reynolds, "Roman Inscriptions, 1971–75," *JRS* 66 (1976): 196; Giovanna Sotgiu, "Un collare di schiavo reinvenuto in Sardegna," *ArchClass* 25–26 (1973–74): 688–97; Jo-Ann Shelton, *As the Romans Did: A Source Book of Roman Social History* (New York: Oxford University Press, 1988), 180.

[31] G. H. R. Horsley et al., eds., *New Documents Illustrating Early Christianity*, vol. 1, *A Review of the Greek Inscriptions and Papyri Published in 1976* (Marrickville, Australia: The Ancient History Documentary Research Centre [Macquarie University], 1981), 140–41. See also idem, eds., *New Documents*, vol. 3, *A Review of the Greek Inscriptions and Papyri*

For instance, eight shackled slaves are depicted on the stele of A. Kapreilius Timotheus.[32]

The epigraphic evidence is mostly funerary since tombstones furnish nearly three-fourths of the entire corpus of Greek and Latin inscriptions. These epitaphs commemorated slaves or ex-slaves, and often record little more than the name of the deceased. (It is important to remember that most slaves were buried or cremated without an inscription.) However, tens of thousands of tombstones offer the historian a few further details, such as age at death and the name and relationship of the commemorator.[33] Such evidence reveals that many commemorated slaves and freedmen/women had families, despite the fact that slaves could not contract a legal marriage.[34] In Latin the term *contubernium* was applied to a slave's matrimonial relationship.[35] Epitaphs of slaves were typically erected by their respective masters. One such necrological notice has importance for understanding ancient slaveholder ideology; it reads, "I am yours, master, even in Hades."[36] Another reads, "To you even now under the earth, yes master, I remain as faithful as before."[37] Evidently the master-slave relationship was thought in some instances to extend beyond death – masters kept their slaves even in Hades. This view that slavery survived into the afterlife was not universal, however. An additional tombstone illustrates this counterpoint. It reads, "I am Zosime who was formerly a slave only with my body; now I have found freedom for my body as well."[38] It seems that while some ancients believed that the master's power

---

Published in 1978 (Marrickville, Australia: The Ancient History Documentary Research Centre [Macquarie University], 1983), 63–64.

[32] M. I. Finley, "Aulos Kapreilios Timotheos, Slave Trader," in *Aspects of Antiquity: Discoveries and Controversies*, 2d ed. (New York: Penguin Books, 1977), 154–66.

[33] Saller and Shaw, "Tombstones," 124. The standard collection of Greek slave inscriptions is Hermann Raffeiner, *Sklaven und Freigelassene: Eine soziologische Studie auf der Grundlage des griechischen Grabepigrams*, Commentationes Aenipontanae 23, Philologie und Epigraphik 2 (Innsbruck: Wagner, 1977).

[34] Bradley, *Slaves and Masters*, 47–80; Dale B. Martin, *Slavery as Salvation: The Metaphor of Slavery in Pauline Christianity* (New Haven: Yale University Press, 1990), 2–7 and 161 (table C).

[35] W. W. Buckland, *The Roman Law of Slavery: The Condition of the Slave in Private Law from Augustus to Justinian* (1908; reprint, New York: AMS Press, 1969), 76; A. M. Duff, *Freedmen in the Early Roman Empire*, 2d ed. (Cambridge: W. Heffer & Sons, 1958), 59. The term *contubernium* also applied to a matrimonial relationship involving free noncitizens.

[36] Horsley et al., *New Documents*, vol. 2, *A Review of the Greek Inscriptions and Papyri Published in 1977* (Marrickville, Australia: The Ancient History Documentary Research Centre [Macquarie University], 1982), 53, dated to the third century B.C.E.

[37] Ibid.

[38] Ibid.

over a slave extended even into the afterlife, others saw death as a means of escape from a master's domination.[39]

The papyrological evidence is specific to Hellenistic and Roman Egypt; although useful, its application to other parts of the ancient Mediterranean world is limited. We have, for example, two official notices of runaway slaves that were posted in Alexandria in 156 B.C.E.[40] Notices similar to these must have been posted by slaveowners throughout the avenues and highways of the ancient world but not preserved, since most were likely written on papyrus or wood. Other papyrological sources are collected in a recent edition of Ptolemaic slave-related papyrus documents.[41] Yet the main problem is again that the evidence is specific to a single geographic region.

Therefore, one turns to literary sources in the hopes of covering more ground. At first, this evidence looks promising; after all, we have more of it than any other source.[42] Because of its bulk, we should divide ancient literature into the following broad categories: legal material, histories, letters, moral literature, advice literature, and imaginative literature (novels, satires, poetry, drama, and the like). Each of these kinds of sources presents particular problems. For instance, concerning the available laws, the only two Greek states for which we have direct evidence of the legal status of slaves are Athens and the Dorian Cretan city of Gortyn. Gortynian and Athenian slaveries differed significantly; Gortyn gave slaves certain personal privileges that were, in Athens, permitted only to citizens. In Gortyn, slaves could acquire property in their own right not subject to confiscation by the master, had a right of inheritance in the master's property, and could legally contract marriages; Athenian slaves had none of these rights.[43] We know of the slave laws for

---

[39] On suicide as a form of slave resistance and escape, see Sen. *Ep.* 4.4 (runaway slaves); *Ep.* 70.19–26 (gladiators); *Ep.* 77.15 (Spartan boy who killed himself to avoid enslavement); *CIL* 13.7070 (*servus homicida*, of a slave who killed his master and himself); Bradley, *Slaves and Masters*, 113 n. 3; idem, *Slavery and Rebellion in the Roman World: 140 B.C.–70 B.C.* (Bloomington: Indiana University Press, 1989), 89; Anton J. L. van Hoof, *From Autothanasia to Suicide: Self-Killing in Classical Antiquity* (London: Routledge, 1990), 16–21, 28, 75, 78, 93, 111, 151, 162, 184–85.

[40] *UPZ* 1.121.566–567; Westermann, *Slave Systems*, 39; see also the example found in the useful sourcebook by Thomas E. J. Wiedemann, *Greek and Roman Slavery* (1981; reprint, London: Routledge, 1988), 192.

[41] Reinhold Scholl, ed., *Corpus der ptolemäischen Sklaventexte*, 3 vols., Forschungen zur antiken Sklaverei Beiheft 1 (Stuttgart: Franz Steiner, 1990); note the critical reviews by Joachim Hengstl, *BASP* 29 (1992): 183–89, and Dorothy J. Thompson, *CR* 42 (1992): 164–66.

[42] R. H. Barrow, *Slavery in the Roman Empire* (London: Methuen, 1928), 237–45, offers a useful but not exhaustive appendix citing the literary evidence.

[43] Robert Schlaifer, "Greek Theories of Slavery from Homer to Aristotle," in Finley, *Slavery in Classical Antiquity*, 110–11; Ronald F. Willetts, *The Law Code of Gortyn*, Kadmos Suppl. 1 (Berlin: Walter de Gruyer, 1967), 13–17; idem, "Freedmen at Gortyna," *CQ* 4

classical Athens mainly from Plato.[44] The Roman legal evidence has a much wider base of source material, the Justinianic compilation called the *Corpus Iuris Civilis* (containing the *Digest*, *Institutes*, and *Code*) and an extant second-century law school textbook, the *Institutes* of Gaius.[45] The compendium of Gaius, for example, reveals the enormous importance of slaves for commercial and other acquisitions.[46] In the use of these materials, however, one must always guard against mistaking law codes for social description.

Similarly, histories pose problematics. Because ancient historiography concerned itself with politics, wars, and great personalities, such narratives frustrate efforts to reconstruct the lives of the majority of the population, which lived below the aristocratic senatorial and equestrian orders. Much of the historical material on slaves is anecdotal and mentioned only in passing, since senators and equestrians considered writing about the lives of individual slaves beneath the appropriate dignity of a historian.[47] One of the longest surviving

---

(1954): 216–19; Michael Gagarin, "The First Law of the Gortyn Code," *GRBS* 29 (1988): 335–43.

[44] Glenn R. Morrow, *Plato's Law of Slavery in Its Relation to Greek Law*, Illinois Studies in Language and Literature 25.3 (Urbana: University of Illinois Press, 1939); idem, "The Murder of Slaves in Attic Law," *CP* 32 (1937–38): 210–27; Gregory Vlastos, "Slavery in Plato's Thought," in Finley, *Slavery in Classical Antiquity*, 133–49; idem, "Does Slavery Exist in Plato's Republic?" *CP* 63 (1968): 291–95.

[45] Buckland, *Roman Law of Slavery*; J. A. Crook, *Law and Life of Rome, 90 B.C.–A.D. 212*, Aspects of Greek and Roman Life (Ithaca: Cornell University Press, 1967), esp. 55–57, 179–91; Barry Nicholas, *An Introduction to Roman Law*, 3d ed., Clarendon Law Series (Oxford: Clarendon Press, 1987), esp. 69–80; Alan Watson, "Morality, Slavery and the Jurists in the Later Roman Republic," *Tulane Law Review* 42 (1967–68): 289–303; idem, "Roman Slave Law and Romanist Ideology," *Phoenix* 37 (1983): 53–65; idem, *Roman Slave Law* (Baltimore: Johns Hopkins University Press, 1987); Keith R. Bradley, "Roman Slavery and Roman Law," *Historical Reflections/Réflexions historiques* 15 (1988): 477–95; Franz Wieacker, *Römische Rechtsgeschichte: Quellenkunde, Rechtsbildung, Jurisprudenz und Rechtsliteratur*, pt. 1, *Rechtsgeschichte des Altertums*, Handbuch der Altertumswissenschaft 3.1 (Munich: C. H. Beck, 1988), 362–67 with extensive material in notes. New English translations of the standard legal sources are *The Digest of Justinian*, ed. Theodor Mommsen with Paul Krueger, trans. Alan Watson (Philadelphia: University of Pennsylvania Press, 1985); and *The Institutes of Gaius*, trans. with an introd. by W. M. Gordon and O. F. Robinson, Latin text ed. Seckel and Kuebler, Texts in Roman Law (Ithaca: Cornell University Press, 1988). However, Watson's edition must be used with caution and the translation checked for accuracy. English legal terms chosen are not always the best for the Latin context, and, at times, whole sentences are omitted from the translation.

[46] Watson, *Slave Law*, 105.

[47] On the inherent dignity of history (as opposed to other genres, such as biography) in Greco-Roman understanding, see Arnoldo Momigliano, *The Development of Greek Biography*, expanded ed. (Cambridge: Harvard University Press, 1993), 39–42, 65–100. Richard P. Saller, "Slavery and the Roman Family," in *Classical Slavery*, ed. M. I. Finley, Slavery and Abolition Special Issue 8 (London: Frank Cass, 1987), 65–87; Iiro Kajanto, "Tacitus on the Slaves," *Arctos* 6 (1970): 43–60.

passages by a Latin historian describing an episode concerning slaves is only two pages in length; and Tacitus only includes it in his narrative to make a rhetorical point about an attempt by the populace to influence polity.[48] Because it considers slaves socially dead and uninteresting, ancient historiography frustrates our investigation.

We turn, then, to letters as a more promising source. The correspondence of Cicero, for example, gives us the fullest available impression of the constant use of slaves in nonproductive services, such as letter carrying.[49] One of the best documented of all freedmen/women is Cicero's Tullius Tiro, known from Cicero's letters.[50] The Pauline epistles (especially Philemon) also mention slaves. Letters, like Paul's or Cicero's, provide important personal details of how slaves functioned in domestic service. Yet letters are only one half of a dialogue. Often, the other half is lost, and this loss presents an obstacle for the historian.

Moral exhortation literature, the fourth genre, offers additional evidence, yet also presents obstacles of its own. The writings of Plato and Seneca fall into this category. One of the most sustained discussions of slavery by an ancient moralist is Seneca's *Epistle* 47, in which he delineates the elements of the model master-slave relationship according to Stoicism. Seneca condemns "harsh" physical punishment of slaves as beneath the dignity of the self-controlled Stoic, but sees no problem with more moderate, regular disciplining of one's slaves.[51] Such calls to kindness toward slaves were not criticisms of the institution, but of its abuse by arrogant masters not abiding by Stoic ideals. The concerns are analogous to the motivations behind our modern legislation in the United States protecting animals (mostly domesticated) against cruelty.[52] Because they were chattel, slaves were not considered, by Seneca or other Stoics, to be of equal political rank or social standing to masters. These statements calling for humane treatment of slaves were articulated to streng-

---

[48] Tac. *Ann.* 14.42–5; Saller, "Slavery and the Roman Family"; Joseph Georg Wolf, *Das Senatusconsultum Silanianum und die Senatsrede des C. Cassius Longinus aus dem Jahre 61 n. Chr.*, SHAW 2 (Heidelberg: Carl Winter, 1988).

[49] Westermann, *Slave Systems*, 74 n. 116; Andrew Garland, "Cicero's *Familia Urbana*," *G & R* 39 (1992): 163–73.

[50] Susan Treggiari, *Roman Freedmen during the Late Republic* (Oxford: Clarendon Press, 1969), 11.

[51] Bradley, *Slaves and Masters*, 119, writes that Seneca's "apparent distaste" for this kind of cruelty was "virtually exceptional." Yet Bradley overstates the case here given that others (e.g., Lucian of Samosata and Epictetus) also rejected the cruel treatment of slaves by owners.

[52] Nicholas, *Roman Law*, 69.

then the institution, not to abolish it.[53] They also tell more about the Stoic philosophy of large slaveholders than about the slaves themselves.

Philosophers wrote much of the moral exhortation literature. The philosophical discussion by Dio Chrysostom forms the longest treatment of slavery in all of extant classical literature.[54] Yet it is the philosophy of Aristotle that supplies the discussion that is best known today. He claimed that "the slave is a kind of animate possession" (ὁ δοῦλος κτῆμά τι ἔμψυχον) and that some human bodies, by virtue of their very anatomy, were biologically built for servility – hunched over for deference, with large body frames suited for manual labor.[55] Yet Aristotle's theory of natural slaves did not convince the Roman jurists, who held that slavery was an institution of the law of nations (*ius gentium*) by which, contrary to nature (*contra naturam*), a person is subjected to the power (*dominium*) of another.[56] Slavery is remarkably the only case in the entire extant corpus of Roman private law in which the *ius gentium* and the *ius naturale* are in conflict.[57] To the jurists and the majority of Roman authors, it was fate, not nature, that made certain people slaves. Aristotelian arguments of biological determinism for natural slaves did not convince antiquity in general.[58] I say "in general" because, as will become apparent in the excursus on Jewish freedmen/women, certain authors shared the Aristotelian notion of

---

[53] Miriam T. Griffin, *Seneca, a Philosopher in Politics* (Oxford: Clarendon Press, 1976), 256–85, 458–61; Brent D. Shaw, "The Divine Economy: Stoicism as Ideology," *Latomus* 44 (1985): 16–54; Keith R. Bradley, "Seneca and Slavery," *C & M* 37 (1986): 161–72; idem, *Slaves and Masters*, 113–37. *Pace* Will Richter, "Seneca und die Sklaven," *Gymnasium* 65 (1958): 196–218; G. Rocca-Serra, "Le stoicisme pré-imperial et l'esclavage," *CRDAC* 8 (1976–77): 205–22; William Watts, "Seneca on Slavery," *DR* 90 (1972): 183–95; C. E. Manning, "Stoicism and Slavery in the Roman Empire," *ANRW* 2.36.3 (1989): 1518–43.

[54] Dio Chrys. *Or.* 14–15; P. A. Brunt, "Aspects of the Social Thought of Dio Chrysostom and the Stoics," *PCPhS* 19 (1973): 9–34.

[55] Arist. *Pol.* 1.1–7 (1252a–56a); Robert Schlaifer, "Greek Theories of Slavery," 127–29; Hans Kless, *Herren und Sklaven: Die Sklaverei in oikonomischen und politischen Schriften der Griechen in klassischer Zeit*, Forschungen zur antiken Sklaverei 6 (Wiesbaden: Franz Steiner, 1975), 181–227; Nicholas D. Smith, "Aristotle's Theory of Natural Slavery," *Phoenix* 37 (1983): 109–22; Giuseppe Cambiano, "Aristotle and the Anonymous Opponents of Slavery," trans. Mario di Gregorio, in Finley, *Classical Slavery*, 22–42. David Brion Davis, *The Problem of Slavery in Western Culture* (1966; reprint, New York: Oxford University Press, 1988), 75 n. 38 (*contra* Schlaifer). Ekaterini Synodinou, "On the Concept of Slavery in Euripides" (Ph.D. diss., University of Cincinnati, 1974), 168–72, identifies Aristotle's unnamed opponent as Euripides.

[56] *Inst.* 1.3.2; *Digest* 1.5.4.1 (Florentinus).

[57] Buckland, *Roman Law of Slavery*, 1; Watson, *Roman Slave Law*, 7–8.

[58] Cic. *Paradoxa stoicorum* 33–34 (paradox 5); Dio Chrys. *Or.* 15; Hor. *Sat.* 2.7.75–94; Philo, *Quod omn. prob. lib. sit.* 36–40; Arr. *Epict. diss.* 3.24.66; Sen. *Dial.* 9.10.3; Sen. *Ep.* 47; Sen. *Ben.* 3.17–28; Aul. Gell. *NA* 2.18; ps.-Heraclit. *Ep.* 9 (trans. in Abraham J. Malherbe, *The Cynic Epistles: A Study Edition*, SBLSBS 12 [Missoula, Mont.: Scholars Press, 1977], 210–15). Cf. esp. Job 31:13–15 and Prov 17:2 for similar views that slaves were not biological inferiors.

natural slaves. Thus Cicero considered the Jews and Syrians, for instance, naturally good slaves. Yet the ancient critics of Aristotle, who were not critics of slavery *per se* but of Aristotle's particular view about it being natural, believed that risk of personal enslavement was common to all human beings. Such critics (mostly Stoic) were clearly not calling for slavery's abolition. In antiquity, to argue that slavery was *contra naturam* meant only that there were no particular ethnic groups anatomically born servile. The Stoic philosophers, in particular Seneca, found piracy, kidnapping, and other forms of abduction a compelling argument against the Aristotelian notion of biologically determined ("natural") slaves. Noble figures such as Julius Caesar, Hecuba, Darius's mother, Plato (who was captured and ransomed at Aegina), and even the Cynic sage Diogenes all were reported to have been taken into captivity at some point in their lives. To Seneca, that even these greats suffered a twist of fortune and were at some time enslaved proved the unpredictable character of human life. Every human being was a potential slave. Not even the archetypal sage Diogenes could escape this possibility. Although Seneca clearly considered slavery itself a natural part of human civilization, he certainly did not view particular people as natural slaves. Fate, not one's anatomy, determined who became slaves and who became masters. Seneca warned that a reversal of fortune could easily have made the master the slave and the slave the master. From this recognition that fate spared none, Stoics like Seneca exhorted humane treatment for slaves. In actuality, slaves were fellow human beings who just happened to have had bad luck.[59]

Related to moral literature is advice literature on household management. One particularly important form, the handbook, brings with it its own difficulties. There were two kinds of handbook: first, writings from classical authors on how to run a large agricultural estate (Latin: *latifundium*); and second, domestic codes (German: *Haustafeln*) in literature that address urban household management, large or small.[60] The agricultural manuals were economic works in the technical Greek sense of the word recommending how a senator or equestrian ought to manage his rural estate. Our knowledge of agricultural slavery stems mostly from authors in this category: Cato the Elder (Censor),

---

[59] Sen. *Ep.* 47. Other authors share this argument on piracy as a major source of slaves; Philo, *Quod omn. prob. lib. sit* 36–40. Arr. *Epict. diss.* 3.24.66 speaks of Diogenes as the archetype of the wise, free man being sold as a slave in Corinth.

[60] On the NT *Haustafeln*, see Dieter Lührmann, "Neutestamentliche Haustafeln und antike Ökonomie," *NTS* 27 (1980–81): 83–91; Peter Fiedler, "Haustafel," *RAC* 13 (1986): 1063–73; David L. Balch, *Let Wives Be Submissive: The Domestic Code in 1 Peter*, SBLMS 26 (Chico, Calif.: Scholars Press, 1981); idem, "Household Codes," in *Greco-Roman Literature and the New Testament*, ed. David E. Aune, SBLSBS 21 (Atlanta: Scholars Press, 1988), 25–50; David E. Aune, *The New Testament in Its Literary Environment*, Library of Early Christianity (Philadelphia: Westminster Press, 1987), 196, 217.

Varro, and Columella.[61] In particular, Columella's agricultural handbook on how to run an estate furnishes occasional, extended passages on rural slavery. Yet this ancient "how to" literature paints a picture of how things *should be* as opposed to what they actually *are*, and so should not be read as social description.

The same caveat applies to imaginative literature: poetry, drama, parables, proto-novels, and satires.[62] The problem revolves around how to read this evidence historiographically. For example, we have Athenaeus, the author of *Deipnosophistai*, a symposium on encyclopedic topics. He offers one of the few passages of appreciable length in all of extant sources dealing with slavery.[63] At first glance its length suggests a great find. Yet there is a problem of method. How do interpreters make statements of historical fact from evidence that was written to be fiction? This question applies to all fictional depictions of slaves and freedmen/women, such as those found in the dream

---

[61] See Kenneth D. White, "Roman Agricultural Writers I: Varro and His Predecessors," *ANRW* 1.4 (1973): 439–95; Ross Samson, "Rural Slavery, Inscriptions, Archaeology, and Marx: A Response to Ramsay MacMullen's 'Late Roman Slavery,'" *Historia* 38 (1989): 99–110. For classical Athens, see Michael H. Jameson, "Agriculture and Slavery in Classical Athens," *CJ* 73 (1977–78): 122–45; G. E. M. de Ste. Croix, *The Class Struggle in the Ancient Greek World: From the Archaic Age to the Arab Conquest* (1981; reprint with corr., Ithaca: Cornell University Press, 1989), 140–74, 505–9; Ellen M. Wood, *Peasant-Citizen and Slave: The Foundations of Athenian Democracy* (London: Verso Press, 1988), 51–80.

[62] C. W. Amerasinghe, "The Part of the Slave in Terence's Drama," *G & R* 19 (1950): 62–72; Philip W. Harsh, "The Intriguing Slave in Greek Comedy," *TAPA* 86 (1955): 135–42; Peter P. Spranger, *Historische Untersuchungen zu den Sklavenfiguren des Plautus und Terenz*, Forschungen zur antiken Sklaverei 17 (Wiesbaden: Akademie Mainz, 1960); C. Stace, "The Slaves of Plautus," *G & R* 15 (1968): 64–77; W. Thomas MacCary, "Menander's Slaves: Their Names, Roles, and Masks," *TAPA* 100 (1969): 277–94; David Bain, *Masters, Servants, and Orders in Greek Tragedy: A Study of Some Aspects of Dramatic Technique and Convention* (Manchester: Manchester University Press, 1981); M. Garrido-Hory, *Martial et l'esclavage*, Annales littéraires de l'Université de Besançon 255, Centre de recherches d'histoire ancienne 40 (Paris: Les Belles Lettres, 1981); David Wiles, "Greek Theatre and the Legitimation of Slavery," in *Slavery and Other Forms of Unfree Labour*, ed. Léonie J. Archer, History Workshop Series (London: Routledge, 1988), 53–67; Holt Parker, "Crucially Funny or Tranio on the Couch: The *Servus Callidus* and Jokes about Torture," *TAPA* 119 (1989): 233–46; Mary Ann Beavis, "Ancient Slavery as an Interpretive Context for the New Testament Servant Parables with Special Reference to the Unjust Steward (Luke 16:1–8)," *JBL* 111 (1992): 37–54; J. R. Morgan and Richard Stoneman, eds., *Greek Fiction: The Greek Novel in Context* (New York: Routledge, 1994). For an excellent sourcebook, see B. P. Reardon, *Collected Ancient Greek Novels* (Berkeley and Los Angeles: University of California Press, 1989).

[63] Ath. *Deipnosophistai* 6.262–73; William L. Westermann, "Athenaeus and the Slaves of Athens," in Finley, *Slavery in Classical Antiquity*, 73–92; Pierre Vidal-Naquet, "Reflections on Greek Historical Writing about Slavery," in *The Black Hunter: Forms of Thought and Forms of Society in the Greek World*, trans. Andrew Szegedy-Maszak (Baltimore: Johns Hopkins University Press, 1986), 165–88.

handbook of Artemidorus.[64] An answer is to check references in fiction against other kinds of evidence. For example, the best known of all Roman freed-men/women is a fictional character, the boorish Trimalchio of Petronius's *Satyricon*. In order to carry his message, Petronius exploited stereotypes recognizable from the daily experience of his intended audience; otherwise his narrative would not have been found hilarious. Yet claims of fact based on fiction are still dubious. Seneca, however, can help in this regard. He describes a real-life counterpart to Trimalchio, the boorish Calvisius Sabinus who is said to have paid great sums for slaves who had memorized all the works of Homer and Hesiod.[65] This real-life counterpart supports historiographical use of Petronius, albeit within limits. With care, imaginative literature can yield important historical insights.

For example, Lucian of Samosata offers many insights into how he and other ancients from the propertied classes understood slavery in their society; indeed humor often serves as a vehicle for communicating cultural values and mores within a society. In his *Fugitivi*, Lucian brings a comical outlook to the plight of slave runaways.[66] In his *Vitarum auctio*, he presents a fictitious slave auction, with certain philosophies on sale bringing higher prices than others.[67] The loud-mouthed slave auctioneer, the stripped slave (for sale), and the celebrants of the festival Saturnalia are all characters important to Lucian and his humor.[68] Lucian's accounts of these fictional characters must be read critically, as one would read the literary figures in other satires, such as those by Juvenal and Martial, which deliver helpful but nevertheless anecdotal information regarding the lives of actual slaves.

In the end, we find that none of our sources fulfills our expectations; together, they allow a reconstruction of slavery that few historians specializing in modern periods would find satisfactory. Archaeology provides information on living quarters and some items of the trade, such as shackles, but can be

---

[64] Artemidorus, *The Interpretation of Dreams (Oneirocritica)*, trans., and commentary by Robert J. White (Park Ridge, N.J.: Noyes Press, 1975); Martin, *Slavery as Salvation*, 20–22, 32–35, 45–46, 74–75, draws attention to this important work, yet I disagree with Martin's conclusion that the passages illustrate the honor that certain managerial slaves held in Roman society.

[65] Sen. *Ep.* 27.5; Garnsey and Saller, *Roman Empire*, 120–21.

[66] Lucian, *Fug.*; Graham Anderson, *Lucian: Theme and Variation in the Second Sophistic*, Mnemosyne Bibliotheca Classica, Batava Supplementum 41 (Leiden: E. J. Brill, 1976), 107–9. On the professional slave-catcher, see David Daube, "Slave-Catching," *Juridical Review* 64 (1952): 12–28.

[67] Lucian, *Vit. auct.* (in this work Lucian also mentions the role of pirates in the slave trade).

[68] Lucian, *Pro Merc. Cond.* 23–25 (which also contains references to pirates, with a discussion of liberty and slavery); *Eun.* 12 (inspection of slaves like that of cattle); see also *Sat.* passim.

misused, as it might be when arguing for the rise of slavery from an observed decline in back problems. Inscriptions offer insights into the view that slavery survived the afterlife, but there are counterexamples that not all believed this. Papyrology offers promising evidence, such as "slave wanted" posters, yet its application to areas outside Egypt is limited. Laws do not necessarily reflect social practice; histories care little for slaves; and letters contain only one half of a dialogue. Moral exhortation literature tells more about the Stoic philosophy of large slaveholders than the lives of slaves. Agricultural handbooks advise what ancient farming *ought* to have been, not necessarily what it *was*. Finally, because poetry, drama, parables, myths, and proto-novels are pieces of fiction, our use of them must reckon with the limitations of using imaginative literature to support historical claims. Although frustrated by this sobering discovery, we are not reduced to silence. We can still state some historical facts about ancient slavery, based on careful use of the evidence itemized above. We begin with the question of slave origins.

The Sources of Slaves

The main sources of ancient slaves were warfare, piracy, brigandage, the international slave trade, kidnapping, infant exposure, some breeding, and the punishment of criminals.[69] To be sure, some freeborn people did sell themselves or their children into slavery. The Christian author of *First Clement* writes: "We know that many among ourselves have given themselves to bondage that they might ransom others. Many have delivered themselves to slavery, and provided food for others with the price they received for themselves."[70] However, this activity was neither regular in Rome nor widespread throughout its empire; at no time did self-sale provide a major supply of slaves. Some New Testament scholars have argued that the large number of people selling themselves into slavery constitutes evidence of how humane (or attractive a lifestyle) ancient slavery was.[71] At first glance, several pieces of evidence appear to support such claims. In the *Satyricon* the fictional freedman character

---

[69] See the excellent collection in Wiedemann, *Greek and Roman Slavery*, 106–21.

[70] *1 Clem.* 55.2; Henneke Gülzow, *Christentum und Sklaverei in den ersten drei Jahrhunderten* (Bonn: Rudolf Habelt, 1969), 105–6; Peter Lampe, *Die stadtrömischen Christen in den ersten beiden Jahrhunderten*, 2d expanded ed., WUNT 18, 2d ser. (Tübingen: J.C.B. Mohr [Paul Siebeck], 1989), 68–69, 72, 113–14, 346, 348; Andreas Lindemann, *Die Clemensbriefe*, HNT 17, *Die Apostolischen Väter* (Tübingen: J.C.B. Mohr [Paul Siebeck], 1992), 155.

[71] E.g., S. Scott Bartchy, *ΜΑΛΛΟΝ ΧΡΗΣΑΙ: First-Century Slavery and the Interpretation of First Corinthians 7:21*, SBLDS 11 (1973; reprint, Atlanta: Scholars Press, 1985), 45–46, who accepts uncritically the cliometric calculations of A. H. M. Jones.

Trimalchio tells why he became a slave. His explanation seems to support the view that self-sale was attractive to some non-Romans in the early Empire: "'Why are you a freedman?' did you ask? Because I put myself into slavery. I wanted to be a Roman citizen, not a provincial with taxes to pay."[72] Yet this statement is meant to be comical and absurd; to take the passage seriously as historical evidence of social practice is methodologically questionable.

Another piece of evidence often adduced is Dio Chrysostom, who writes an imaginary dialogue between a slave and a citizen. The slave character says: "I mean that great numbers of people, we may suppose, who are freeborn sell themselves, so that they are slaves by contract [δουλεύειν κατὰ συγγραφήν], sometimes on no easy terms but the most severe imaginable."[73] At first reading, the passage appears to suggest that self-sale was a major slave source. The interlocutor, however, refers to educated Greeks who contract themselves not into *chattel* bondage but a kind of *indentured* servitude (δουλεύειν κατὰ συγγραφήν) for a specified time. Presumably, the indentured servants neither contracted themselves permanently nor included their children, both of which are essential to chattel slavery. Like Petronius, Chrysostom aims to satirize the higher orders of society. Chrysostom uses the language of slavery and freedom metaphorically in an attempt to condemn moral vices (such as greed, gluttony, and so forth) and to promote the virtues practiced by the Stoic. It is telling that the non-Christian parallels to *1 Clem.* 55.2 are fictional. Recent investigations of Roman historians have shown how historically unreliable such evidence is, and have discredited the scholarly commonplace, based on this evidence, that large numbers of freeborn persons sold themselves as chattels.[74] The closest parallel, Dio Chrys. *Or.* 15.23, suggests that Clement refers to indentured servants, not chattel slaves. There are, then, no grounds for seeing self-sale as a major source of slaves or as evidence for ancient slavery's relatively humane character.

Above all else, warfare remained throughout classical antiquity an important supplier of slaves.[75] According to Dio Chrysostom, the original ways of

---

[72] Petron. *Cena* 57. Trimalchio refers to the legal rule that formal manumission normally conferred citizenship on the freedman/woman if the manumittor was a Roman citizen. On this rule see chapter 4.

[73] Dio Chrys. *Or.* 15.23; see the note in the LCL edition (165 n. 3).

[74] William V. Harris, "Towards a Study of the Roman Slave Trade," in *The Seaborne Commerce of Ancient Rome: Studies in Archaeology and History*, ed. J. H. D'Arms and E. C. Kopff, Memoirs of the American Academy in Rome 36 (Rome: The Academy, 1980), 124. *Pace* Gülzow, *Christentum*, 105–6; Lampe, *Stadtrömischen Christen*, 68–69; Lindemann, *Clemensbriefe*, 155.

[75] For Greece, see A. H. Jackson, "Some Recent Work on the Treatment of Prisoners of War in Ancient Greece," *Talanta* 2 (1970): 37–53; Yvon Garlan, "War, Piracy, and Slavery in the Greek World," trans. Marie-Jo Roy, in Finley, *Classical Slavery*, 7–21; idem, *Slavery in Ancient Greece*, rev. and expanded ed., trans. Janet Lloyd (Ithaca: Cornell University

obtaining slaves were by capture in war and by land or sea brigandage.[76] In his campaigns in Gaul between 58 and 51 B.C.E. alone, Julius Caesar is reported to have shipped back to peninsular Italy nearly one million enslaved Gallic prisoners of war.[77] Slaves by the tens of thousands poured into the markets of Sicily and peninsular Italy as early as the First Punic War (264–241 B.C.E.), a direct result of the annual pattern of warfare and military expansion of Rome's borders during the late Republic.[78] The classic statement on warfare as a slave source comes from the imperial jurist Florentinus, who wrote about the etymological root of the Latin word for slave. The *Digest* quotes: "Slaves [*servi*] are so called because commanders generally sell the people they capture and thereby save [*servare*] them instead of killing them. The word for property in slaves [*mancipia*] is derived from the fact that they are captured from the enemy by force of arms [*manu capiantur*]."[79] Indeed, Florentinus correctly states that one important source of slaves was the steady stream of prisoners of war, although his etymologies are probably false.

Yet we are not then permitted to claim, as traditional Marxist historians do, that the need for slaves was the true origin of the whole history of Roman war and expansion.[80] Without any primary evidence for it, such a claim cannot be proved and is highly unlikely. Indeed, no Marxist scholar has yet been able to show in adequate detail how the entire phenomenon of warfare could have

---

Press, 1988), 47–48; M. M. Austin and P. Vidal-Naquet, *Economic and Social History of Ancient Greece: An Introduction*, 2d ed., trans. and rev. M. M. Austin (Berkeley and Los Angeles: University of California Press, 1977), 13, 18–19.

[76] Dio Chrys. *Or.* 15.25, where he lists the ways in which slaveowners acquired slaves; Varr. *R.R.* 2.10.4 provides a similar list; Harris, "Towards a Study," 121–22, 136 n. 47.

[77] Plut. *Vit. Caes.* 15.3; Appian, *Gall.* 1.2; M. I. Finley, *The Ancient Economy*, Sather Classical Lectures 43, 2d ed. (Berkeley and Los Angeles: University of California Press, 1985), 72, calls one million "a not wildly incredible figure"; Keith Hopkins, *Conquerors and Slaves*, Sociological Studies in Roman History 1 (New York: Cambridge University Press, 1978), 1–15, 99–115. Caesar regularly gave Gallic prisoners of war to his troops as slaves, Suet. *Iul.* 26.3; Treggiari, *Roman Freedmen*, 9–10.

[78] Livy, *Epit.* 26.40.13; 27.16.7; 31.30.2–3; 41.11.8; 41.28.8–9; 45.34.5; Livy, *Per.* 68; Polyb. 30.15 (= Strabo 7.322); Strabo 5.224; Appian, *Pun.* 15, 23, 26, 36, 48; Appian, *Iber.* 68; Plut. *Vit. Aem.* 29; Suet. *Gal.* 3; Sall. *Iug.* 91.7; William V. Harris, *War and Imperialism in Republican Rome, 327–70 B.C.* (Oxford: Clarendon Press, 1979), 74–75, 81; P. A. Brunt, "Laus imperii," in *Imperialism in the Ancient World*, ed. P. D. A. Garnsey and C. R. Whittaker, Cambridge Classical Studies (Cambridge: Cambridge University Press, 1978), 190.

[79] *Digest* 1.5.4.2–3, trans. in Wiedemann, *Greek and Roman Slavery*, 15.

[80] E. M. Štaerman, *Die Blütezeit der Sklavenwirtschaft in der römischen Republik*, trans. Maria Bräuer-Pospelova, Übersetzungen ausländischer Arbeiten zur antiken Sklaverei 2 (Wiesbaden: Franz Steiner, 1969), 36–70; Max Dieckhoff, *Krieg und Frieden im griechisch-römischen Altertum*, Lebendiges Altertum 10 (Berlin: Akademie-Verlag, 1962), 1–58; see also a non-Marxist, J. A. Hobson, *Imperialism: A Study*, rev. with new introd. by Philip Siegelman (Ann Arbor: University of Michigan Press, 1965), 247–48; cited by Harris, *Imperialism*, 83 n. 5.

grown out of conflicts over the means of production within the Roman empire.[81] The causes of Roman imperialism are complex, as William V. Harris correctly points out:

An adequate supply of slaves at reasonable prices was not likely to be forthcoming in peaceful conditions. ... thus for a satisfactory slave supply war, or rather periodic successful war, was indeed highly desirable. This, however, was only one of the economic benefits which were assumed to grow from successful warfare, and there is no rational justification for reckoning it the only important one, still less for treating the demand for slaves as the root of Roman imperialism.[82]

Harris is surely correct in his criticism of Marxist explanations for the etiology of war; economics alone do not explain enslavement as a human phenomenon.[83] No identifiable economic motives for military expansion can be found in the ancient sources. In fact, Rome's military actions at times worked against any supposed overarching strategy to secure control over the conditions of production in subject communities.[84]

---

[81] Harris, *Imperialism*, 83–85.

[82] Harris, *Imperialism*, 84–85.

[83] Finley, *Ancient Slavery and Modern Ideology*, 83–86; Erich S. Gruen, *The Hellenistic World and the Coming of Rome* (Berkeley and Los Angeles: University of California Press, 1984), 1:297–99. Yet this kind of argumentation is found not only in Marxists, but also in the writings of eighteenth-century mercantilists, who emphasized the need for trade routes and markets as an explanation for war and enslavement. Even Max Weber claimed ancient wars to be essentially "slave hunts" (*The Agrarian Sociology of Ancient Civilizations*, trans. R. I. Frank, Foundations of History Library [London: N.L.B., 1976], 393).

[84] That two potentially useful urban market centers, Carthage and Corinth, were destroyed by Roman troops suggests that neither obtaining market centers nor commanding trade were at issue in those campaigns. Roman commanders were less likely motivated by trade or market concerns than by prospects for public acclaim and personal *dignitas*, and by aristocratic competition in triumph hunting. There are also four penetrating methodological points against certain modern attempts to discern motives behind the actions of ancient people. The first problem is a reliance upon sources that are not only quite late for the early Republic (e.g., the writings of Livy), but also by their very nature biased with particular historiographical goals. A second problem is the complexity involved in reconstructing the cultural context in which actions have meaning. A third concern is that there may have been underlying personal motivations, of which even the commanders may not have personally been aware. (Even modern people, in the age of psychologists, admit that sometimes they do not know why they choose to do certain things.) Lastly, it is not likely that military actions stemmed from only one motive. That several layers of motives lie behind decisions for military conflict was recognized even by ancient authors. Polybius writes that in its decision to march against the Dalmatians in Illyria (157 B.C.E.), the Senate publicly stated the cause for war lay in Dalmatian insult to Roman ambassadors, while their private motivation lay in gaining an opportunity to keep the Roman citizen body militarily fit (Polyb. 31.23). Whereas some kinds of wars were perceived to be profitable, there was also an appreciation that going to war entailed a great deal of uncertainty. Republican decisions to march came only after discussions in the Roman Senate. The Senate did avoid war at times (e.g., 155/154 B.C.E. in Bithynia; A. N. Sherwin-White,

However, historians continue to debate at which particular period warfare served as Rome's primary source of slaves. After 14 c.e., there was no continuous expansion of the Roman empire.[85] Therefore, a number of scholars argue that in the Republican period warfare was the primary source of slaves and that in the Principate it was breeding.[86] "Slave breeding" means the raising of offspring parented by one's existing slave population. It is doubtful that Roman slaveholders systematically engaged in slave breeding, although it probably always served as a source for their slaves whose importance varied at different times.[87] Other scholars, opposing the hypothesis that breeding replaced warfare as the primary source of slaves under the Principate, contend that although continuous expansion ceased, wars and other conflicts did not; thus, the enslavement of Roman enemies after battles continued to be an important source of slaves even after the late Republican wars of expansion.[88] The significance of this debate will become apparent in chapter 2, which will challenge an idea popular among New Testament scholars that under the Principate slaves were treated kindly because they were raised in homes and not taken by violence in battle. But slave populations rarely reproduce enough

---

Roman Foreign Policy in the East, 169 b.c. *to* a.d. *1* [Norman: University of Oklahoma Press, 1983], 45). One senator may have voted for war because he would have been the chosen commander. A second, aged senator might have voted against a campaign because, if Rome did go to war, he would have to deal with the added competition caused by the triumphing of another, younger senator. These four problems betray the simplicities behind the Marxist interpretation that the Roman market demand for slaves singularly caused Roman imperialism. For an insightful analysis of Roman imperialism as a cultural phenomenon peculiar to the Roman values of *virtus* and *dignitas* and not simply a product of generic human impulses (e.g., for power), see E. Badian, *Roman Imperialism in the Late Republic* (Oxford: Basil Blackwell, 1968); Harris, *Imperialism*; Hopkins, *Conquerors*, 1–98 (on the extraordinary amount of military mobilization in Roman society).

[85] There was expansion under Claudius (Britain) and Trajan (Dacia).

[86] The first direct evidence of large-scale slave breeding is Nep. *Att.* 13.3 and Hor. *Epod.* 2.65. See also Varro, *R.R.* 1.17.5; 2.10.6; Columella, *R.R.* 1.8.5; 1.8.19; Cic. *Fin.* 1.12.

[87] Keith R. Bradley, "On the Roman Slave Supply and Slave Breeding," in Finley, *Classical Slavery*, 55; Harris, "Towards a Study," 120–21.

[88] The best study remains Bradley, "Slave Breeding," 42–64, who summarizes the scholarly opinions of Roman historians; see also idem, *Slaves and Masters*, 62–63. Bradley, 54, argues that "there is no convincing reason to believe that natural reproduction among slaves could not have been a significantly contributing element in Rome's slave supply as early as 200 b.c." However, I do not accept all of Bradley's conclusions. He contends, for example, by using a table (table 1, "Slave Breeding," 45), that records of mass enslavements end around 142 b.c.e. Closer examination of his evidence (mainly, the writings of Livy) reveals that the records end around 142 b.c.e. because Livy's narrative breaks off shortly before that time. Rome did not suddenly stop enslaving cities in 142 b.c.e. The evidence, therefore, is inconclusive, and cannot be used to prove that mass enslavements in war ended in 142 b.c.e..

to replace themselves. Furthermore, while the antebellum U.S. South is a prominent exception on this point, no American historian claims that breeding slaves caused masters to treat them kindly. It seems reasonable to conclude, then, that both breeding and warfare contributed to the slave supply to varying degrees throughout the whole of Roman history.

Another source of slaves was piracy. Cilician pirates abducted young Julius Caesar, who was sailing to Rhodes, and detained him for nearly forty days for a ransom of fifty talents.[89] Abduction by bandits (*latrones*), kidnappers (*plagiarii*), or common thieves (*fures*) was a real danger for travelers, no matter how much private protection they mustered. Although the army did sometimes seek to maintain internal peace and order, Rome still lacked anything comparable to modern police forces or investigative agencies.[90] The Roman government concentrated its hegemony over cities and borders, leaving whole geographic regions surrounded by its forces but otherwise inadequately protected by its institutions.[91] Within rural regions, violent renegades organized to seize indiscriminately both slave and freeborn. Victims of kidnapping often found themselves thrown into the slave prisons (*ergastula*) on the estates of wealthy landowners, never to be heard from again.[92]

Yet piracy in the ancient world should not be thought of in its modern sense of individual renegade outlaws working independently of any governmental sponsorship.[93] Ancient pirates enjoyed the support of monarchs and magnates, such as those of the Illyrian kingdom, Asia Minor, and the outlying areas of the Black Sea. Rulers worked hand in hand with slave-dealing pirates.[94] Cilicia in southern Asia Minor, the home base of Caesar's abductors, was particularly notorious for harboring pirates.[95] The economies of some ancient states depended on the success of piracy, and Rome was no excep-

---

[89] The pirates threatened to sell Caesar into slavery if the ransom money did not come; Plut. *Vit. Caes.* 1; Suet. *Iul.* 4; Henry A. Omerod, *Piracy in the Ancient World* (1914; reprint, New York: Doreset Press, 1987), 20.

[90] The army's internal policing role remains one of the most neglected of subjects in works on Roman military history; B. D. Shaw, "Bandits in the Roman Empire," *P & P* 105 (1984): 18. See also idem, "Bandits," in Giardina, *The Romans*, 300–341.

[91] Shaw, "Bandits in the Roman Empire," 30; Ramsay MacMullen, *Enemies of the Roman Order: Treason, Unrest, and Alienation in the Empire* (Cambridge: Harvard University Press, 1966), 192–241.

[92] Suet. *Tib.* 8; Wiedemann, *Greek and Roman Slavery*, 114; Shaw, "Bandits in the Roman Empire," 33.

[93] Finley, "Aulos Kapreillios Timotheos," 161.

[94] Westermann, *Slave Systems*, 6, 28–29, 60, 63–69; M. I. Finley, "The Black Sea and Danubian Regions and the Slave Trade in Antiquity," *Klio* 40 (1962): 51–59; Shaw, "Bandits in the Roman Empire," 14, 33–39, 41; Garlan, "War, Piracy, and Slavery," 7–21.

[95] Ormerod, *Piracy*, 190–247; Westermann, *Slave Systems*, 126.

tion.[96] In 67 B.C.E., in an uncomplicated naval exercise, Pompey the Great cleared the eastern Mediterranean seaboard of a considerable infestation of Cilician pirates. How did Pompey manage to clear the seas of pirates in only a few months when no Roman had made any impact for the preceding hundred years? The answer lies in a conflict of interests. With their extensive kidnapping-slaving operation, Cilician pirates had transported a welcome and plentiful number of slaves to Italy and Sicily. Only when piratical activity in the Adriatic threatened the corn supply to the city of Rome did the Senate finally take action.[97] Ironically, Sextus Pompeius, the son of Pompey the Great, grew up to command fleets of pirates and mercenaries (possibly the very descendants of Pompey's Cilician piratical adversaries) in the civil wars against Octavian from 38 to 36 B.C.E.[98]

Piracy went hand in glove with the international slave trade. The literary sources mention surprisingly little about this activity; a reference in the New Testament to the human cargo of slave merchants is found in the Apocalypse:

> And the merchants of the earth weep and mourn for her, since no one buys their cargo anymore, cargo of gold, silver, jewels and pearls, fine linen, purple, silk and scarlet, all kinds of scented wood, all articles of ivory, all articles of costly wood, bronze, iron, and marble, cinnamon, spice, incense, myrrh, frankincense, wine, olive oil, choice flour and wheat, cattle and sheep, horses and chariots, slaves – and human lives. (Rev 18:11–13)

The author's perspective may be due to his knowledge about or personal experience of the Jewish War of 66–70/73 C.E.[99] Discussion of the slave trade occurs mostly when some special circumstance attracted a writer (this seems true of Rev 18 as well), such as Thucydides' exceptional narrative of how the Athenians removed the entire population of the Sicilian town of Hyccara,

---

[96] E. Maróti, "Der Sklavenmarkt auf Delos und die Piraterie," *Helikon* 9 (1969): 24–42; A. H. Jackson, "Privateers in the Ancient Greek World," in *War and Society: Historical Essays in Honour and Memory of J. R. Western*, ed. M. R. D. Foot (London: Paul Elek, 1973), 241–53; Pierre Brulé, *La piraterie Crétoise hellénistique*, Annales littéraires de l'Université de Besançon 223, Centre de recherches d'histoire ancienne 27 (Paris: Les Belles Lettres, 1978), 117–38; M. H. Crawford, "Republican Denarii in Romania: The Suppression of Piracy and the Slave Trade," *JRS* 67 (1977): 117–24.

[97] Finley, *The Ancient Economy*, 156; H. H. Scullard, *From the Gracchi to Nero: A History of Rome 133 B.C. to A.D. 68*, 5th ed. (London: Methuen, 1982), 97–98, 421 n. 16; Egon Maróti, "Die Rolle der Seeräuber in der Zeit der Mithradatischen Kriege," in *Ricerche stoiche ed economiche in memoria di Corrado Barbagalla a cura di Luigi de Rose*, vol. 1 (Naples: Edizioni Scientifiche Italiane, 1970), esp. 488–93; Hermann Strasburger, "Poseidonius on Problems of the Roman Empire," *JRS* 55 (1965): 42–43, 50–52; Shaw, "Bandits in the Roman Empire," 39–41.

[98] Scullard, *Gracchi to Nero*, 163–64; A. H. Jackson, "Privateers," 243; Shaw, "Bandits in the Roman Empire," 33–34.

[99] On the social identity of the author, see Adela Yarbro Collins, *Crisis and Catharsis: The Power of the Apocalypse* (Philadelphia: Westminster Press, 1984), 25–53.

shipped the people to the market at Catania, and sold them for 120 talents.[100] Yet as M. I. Finley remarks, "The absence of evidence about the slave trade may prove something about the attitudes and interest of ancient writers, but it proves nothing about the existence of a slave trade or its character or scale."[101] Despite the lack of direct literary references to the slave trade, scholars have been able indirectly to glean information on where slaves were bought and sold.[102] In this regard, Finley offers a useful distinction between the regular slave markets and the activities of itinerant slave traders.[103] Building upon Finley's work, William Harris identifies four settings in which slaves changed hands: individual transactions, opportunistic markets, periodic markets, and regular metropolitan markets.

The first two of these settings, individual transactions and opportunistic markets, were *ad hoc* arrangements. In nearly every neighborhood of a town, individual owners sold slaves to one another in small-scale transactions. In Egypt, for instance, a buyer did not need to go to Alexandria to purchase a single slave: papyrus and parchment fragments record personal sales in smaller nomes, such as Hermopolis, Oxyrhynchus, Ptolemais, Euergetis, and Socnopaiou Nesos. Yet it does appear that if one desired to buy or sell a large number of slaves, one had to go to a major metropolitan port such as Alexandria.[104] Opportunistic markets formed around frontier army camps, where a parasitic settlement of traders, veterans, and lower sorts sold the prisoners of war after successful campaigns.[105] These "camp followers" (*canabae*) worked deals with the military to operate wholesale bazaars to auction off the always plentiful war captives. When the army marched on a campaign, the *canabae* followed closely behind, preparing to enrich themselves after successful battles (or to flee after unsuccessful ones).[106] *Canabae* profited after Pompey's capture of Jerusalem in 63 B.C.E., Jerusalem's second sacking by the Roman general Gaius Sosius and his two Syrian legions in 37 B.C.E., the Jewish War of 66–70/ 73 C.E., and the Bar-Kokhba revolt of 132–135 C.E. All of these Roman military victories placed huge numbers of Jewish prisoners of war into the hands of *canabae*; most were subsequently shipped to Rome for retail auction as slaves.[107] As a consequence, overwhelming numbers of Jewish prisoners of

---

[100] Thuc. 6.62; 7.13; Finley, "Slave Trade," 167.

[101] Finley, "Slave Trade," 168.

[102] Keith R. Bradley, "Social Aspects of the Slave Trade in the Roman World," *MBAH* 5 (1986): 49–58.

[103] Finley, "Aulos Kapreillios Timotheos," 163–64; so noted by Harris, "Towards a Study," 137 n. 83.

[104] Harris, "Towards a Study," 125.

[105] *CIL* 3.940.19; 3.959.18; 13.1954; *Oxford Latin Dictionary*, s.v. "canabae."

[106] Harris, "Towards a Study," 125.

[107] H. St. Hart, "Judaea and Rome: The Official Commentary," *JTS* n.s. 3 (1952): 176–84; Emil Schürer, *The History of the Jewish People in the Age of Jesus Christ (175 B.C.–*

war poured into the Italian and Sicilian slave markets.[108] The trafficking in
Jewish slaves by camp followers took place also in earlier wars and battles, such
as those under the Hasmoneans.[109] These examples illustrate the role of *canabae* in the wholesale slave trade.[110]

The periodic and regular metropolitan markets sold large numbers of slaves
on the retail level. "Periodic market" refers to slave sales that took place in
conjunction with calendric festivals. The central Grecian town of Tithorea,
for example, held a slave sale twice a year during the semi-annual festival in
honor of Isis.[111] "Regular market" denotes large-scale, continuing operations
in major metropolitan ports, such as Roman Corinth and the island of Delos.
In some cases, there may have been a periodic element to the regular metropolitan market. The Syrian town of Baetocaese, for instance, opened a slave
market only twice monthly.[112] In either setting, the physical place where
slaves were sold was not isolated from other squares of the marketplace. Slaves
were part and parcel of regular seaborne commerce and were not considered
"peculiar" commodities that they were thought to be in the antebellum U.S.
South. (The square where slaves were sold in the South was nearly always
separated off from other squares in the marketplace.) Auction served as the
regular means of actual sale. Tombstones often provide pictorial representa-

---

A.D. *135),* new ed., rev. Geza Vermes, Fergus Millar, and Martin Goodman (Edinburgh:
T. & T. Clark, 1973), 1:240–42, 552–53; E. Mary Smallwood, *The Jews under Roman
Rule: From Pompey to Diocletian,* SJLA 20 (Leiden: E. J. Brill, 1976), 519; G. Fuks, "Where
Have All the Freedmen Gone? On an Anomaly in the Jewish Grave-Inscriptions from
Rome," *JJS* 36 (1985): 25–29.

[108] Josephus, *JW* 1.7.6–7 §154–158 (= *Ant.* 14.4.4–5 §71–79); *JW* 1.17.8–18.2 §343–
353 (= *Ant.* 14.15.14–16.2 §465–481); *JW* 3.7.31–36 §304–337 (cf. *JW* 3.10.10 §540–
542 on Jewish slaves sent to cut a canal through the isthmus of Corinth); *JW* 6.9.2 §417–
418; 7.5.3 §118; *Psalms of Solomon* 2:6; 8:21; 17:12; Luke 21:20–24; Plut. *Vit. Pomp.*
45.1–5; Appian, *Mith.* 12.17.117; Roman coinage depicting a Jewish slave with the inscription *IUDAEA CAPTA* (Edward A. Sydenham, *The Coinage of the Roman Republic*
[London: Spink & Son, 1952], 199 no. 1272); Jerome (Hieronymus), *In Hieremiam* 6
(CCSL 74.307); idem, *In Zachariam* 3.9.4.5 (CCSL 76.1.851); *Chronicon Paschale,* ed. L.
Dindorf, Corpus Scriptorum Historiae Byzantinae (Bonn: Impensis Ed. Weberi, 1832),
1:474.

[109] Ezek 27:13; Joel 3:6; *Letter of Aristeas* 12–14; 1 Macc 3:41 (= Josephus, *Ant.* 12.7.3
§298–299); 2 Macc 8:10–11; 3 Macc 2:28–29; *CII* 709 (157/156 B.C.E.); *CII* 710 (162
B.C.E.); *CII* 711 (119 B.C.E.); D. M. Lewis, "The First Greek Jew," *JSS* 2 (1957): 264–66;
Victor Tcherikover, *Hellenistic Civilization and the Jews,* trans. S. Applebaum (Philadel-
phia: Jewish Publication Society of America, 1959), 342; Schürer, *History of the Jewish
People,* 1:159.

[110] Finley, "Aulos Kapreillios Timotheos," 160.

[111] Paus. 10.32.15; cf. *IG* 9².1.583 at lines 32–34, concerning slave sales in conjunction
with the Temple of Apollo at Actium; Finley, "Aulos Kapreillios Timotheos," 163–64;
Harris, "Towards a Study," 126.

[112] *OGI* 262.26–27; Harris, "Towards a Study," 126.

tions of such degrading experiences. Other stones from Capua and from Arles depict scenes of slaves in single garments standing on rotating platforms with potential buyers checking underneath the slaves' clothes. Seneca observed, "When you buy a horse, you order its blanket removed; so, too, you pull the garments off slaves."[113] As a further sign of dishonor, auctioneering dealers typically used chalk to mark the feet of fresh overseas slaves to set them apart from the more domesticated homebred slaves.[114] Slave dealers in antiquity enjoyed a reputation similar to that of used-car sellers today. John Chrysostom evinces ancient society's contempt for slave dealers when he writes, "Just as slave dealers show sweets and cakes, dice and other things to small children to entice them and deprive them of their freedom and even of their lives; so also demons, promising to heal the sick limbs of our body, completely destroy the health of the soul."[115] To compound their ill repute, slave dealers often made dishonest claims about the quality, service, and history of their merchandise. They were not above lying about the national origin of the slaves that they sold.[116] The elder Pliny reports that the infamous dealer Toranius sold, for a good price, two slave boys to the triumvir Marcus Antonius (Mark Anthony) as twins, even though one came from Asia and the other from Gaul.[117] The *Digest* tried to regulate such unscrupulous slave dealing: "Those selling slaves should declare their nationality when making the sale; for the slave's nationality may often induce or deter a purchaser; therefore, we have an interest in knowing the nationality; for there is a presumption that some slaves are good, coming from a race with no bad repute, while others are thought bad, since they come from a notorious people."[118] In the purchasing of slaves, one had to follow the adage "caveat emptor."

Related to the Mediterranean slave trade and piracy was infant exposure. Child abandonment was regular in the ancient Mediterranean world and led to foundlings being circulated in Roman trade.[119] Tacitus thought the absence

---

[113] Sen. *Ep.* 80.9; Finley, "Aulos Kapreillios Timotheos," 164; see also Lucian, *Eun.* 12.

[114] Pliny, *HN* 35.38; Wiedemann, *Greek and Roman Slavery*, 111–12.

[115] Chrys. *Jud.* 1.7 (*PG* 48.855); trans. in Wayne A. Meeks and Robert L. Wilken, *Jews and Christians in Antioch in the First Four Centuries of the Common Era*, SBLSBS 13 (Missoula, Mont.: Scholars Press, 1978), 102. See also 1 Tim 1:10.

[116] Finley, "Aulos Kapreilios Timotheos," 155–56.

[117] Pliny, *HN* 7.12.56; Wiedemann, *Greek and Roman Slavery*, 104; Bradley, *Slaves and Masters*, 62.

[118] *Digest* 21.1.31.21 (Ulpian).

[119] For the epigraphical evidence, see A. Cameron, "ΘΡΕΠΤΟΣ and Related Terms in the Inscriptions of Asia Minor," in *Anatolian Studies Presented to William Hepburn Buckler*, ed. W. M. Calder and J. Keil (Manchester: Manchester University Press, 1939), 27–62; T. G. Nani, "θρεπτοί," *Epigraphica* 5–6 (1943–44): 45–84; Beryl Rawson, "Children in the Roman *Familia*," in *The Family in Ancient Rome: New Perspectives*, ed. idem (Ithaca: Cornell University Press, 1986), 173–86; cf. Kudlien, *Sklaven-Mentalität*, 165–67. The allegory of

of exposure in Jewish and German society strange; Aelian found the Theban practice to prevent it odd; Strabo considered Egyptians peculiar because they raised every baby that was born.[120] Exposure of unwanted children was not considered identical to infanticide; literary sources reveal that people expected that an abandoned baby would be picked up and enslaved.[121] Justin Martyr mentions the evils of exposure because slave dealers hunted for foundlings precisely to supply their prostitution industry; Justin claims that someone going to a prostitute might commit incest with a child that he had exposed years ago.[122] Greco-Roman moralists also offered arguments against the exposure of infants. Gaius Musonius Rufus, the Stoic teacher of Epictetus, exhorted that every child must be raised, and not aborted or abandoned, in an effort to encourage marriage and reproduction in the senatorial and equestrian orders.[123] Although there were conflicting attitudes about the economic

---

Ezek 16 may reflect the practice of exposure in Palestine in the sixth century B.C.E. or thereabouts; Walther Zimmerli, *Ezekiel 1: A Commentary on the Book of the Prophet Ezekiel, Chapters 1–24*, trans. Ronald E. Clements, ed. Frank Moore Cross and Klaus Baltzer with Leonard Jay Greenspoon, Hermeneia (Philadelphia: Fortress Press, 1979), 336, 338–39, 348.

[120] Tac. *Hist.* 5.5; *Germ.* 19; Ael. *VH* 2.7; Strabo 17.2.5; Harris, "Towards a Study," 123; P. W. van der Horst, *The Sentences of Pseudo-Phocylides* (Leiden: E. J. Brill, 1978), 232–34.

[121] Pliny, *Ep.* 10.65; 10.66; La Rue Van Hook, "The Exposure of Infants at Athens," *TAPA* 51 (1920): 145; Max Radin, "The Exposure of Infants in Roman Law and Practice," *CJ* 20 (1924–25): 340; Garnsey and Saller, *The Roman Empire*, 138; Saller, "Slavery and the Roman Family," 69; Harris, "Towards a Study," 123; Bradley, *Slaves and Masters*, 57–58; Mark Golden, "Demography and the Exposure of Girls at Athens," *Phoenix* 35 (1981): 330–31; Cynthia Patterson, "'Not Worth Rearing': The Causes of Infant Exposure in Ancient Greece," *TAPA* 115 (1985): 103 n. 1, 104–7, 121–22; John E. Boswell, "*Expositio* and *Oblatio*: The Abandonment of Children and the Ancient and Medieval Family," *AHR* 89 (1984): 13; idem, *The Kindness of Strangers: The Abandonment of Children in Western Europe from Late Antiquity to the Renaissance* (New York: Pantheon Books, 1988), 25, 41–41, 54 n. 2, 59 n. 11, 69 n. 51, 170, 176 n. 128, 196, 353.

[122] Just. *1 Apol.* 27 (Goodspeed, 44). For the Christian material on child abandonment, see Boswell, *Kindness of Strangers*, 157–79. Boswell, however, is too optimistic in his appraisal of how foundlings were treated; the slavery of such foundlings was brutal.

[123] Musonius Rufus, F 15a–b (ed. O. Hense) with additional segments supplied by a papyrus fragment (*PHarris* 1) discovered after Hense's edition; trans. in Cora E. Lutz, "Musonius Rufus: 'The Roman Socrates,'" *YClS* 10 (1947): 96–101; commentary in A. C. van Geytenbeek, *Musonius Rufus and the Greek Diatribe*, Wijsgerige Teksten en Studies 8, rev. ed. trans. B. L. Hijmans (Assen, Netherlands: van Gorcum, 1963), 78–89; Keith Hopkins, "A Textual Emendation in a Fragment of Musonius Rufus," *CQ* 15 (1965): 72–74; idem, "Contraception in the Roman Empire," *CSSH* 8 (1965–66): 141; Robert Etienne, "La conscience médicale antique et la vie des enfants," *Annales de démographie historique* (1973): 18, 23. For literature on *PHarris* 1, the only text of Musonius found in any papyrus, see J. Enoch Powell, "Musonius Rufus: Εἰ πάντα τὰ γινόμενα τέκνα θρεπτέον in P. Harr. 1," *APF* 12 (1937): 175–78; Bruno Snell, "The Rendel Harris Papyri of Woodbrooke College, Birmingham," *Gnomon* 13 (1937): 578; W. G. Waddell, review of

value of children, Greek and Roman authors often used exposure as a *topos* of social criticism; their statements, however, about other ethnic groups' not practicing it were not usually based on actual observation.[124] The value of such statements lies not in establishing the rate of occurrence in quantitative terms, but in understanding how accepted a practice exposure was in antiquity. Most often, the unwanted child would be left at a visible place known for foundlings, such as a temple of Asclepius, or an area where slave dealers were known to linger. Some scholars have suggested that, especially in Greco-Roman Egypt, the public dunghill (κοπρία) often served as one such place, as attested by the frequency of copronyms (Κοπρεύς, Κοπριαίρετος).[125] Sarah Pomeroy, however, has demonstrated that such uncomplimentary nicknames (*Spitznamen*) were common and cannot be adduced as evidence for exposure of infants in Greco-Roman Egypt before the Roman period.[126] Apparently baby girls were more likely to be exposed than baby boys, but the evidence is admittedly limited in value for reconstructing the demographic structure of ancient populations, for which little reliable census data exist.[127] As the third-century B.C.E. comic poet Posidippus wrote: "Everyone raises a son even if he is poor, but exposes [ἐκτίθησι] a daughter even if he is rich."[128]

Penal slavery served as another slave source. In Roman criminal law, the *servus poenae* ("the slave of his punishments") described a free person who became a slave (and lost any citizenship) as a result of capital punishment. It was "capital" because one lost one's *caput*, the aggregate of personal political,

---

The Rendel Harris Papyri, ed. J. Enoch Powell, CR 51 (1937): 70; Alfred Körte, "Literarische Texte mit Ausschluss der Christlichen," APF 13 (1939): 112.

[124] A. Cameron, "The Exposure of Children in Greek Ethics," CR 46 (1932): 113.

[125] Emil Eyben, "Family Planning in Graeco-Roman Antiquity," trans. Berthold Puchert, AncSoc 11–12 (1980–81): 25 n. 72. Iza Bieżunska-Małowist, "Die Expositio von Kindern als Quelle der Sklavenbeschaffung im griechisch-römischen Ägypten," *JWG* (1971): 2:129–33, summarizes the Oxyrhynchus papyrus/parchment evidence.

[126] Sarah B. Pomeroy, "Copronyms and the Exposure of Infants in Egypt," in *Studies in Roman Law in Memory of A. Arthur Schiller*, ed. Roger A. Bagnall and William V. Harris (Leiden: E. J. Brill, 1986), 161–62. In classical Athens, unwanted infants were commonly placed in pots (χύτρα), the practice of which, some scholars conjecture, developed into a specialized occupation of professional nurses who were called ἐγχυτρίστριαι ("in-potters"). However, H. Bolkestein, "The Exposure of Children at Athens and the ἐγχυτρίστριαι," CP 17 (1922): 237, discredits this theory, arguing no evidence exists that a regular occupation developed from the Athenian custom of infant exposure.

[127] Donald Engels, "The Problem of Female Infanticide in the Greco-Roman World," CP 75 (1980): 114; Patterson, "'Not Worth Rearing,'" 119–23; William V. Harris, "The Theoretical Possibility of Extensive Infanticide in the Graeco-Roman World," CQ 32 (1984): 114–16; Sarah B. Pomeroy, *Goddesses, Whores, Wives, and Slaves: Women in Classical Antiquity* (New York: Schocken Books, 1975), 140, 164–65, 228; idem, "Infanticide in Hellenistic Greece," in *Images of Women in Antiquity*, ed. Averil Cameron and Amélie Kuhrt (Detroit: Wayne State University Press, 1983), 207–22.

[128] 11 E. = Stob. *Flor.* 77.7; Golden, "Demography," 316.

legal, and social rights. Such a condemned criminal typically was sentenced to labor in the public works, the mines, or the gladiatorial troops.[129]

Even the limited evidence can yield positive answers to the question of slave origins. Warfare supplied the greatest source of slaves, especially because of the *canabae*. Yet it is a mistake to equate the goals of the *canabae* with those of the military commanders: ancient wars were not the "slave hunts" that Max Weber claimed them to be. Other sources included piracy on sea, brigandage on land, exposure of infants, kidnapping, the international slave trade in both periodic and regular markets, some breeding, and criminal punishment. This investigation leads to the question of the slave population itself.

The Number and Position of Slaves

Scholars of slavery often make a distinction between genuine slave societies and societies that simply contained slaves.[130] Such specialists maintain that in the history of Western civilization there have been only five genuine slave societies: two in antiquity (classical Athens and classical Italy) and three in the modern New World (the Caribbean, Brazil, and the southern United States).[131] These five cultures bear this designation not for the slaves' actual numbers so much as for the slaves' integration into their economies and societies. Scholars have long acknowledged that the actual number of slaves in any given society is rarely known, and this especially holds true in classical antiquity. Unlike those studying modern America, ancient historians lack the raw material of cliometrics: there is no evidence on the basis of which the scholar can combine history of the traditional kind – dealing with qualitative material and episodes – with a mathematical and economic interpretation of data. Calculating ancient statistics without any initial measurable, hard data provides, at best, highly speculative numbers and, at worst, figures that dangerously mislead because of a specious sense of "scientific" accuracy.

Some scholars play what M. I. Finley calls the "numbers game." Finley argues that attempts to calculate ancient servile population and arguments

---

[129] Buckland, *Roman Law of Slavery*, 277–78; Adolf Berger, *Encyclopedic Dictionary of Roman Law*, TAPhS 43.2 (Philadelphia: The Society, 1953), 705–6; Crook, *Law and Life of Rome*, 57, 272–73; Peter Garnsey, *Social Status and Legal Privilege in the Roman Empire* (Oxford: Clarendon Press, 1970), 132, 155, 165; Fergus G. B. Millar, "Condemnation to Hard Labour in the Roman Empire, Augustus to Constantine," *PBSR* 52 (1984): 124–47; Joan Burdon, "Slavery as a Punishment in Roman Criminal Law," in Archer, *Slavery and Other Forms of Unfree Labour*, 68–85.

[130] Finley, *Ancient Slavery and Modern Ideology*, 79. Patterson, *Slavery and Social Death*, 350–64 (appendices B and C), lists 66 slaveholding societies and 141 large-scale slave systems.

[131] Finley, *Ancient Slavery and Modern Ideology*, 9.

against the profitability of slavery based on such dubious statistics present equations that fall short of genuine quantification.[132] A comparison of Finley with A. H. M. Jones on the particular question of whether or not classical Athenian slavery was profitable illustrates this point.[133] Jones offers a classic cliometric argument that classical slavery was not profitable in agricultural production, except after wars when slaves could be bought cheaply and in mass numbers (which Jones purports to calculate). Finley, by contrast, argues not from economics but from social psychology that authors of ancient agricultural manuals assumed slavery to be profitable. Finley correctly points out that ancients lacked the accounting technology to know the real maintenance cost of a slave, which Jones calculates. For example, they did not have double-entry bookkeeping; and although they were certainly acquisitive, they did not exhibit capitalistic concern for monetary return. "Capitalistic" means making accounting decisions characterized exclusively by profit maximization (watching the "bottom line"), with profits measured only in monetary units. "Acquisitive" means seeking profit not solely to gain more money, but also to gain honor from public displays of conspicuous material consumption. Because profitability was more intuited than calculated in antiquity, the actual number of slaves means very little in the determination of ancient society as a slave society.[134]

However problematic cliometrics are to ancient historical investigation, I nonetheless recognize the need to conjecture probable minimum numbers. Here careful comparative studies can aid the ancient historian. As already stated, the actual totals of slaves are rarely known. The exception to this rule is the American South, where government census documents provide reliable data.[135] Of the estimated ten million slaves shipped to the Western hemisphere from Africa in the Atlantic slave trade, the majority went to the West Indies and South America; only a small percentage (400,000 slaves) came directly to the United States. The official closure of the Atlantic slave trade came in 1809. Yet by 1860, slaves made up 33 percent of the total population in the Confederate slave states. As we saw above, in the world history of slavery only the American South had a slave population that reproduced itself.[136] The first scientific scholar of ancient slavery, Henri Wallon, estimated the Athenian slave population to be 400,000, but Finley has since discredited this figure as

---

[132] Finley, *Ancient Slavery and Modern Ideology*, 79–80.

[133] A. H. M. Jones, "Slavery in the Ancient World," in Finley, *Slavery in Classical Antiquity*, 1–15; Finley, "Was Greek Civilization Based on Slave Labour?" in *Slavery in Classical Antiquity*, 53–72.

[134] Finley, *Ancient Economy*, 83–84.

[135] Philip D. Curtin, *The Atlantic Slave Trade: A Census* (Madison: University of Wisconsin Press, 1969).

[136] Finley, "Slavery," 310; Harris, "Towards a Study," 119, 121.

both ridiculously high and based on a false assumption that one must have huge numbers of slaves to justify the label "slave society."[137] Recent numbers for classical Athens have ranged from 20,000 slaves (or one-tenth of the population) to 100,000 (one-third). Thucydides claims that in the Spartan occupation during the Peloponnesian War, "more than 20,000 slaves escaped from Attica."[138] The Athenian silver and lead mines at Laurium were said to have employed more than 10,000 slaves, and excavated remains of extensive slag heaps indicate a huge operation that validates this figure.[139] For classical Italy, out of an estimated population of seven million at the time of Augustus, two to three million persons were slaves.[140] Augustus claims in his *Res Gestae* to have returned 30,000 slaves, who "had taken up arms against the Republic" during the civil wars, to their rightful owners.[141] The physician Galen reports that his city of Pergamum in Asia Minor contained 120,000 adults, of whom 40,000 (33 percent) were slaves.[142] To get an idea of how pervasive slaves were in Roman society, consider Seneca's remark: "A proposal was once made in the Senate to distinguish slaves from free men by their clothing. It then became apparent how great would be the impending danger if our slaves should begin to count their number."[143] To be sure, numbers in literary texts were notoriously easy to miswrite, and we must ask whether the ancient author was in a position to know the actual numbers he gives or even whether a meaningful series of numbers is presented. Yet Seneca's remark, together with the numbers given in the literary sources, does suggest that slaves were commonplace in Roman society, perhaps making up one-third of the population, similar to the demographics of the American South.[144] I say "similar" but there is one importance difference – position. According to the American historian Kenneth Stampp, the average Southerner had little personal contact with slaves: "nearly three-fourths of all free Southerners had no connection with slavery through either family ties or direct ownership. The 'typical'

---

[137] Henri Wallon, *Histoire de l'esclavage dans l'antiquité*, 2d ed. (Paris: Hachette, 1879), 1:221–83; cf. 2:67–158 (for Rome); Finley, *Ancient Slavery and Modern ideology*, 31, 64, 79–80.

[138] Thuc. 7.27.5; Victor Hansen, "Thucydides and the Desertion of Attic Slaves during the Decelean War," *ClAnt* 11 (1992): 210–28.

[139] Siegfried Lauffer, *Die Bergwerkssklaven von Laureion*, 2d ed., rev., Forschungen zur antiken Sklaverei 11 (Wiesbaden: F. Steiner, 1979).

[140] Hopkins, *Conquerors and Slaves*, 7–8; P. A. Brunt, *Italian Manpower, 225 B.C.–A.D. 14* (Oxford: Clarendon Press, 1971), 22, 67, 121–5, 702–3.

[141] *Res Gestae* 25.1 (Brunt and Moore, 50). Augustus alludes to his victory in 36 B.C.E. over Sextus Pompey, whose pirate fleets were manned largely by slaves; see Brunt and Moore, 66.

[142] Galen, *De cogn. curand. animi morbis* 9 (Kühn 5.49); Wiedemann, *Greek and Roman Slavery*, 79; Ste. Croix, *Class Struggle*, 242.

[143] Sen. *Clem.* 1.24.1.

[144] Finley, *Ancient Slavery and Modern Ideology*, 80; Garlan, *Slavery*, 59–60.

Southerner was not only a small farmer, but also a nonslaveholder."[145] For classical Athens and Italy, the situation was dramatically different: there is every indication that slaveholding was not the exclusive domain of the very wealthy, but extended far down the social scale.[146] Even persons of modest means owned slaves. Martial recounts that not only patrons, but also their clients had slaves.[147] Slaves in Roman society could even own slaves themselves.[148] The impression gained from these minimum numbers is that the average Roman had greater likelihood of personal contact with and ownership of slaves than the average American Southerner.

Advancing from the minimum numbers to projecting the size of average individual slave holdings in antiquity is, of course, a precarious move, yet some specific figures are given in the sources. We hear of a certain Nikias in Athens who owned one thousand slaves and hired them out to Sosias the Thracian for an obol per slave per day to work in the largest mines in the Greek world, those at Laurium.[149] Certainly Nikias was the exception. Demosthenes, considered one of the wealthiest Athenians of his day, had up to thirty-three slaves in just one workshop.[150] Plato had five slaves; Aristotle little more than thirteen, all of whom he is reported to have eventually freed by testamentary manumission (which prompts us to wonder about his commitment to his own natural slave theory).[151] The orator Lysias and his brother jointly owned a shield factory and employed over one hundred slaves, which makes the operation the largest single factory on record in antiquity.[152] In contrast, Roman aristocrats regularly possessed whole herds of chattel slaves both in country estates and urban townhouses.[153] By "herds" I mean dozens, hundreds, and even thousands. Lucius Pedanius Secundus, the prefect of the city of Rome under Nero, had over four hundred slaves in his townhouse alone.[154] The Roman aqueducts required a permanent staff of seven hundred

---

[145] Kenneth M. Stampp, *The Peculiar Institution: Slavery in the Ante-Bellum South* (New York: Vintage Books, 1956), 30; cited in Finley, "Slavery," 310.

[146] Garnsey and Saller, *Roman Empire*, 73; Garlan, *Slavery*, 61; Juv. *Sat.* 3.167; E. Courtney, *A Commentary on the Satires of Juvenal* (London: Athlone Press, 1980), 178.

[147] Mart. 2.18; 3.36; 3.38; 3.46.

[148] Erman N. Epp, *Servus vicarius: L'esclave de l'esclave romain* (Lausanne: F. Rouge, 1896), remains the standard work.

[149] Athenaeus, *Deipnosophistai* 6.272c–d; Wiedemann, *Greek and Roman Slavery*, 90.

[150] Dem. 27.9 (*Against Aphobus*, I), in LCL 4:13.

[151] Garlan, *Slavery*, 62. For the argument that Aristotle's testamentary manumission act betrays his uneasiness about the natural slavery he so ardently defended, see Smith, "Aristotle's Theory," 111.

[152] Lysias 12.19; Finley, *Ancient Slavery and Modern Ideology*, 80; Wiedemann, *Greek and Roman Slavery*, 99.

[153] Garlan, *Slavery*, 62; Bradley, *Discovering*, 90–93.

[154] Tac. *Ann.* 14.42–5; Saller, "Slavery and the Roman Family," 65; Finley, *Ancient Slavery and Modern Ideology*, 80.

public slaves (that is, owned by the Roman state), including slave architects.[155] Among the very wealthy in Roman society, some masters held upwards to four thousand slaves. Of course the greatest slaveowner was the emperor, who commanded thousands upon thousands of imperial slaves in his *familia Caesaris* scattered in administrative posts throughout the Empire.[156] The Apostle Paul met one of them, Felix, the imperial freedman of Claudius, who served as Roman procurator of Judaea, a position of equestrian rank (Acts 24:22–27). In sum, then, slave holdings of Athenians were considerably smaller than those of their Roman counterparts. But aside from this finding, what further conclusions can we draw from these figures? Do they add up to a "slave society"? Not necessarily: I agree with Finley that playing the numbers game ultimately leads to unproductive research. The importance lies not with slave totals, which are in any case beyond cliometric calculation, but with slave position in the ancient society and economy.

Examination of slave position supports the characterization of classical Italy as a "slave society." We find that, as a general rule, Roman slaves did everything, except serving in politics and the military, although even these two occupations, at times, were had by slaves or ex-slaves.[157] Apart from mining and domestic service, there were no employments specifically reserved for slaves.[158] Despite the claims of moralists like Aristotle and Cicero that manual labor was beneath their contempt, the vast majority of the free population lived in an agrarian economy at near subsistence level; they had to work for a living. In the small farms, workshops, and businesses that dotted the ancient world, masters and slaves regularly worked together. Xenophon reports that

---

[155] Finley, *Ancient Slavery and Modern Ideology*, 80. On public slaves, see Walter Eder, *Servitus Publica*, Forschungen zur antiken Sklaverei 13 (Wiesbaden: Franz Steiner, 1980).

[156] Bradley, *Slaves and Masters*, 16; the standard work on imperial slaves and freedmen/ women remains P. R. C. Weaver, *Familia Caesaris: A Social Study of the Emperor's Freedmen and Slaves* (Cambridge: Cambridge University Press, 1972). See also Gérard Boulvert, *Les esclaves et les affranchis impériaux sous le Haut-Empire romain*, 2 vols. in 1 (Aix-en-Provence: Centre régional de documentation pédagogique, 1964); idem, *Domestique et fonctionnaire sous le Haut-Empire romain: La condition de l'affranchi et de l'esclave du prince*, Annales littéraires de l'Université de Besançon 151 (Paris: Belles Lettres, 1974); Duff, *Freedmen*, 143–86; Heinrich Chantraine, "Freigelassene und Sklaven kaiserlicher Frauen," in *Studien zur antiken Sozialgeschichte: Festschrift Friedrich Vittinghof*, ed. Werner Eck, Hartmut Galsterer, and Hartmut Wolff, Kölner historische Abhandlungen 28 (Cologne: Böhau, 1980), 389–416.

[157] Livy 10.21.4. Although some slaves and freedmen (such as Felix, of the imperial household) did participate in Roman administration, they were barred from Roman politics. By "administration," I mean performing secretarial work for Roman magistrates or serving as a legate for the emperor in the provinces. By "politics," I mean admission to the upper equestrian and senatorial orders and the attainment of public office in Rome (such as the consulship).

[158] Finley, *Ancient Slavery and Modern Ideology*, 81; cf. Lionel Casson, "Galley Slaves," *TAPA* 97 (1966): 35–44.

when the Erechtheum temple was constructed on the Athenian Acropolis, slave and free worked hand in hand and were paid an identical amount regardless of legal status.[159] Unlike their counterparts in the modern slave societies of the New World, Roman slaves were not segregated from freeborns in work or types of job performed, with the notable exception of mining operations.[160] Some slaves held positions of considerable power not only over fellow slaves, but also over freeborns. Two examples are imperial slaves who held administrative authority, most notably the Claudian freedmen Pallas and Narcissus, and armed Scythian slaves who were retained as police for Athens during the classical period.[161] In modern slavery, slave illiteracy was often required by law, though not always enforced; in ancient slavery, an educated slave was prized.[162] In cities throughout the ancient Mediterranean world, slaves were trained and served as physicians, architects, craftsmen, shopkeepers, cooks, barbers, artists, thespians, magicians, prophets (e.g., Acts 16:16–24), teachers, professional poets, and philosophers. Some slaves could accumulate considerable wealth from their occupations. However, most slaves were of quite modest means and worked as ordinary laborers or specialized domestics (larger households even had slaves whose sole job was to fold fancy dinner napkins).[163] Because slaves could be found in all economic levels of society, they had no cohesion as a group and lacked anything akin to class consciousness. Finley correctly argues, "Slaves were a logical class and a juridi-

---

[159] Xen. *Mem.* 2.3.3; R. H. Randall, "The Erechtheum Workmen," *AJA* 57 (1953): 199–210; Garlan, *Slavery*, 65; Finley, *Ancient Slavery and Modern Ideology*, 101.

[160] On mining, see the admittedly highly rhetorical passage on its horrors in Apul. *Met.* 9.12; Diod. Sic. 5.36.3; 5.38.1; Wiedemann, *Greek and Roman Slavery*, 176–77; Bradley, *Slaves and Masters*, 119; Fergus B. G. Millar, "The World of the Golden Ass," *JRS* 71 (1981): 65.

[161] Garlan, *Slavery*, 68; A. Plassart, "Les archers d'Athènes," *REG* 16 (1913): 151–213; M. F. Vos, *Scythian Archers in Archaic Attic Vase-Painting*, Archaeologica Traiectina 6 (Groningen: J. B. Wolters, 1963), 61–69.

[162] Clarence A. Forbes, "The Education and Training of Slaves in Antiquity," *TAPA* 86 (1955): 321–60; Alan D. Booth, "The Schooling of Slaves in First-Century Rome," *TAPA* 109 (1979): 11–19; William V. Harris, *Ancient Literacy* (Cambridge: Harvard University Press, 1989), 111, 197, 199, 238, 247–53, 255–59, 277.

[163] Bradley, *Discovering*, 113–16; Martin, *Slavery as Salvation*, 11–15; Garland, "Cicero's *Familia*," 163–73; Susan Treggiari, "Jobs in the Household of Livia," *PBSR* 43 (1975): 48–77. I am aware of the differences in slave employments between classical Athens and Rome. Slaves infrequently served as physicians in Athenian society, for example, but were quite common in the Roman medical profession (note the polemic in Pliny, *HN* 29.6–8); Vogt, *Ideal of Man*, 114–20; Klaus-Dietrich Fischer, "Zur Entwicklung des ärztlichen Standes im römischen Kaiserreich," *Medizin-historisches Journal* 14 (1979): 165–75; Giuseppe Penso, *La médecine romaine: L'art d'Esculape dans la Rome antique* (Paris: Roger Dacosta, 1984), 99–100; Fridolf Kudlien, *Die Stellung des Arztes in der römischen Gesellschaft: Freigeborene Römer, Eingebürgerte, Peregrine, Sklaven, Freigelassene als Ärzte*, Forschungen zur antiken Sklaverei 18 (Stuttgart: Franz Steiner, 1986), 92–118.

cal class but not, in any usual sense of that term, a social class."[164] Finley's
analysis clearly differs from Marxist interpretations that lump slaves into a
single economic class and identify a so-called slave mode of production.[165]
Class as a heuristic category is here problematic.

Finley's correct assessment that class fails as an interpretive model of ancient
slavery raises important considerations for studying ancient societies. The
three sociological categories of class, order, and status must be kept clearly
distinct and used with control. *Classes* are modern constructs of historians and
sociologists that indicate how individuals in a given society relate to a system
of production; those who own the factories and farms belong to the upper
class, for example. *Orders* are groups formally defined within a state; they are
distinguished by different legal rights and include categories such as resident
aliens, citizens, prisoners, and so forth. *Status* is an individual's own idea of his
or her personal prestige. A lower-stratum person may become a local hero,
thereby increasing the person's status in the community. The formal orders in
Augustan Rome included senators at the top, required by law to be millionaires (measured in sesterces); then, equestrians, with a property requirement
of four hundred thousand sesterces; next, local municipal notables (decurions,
sometimes called "senators") who belonged to ruling families ranked aristo-

---

[164] Finley, *Ancient Slavery and Modern Ideology*, 77; see also Vidal-Naquet, *Black Hunter*,
159–67, *pace* Ste. Croix, *Class Struggle*, 63–65.

[165] Karl Marx wrote only scattered and brief comments on slavery, amounting to no
more than a few pages; Karl Marx, *Grundrisse der Kritik der politischen Ökonomie (Rohentwurf) 1857–1858, Anhang 1850–1859*, 2d ed. (Berlin [East]: Dietz Verlag, 1974), 375–
413. These writings received little attention before the 1950s, at the height of the Cold
War era; Finley, *Ancient Slavery and Modern Ideology*, 40; Michael Grant, *Social History*, 137–
39. Although his writings on the subject were few, Marx's impact and influence became
enormous. The Italian scholar Ettore Ciccotti was the first Marxist historian to give a full-
scale economic account of the decline of slavery, using Marx's category of an Asiatic mode
of production. Ciccotti critiqued in detail Paul Allard's view (*Les esclaves chrétiens, depuis les
premiers temps de l'eglise jusqu'à la fin de la domination romaine en occident*, 6th ed. [Paris: Victor
Lecoffre, 1914]), and to a lesser extent Henri Wallon's (*Histoire de l'esclavage*), that Christianity, Stoicism, or any other religious-ethical system had caused ancient slavery's demise.
His alternative model for the decline pointed not to ethical, but to economic changes in
the Roman Empire. According to Ciccotti, these changes effectively rendered slavery a
handicap in the Roman system of economic production, which doomed slavery to ex-
tinction in a manner akin to biological natural selection (*Il tramonto della schiavitù nel mondo
antico*, 2d ed. [Udine: Instituto delle Edizioni Academice, 1940], 231–441). Ciccotti was
obsessed with both the inadequacy of slave labor as a vehicle of production and the moral
flaw of slavery. In this way, he had much in common with the abolitionists; Finley, *Ancient
Slavery and Modern Ideology*, 42–43. Although not a Marxist, Barrow, *Slavery*, 97, echoes
Ciccotti's view that slavery failed because it was too expensive and inefficient. Finley
explodes the myth that slavery ended because it was nonproductive or unprofitable. Such
arguments, Finley, reveals, are products of modern ideological debates, not critical investigation of ancient slavery.

cratic; below them, full Roman citizens, who retained important legal rights that separated them in law from Junian Latins and the general population; then, noncitizens, who were the vast majority; and at the bottom, slaves, who were considered (to use Patterson's term) socially dead. Although they were ranked below all, some slaves nonetheless did manage businesses and farms for their masters, making them members of what modern scholars call the "upper class." Such slaves experienced what Finley calls "status crisscrossing," or what sociologists term "status inconsistency."[166] The high status of these slaves was inconsistent with their low rank. Similarly, freedmen/women did not fit neatly into the formal orders of Rome. Some gained citizenship, and some became millionaires, even billionaires; Petronius's novel *Satyricon* lampoons a fictional example, the freedman millionaire Trimalchio. As a control for the use of this imaginative literature, we have real-life examples such as the procurator Felix and Seneca's Calvisius Sabinus.

Another group, freeborn women, were excluded (as were slaves) from public service and the military, and so were not included in the hierarchy of formal orders. Some women gained high status, like Cicero's wife Terentia, who controlled Cicero's estates until he divorced her, and Germanicus's wife Agrippina, who assumed the duties of a general in the heat of a battle to prevent the destruction of the Roman Rhine bridge.[167] In his biography of Agricola, Tacitus remarks that Agricola's mother owned a large estate and was a source of patrimony.[168] Roman women could gain high status by donating large sums of money to their hometowns, with the cities in return making the matrons' birthdays public holidays.[169] Women also gained charismatic leadership roles in the early church and synagogue.[170] Employing the three sociological categories of class, order, and status removes confusion and reveals the

---

[166] Finley, *Ancient Economy*, 35–61; Garnsey and Saller, *Roman Empire*, 109–23; Wayne A. Meeks, *The First Urban Christians: The Social World of the Apostle Paul* (New Haven: Yale University Press, 1983), 22–23, 191, 215 n. 20, 240 n. 28.

[167] Tac. *Ann.* 1.69.

[168] Tac. *Agr.* 7.

[169] Ramsay MacMullen, *Changes in the Roman Empire: Essays in the Ordinary* (Princeton: Princeton University Press, 1990), 162–76.

[170] Antoinette Clark Wire, *The Corinthian Women Prophets: A Reconstruction through Paul's Rhetoric* (Minneapolis: Fortress Press, 1990), esp. 188–95; Ben Witherington III, *Women in the Earliest Churches*, SNTSMS 59 (Cambridge: Cambridge University Press, 1988); Bernadette J. Brooten, "'Junia ... Outstanding among the Apostles' (Rom. 16:7)," in *Women Priests: A Catholic Commentary on the Vatican Declaration*, ed. Leonard Swindler and Arlene Swindler (New York: Paulist Press, 1977), 141–44; idem, *Women Leaders in the Ancient Synagogues*, BJS 36 (Chico, Calif.: Scholars Press, 1982); Wayne A. Meeks, "The Image of the Androgyne: Some Uses of a Symbol in Earliest Christianity," *HR* 13 (1974): 165–208. Elizabeth A. Clark, *Women in the Early Church*, Messages of the Fathers 13 (1983; reprint, Collegeville, Minn.: Liturgical Press, 1990), provides a useful sourcebook of primary material; as does Ross Shepard Kraemer, *Her Share of the Blessings: Women's Religions among*

methodological problems in Marxist interpretations based exclusively on class analysis. Slaves in antiquity were neither a homogeneous social class nor in identical positions with respect to the economic means of production. Slaves of the aristocratic elite, such as the philosopher Epictetus tied to the Imperial household, certainly had the same disdain for manual-labor slaves as any member of the upper Roman orders. The slave physician had little in common with a slave agricultural fieldhand. Slaves worked in all levels of society and shared no sense of class solidarity with each other or (as Marxists claim) the urban poor or rural peasantry.[171]

What conclusion, then, do we draw about the term "slave society" as applied to antiquity? We must exercise great care to avoid unwarranted generalizations about the numbers and positions of slaves in classical Athens and Rome. If we mean by "Rome" peninsular Italy and Sicily of the late Republic and Principate, then we can safely call Rome a slave society. Yet the entire ancient Mediterranean world certainly cannot be characterized as one huge slave society. Although slavery apparently dominated agrarian production in peninsular Italy and Sicily, it never was so vital in agriculture of the most populous regions of the Empire: North Africa, Egypt, Greece, and the Near East.[172] In the ancient economy, most of the workforce consisted of peasants.[173] Claims that slavery was the sole form of dependent labor are problematic.

We have considered labor in antiquity, the position of slaves and the extent of their socio-economic integration, and the three sociological categories of class, order, and status. We found that statistics and class analysis are problematic because of the limitations of the evidence. A positive solution to this calculation and classification problem is to shift our focus from totals to tasks. Slaves did nearly everything in antiquity, except politics and military service (although some exceptions occurred, such as the procurator Felix). In the

---

Pagans, Jews, and Christians in the Greco-Roman World (New York: Oxford University Press, 1992), esp. 174–90.

[171] *Pace* Martin, *Slavery as Salvation*, 1–49 (see J. Albert Harrill, review of *Slavery as Salvation*, by Dale Martin, *JR* 72 [1992]: 426–27); Ste. Croix, *Class Struggle*, 63–53; Dimitris J. Kyrtatas, *The Social Structure of the Early Christian Communities* (New York: Verso Press, 1987), 21–24; Garlan, *Slavery*, 10, 176–91, 207–8.

[172] Neal Wood, *Cicero's Social and Political Thought* (Berkeley and Los Angeles: University of California Press, 1988), 20–21; E. M. Štaerman et al., *Die Sklaverei in den westlichen Provinzen des römischen Reiches im 1.–3. Jahrhundert*, trans. Jaroslav Kriz, Übersetzungen ausländischer Arbeiten zur antiken Sklaverei 4 (Stuttgart: Franz Steiner, 1987), 1–146. Wood considers the western provinces of Gaul and Spain also to be "slave societies." Yet it is doubtful that these provinces can be called "slave societies" – maybe Narbonensis and Baetica, but the evidence is slender.

[173] Peter Garnsey, *Famine and Food Supply in the Graeco-Roman World: Responses to Risk and Crisis* (Cambridge: Cambridge University Press, 1988), 44.

end, we found that the designation "slave society" refers not to a society with numerous slaves, but to one with slaves in every working environment and social position.

Slaves and Children

We now proceed to a discussion of slaves in their most common working environment, the home. This section argues three things: that the presence of slaves in the home affected family relations, that slaves were not treated as children, and that racism played no part in the ancient ideology of slavery. We begin with the literary evidence.

Tacitus saw servile influence as negative and particularly dangerous to free-born children (*liberi*). He writes that in earlier times a chaste mother, not a purchased nurse in her chamber, raised sons and daughters in the strict discipline of Roman ancestral custom. The great matrons of older, golden days such as Cornelia (mother of the Gracchi), Aurelia (mother of Caesar), and Atia (mother of Augustus) directed their children's education and so reared the greatest sons (and daughters). With his rhetorical flare, Tacitus further describes the problems of the present age: "But in our day, we entrust the infant to a little Greek slave-girl who is attended by one or two others, commonly the worst of all slaves, creatures utterly unfit for any important work. Their stories and their prejudices from the outset fill the child's tender and unrestricted mind."[174] Tacitus blames Rome's vices on its wet-nurse slaves, whose hands rock the cradles of Roman children and whose voices whisper non-Roman (and so corrupting) bedtime stories into the infants' ears. This is strong testimony to how influential slaves were considered to be in the nuclear family. Tacitus's remarks, however, must be recognized as polemic. To be sure, the passage reveals a great deal about the ideology of slaveholders such as Tacitus and other Roman senators. Yet granted its polemical status, the passage nevertheless demonstrates that even the ancients understood that having slaves under the same roof inevitably affected family relations.[175]

Ancient attitudes toward slaves differed significantly from attitudes toward children. Often the term "paternalistic" is used in the secondary literature to describe slaveholding ideology in general. Ancient slaveholders were not pa-

---

[174] Tac. *Dial.* 28–29.

[175] Keith R. Bradley, "Wet-Nursing at Rome: A Study in Social Relations," in Rawson, *Family in Ancient Rome*, 201–29; Sandra R. Joshel, "Nurturing the Master's Child: Slavery and the Roman Child-Nurse," *Signs* 12 (1986): 3–22; Peter Garnsey, "Child Rearing in Ancient Italy," in *The Family in Italy: From Antiquity to the Present*, ed. David I. Kertzer and Richard P. Saller (New Haven: Yale University Press, 1991), 48–65; Bradley, *Discovering*, 13–36, 143–45 (on male domestics as childminders).

ternalistic, however, and applying the term to them stems from a conflation of the ancient and modern ideologies of slavery. Modern New World slavery contained a component not found in antiquity – racism. American slave-holders justified their position of authority and control by labeling the African American essentially a subhuman and an infantile adult. Although ancient masters customarily addressed male slaves of any age as "boy" (παῖς/*puer*),[176] they did not justify their slaveholding as parenting, for they saw no need to justify it in any way. They clearly thought of their two roles, parent and master, as two different modes of authority. Richard Saller argues that classical Ro-man authors, far from advocating the virtue of corporal punishment for chil-dren and slaves alike, condemned the use of the whip on children precisely because it was important to differentiate children from slaves.[177] In their idiom of rule, Roman slaveholders were neither paternalistic nor racist in the modern sense of the term. Race itself is a modern construct: although there were views about differing ethnicities in antiquity (the elder Pliny's tirades against the Greeks, for example), there was no so-called scientific theory of skin-colored race until the nineteenth century.[178] Racism entered the mod-ern ideology of rule partially as a result of eighteenth-century egalitarian liberalism. As the American historian of slavery James Oakes writes, "It was no accident that the first systematically racist analysis of black slaves was written by the master [Thomas Jefferson] who wrote the Declaration of Independ-ence."[179] Because many revolutionary leaders saw an inherent conflict be-tween their liberal ideals and their holding of African-American slaves, these slaveholders had to exclude African Americans from their definition of nor-mal human beings. African Americans were classified as biologically inferior to European Caucasians. Thus Southerners downplayed the Roman legal definition, with its Stoic influences, of slavery being *contra naturam* and em-braced instead the Aristotelian notion of natural slaves. Racism thus crept into the ideology of slavery only in the modern era. An important conclusion from this comparative exercise is that neither race nor color prejudice adequately explains the origins of slavery. Racism is neither a necessary precursor, nor

---

[176] Finley, *Ancient Slavery and Modern Ideology*, 96.

[177] Richard P. Saller, *Patriarchy, Property, and Death in the Roman Family* (Cambridge: Cambridge University Press: 1994), 142–53.

[178] For ancient understandings of, and prejudices against, ethnic (but not skin color) differences, see A. N. Sherwin-White, *Racial Prejudice in Imperial Rome* (Cambridge: Cambridge University Press, 1967), esp. 57–60, 93; Frank M. Snowden Jr., *Blacks in Antiquity: Ethiopians in the Greco-Roman Experience* (Cambridge: Harvard University Press, Belknap Press, 1970), esp. 169–95; idem, *Before Color Prejudice: The Ancient View of Blacks* (Cambridge: Harvard University Press, 1983).

[179] James Oakes, *The Ruling Race: A History of American Slaveholders* (New York: Vintage Books, 1983), 30–31.

component, nor outgrowth of slavery.[180] Indeed, scholars of American slavery have long recognized that racism and slavery do not necessarily go together, and that neither of the two phenomena serves as the exclusive explanation for the other's existence.

We have seen that the presence of slaves affected family relations and that slaves were not treated as children. The term "paternalism" is problematic when applied to ancient slavery, a system in which the roles of father and master were clearly differentiated. The nineteenth-century "scientific" concept of race is alien to ancient slaveholding ideology. Any etiology of slavery that necessitates race as a precondition fails. Unlike modern slaveholders, Roman slaveholders saw no need for apologetics such as paternalism or racism.

Manumission

Besides racism, a further anachronism arises when we read modern or Athenian manumission ideology into the Roman evidence. In Roman slavery, manumission — master-sanctioned release from slavery — was regular. This regularity is remarkable when we compare it with manumission in American slavery, which was extremely rare. When slaveholders in the U.S. South did manumit, the position of the black freedman/woman was extremely limited and controlled. Likewise Athenian freedmen[181] were denied citizenship and thus (unlike their Roman counterparts) excluded from political life, ineligible for all magistracies, forbidden to own land, and prohibited from acquiring mortgage loans; their male children remained noncitizens. The freedman's position was similar although not identical to that of the Athenian metic (resident alien).[182] Only a handful of Athenian freedmen are actually known, the most notable being the bankers Pasion and Phormion. These two, however, are very rare birds: they were favored with citizenship by decree of the Athenian assembly because of special circumstances. Most Athenian slaves never achieved this kind of liberation.[183] By contrast, the Romans regularly granted

---

[180] How could ancient slavery have a racist basis when Romans could not even tell a slave from a free person walking along the street? See Pliny, *Ep.* 10.29–30 (runaway slaves discovered serving as impostors in the army); Appian, *BC* 2.17 (on clothing); Dion. Hal. 4.24 (freedmen/women melting into society); Tac. *Ann.* 12 (problem of mixed marriages, imperial slaves); Sen. *Clem.* 1.24. For the lack of color distinctions between Athenians and their slaves, see ps.-Xen. *De re publica Atheniensium* 1.10 (Hartvig Frische, *The Constitution of the Athenians: A Philological-Historical Analysis*, Classica et Mediaevalia Dissertationes 2 [Copenhagen: Gyldendalske Boghandel, Nordisk Forlag, 1942], 16–17, 207–8); Xen. *Oec.* 13.10; Garlan, *Slavery*, 147–48; Patterson, *Freedom*, 138.

[181] Freedwomen, like all women, were never citizens in classical Athens.

[182] Garlan, *Slavery*, 80–82.

[183] Garlan, *Slavery*, 83.

citizenship to freedmen/women who had been formally manumitted by a citizen master. Yet it is important to qualify this statement with the understanding that one or at the most two generations were necessary before complete integration occurred in Roman society. As the son of a freedman, the poet Horace serves as an example.[184] This dissimilarity between Athenian and Roman slavery is too often overlooked or conflated by nonspecialists.

Athenian manumission procedures are difficult to reconstruct. Most of the evidence is epigraphic and specific to temple settings, although some civic registers survive. The sacred precinct of Delphi recorded the manumission of slaves sold to Apollo, a transaction that was considered a legal fiction; the city of Athens posted lists of liberated slaves manumitted in a similar legal procedure of fictitious sale. In nearly every case, the ex-slave was required to remain with the former master for a specified length of time before the manumission became effective. This phenomenon was called "*paramonē*," and the documents "*paramonē* contracts"; the practice survived into Hellenistic and Roman times. In areas of the Roman East, such as Asia Minor where Ignatius of Antioch wrote about the manumission of Christian slaves, *paramonē*, was the most common way to liberate a slave and so will require detailed study in chapter 4.

Roman manumission took many known forms, both formal and informal. The formal ceremony had three varieties. *Manumissio vindicta* ("by the magistrate's rod") occurred before a Roman magistrate in a legal proceeding. *Manumissio censu*, a Republican form that eventually fell into disuse, transpired when the censor placed the slave on the roll of Roman citizens. *Manumissio testamento*, which is generally considered by specialists the most common form, although admittedly no tangible evidence exists to substantiate this view, required a statement of liberation in a master's last will and testament. The informal forms were two. *Manumissio per epistulam* took place when the master wrote a letter to a friend stating that his slave was liberated. *Manumissio inter amicos* was a ceremony conducted by the master "before friends," who served as witnesses that the slave had been liberated.[185]

There were also degrees of Roman manumission, ranging from full enfranchisement (Roman citizen) to partial (Junian Latin). In his second-century textbook of Roman law, the jurist Gaius outlines the differences between a Roman citizen and a Junian Latin:

---

[184] Hor. *Sat.* 1.6.65–92; Finley, *Ancient Slavery and Modern Ideology*, 97; Treggiari, *Roman Freedmen*, 52–64; Peter Garnsey, "Descendants of Freedmen in Local Politics: Some Criteria," in *The Ancient Historian and His Materials: Essays in Honor of C. E. Stevens on His Seventieth Birthday*, ed. Barbara Levick (Westmead, England: D. C. Heath, Gregg International, 1975), 167–80.

[185] Buckland, *Roman Law of Slavery*, 437–597; Bradley, *Slaves and Masters*, 81–112; Kyrtatas, *Social Structure*, 55–74.

For any person who fulfills three conditions – that he is above the age of thirty, that he is in the quiritary[186] ownership of his master, and that he is freed by means of a lawful and legally recognized manumission (that is, by rod, by inclusion in the census, or by will) – becomes a Roman citizen; but if any of those conditions is lacking he will be a [Junian] Latin.[187]

The specific grant of full or partial enfranchisement depended on the slave's age, his or her legal relation to the master, and the form of ceremony. The creation of Junian Latins became common under the Principate because of efforts to bar slaves from full Roman citizenship. A Junian Latin had *commercium* (right to enter into Roman contracts) but neither *conubium* (right to a recognized marriage with a Roman citizen) nor *testamenti factio* (right to make and take under a Roman will).[188] A Junian Latin could, therefore, function as an agent of his or her patron without the right to live and work as an independent freedman/woman, a restriction that appealed to slaveholders.

Slaves could not start their own families. To be sure, slaves had what they (and their masters) considered spouses and families, but such unions had no recognition in law, and so were subject to separation by sale to different owners.[189] An important difference between slaves and freedmen/women was that freedmen/women usually gained some control over their personal family life. I say "usually" because release from chattel slavery did not normally mean release from continuing obligations to the former master, even for freedmen/women fully enfranchised as Roman citizens. In the Roman system of slavery, freedmen/women (both the fully enfranchised citizens and the lesser enfranchised Junian Latins) owed deference (*obsequium*) and specific work duties (*operae*) to their ex-master, now their patron. The question of whether there were "independent" freedmen/women remains. We shall return to this question in chapter 4.

Of the many problems, debates, and controversies surrounding the essential elements of ancient slavery, none deserves more attention than those over manumission. The Roman evidence differs dramatically from the Athenian and American, especially in regard to the regularity of manumission. The geographic distribution along Romanized and non-Romanized lines must also be recognized. In Romanized areas, the legal procedures included three formal forms (*manumissio vindicta*, *manumissio censu*, and *manumissio testamento*)

---

[186] "Quirites" is an archaic name for Roman citizens. "Quiritary ownership" means bare possession as opposed to possession by title in an estate; *Institutes of Gaius*, trans. Gordon and Robinson, 552.

[187] Gaius, *Inst.* 1.17 (the *lex Junia*, ca. 19 C.E.); *Institutes of Gaius*, trans. Gordon and Robinson, 25–27. P. R. C. Weaver, "Where Have All the Junian Latins Gone? Nomenclature and Status in the Early Empire," *Chiron* 20 (1990): 276–305.

[188] Nicholas, *Roman Law*, 64–65, 74–75.

[189] Bradley, *Slaves and Masters*, 47–80; Finley, *Ancient Slavery and Modern Ideology*, 93–122.

and two informal forms (*manumissio per epistulam* and *manumissio inter amicos*). There were also two degrees of enfranchisement: Junian Latins and Roman citizens. In non-Romanized areas, we find Hellenistic manumission forms with their own particulars, such as *paramonē* contracts recorded as fictitious sales of slaves to gods.

Yet in order to understand how manumission operated in early Christianity, we also need to consider the Jewish evidence. To this end, the excursus below investigates the social and economic position of Jewish freedmen/women in the city of Rome, where our evidence is most plentiful. This excursus has two functions. First, it supplies information necessary to understand the precursors of the early Christian practice. Second, it fills a gap in the secondary literature, which contains surprisingly little discussion of Jewish freedmen/women as an identifiable group in classical antiquity. The excursus documents vertical (client–patron) and horizontal (client–client) social networks among Jews in Rome.

Excursus: Jewish Freedmen/women

The position of liberated slaves in the economy and society of ancient Rome has often caught the interest of scholars.[190] Yet of their many studies, startlingly few concern freedmen/women who were self-identified as Jewish either by ethnic origin or community affiliation.[191] As Arnaldo Momigliano once wrote, even M. I. Finley, whose imagination and energy contributed much to the academic study of ancient slavery, had little to say about Jews.[192] When scholars do mention Jewish freedmen/women, many typically repeat the commonplace that Roman masters found Jewish slaves to be "troublesome," because of their dietary and Sabbath observances, and so were motivated to manumit them.[193] This has become standard to explain why the literary sources refer to Rome having a sizable Jewish freedman/woman population. The issue, however, proves more complex.

---

[190] Duff, *Freedmen*; Treggiari, *Roman Freedmen*; Weaver, *Familia Caesaris*; Georges Fabre, *Libertus: Recherches sur les rapports patron-affranchi à la fin de la république romaine*, Collection de l'École Française de Rome 50 (Paris: École Française de Rome, 1981); Wolfgang Waldstein, *Operae Libertorum: Untersuchungen zur Dienstpflicht freigelassener Sklaven*, Forschungen zur antiken Sklaverei 19 (Stuttgart: Franz Steiner, 1986). Of these monographs, only Treggiari, 205–7, attempts an extended discussion of Jewish freedmen/women, but even that discussion is brief – only three pages.

[191] A notable exception is Fuks, "Freedmen."

[192] Arnaldo Momigliano, "Moses Finley and Slavery: A Personal Note," in Finley, *Classical Slavery*, 2–3.

[193] Salo Wittmayer Baron, *A Social and Religious History of the Jews* (Philadelphia: Jewish Publication Society of America, 1952), 1:259; Smallwood, *The Jews under Roman Rule*,

For example, what identified a man or woman as "Jewish" in the ancient Mediterranean world? This conundrum runs deeper than the question of whether such people as Gentile converts to Judaism, Jewish sympathizers, Judaizers, or so-called God-fearers can be classed with persons born to a Jewish parent (whether the father or mother, or both). Indeed, many converts, called proselytes, apparently considered themselves to be fully Jewish.[194] The popularity of Jewish names, especially biblical names, among early Christians compounds the problem.[195] Yet even where we have explicit testimony that a person was a "Jew," we still may have no clue as to in what sense (religious, ethnic, linguistic, political, or geographical) that ancient individual may have understood the term.[196] For example Ἰουδαῖος / Ἰουδαία or *Iudaeus/Iudaea* might have signified geographical origin rather than religious or ethnic affiliation.[197] When no explicit self-identification exists, as is often the case in ancient Jewish epigraphy, the question becomes even more difficult. Perhaps we have only a name on a tombstone that "sounds" Jewish (or at least "Semitic") to us. In those instances, we must determine Jewishness by relying on hazy and uncontrolled criteria, which are usually derived from unsubstantiated and unexamined assumptions about what made and makes a person "Jewish."

One first-century C.E. marble tombstone inscription found at the fifth mile marker along the Via Appia is illustrative. It reads:

L·VALERIVS·L·L
BARICHA
L·VALERIVS·L·L
ZABDA
L·VALERIVS·L·L
ACHIBA[198]

131; Emil Schürer, *The History of the Jewish People in the Age of Jesus Christ (175 B.C.–A.D. 135)*, new ed., rev. Geza Vermes, Fergus Millar, and Martin Goodman (Edinburgh: T. & T. Clark, 1986), 3.1:75.

[194] Laurence H. Kant, "Jewish Inscriptions in Greek and Latin," *ANRW* 2.20.2 (1987): 686–67. While circumcision determined Jewishness for males, the situation of female converts is harder to reconstruct; Paula Fredriksen, "Judaism, the Circumcision of Gentiles, and Apocalyptic Hope: Another Look at Galatians 1 and 2," *JTS* 42 (1991): 546.

[195] Naomi G. Cohen, "Jewish Names as Cultural Indicators in Antiquity," *JSJ* 7 (1976): 127–28 n. 137.

[196] Or how the engraver, or the person who commissioned the engraver, understood the term.

[197] A. Thomas Kraabel, "The Roman Diaspora: Six Questionable Assumptions," *JJS* 33 (1982): 445–64; cited in Ross S. Kraemer, "Jewish Tuna and Christian Fish: Identifying Religious Affiliation in Epigraphic Sources," *HTR* 84 (1991): 144.

[198] *CII* 70* (= *CIL* 6.27959).

P. Jean-Baptiste Frey writes that because all the names are Jewish sounding, "selon toute probabilité, il s'agit ici de trois Juifs, affranchis par L(ucius) Valerius."[199] He bases this conclusion on the hypotheses that *Baricha* corresponds to the Aramaic name *Baruch*, that *Zabda* is an abridged form of *Zebadiah* or *Zebedee*, and that *Achiba* is a homonym for Aqiba. Harry J. Leon agrees with Frey that this is "an epitaph of three Jewish freedmen" of a certain L. Valerius.[200] Having decided that these three names identify Jews (not merely "Semitic" persons), one then reads this epitaph in conjunction with another inscription: a lengthy funerary notice from Rome mentions a certain L. Valerius Zabda, a name identical to that above, perhaps referring to the same person.[201] The tombstone dates after Ovid and commemorates a certain Aries, one of Zabda's freedmen. It indicates Zabda's profession – a slave trader (*mercator venalicius*). Using the onomastic criterion that the name Zabda indicates Jewishness in its user, we identify this other Zabda as also "Jewish." Yet the first inscription is included in Frey's *Corpus Inscriptionum Iudaicarum*, but the second is not. Frey evidently overlooked it, or did not consider it to be Jewish. The implications for identifying the second epitaph as Jewish are broad. If this second Zabda was a Jew (as Frey considers the first Zabda to have been), then we would have direct testimony that Jews actively engaged in the Roman slave trade as dealers. Yet neither positive nor negative indicators of L. Valerius Zabda's "Jewishness" are present in the text, except for his name.[202] All we can say for sure about the name is that it sounds Semitic and belongs to a slave trader.[203] If the two Zabdas are the same person, then we would have an example of a former slave who publicly expressed pride in becoming slave trader.[204]

---

[199] P. Jean-Baptiste Frey, *Corpus of Jewish Inscriptions: Jewish Inscriptions from the Third Century B.C. to the Seventh Century A.D.*, vol. 1, *Europe*, Library of Biblical Studies (1936; reprint with prolegomenon by Baruch Lifshitz, New York: Ktav, 1975), 572. The first-century date is given by Frey.

[200] Harry J. Leon, *The Jews of Ancient Rome*, The Morris Loeb Series (Philadelphia: Jewish Publication Society, 1960), 142 n. 2.

[201] *CIL* 6.9632 (= 6.33813); all but the first line is a quotation from Ov. *Trist.* 1.11.11.4–10. *Corpus Inscriptionum Latinarum*, vol. 6, pt. 6, *Indices*, fasc. 6, ed. L. Vidman (Berlin: Walter de Gruyter, 1980), 352, lists 17 occurrences of Zabda/Sabda/Zavda, 10 of which belong to *liberti*. The name Valerius is practically useless for prosopography because of its ubiquity. To identify the two Zabdas here as the same person, although certainly a possibility, seems risky.

[202] Kraemer, "Jewish Tuna and Christian Fish," 142–61, itemizes typical "positive" and "negative" indicators of Jewishness in epigraphical classification. I concentrate here on the onomastic indicators.

[203] So Harris, "Towards a Study," 130.

[204] For a further example of this phenomenon, see Finley, "Aulos Kapreilios Timotheos," 154–66.

The question of who Zabda was reveals the difficulty of ancient Jewish onomastics. Roman servile naming practices present additional problems of their own. Slaves almost always bore not their self-chosen names, but ones given them by their masters, and masters were always free to choose and change at will the names of their slaves. So, the freedmen Zabda, Baricha, and Achiba may have originally been sold by a slave dealer who claimed, either truthfully or falsely, that all three were Jewish and thus came from the same region, by chance a region known to produce good slaves. There was, in fact, a perception among the Romans that Orientals, especially Jews and Syrians, made naturally good slaves. Cicero calls Jews and Syrians people "born to be slaves."[205] The passage is, of course, rhetorical, but plays upon and so reveals the prejudices and perceptions of the upper equestrian and senatorial orders.[206] Indeed, the slave population of the empire was proverbially Oriental.[207] This anecdotal material undermines the belief held dear by many scholars that Romans generally perceived Jews to be "troublesome" slaves. The Roman perception, at least as represented by Cicero, was that far from being troublesome, Jews (like Syrians) made exceptionally good slaves – so good, in fact, that the servility of the Jews became proverbial and a *topos* in Roman political oratory. These anecdotes also show that Aristotle's theory of natural slaves did not completely die out in antiquity, despite competing Stoic views that fate (not physique) made slaves, which continued to dominate Roman philosophical exhortations for better servile treatment.

Furthermore, Zabda and his fellow freedmen could have received their monikers from a master who preferred the exotic and luxurious quality of Oriental names. Or the names could simply have been those given by their parents, indicating Semitic ethnicity (or at least affiliation) but not necessarily birth in a Semitic land. There is some evidence in the epigraphical sources, however, that Roman masters did exhibit a reluctance to use Oriental names for their slaves, mainly because these names were foreign to them, difficult to pronounce, and not as commonly known as the stock supply of Greek and Latin slave names.[208] So Zabda could have been a Jew after all. My goal here

---

[205] Cicero, *Prov. Cons.* 5.10 (= Menachem Stern, ed., *Greek and Latin Authors on Jews and Judaism* [Jerusalem: Israel Academy of Sciences and Humanities, 1974], 1:202–4 no. 70).

[206] Compare Appian, *BC* 2.74.308: ἀνδράποδα ταῦτ' ἐστὶ Σύρια καὶ Φρύγια καὶ Λύδια, φεύγειν αἰεὶ δουλεύειν ἕτοιμα; Livy, 34.17.5: *vilissima genera hominum et servituti nata.*

[207] Mary L. Gordon, "The Nationality of Slaves under the Early Roman Empire," in Finley, *Slavery in Classical Antiquity*, 172–73; Heikki Solin, "Juden und Syrer im westlichen Teil der römischen Welt: Eine ethnisch-demographische Studie mit besonderer Berücksichtigung der sprachlichen Zustände," *ANRW* 2.29.2 (1984): 590–789.

[208] Heikki Solin, "Die Namen der orientalischen Sklaven in Rom," in *L'onomastique latine*, ed. Noël Nuval, Colloques internationaux de Centre National de la Recherche Scientifique 564 (Paris: Centre National de la Recherche Scientifique, 1977), 205.

is only to demonstrate the methodological difficulties involved in any study of Jewish freedmen/women: names are possible but not secure indicators of Jewishness.[209]

One further caveat remains: Jews did not necessarily have "Jewish-sounding" names. It was standard Roman practice for slaveholders to bestow their Gentile names upon slaves after manumission. In addition, freedmen/women sensitive to the prejudices of their social betters often adopted typical Roman names to blend into freeborn society.[210] Other Jews, freedmen/women or not, simply took on Roman names because of cultural syncretistic tendencies.[211] Of the thousands of extant freedmen/women inscriptions, we shall never know how many masked elusive Jews behind Roman names. With these methodological considerations and cautions, we proceed to the primary evidence.

The sources for Jewish freedmen/women in Rome fall into two broad categories: first, descriptions of enslaved and liberated Jews as a group; and second, reports of individual Jewish slaves and freedmen/women either explicitly called Jewish or identified as such by modern scholars using the criterion, discussed above, of Jewish-sounding names.

The evidence in the first category includes the following:

1. Tacitus (*Ann.* 2.85.4) reports the expulsion of Jews from Italy under Tiberius, with four thousand of them "from the freedmen/women order" (*libertini generis*) being transported to the island of Sardinia to quell brigandage.[212]

---

[209] Kant, "Jewish Inscriptions," 682, calls "typical Jewish names" the "least clear of the categories" for determining Jewish cultural identity, yet he acknowledges that all scholars employ names in identifying Jews in inscriptions.

[210] Suet. *Vesp.* 23 (a wealthy freedman changing his name to pass as freeborn); cf. Suet. *Claud.* 25.1. An example of this freeborn prejudice against serviles is found in the episode involving the freedman Hermeros in Petron. *Cena* 57–58 (cf. 38); Garnsey and Saller, *Roman Empire*, 121.

[211] Scholars often forget this fact. For example, in the first edition of his *Roman Ostia* (1959), Russell Meiggs had argued that no good evidence survives to suggest that the number of Jews in Ostia was ever large. In the second edition (1973), however, he corrects himself because of a new funerary inscription discovery of an archisynagogus, Plotius Fortunatus. Meiggs states with candor: "The name helps to explain why the Jews of Ostia were so elusive: I overlooked the fact that it was common Jewish practice to adopt Roman names" (*Roman Ostia*, 2d ed. [Oxford: Clarendon Press, 1973], 588). The same oversight is easy to make regarding the Jews of Rome.

[212] Stern, *Greek and Latin Authors*, 2:68–73; Elmer T. Merrill, "The Expulsion of Jews from Rome under Tiberius," *CP* 14 (1919): 365–72; W. A. Heidel, "Why Were the Jews Banished from Italy in 19 A.D.?" *AJP* 41 (1920): 38–47; Smallwood, *Jews under Roman Rule*, 201–10. Other expulsion accounts neglect to mention the detail that the Jews banished to Sardinia were "from the freedmen/women class": Seut. *Tib.* 36; Josephus, *Ant.* 18.3.5 §81–84; Philo, *Leg.* 24.159–61; Sen. *Ep.* 108.22; Dio Cassius 57.18.

2. Philo (*Leg.* 23.155–57) describes the ethnically diverse and crowded trans-Tiber district of Rome as inhabited by Jews, the majority of whom were freedmen/women originally brought to Italy as prisoners of war and subsequently manumitted by their Roman citizen owners.[213]

3. Acts 6:9 mentions a "synagogue of the freedmen/women" in Jerusalem, which commentators since John Chrysostom have considered to refer to Jewish freedmen/women from Rome.[214] Yet this is admittedly a conjecture based on the supposition that the Greek transliteration λιβερτῖνοι for the Latin *libertini* indicates a Roman (or at least Latin-speaking) place of origin for these freedmen/women.[215] In any event, the fact that a synagogue could have been composed entirely or mainly of freedmen/women and their descendants is interesting in itself and parallels the phenomenon of *collegia tenuiorum* made up

---

[213] E. Mary Smallwood, ed. and trans., *Philonis Alexandrini: Legatio ad Gaium*, 2d ed. (Leiden: E. J. Brill, 1970), 92 (for commentary, see 234–42); Treggiari, *Roman Freedmen*, 205–6.

[214] Chrys. *Hom. 15 in Ac.* (*PG* 60.120); John Calvin, *The Acts of the Apostles, 1–13*, trans. John W. Fraser and W. J. G. McDonald, Calvin's Commentaries (London: Oliver & Boyd, 1965), 165; Daniel Schenkel, *Bibel-Lexikon: Realwörterbuch zum Handgebrauch für Geistliche und Gemeindeglieder* (Leipzig: Brockaus, 1872), 4:38; Heinrich August Wilhelm Meyer, *Critical and Exegetical Handbook to the Acts of the Apostles*, 2d ed., trans. Paton J. Gloag, trans. rev. and ed. William P. Dickson (New York: Funk & Wagnalls, 1884), 127–29; Fred C. Conybeare, "On the Western Text of the Acts as Evidenced by Chrysostom," *AJP* 17 (1896): 152; Friedrich Blass, *Philology of the Gospels* (London: Macmillan, 1898), 69–73; J. Rendell Harris, "The History of a Conjectural Emendation," *Expositor* 6 (1902): 379–85; Samuel Krauss, "Slaves and Slavery – Freedmen," *The Jewish Encyclopedia*, ed. Isidore Singer (New York: Ktav, 1905), 11:407–8; L.-K. Vincent, "Découverte de la 'synagogue des affranchis' à Jérusalem," *RB* 30 (1921): 258–60; *A Dictionary of the Bible*, ed. James Hastings (New York: Charles Scribner's Sons, 1923), 3:110; E. Jacquier, *Les Actes des Apôtres*, Ebib (Paris: Gabalda, 1926), 196; Adolf Deissmann, *Light from the Ancient Near East: The New Testament Illustrated by Recently Discovered Texts of the Graeco-Roman World*, 2d ed., trans. R. M. Strachan (London: Hodder & Stoughton, 1927), 441; F. J. Foakes Jackson and Kirsopp Lake, *The Beginnings of Christianity*, pt. 1, *The Acts of the Apostles*, trans. and comment. Kirsopp Lake and Henry J. Cadbury (London: Macmillan, 1933), 4:66–68 n. 9; Theodor Nissen, "Philologisches zu Act. apost. 6,9," *Philologus* 95 (1942–43): 310–13; F. F. Bruce, *The Acts of the Apostles* (Grand Rapids, Mich.: William B. Eerdmans, 1952), 156; Schürer, *History of the Jewish People*, 3.1:133; Treggiari, *Roman Freedmen*, 206–7; Ernst Haenchen, *The Acts of the Apostles: A Commentary*, trans. R. M. Wilson (Philadelphia: Westminster Press, 1971), 271 n. 1; Hans Conzelmann, *Acts of the Apostles: A Commentary on the Acts of the Apostles*, Hermeneia, trans. James Limburg, A. Thomas Kraabel, and Donald H. Juel (Philadelphia: Fortress Press, 1987), 47.

[215] *Liberti* meant freedmen/women in relation to their patron(s), *libertini* in relation to everybody else and to the state; Treggiari, *Roman Freedmen*, 37 n. 5, 52–53; Nicholas, *Roman Law*, 75.

solely of *liberti.*[216] There may also have been a similar "synagogue of freed-men/women" in Pompeii.[217]

4. *CII* 365, 425, and 503 are Roman catacomb inscriptions that identify a first-century synagogue of the Agrippesians ('Αγριππησίων), whose members possibly were originally Jewish slaves and freedmen/women belonging to the household of Marcus Agrippa.[218] The dating of the Jewish catacombs, however, is a source of much debate, with some scholars arguing for extremely late dates (fourth, fifth, or even sixth centuries of the common era).[219]

5. *CII* 284, 301, 338, 368, 416, and 496 are Roman catacomb inscriptions that emanate from a synagogue of the Augustesians (Αὐγουστησίων), whose members perhaps originated as slaves and freedmen/women of the imperial household.[220]

6. *CII* 318, 383, 389, and 494 are catacomb inscriptions that mention a synagogue of the Vernaclesians (Βερνάκλων, Βερνακλώπων, Βερνακλησών), whose members called themselves *Vernacli* or *Vernaclenses* (perhaps from the Latin word *verna*), possibly indicating that its congregation arose from Jewish

---

[216] Jean-Pierre Waltzing, *Étude historique sur les corporations professionnelles chez les Romains depuis les origines jusqu'à la chute de l'empire d'occident* (1900; reprint, Bologna: Forni, 1968), 4:153–80; R. Donceel, "Une inscription inédite de Nole et la date du sénatus-consulte 'de collegiis tenuiorum,'" *BIBR* 42 (1972): 27–71.

[217] J.-B. Frey, "Les Juifs à Pompéi," *RB* 42 (1933): 370–72.

[218] Romano Penna, "Les Juifs à Rome au temps de l'Apôtre Paul," *NTS* 28 (1982): 328. Penna also dates the synagogues of the "Augustesians" and the "Vernaclesians" to the first century. Nikolaus Müller, *Die jüdische Katakombe am Monteverde zu Rom, der älteste bisher bekannt gewordene jüdische Friedhof des Abendlandes* (Leipzig: G. Fock, 1912), 108; Eugène Bormann, "Zu den neuentdeckten Grabschriften jüdischer Katakomben zu Rom," *WS* 34 (1912): 363; Schürer, *History of the Jewish People*, 3.1:96. Leon, *Jews of Ancient Rome*, 141, contends, however, that "We must discard [this] suggestion … since there is no basis for such a view." See also P. W. van der Horst, *Ancient Jewish Epitaphs: An Introductory Survey of a Millennium of Jewish Funerary Epigraphy (300 B.C.E.–700 C.E.)*, Contributions to Biblical Exegesis 2 (Kampen, The Netherlands: Kok Pharos, 1991), 95 (on προστάτης).

[219] A. Ferrua, "Sulla tomba dei Cristiani e su quella degli Ebrei," *Civiltà Cattolica* 87 (1936): 298–311; Iiro Kajanto, *Onomastic Studies in the Early Christian Inscriptions of Roman and Carthage*, Acta Instituti Romani Finlandiae 2.1 (Helsinki: Tilgmann, 1963); Heikki Solin, "Onomastica ed epigrafia: Riflessioni sull'esegesi onomastica delle iscrizioni romane," *QUCC* 18 (1974): 105–32; Leonard Victor Rutgers, "Überlegungen zu den jüdischen Katakomben Roms," *JAC* 33 (1990): 140–57; Tessa Rajak, "Inscription and Context: Reading the Jewish Catacombs of Rome," in *Studies in Jewish Epigraphy*, ed. Jan Willem van Henten and Pieter W. van der Horst, Arbeiten zur Geschichte des antiken Judentums und des Urchristentums 21 (Leiden: E. J. Brill, 1994), 226–41.

[220] Lampe, *Stadtrömischen Christen*, 66–67, is very secure in this knowledge. Yet Leon, *Jews of Ancient Rome*, 142, concludes that "we should reject the view that its members originated from slaves and freedmen of the imperial household." Leon's language is quite strong here: "The theory must remain a hypothesis for which there is not a particle of evidence" (142 n. 2). Leon mainly attacks the view of Schürer, *History of the Jewish People*, 3.1:96. Yet Schürer does offer parallels from Roman *collegia* to support his view.

slaves born in Roman households as opposed to a foreign–born slaves from Judaea or elsewhere.[221] It was proverbial that *vernae* made the best slaves and that a master surrounded by them was a master most at ease.[222] Yet *verna* may also simply refer to a Jew born in Rome, whatever his or her legal status.[223]

The evidence in the second category includes the following:

7. Plutarch (*Life of Cicero* 7.5) speaks of a freedman quaestor of Sicily, under the corrupt governor Verres (73–71 B.C.E.), named Q. Caecilius Niger, who was "suspected of Jewish practices." Plutarch may have confused this figure with the rhetor and Greek historian Caecilius from Calacte, Sicily, in the time of Augustus. The *Suidas* calls the rhetor Caecilius a Jew who was formerly a slave. But the reliability of the *Suidas* is always a question.[224]

8. Cicero (*Att.* 14.19.1) tells of a certain Barnaeus, his domestic letter-carrier, either a slave or a freedman. Barnaeus's "Jewishness" is based solely on his Semitic name.[225]

9. Martial (7.35) comments on his circumcised slave, perhaps a Jew.[226]

10. Josephus (*Ant.* 17.5.7 §141; *JW* 1.32.6 §641) mentions Acme (Akme), the Jewish imperial slave of the Empress Livia.[227]

---

[221] George La Piana, "Foreign Groups in Rome during the First Centuries of the Empire," *HTR* 20 (1927): 352. Leon, *Jews of Ancient Rome*, 155–57, reviews La Piana's and others' theories, but again writes, "Misled by the fact that the Latin word *verna* means a houseborn slave, most authorities have represented the members as having been of servile origin" (155). On the contrary, Leon contends, the word *vernaculus* denoted only "native" or "indigenous" Jews born in Rome.

[222] Hor. *Sat.* 2.6.66; *Epod.* 2.65; Tib. 1.5.26; 2.1.23; Mart. 3.58.22; Tac. *Ann.* 14.44; Harris, "Towards a Study," 118–19.

[223] A similar situation is discussed by P. R. C. Weaver, "Misplaced Officials," *Antichthon* 13 (1979): 78, where the inscription *Ti. Claudius Romanus verna* need not refer to a house-born freedman/woman, but may only mean "born and reared in the household" or "born in Rome" and could refer to a freeborn.

[224] Ada Adler, ed., *Suidae Lexicon*, s.v. Καικίλιος, 3:83; *FGH* 2B:183, T I; cited in M. Stern, "The Jewish Diaspora," in *The Jewish People in the First Century: Historical Geography, Political History, Social, Cultural and Religious Life and Institutions*, ed. S. Safrai and M. Stern, CRINT 1.1 (Philadelphia: Fortress Press, 1974), 1:169; Solin, "Juden und Syrer," 658; D. A. Russell, "Caecilius (4)," *OCD* 187; Leon, *Jews of Ancient Rome*, 15–16; Stern, *Greek and Latin Authors*, 1:566.

[225] Solin, "Juden und Syrer," 677. D. R. Shackleton Bailey, *Cicero's Letters to Atticus* (Cambridge: Cambridge University Press, 1967), 6:324, makes no presumption about the ethnicity of Barnaeus, writing only that "the name occurs in inscriptions."

[226] Stern, *Greek and Roman Authors*, 1:525. Dwora Gilula, "Did Martial Have a Jewish Slave? (7.35)," *CQ* 37 (1987): 532–33, casts doubts upon the view that the slave must necessarily have been Jewish.

[227] Schürer, *History of the Jewish People*, 3.1:78 n. 97; Solin, "Juden und Syrer," 658. On imperial slaves of the Empress, see Chantraine, "Freigelassene," 389–416.

11. Josephus (*Ant.* 13.6.4 §167) reports that a Samaritan imperial freedman (perhaps named Thallus) lent a large sum of money to Agrippa I in Rome.[228] The standard critical edition (ed. B. Niese, reproducing exactly the 1544 *editio princeps* of Arlenius) of the text reads: καὶ γὰρ ἦν ἄλλος Σαμαρεὺς γένος Καίσαρος δὲ ἀπελεύθερος. The predominant assumption has been that the manuscript must be corrupt here, because ἄλλος is impossible Greek in this context. With the exception of Niese, every editor of Josephus since J. Hudson in the eighteenth century has emended this passage to read Θάλλος, following E (the epitome text). In an excellent essay, Horace A. Rigg Jr. articulates a cogent case for reading ἄλλος against Θάλλος, translating: "Now there was another, namely a Samaritan by race (birth), a freedman of Caesar."[229] With either textual reading, the social significance remains that the passage provides a historical example of an enslaved Semitic person related to Judaism who eventually became a wealthy, politically influential imperial freedman.

12. *CII* 105, 172, 212, 234, and 235 all exhibit Flavian names, suggesting possible identification of liberated imperial slaves of the Flavian household, some originally brought to Rome after the Jewish War of 66–70/73 C.E.[230]

13. *CII* 35* records a certain Nunnus, deceased when only seven years and two months old, called a *verna*, which may refer (as above) to a home-born slave.[231]

14. *CII* 256 commemorates a Jewish proselyte named Nicetas; it was set up by a patroness identified as a certain Dionysias. The term *patrona* may denote Dionysias as Nicetas's former master.

15. *CII* 462 memorializes two female proselytes, a child named Felicitas (who died at age six) and Peregrina (who died at age forty-seven, perhaps Felicitas's mother). The stone was set up by an unnamed patroness (*patrona*) who, as in the example above, might have been their ex-master.[232]

---

[228] Schürer, *History of the Jewish People*, 3.1:81, considers the Samaritan to be named Thallus.

[229] Horace A. Rigg Jr., "Thallus: The Samaritan?" *HTR* 34 (1941): 114–19; note also Pierre Prigent, "Thallos, Phlégon et le testimonium flavianum témoins de Jésus?" in *Paganisme, Judaïsme, Christianisme: Influences et affrontements dans le monde antique. Mélanges offerts à Marcel Simon* (Paris: Boccard, 1978), 329 n. 1.

[230] Suzanne Collon, "Remarques sur les quartiers juifs de la Rome antique," *MEFRA* 57 (1940): 92. James S. Jeffers, *Conflict at Rome: Social Hierarchy in Early Christianity* (Minneapolis: Fortress Press, 1991), 60, makes related onomastic arguments for T. Flavius Clemens and his family.

[231] Antonio Ferrua, "Addenda et corrigenda ad Corpus Inscriptionum Iudaicarum," *Epigraphica* 3 (1941): 45; Frey, *Corpus of Jewish Inscriptions*, 552, calls Nunnus an "esclave (né dans la maison)"; Fuks, "Freedmen," 30 n. 37.

[232] Leon, *Jews of Ancient Rome*, 235; van der Horst, *Ancient Jewish Epitaphs*, 72. These references also discuss *CII* 256.

16. *CII* 75* (= *CIL* 10.1931) is an epitaph of a first-century c.e. freedman named Acibas, an iron and vineyard merchant buried in Puteoli. Acibas is considered Jewish by scholars because of his name.[233]

17. Certain names in the Jewish catacomb inscriptions are believed to be of servile origin.[234]

18. Numerous other freedmen/women funerary inscriptions found in Rome exhibit Semitic names.[235] Most of those listed below belong to pagan burial *columbaria* (or "condominiums of the dead"), for ex-slaves of a single household, which were set up by a personal patron (usually the former master):

l. Abinnaeus: CIL 6.9102 (a good example of a freedman/woman *columbarium* epitaph);

l. Ac[h]iba: CIL 6.19250; 6.19798;

l. Acraba: CIL 6.8962 (*T. Flavius Aug. l. Acraba*);

l. Bagatus, Bargates, Bargatus: CIL 6.5684; 6.12692; 6.25219; 6.26302; 6.26361; 6.35310;

l. Barcne: CIL 6.25867;

l. Barna, Barnus, Barnes, Barnaeus: CIL 6.1892; 6.4289; 6.4597; 6.7219; 6.8371; 6.10407; 6.11177; 6.12245; 6.12333; 6.16302; 6.19078; 6.19873; 6.22186; 6.23515; 6.25339; 6.26104; 6.26497; 6.34434; 6.34513; 6.35103; 6.35162; 6.37916; 6.38376;

l. Malchio: CIL 6.1939; 6.3999; 6.4963; 6.9170; 6.9933; 6.14277; 6.20972; 6.21867; 6.22082; 6.23690; 6.25177; 6.26167; 6.29624; 6.31183; 6.35669; 6.36019; 6.36127; 6.37761; 6.38965;

l. Mart[h]a: CIL 6.5582; 6.6050; 6.6184; 6.6572; 6.19755; 6.19521; 6.21145; 6.21644; 6.22443; 6.37487;

l. Massa: CIL 6.22272;

l. Ragia: CIL 6.33;

l. Sabbis, Sabbio, Sabbat[h]is: CIL 6.4779; 6.5543; 6.10127; 6.11665; 6.16302; 6.20252; 6.21666; 6.22928; 6.23226; 6.23859; 6.24504; 6.26153; 6.34288; 6.37594;

l. Zabda, Zavda, Sabda: CIL 6.4787; 6.6330; 6.11457; 6.16759; 6.18520; 6.24891; 6.24918; 6.27959; 6.34566; 6.37616;

l. Zabina, Sabina: CIL 6.12236; 6.16330; 6.37171.[236]

---

[233] S. Applebaum, "The Social and Economic Status of the Jews in the Diaspora," in *Jewish People in the First Century*, ed. S. Safrai and M. Stern, CRINT 1.2 (Amsterdam: Van Gorcum, 1976), 2:722.

[234] Fuks, "Freedmen," 31 nn. 41, 42, following the slave-name list in Duff, *Freedmen*, 110. Duff's methodological assumptions in compiling his list, however, have fallen under severe criticism and should not be followed uncritically; P. R. C. Weaver, "Cognomia Ingenua: A Note," *CQ* 14 (1964): 311, writes: "One of the gains to be reckoned from the study of nomenclature in the sepulchral inscriptions of the early empire is the gradual abandonment of attempts to distinguish between slave and freeborn on the basis of cognomen alone, especially when this is of Latin derivation."

[235] Following the methodology used to interpret *CII* 70* (= *CIL* 6.27959), the three Jewish freedmen, Baricha, Zabda, and Achiba, discussed above.

[236] Compiled from Solin, "Juden und Syrer," 676–79, in conjunction with Vidman's name index to *CIL* 6, although in each case I have gone back to check and read the texts printed in *CIL*.

Even if only a small percentage of these Semitic names belonged to Jews, the nature of the evidence still suggests that many Jewish freedmen/women populated Rome, not only in the ethnically diverse trans-Tiber region that Philo mentions but throughout the entire metropolitan area.

Although there are explicit testimonies to the existence of large numbers of Jewish freedmen/women as a group, explicit testimony to individual Jewish freedmen/women by the designation *lib.* is limited to the *Suidas*. How this discrepancy might be explained remains an open question. Perhaps Jews avoided calling attention to their dependence upon pagans.[237] Part of the problem is surely the general difficulty with identifying any Roman as part of a population group solely on the basis of a name in a commemoration. At any rate, this excursus illustrates vertical (client – patron) and horizontal (client – client) social networks among Jews in Rome.[238] Examples 4, 5, 8, 12, 14, 15, and 18 document vertical networks between patrons, either Jewish or non-Jewish, and Jewish clients; examples 3, 4, 5, and 6 document horizontal networks among fellow Jewish freedmen/women.

Summation

Our investigation has discovered that among the many problems, debates, and controversies surrounding the essential elements of ancient slavery, none deserves more attention than those over manumission. We introduced the intellectual problem of slavery and its definition. We defined "slave" using the

---

[237] Dale Martin ("Slavery in the Ancient Jewish Family," in *The Jewish Family in Antiquity*, ed. Shaye J. D. Cohen, BJS 289 [Atlanta: Scholars Press, 1993], 120–21 n. 24) questions my previous interpretation of the Jewish evidence, which I made in "The Social and Economic Position of Jewish Freedmen in Rome," a paper to the SBL Group on the Social World of Formative Judaism and Christianity, Annual Meeting of the Society of Biblical Literature (San Francisco, California, 23 November 1992). I had argued that the rarity of the *lib.* status indicator in the Jewish catacomb inscriptions reflected an effort to avoid a public symbol of dependence upon non-Jewish patrons. I agree with Martin that the dating of the inscriptions is problematic, and that the absence of the *lib.* may be simply following the trend, from the second-century c.e. onwards, to drop all servile status indicators. However, I still maintain that the ancient synagogue as a corporate institution could have provided an alternative source of patronage to Jewish ex-slaves who otherwise would have been dependent on the *domus* of a non-Jewish patron for daily support. The situation is similar to the role Greco-Roman voluntary associations took as corporate patrons of freedmen/women. I discuss the evidence for this in chapters 3 and 4.

[238] For an investigation of social networks as a feature of social history within early Christianity, see L. Michael White, "Finding the Ties that Bind: Issues from Social Description," in *Social Networks in the Early Christian Environment: Issues and Methods for Social History*, ed. idem, Semeia 56 (Atlanta: Scholars Press, 1992), 3–36.

"social death" hermeneutic of Orlando Patterson and the dependent labor (or "chattel") hermeneutic of M. I. Finley. Then, we investigated the availability and limitations of the evidence, and the process of using such evidence to trace the enslavement process from bondage to (perhaps) freedom in manumission. Despite frustratingly little evidence, interpreters can make positive statements about manumission. Such statements reconstruct social history, as history "from below," and provide clues to solving the crux of 1 Corinthians 7:21 and of Ignatius, *Ad Polycarp.* 4.3.

Chapter 2

The Interpretive Crux of 1 Corinthians 7:21

This chapter investigates the philological and contextual problems of 1 Cor 7:17–24. Generations of New Testament scholars have considered these verses, especially 7:21b, the classic proof text, or *locus classicus*, for assessing the Pauline position on slavery. Many scholars today still uphold this claim. Yet nothing in the passage implies that Paul considered the question of whether the institution of slavery ought to be abolished or not. Paul's explicit topic is the manumission of baptized slaves. Ethical inferences about slavery as a general phenomenon of the Greco-Roman world should be drawn from Paul's words only with great caution.

The verse 7:21b presents serious interpretive difficulties, which begin with a problem in the text: How is one to translate the clause μᾶλλον χρῆσαι? The verse reads: "You were called as a slave. Do not worry about it. But if you can indeed become free, μᾶλλον χρῆσαι [rather use ...]." Because Paul omits an object (a rhetorical device called "brachylogy"), the meaning of the Greek clause is unclear. The first part of this chapter, after some historical background, describes in detail the history of its interpretation from John Chrysostom to the present. The second part presents detailed exegesis of the passage, which includes both a philological analysis and an examination of the argumentative context. This chapter argues that the preponderance of philological evidence supports an adversative translation of the brachylogy in μᾶλλον χρῆσαι, and that the context does not exclude this reading. By "adversative," I mean expressing opposition not to its protasis (if-clause: "if you can *indeed* become free"), but to the previous apodosis (result-clause: "do not worry about it"). The translation proposed is "If you can indeed become free, *use instead* [freedom]."

Before analyzing the text, however, it is necessary to map out the terrain of Greco-Roman background material and provide a brief overview of the ancient city of Corinth, looking at both its history and its position in the Roman Empire. This survey provides a useful context against which to read Paul's letter to the Corinthians.

The Ancient City of Corinth

The terms "Corinth" and "Corinthia" refer to the city proper (ἄστυ) and its surrounding countryside (χώρα), both of which composed its city-state (πόλις).[1] Corinth was located (as it is today) on the isthmus that connects Boeotia/Attica to the Peloponnesus. The Dorians, the last of the northern invaders of Greece during the Dark Age (ca. 1200–800 B.C.E.), founded and occupied the isthmian site as a result of their conquest circa 1100 B.C.E. These Dorian settlers situated the city strategically on the piedmont of Acrocorinth, a name that refers both to the imposing mountain that dominates the topography of the entire area and to the citadel on its summit. In classical scholarship, Corinthia designates the area ruled by the Corinthians after they had expanded to Crommyonia and Peraea around 570/560 B.C.E. In modern Greek, however, Corinthia names a much larger region, which encompasses territories that in classical antiquity belonged to Epidauria, Cleonaea, Phleiasia, Sikyonia, and the two Achaean city-states of Pellene and Aegeira. We must keep the ancient and modern designations distinct; this chapter uses the term Corinthia only in its classical sense to designate the χώρα of greater Corinth bounded by Megara on the north, Sikyon on the west, the Saronic Gulf on the east, and the cities of Cleonae, Argos, and Epidauros on the south.[2] The ancient Corinthia contained two ports: Lechaion, on the Corinthian Gulf, stood as one of the largest artificial harbors in the Roman world; Kenchreai, on the Saronic Gulf, served as the eastern seaport. Both accommodated bustling commercial activity in the time of the Apostle Paul.[3]

---

[1] My discussion in this section reflects conversations with Elizabeth R. Gebhard on the present state of archaeological excavation at Corinth.

[2] M. B. Sakellariou and N. Faraklas, *Corinthia–Cleonaea* (Athens: Athens Center of Ekistics, 1971), 1. See also T. Lenschau, "Korinthos," PWSup 4 (1924): 991–1036; Harold N. Fowler, "Corinth and the Corinthia," in *Corinth: Results of Excavations Conducted by the American School of Classical Studies at Athens*, ed. Harold N. Fowler and R. Stillwell, vol. 1, *Introduction, Topography, Architecture* (Cambridge: The American School, 1932), 18–114; James Wiseman, *The Land of the Ancient Corinthians*, Studies in Mediterranean Archaeology 1 (Göteborg: Paul Åströms Förlag, 1978), 9–15; J. B. Salmon, *Wealthy Corinth: A History of the City to 338 B.C.* (Oxford: Clarendon Press, 1984), 1–37.

[3] Robert L. Hohlfelder, "Kenchreai on the Saronic Gulf: Aspects of Imperial History," *CJ* 71 (1976): 223; Donald Engels, *Roman Corinth: An Alternative Model for the Classical City* (Chicago: University of Chicago Press, 1990), 11–12. Engels must be used with caution; see the critical reviews by Richard P. Saller, *CP* 86 (1991): 351–57; and Mary E. Hoskins Walbank, *JRS* 81 (1991): 220–21. See also Victor Paul Furnish, *II Corinthians*, AB 32A (New York: Doubleday, 1984), 4–22. In Rom 16:1, Paul writes that a certain woman named Phoebe served as a "deacon" (διάκονος) of the church at Kenchreai.

The story of ancient Corinth begins as a tale of two cities.[4] The first Corinth, classical Corinth, was an independent city-state governed by a constitutionally based oligarchy, which flourished from the time of the overthrow of the tyrants (550/540 B.C.E.) to the time of the Macedonian conquest and occupation (338 B.C.E.). When republican Rome expanded its military influence into the eastern Mediterranean, the Consul Lucius Mummius and his four consular legions sacked Corinth in 146 B.C.E. and sold its inhabitants into slavery as an example to other Greek cities of how Rome would respond to opposition to its hegemony in Achaea.[5] The second Corinth, Roman Corinth, was a Caesarean colony, founded in 44 B.C.E. by Julius Caesar. This new Corinth, renamed Colonia Laus Iulia Corinthiensis, was settled mainly by Roman freedmen/women from Italy.[6] Although there is some evidence of cultural continuity between classical and Roman Corinth,[7] the two cities were nevertheless markedly different.

Evidence specific to classical Corinth must not be confused with that specific to Roman Corinth. Perhaps the most notorious error of this kind, at least in New Testament studies (as recent commentaries have pointed out), concerns Corinth's reputation for easy living and loose morals. Some biblical scholars wrongly bill Corinth as the "Las Vegas of antiquity" (or, to use a port-city analogy, the "New Orleans of ancient Achaia"),[8] condemning its loose, perverse, and "pagan" character. This interpretation rests upon confusion of classical and Roman Corinth. In classical times, Aristophanes coined the verb κορινθιάζεσθαι (to Corinth-ize), which meant to practice fornication;[9] Plato

---

[4] Corinth's history is, of course, more complex than what I outline here. I omit its prehistory in the Neolithic Age, its chronology during the Early, Middle, and Late Helladic Periods, and the history of archaic Corinth under the tyrants. I also exclude the Hellenistic eras of Macedonian domination (243–222 B.C.E.) and of membership in the Achaean Confederacy (196–146 B.C.E.). For these periods, see Sakellariou and Faraklas, *Corinthia*, 30–71, 107–22; Salmon, *Wealthy Corinth*, 186–229.

[5] For the details, see H. H. Scullard, *A History of the Roman World: 753 to 146 B.C.*, 4th ed. (New York: Methuen, 1980), 290–91.

[6] Oscar Broneer, "Colonia Laus Iulia Corinthiensis," *Hesperia* 10 (1941): 388–90; James Wiseman, "Corinth and Rome I: 228 B.C.– A.D. 267," *ANRW* 2.7.1 (1979): 497. Fritz S. Darrow, "The History of Corinth from Mummius to Herodes Atticus" (Ph.D. diss., Harvard University, 1906), still provides useful historical background.

[7] Richard E. Oster Jr., "Use, Misuse and Neglect of Archaeological Evidence in Some Modern Works on 1 Corinthians (1 Cor 7,1–5; 8,10; 11,2–16; 12,14–26)," *ZNW* 83 (1992): 54–55.

[8] Luke T. Johnson, *The Writings of the New Testament* (Philadelphia: Fortress Press, 1986), 272.

[9] Ar. F 354. The active voice is found in the work of the fifth-century C.E. lexicographer Hesychius of Alexandria. The nominal form, Κορινθιαστής, meaning "whoremonger," forms the titles of plays by the Middle Comedic poet Philetaerus, *Ath.* 13.559a, and the second-century C.E. writer of comedy, Poliochus, *Id.* 7.313c. These attestations,

used the expression Κοϱίνθια κόϱη to denote a prostitute;[10] and Strabo rhetorically describes the thousand temple prostitutes who worked out of the Temple of Aphrodite on the Acrocorinth.[11] From this evidence, some New Testament scholars have argued that sexual "immorality" was rampant in daily Corinthian life. Yet this interpretation not only overplays the intentional exaggeration of these authors, but also is anachronistic since Aristophanes, Plato, and Strabo were speaking not of Roman but of classical Corinth. Furthermore, these authors are highly rhetorical and cannot be taken as reliable evidence even for classical Corinth.[12] In the end, one must sort out the evidence specific to each of the two cities.

The specific social and legal conditions of Roman Corinth's population have relevance to our study of 1 Cor 7:21 and ancient slavery. Roman Corinth was founded as a Caesarean colony of freedmen/women. The Italian settlers who took the city and its Corinthia from the locals, thus displacing the native Corinthian population, apparently evoked bitter resentment from some Greeks, such as the Lesbian poet Crinagoras (born ca. 70 B.C.E.). Crinagoras took part in an embassy to Julius Caesar in 44 B.C.E. and was present when final plans were being drawn up to resettle Corinth as a Roman colony. The poet laments:

What sort of inhabitants, O pitiful city, have you found, and in place of whom? Alas, it is a great misfortune to Greece. Would that you, O Corinth, lay lower than the ground and more desert than the Libyan sands, rather than be a one so completely abandoned to such a mass of good-for-nothing slaves [παλιμπϱήτοισι = "often sold"; i.e., good-for-nothing slaves who pass from owner to owner][13] to distress the bones of the ancient Bacchiadae![14]

This acerbic epigram not only reveals sharp prejudice against slaves and even liberated slaves in Greco-Roman society, but also demonstrates how some members of the Greek aristocratic elite contemporary with Julius Caesar

---

however, reflect later imitation of Aristophanes' diction. For background material, see William S. Anderson, "Corinth and Comedy," in *Corinthiaca: Studies in Honor of Darrell A. Amyx*, ed. Mario A. Del Chiaro and William R. Biers (Columbia: University of Missouri Press, 1986), 44–49.

[10] Pl. *Resp.* 404d.

[11] Strabo 12.3.36.

[12] Gordon D. Fee, *The First Epistle to the Corinthians*, NICNT (Grand Rapids, Mich.: William B. Eerdmans, 1987), 2–3; Jerome Murphy-O'Connor, *St. Paul's Corinth: Texts and Archaeology*, GNS 6 (Collegeville, Minn.: Liturgical Press, 1983), 56; Hans Conzelmann, "Korinth und die Mädchen der Aphrodite: Zur Religionsgeschichte der Stadt Korinth," *NAWG* 8 (1967–68): 247–61; Charles K. Williams II, "Corinth and the Cult of Aphrodite," in Del Chiaro and Biers, *Corinthiaca*, 12–24.

[13] LSJ, s.v. the two-termination adjective παλίμπϱατος, –ον; cf. Pollianus 3.125.

[14] Crinagoras, *Anthologia Graeca* 9.284 (LCL), my translation. Murphy-O'Connor, *Paul's Corinth*, 51; Ferdinand-Joseph De Waele, *Corinthe et Saint Paul*, Les hauts lieux de l'histoire (Paris: Albert Guillot, 1961), 85.

viewed Roman Corinth as somewhat of an embarrassment to the freeborn ancestry of classical Corinth.[15] The evidence for this embarrassment, however, rests solely upon Crinagoras and may reflect his personal biases against Julius Caesar and the Dictator's handling of the colony's founding. According to the colony's charter, freedmen could be elected to be the chief magistrates of the city, the *duoviri iure dicundo*, and could administer the Corinthia.[16] This practice marks a radical departure from both Republican and Principate tradition, which allowed only descendants of freedmen to become decurions.[17] Perhaps it was this or something similar in the colony's charter that prompted Crinagoras to write his biting, almost resentful verses against Roman Corinth.

Another important element concerns the key role of the Corinthia in the international slave trade.[18] Corinth's two seaports, Lechaion on the Corinthian Gulf and Kenchreai on the Saronic Gulf, served as freight way stations that handled high volumes of traffic and vast inventories of merchandise, including human chattel, which were destined for trade markets throughout the ancient Mediterranean world. It has been suggested that Corinth may have replaced the isle of Delos as "the eastern 'clearing house' for the slave trade ... as the [common slave] name 'Corinthus' seems to indicate."[19] Varro writes that

---

[15] James H. Oliver, "Panachaeans and Panhellenes," *Hesperia* 47 (1978): 191. Strabo 8.6.20, however, mentions the Corinthian freedmen/women colonists in a neutral tone and does not appear to share Crinagoras's bitter resentment.

[16] Wiseman, "Corinth and Rome," 498. On the provincial and local magistrates, see John K. Chow, *Patronage and Power: A Study of Social Networks in Corinth*, JSNTSup 75 (Sheffield: Sheffield Academic Press, 1992), 59–60; Anita Bagdikian, "The Civic Officials of Roman Corinth" (master's thesis, University of Vermont, 1953), 1–18. Bagdikian, however, does not discuss freedmen.

[17] Susan Treggiari, *Roman Freedmen during the Late Republic* (Oxford: Clarendon Press, 1969), 52–64. This practice continued into the Principate; Peter Garnsey, "Descendants of Freedmen in Local Politics: Some Criteria," in *The Ancient Historian and His Materials: Essays in Honor of C. E. Stevens on His Seventieth Birthday*, ed. Barbara Levick (Westmead, England: D. C. Heath, Gregg International, 1975), 167–80.

[18] The best study on the Roman slave trade remains William V. Harris, "Towards a Study of the Roman Slave Trade," in *The Seaborne Commerce of Ancient Rome: Studies in Archaeology and History*, ed. J. H. D'Arms and E. C. Kopff, Memoirs of the American Academy in Rome 36 (Rome: The Academy, 1980), 117–40. Harris, however, does not mention the Corinthia's role. Note also M. I. Finley, "Aulos Kapreilios Timotheos, Slave Trader," in *Aspects of Antiquity: Discoveries and Controversies*, 2d ed. (New York: Penguin Books, 1977), 154–66.

[19] S. Scott Bartchy, *MAΛΛON XPHΣAI: First-Century Slavery and the Interpretation of First Corinthians 7:21*, SBLDS 11 (1973; reprint, Atlanta: Scholars Press, 1985), 58 n. 185; he follows Mary L. Gordon, "The Nationality of Slaves under the Early Roman Empire," in *Slavery in Classical Antiquity: Views and Controversies*, ed. M. I. Finley (Cambridge: W. Heffer & Sons, 1960): 172, 177. The name "Corinthus" is found in *CIL* 5.1305; 6.11541; 6.3956; 6.4454; see also P. M. Fraser and E. Matthews, *A Lexicon of Greek Personal Names*, vol. 1, *The Aegean Islands, Cyprus, Cyrenaica* (Oxford: Clarendon Press, 1987), 269.

ancient servile nomenclature often reflected the slave's place of purchase: for example, a master would name a slave "Ephesios" because he was bought in the city of Ephesus.[20] Yet because slave names are in fact not reliable indicators of point of origin or place of original purchase, nomenclature alone is not sound enough evidence upon which to base an argument about Corinth's central role in the eastern Mediterranean slave trade.

Fortunately other evidence exists. In 1929, archaeological investigations of the site of Roman Corinth under the auspices of the American School of Classical Studies at Athens unearthed and excavated a large market north of the hill of the temple of Apollo.[21] The find is remarkably well preserved, and the evidence clearly supports the designation "market" for the excavated site. The area is a rectangular plaza bordered on three sides by a series of shops, containing a row of chambers along its south side, partition walls of rooms at the west, and a paved central plaza with mosaics and a sidewalk. The design resembles that found in other Hellenistic and Roman cities, such as Magnesia, Priene, Pompeii, and Thuburba in North Africa.[22] This business zone (forum) housed, among other things, the Corinthian slave market. Although one might expect to find the slave market in the agora (its location in the classical period), a close look at the location of the architectural remains and road grid of the Roman city provides compelling reasons against this view. The Roman city's central agora does not have the physical layout of a major thoroughfare, or even market. The roads stop short of entering the agora; in fact, they run into steps, which would obstruct chariots, wagons, and other vehicles. There are no ruts on the paving stones, which are made of marble. Marble makes a nice decorative veneer, but not a good road surface. From this physical evidence, classical archaeologists who have worked on the site of Roman Corinth argue that the agora could not, and did not, accommodate the cart traffic necessary for a marketplace. They conclude that the Corinthian agora served as the ceremonial, not market, center of the city. Instead, they point to the Roman market north of the temple of Apollo as the location for the slave markets. This archaeological evidence somewhat supports the widely held (but little documented) theory that Corinth replaced Delos as the home of the eastern slave trade. Yet given the lack of literary evidence, it is probably safest to say only that Corinth, like other major metropolitan areas with seaports, had a viable and large slave market. The Corinthia, with its extensive network of harbors and roads, was a merchant and market center in the an-

---

[20] Varro, *Ling.* 8.21.

[21] Ferdinand Joseph De Waele, "The Roman Market North of the Temple at Corinth," *AJA* 2d ser. 34 (1930): 432–54; Robert L. Scranton, *Corinth: Results of Excavations Conducted by the American School of Classical Studies at Athens*, vol. 1.3, *Monuments in the Lower Agora and North of the Archaic Temple* (Princeton: American School, 1951), 180–94.

[22] De Waele, "Roman Market," 435.

cient Mediterranean world. Corinth's location on the isthmus that connects Boeotia/Attica to the Peloponnesus led to its vital importance. As many commentators have contended, it is against this background that one must interpret Paul's exhortation to slaves in 1 Cor 7:21.[23] Note the marketplace language of 1 Cor 6:20: "For you were bought with a price; therefore glorify God in your body," and 1 Cor 7:23: "You were bought with a price; do not become slaves of human masters." This image of Corinth as a market metropolis of east-west trade and commerce underlies the following discussion.

The evidence specific to Roman Corinth does not support the view that it was the "Las Vegas of antiquity." The city had its origins as a Caesarean colony of freedmen/women, which some Greeks resented. With its location on the isthmus and its two bustling ports, Corinth provided a major center for the trafficking of human chattel. According to classical archaeologists, the slave market was located not in the agora, but in the large Roman market north of the temple of Apollo.

History of Interpretation: Overview

This section summarizes and analyzes the history of interpretation of 1 Cor 7:21, setting out the various options for solving the interpretative crux of the passage as argued in the commentary literature. The options are three: μᾶλλον χρῆσαι means (1) "rather use freedom," (2) "indeed use slavery," or (3) "by all means [as a freedman/woman] live according to [God's calling]."[24] Commentators have considered these translations to be mutually exclusive. In deciding between the first two options, commentators frame the crux of the verse in these terms: either Paul was a "social conservative" on slavery or he was not. Such an "either/or" approach has been posed in terms of two rival pictures of Paul:

1) Paul the "social conservative," whose determination to hold the *status quo* led him so far as to urge slaves to remain in slavery, even if this meant rejecting an opportunity to become free; or
2) Paul the "social realist," who certainly would not have wanted his seemingly conservative-sounding advice in chapter 7 to be taken by slaves who were Christians to mean that they could not accept freedom if it became available.[25]

These pictures of Paul are anachronistic, however, since they wrongly assume that opposition to manumission was a sign of ancient "social conservatism."[26]

---

[23] E.g., Fee, *Corinthians*, 2.

[24] The last is a modified version of Bartchy's translation, *ΜΑΛΛΟΝ ΧΡΗΣΑΙ*, 183.

[25] Bartchy, *ΜΑΛΛΟΝ ΧΡΗΣΑΙ*, 1.

[26] *Pace* Werner Georg Kümmel, *Introduction to the New Testament*, 17th German ed., trans. Howard Clark Kee (1975; reprint, Nashville: Abingdon Press, 1987), 350; J. E.

Cicero, Augustus, Seneca, and other Roman "social conservatives" for whom we have evidence did not oppose the manumission of slaves; quite to the contrary, they widely favored and practiced manumission in their own households. By liberating their slaves and making their homes "crowded houses" of freedmen/women protégés, Roman conservatives hoped to gain public honor in the aristocratic virtue of *dignitas*. When commentators on 1 Cor 7:21 assume that to oppose manumission was the mark of an ancient conservative, their assumption is based less on knowledge about ancient slavery and more on familiarity with modern slavery, specifically the institution and its ideology in the nineteenth-century American South, the Caribbean Islands, and Brazil. In these places, manumission was an extremely rare occurrence; legal statutes were set up and actively enforced to keep black slaves in perpetual bondage. Yet while American conservatives were opposed to manumission, Roman conservatives were not. Urban manumission under Roman rule was a regular and frequent occurrence; Roman freedmen/women were commonplace.[27] Thus, to label Paul a "social conservative" or "social realist" based on his advice to slaves concerning manumission is to evaluate Paul from a modern perspective, not from within his ancient context.

The interpretative crux of the passage is how to interpret the brachylogy and ambiguity of the Greek clause μᾶλλον χρῆσαι. (Brachylogy is brevity of diction and an abbreviated expression or construction.)[28] The sentence reads: "Were you [singular] a slave when called? Do not be concerned about it. But

---

Crouch, *The Origin and Intention of the Colossian Haustafel*, FRLANT 109 (Göttingen: Vandenhoeck & Ruprecht, 1972), 122–29, 158; Gerd Theissen, *The Social Setting of Pauline Christianity*, ed., trans., and with an introd. by John H. Schütz (Philadelphia: Fortress Press, 1982), 105–8; Robert M. Grant, *Augustus to Constantine: The Rise and Triumph of Christianity in the Roman World* (1970; reprint, San Francisco: Harper & Row, 1990), 56, 269; Christophe Senft, *La première épître de Saint Paul aux Corinthiens*, 2d ed., rev., CNT 2d ser. 7 (Geneva: Labor et Fides, 1990), 99–100.

[27] The best study remains Thomas E. J. Wiedemann, "The Regularity of Manumission at Rome," *CQ* 35 (1985): 162–75; correcting Géza Alföldy, "Die Freilassung von Sklaven und die Struktur der Sklaverei in der römischen Kaiserzeit," *RSA* 2 (1972): 97–129, esp. 114–15, who presented a circular argument from epigraphical evidence that not only urban, but also rural slavery exhibited high manumission rates. A. M. Duff, *Freedmen in the Early Roman Empire*, 2d ed. (London: W. Heffer & Sons, 1958), 12–35; Treggiari, *Roman Freedmen*, 1–36; Keith R. Bradley, *Slaves and Masters in the Roman Empire: A Study in Social Control* (1984; reprint with suppl. bibliog., New York: Oxford University Press, 1987), 81–112; Alan Watson, *Roman Slave Law* (Baltimore: Johns Hopkins University Press, 1987), 23–45.

[28] Herbert Weir Smyth, *Greek Grammar*, 2d ed., rev. Gordon M. Messing (Cambridge: Harvard University Press, 1956), 674–77 §§3017–18; F. Blass and A. Debrunner, *A Greek Grammar of the New Testament and Other Early Christian Literature*, trans. and rev. from the 9th–10th German ed. by Robert W. Funk (Chicago: University of Chicago Press, 1961), 255–56 §483; Norbert Baumert, *Ehelosigkeit und Ehe im Herrn: Eine Neuinterpretation von 1 Kor 7*, 2d ed., FB 47 (Würzburg: Echter, 1986), 451–52.

if you can gain your freedom, μᾶλλον χρῆσαι [rather use (it)]." Use what? Does Paul mean that slaves should use their *being a slave*, that is, refuse manumission offers? The immediate context has led most commentators to favor this view. Or does he mean that slaves should now use their *becoming free* and avail themselves of the opportunity for new social status? Or does he mean that slaves should use their *calling* (κλῆσις, nominal form of the verb in verse 7:17) as believers in the congregation regardless of their external, legal position in the larger society? The earliest witness for the only textual variant, the omission of the καί (ἀλλ᾿ εἰ δύνασαι ἐλεύθερος γενέσθαι, μᾶλλον χρῆσαι), is Codex Boernerianus (G) from the ninth century; this significant variant will be discussed later in this chapter.[29] The force of the aorist imperative χρῆσαι might imply embracing a new situation,[30] but some scholars argue that the context (1 Cor 7:17, 20, 24: Paul's refrain to remain in one's calling) implies that the slave should remain a slave.[31] Indeed, most of those scholars who stress grammatical and syntactical considerations prefer the "take freedom" option, whereas most of those who stress context prefer the "use slavery" interpretation.[32] Still other

---

[29] *Pace* Bartchy, *ΜΑΛΛΟΝ ΧΡΗΣΑΙ*, 3 n. 8, who argues that the variant is insignificant. Baumert, *Ehelosigkeit*, 123, stresses the importance of καί in the text. With remarkable acumen, he points out that because the καί presents something of a philological obstacle for the "use freedom" interpretation of μᾶλλον χρῆσαι, both Luther and Joseph Franz Allioli (*Die Heilige Schrift des Alten und Neuen Testaments*, 7th ed. [Munich: Vogel, 1851], 3:554) ignore and do not translate it.

[30] So John Edgar McFadyen, *The Epistles to the Corinthians and Galatians*, Interpreter's Commentary on the New Testament 6 (New York: A. S. Barnes, 1909), 48; Archibald Robertson and Alfred Plummer, *A Critical and Exegetical Commentary on the First Epistle of St Paul to the Corinthians*, 2d ed., ICC 7 (New York: Charles Scribner's Sons, 1925), 147–48; A. Schlatter, *Paulus der Bote Jesu: Eine Deutung seiner Briefe an die Korinther*, 4th ed. (Stuttgart: Calwer, 1969), 231–35; C. F. D. Moule, *An Idiom Book of New Testament Greek*, 2d ed. (Cambridge: Cambridge University Press, 1959), 21; Margaret E. Thrall, *Greek Particles in the New Testament: Linguistic and Exegetical Studies*, NTTS 3 (Leiden: E. J. Brill, 1962), 81–82 (on the Greek particles εἰ καί); F. F. Bruce, *1 and 2 Corinthians*, NCB (London: Oliphants, 1971), 72; Leon Morris, *The First Epistle of Paul to the Corinthians*, rev. ed., Tyndale New Testament Commentaries (Grand Rapids, Mich.: William B. Eerdmans, 1985), 110; Buist M. Fanning, *Verbal Aspect in New Testament Greek*, Oxford Theological Monographs (Oxford: Clarendon Press, 1990), 367–68.

[31] So C. F. Georg Heinrici, *Der erste Brief an die Korinther*, 8th ed., MeyerK 5 (Göttingen: Vandenhoeck & Ruprecht, 1896), 231–33; C. K. Barrett, *A Commentary on the First Epistle to the Corinthians*, 2d ed., Black's New Testament Commentaries (London: Adam & Charles Black, 1971), 170–71; Hans Conzelmann, *Der erste Brief an die Korinther*, 2d ed., MeyerK 5 (Göttingen: Vandenhoeck & Ruprecht, 1981), 160–61; Wayne Meeks, ed., *The Writings of St. Paul*, Norton Critical Editions (New York: W. W. Norton, 1972), 33 n. 4; Robert M. Grant, *Early Christianity and Society: Seven Studies* (San Francisco: Harper & Row, 1977), 90; idem, *Augustus to Constantine*, 56, 269; Jerome H. Neyrey, *Paul, in Other Words: A Cultural Reading of His Letters* (Louisville, Ky.: Westminster/John Knox Press, 1990), 68.

[32] Bartchy, *ΜΑΛΛΟΝ ΧΡΗΣΑΙ*, 23

scholars discount both of these interpretations and favor "use one's calling."[33] In any event, none of these three options has gained overwhelming scholarly support. A most striking example of the lack of consensus in New Testament studies on this crux can be seen by comparing the NRSV text and note and the previous RSV text and note.[34] The NRSV translates "use slavery" in the text and places the alternate translation of "use freedom" in a footnote; the RSV endorses the "use freedom" translation, acknowledging the alternative interpretation, "use slavery," in a footnote. Evidently, the NRSV committee of translators found the crux too uncertain to make a definitive judgment.[35] The ambiguity of the verse is notorious, and its interpretation has a long history going back at least to the fourth century.

Patristic Commentary

Among the few writers prior to the fourth century to comment or allude to this passage, Origen considers 1 Cor 7:21 to refer to marriage, not slavery. He spiritualizes 1 Cor 7:21 by arguing that Paul takes the terms "slavery" and "freedom" as metaphorical references (παραδείγματα) to "marriage" and "chastity." In this context, Origen interprets μᾶλλον χρῆσαι to mean "rather take freedom" from marriage.[36] Tertullian, in his *De monogamia*, takes the clause to mean that actual slaves should remain actual slaves, just as those circumcised should remain circumcised and those married should remain married.[37] Neither Origen nor Tertullian indicates that 1 Cor 7:21b is particularly ambiguous; in the fourth century, however, controversy surrounding the passage is evident.

John Chrysostom (ca. 354–407 c.e.) is the first exegete known to have addressed the problem of what this verse means in terms of chattel slavery. He writes:

---

[33] Bartchy, *ΜΑΛΛΟΝ ΧΡΗΣΑΙ*, 183.

[34] Revised Standard Version of the Bible (RSV), copyrighted 1946 and 1952 by the Division of Christian Education of the National Council of the Churches of Christ in the United States of America; New Revised Standard Version Bible (NRSV), copyrighted 1989 by the Division of Christian Education of the National Council of the Churches of Christ in the United States of America.

[35] There is no published account of the NRSV committee's work on this crux: "I am sorry to say that there is no record of the discussions that led up to the adoption of the NRSV rendering of 1 Cor 7:21. Furthermore, I myself do not have any recollection of the discussions" (Bruce M. Metzger, letter to author, 11 May 1991).

[36] Origen, *Comm. in 1 Cor.* 38 (ed. C. Jenkins, "Origen on I Corinthians, III," *JTS* 9 [1908]: 507–8; *Comm. in Rom.* 1 (*PG* 14.461).

[37] Tertullian, *De monogamia* 11.12 (CCSL 2.1246).

Now I am not ignorant that some say that the words "rather use it" [μᾶλλον χρῆσαι] are spoken with regard to freedom, interpreting it: "if you can become free, become free." But the expression would be very contrary to Paul's manner if he intended this. For he would not, when consoling the slave and signifying that he was in no respect injured, have told him to get free. Since perhaps someone might say, "What then, if I am not able? I am an injured and degraded person." This then is not what he says, but as I said, meaning: to point out that a person gets nothing by being made free, [the Apostle] says, "Although you have it in your power to be made free, remain rather in slavery."[38]

Two issues are immediately apparent: first, Chrysostom is entering a debate that already existed; second, he makes his argument not from grammar, but from context and his understanding of Pauline theology.[39] Paul cannot, to Chrysostom's mind, be advising every Christian slave to become free: that capacity lies beyond the reach of many, and Paul's theology must be addressed to all. Chrysostom's Paul advises every Christian slave, including the "injured and degraded," to make the best of remaining in their assigned station.[40]

The overwhelming majority of commentators before the modern period sided with Chrysostom and the "use slavery" option. In making their claim, many of these patristic authors felt it necessary to explain why Paul would have advised a slave to remain in bondage. Severian, the bishop of the Syrian city of Gabala (d. ca. 408 C.E.), states that a slave should remain in slavery so that the world could see that there is no disadvantage for a Christian to be a slave.[41] Cyril of Alexandria (d. 444 C.E.) tells slaves to remain in their state because bearing such a yoke of servitude would bring future rewards, especially if endured under cheerful disposition.[42] Pelagius (ca. 350–ca. 425 C.E.) makes Paul's language clear in his *Commentary on Thirteen Pauline Epistles*, where, after quoting the Vulgate's version of the Pauline clause "rather use ..." (*magis utere*), he completes the ellipsis with "rather use slavery" (*magis utere*

---

[38] John Chrysostom, *Hom. 19 in epist. I ad Cor.* 5 (PG 61.164). Cf. *Hom. in epist. ad Philem.* argumentum: μᾶλλον χρῆσαι· τουτέστι, τῇ δουλείᾳ παράμενε (PG 62.773); *Sermo 5 in Gen.* 1: μᾶλλον χρῆσαι, τουτέστι, μᾶλλον μένε ἐν τῇ δουλείᾳ. ... μᾶλλον χρῆσαι· τουτέστι, μένε δοῦλος (PG 54.666).

[39] Baumert, *Ehelosigkeit*, 116.

[40] Adolf Martin Ritter, "Zwischen 'Gottesherrschaft' und 'einfachem Leben': Dio Chrysostomus, Johannes Chrysostomus und das Problem einer Humanisierung der Gesellschaft," *JAC* 31 (1988): 137–39; Elizabeth A. Clark, *Jerome, Chrysostom, and Friends: Essays and Translations,* Studies in Women and Religion 1 (New York: Edwin Mellen Press, 1979), 22–23 n. 7; idem, "Comment: Chrysostom and Pauline Social Ethics," in *Paul and the Legacies of Paul,* ed. William S. Babcock (Dallas: Southern Methodist University Press, 1990), 193–99; Wulf Jaeger, "Die Sklaverei bei Johannes Chrysostomus" (doctoral diss., Kiel, 1974), 145–50.

[41] John Anthony Cramer, comp., *Catenae Graecorum Patrum in Novum Testamentum* (1841; reprint, Hildesheim: Georg Olms, 1967), 5:141; Bartchy, *ΜΑΛΛΟΝ ΧΡΗΣΑΙ,* 14 n. 30.

[42] Cyril, *Com. in Joannis evangelium* 10 (PG 74, 878); Bartchy, *ΜΑΛΛΟΝ ΧΡΗΣΑΙ,* 14 n. 30.

servitio).[43] An important twelfth-century monastic, Hervaeus of Bourgdieu (whose commentary was falsely attributed to Anselm of Canterbury), exhorts slaves to remain slaves because slavery, he claims, is a useful and good thing. It encourages humility and patience and will earn a great reward from God.[44] This brief sketch of pre-modern exegetes shows the importance of 1 Cor 7:20–24 to the ancient and medieval slaveholders' ideology that slavery was good for slaves. Christian slaves ought to remain slaves, they argue, because their obedience and humility are great virtues.[45] Before the beginning of critical inquiry into the New Testament, the verse was nearly universally interpreted as "slaves must remain slaves"; this interpretation respected previous commentators and served the slaveholding ideology.

I say "nearly" because the Reformers broke from Catholic exegetical tradition of this verse: both John Calvin and Martin Luther disagreed with John Chrysostom. In their commentaries on 1 Corinthians, these Reformation leaders opted for the "use freedom" interpretation. Calvin writes: "I exhort slaves to be of good courage, though a state of freedom is preferable [*soit beaucoup meilleur*], if one has it in his choice."[46] Calvin, however, is unsure whether Paul is speaking directly to slaves or only exhorting their masters. Luther is more sure that the passage is a direct exhortation to slaves. He writes:

[F]or at that time there were many bondsmen, as there are still in many places, now termed serfs, whom St. Paul calls slaves. ... "But," St. Paul says, "if you can gain your freedom, avail yourself of the opportunity." This does not mean that you should rob your master of your person and run away without his knowledge and consent, but it means you are not to interpret the words of St. Paul, when he says that everyone should remain in the estate in which he was called, to mean that you must remain a serf, even though you could gain your freedom with the knowledge and consent of your master.

---

[43] *Pelagi expositio in I Corinthios* 7.21 (Alexander Souter, ed., *Pelagius's Expositions of Thirteen Epistles of St Paul*, pt. 2, *Text and Apparatus Criticus*, Texts and Studies 9.2 [Cambridge: Cambridge University Press, 1929], 165.14). On how Pelagius's Pauline text largely corresponds to the Vulgate version (including certain variants of the Old Latin I-type text), see now Theodore de Bruyn, *Pelagius's Commentary on St Paul's Epistle to the Romans: Translated with Introduction and Notes*, OECS (Oxford: Clarendon Press, 1993), 7–8; J. Albert Harrill, review of *Pelagius's Commentary*, by de Bruyn, *EMC* 13 (1994): forthcoming.

[44] Hervaeus of Bourgdieu, *Com. in epist. Pauli – in epist. 1 ad cor.* 7 (PL 81.880–83); Bartchy, *ΜΑΛΛΟΝ ΧΡΗΣΑΙ*, 14 n. 30.

[45] Maurice Goguel, *The Primitive Church*, trans. H. C. Snape (London: George Allen & Unwin, 1964), 554–55 n. 2; J. B. Lightfoot, *Notes on Epistles of St Paul from Unpublished Commentaries* (London: Macmillan, 1895), 229; Heinrich August Wilhelm Meyer, *Critical and Exegetical Handbook to the Epistles to the Corinthians*, trans. D. Douglas Bannerman (New York: Funk & Wagnalls, 1884), 166–67; L. I. Rückert, *Die Briefe Pauli an die Korinther* (Leipzig: R. Röhler, 1836), 1:195–97, declared that the patristic interpretation favoring "use slavery" was against the spirit of the Apostle.

[46] John Calvin, *Commentary on the Epistles of Paul the Apostle to the Corinthians*, trans. John Pringle, Calvin's Commentaries 20 (1848; reprint, Grand Rapids, Mich.: Baker Book House, 1984), 249.

St. Paul wants only to instruct your conscience, so that you know that before God both estates are free, whether you are a bondsman/woman or a freedman/woman. He does not want to hold you back from gaining your freedom, if you can do so with the consent of your master.[47]

This interpretation marks an important break with patristic authority. These Reformers turn the tide of subsequent interpretation of this verse. In particular, Luther's position greatly influenced early modern German scholarship.

Earlier Modern Scholarship

During the mid-nineteenth century, when slavery was still very much an issue in contemporary politics, Henri Wallon, a historian and in his day the recognized authority on ancient slavery, interpreted the crux of 1 Cor 7:21 as "take freedom."[48] Wallon himself was personally devoted to the abolitionist cause in France and became one of the prime movers in the political campaign to end slavery in the French colonies, particularly the West Indies. That the first edition of his work (1847) was published virtually on the eve of the French Abolition Bill should not be overlooked.[49] Wallon had great faith in the power of moral truth to guide the course of history. In a lengthy introduction, which takes up nearly a third of volume 1, he makes a passionate plea for abolition and attacks modern colonial slavery. He attributes progress in Western civilization toward abolition to the spread and influence of Christianity and uses 1 Cor 7:21 to show Christianity's anti-slavery tendencies.[50]

Following in the footsteps of Wallon, an ecclesiastical historian, Paul Allard, composed his own book on Christianity and slavery, which went through six editions after it first appeared in 1876; he also interprets 1 Cor 7:21 as "use

---

[47] Martin Luther, *Luther's Works*, vol. 28, *Commentaries on 1 Corinthians 7, 1 Corinthians 15, Lectures on 1 Timothy*, trans. modified from Edward Sittler (Saint Louis: Concordia Publishing House, 1973), 42–43. Considering Luther's tortured relations with rebellious peasants, this quotation is interesting. In his anti-serf writings of the Peasants' War of 1524–25, Luther refers to 1 Cor 7:21–22 to argue that serfdom should not be abolished; idem, *Admonition to Peace: A Reply to the Twelve Articles of the Peasants in Swabia* (1525), trans. Charles M. Jacobs, rev. R. Schultz, in *Luther's Works*, vol. 46, *The Christian in Society III* (Philadelphia: Fortress Press, 1967), 38–39; Paul Althaus, *The Ethics of Martin Luther*, trans. Robert C. Schultz (Philadelphia: Fortress Press, 1972), 146–47.

[48] H. Wallon, *Histoire de l'esclavage dans l'antiquité*, 2d ed. (Paris: Hachette, 1879), 3:5 n. 1.

[49] Yvon Garlan, *Slavery in Ancient Greece*, trans. Janet Lloyd (Ithaca: Cornell University Press, 1988), 1–2; Zvi Yavetz, *Slaves and Slavery in Ancient Rome*, trans. Adam Vital (New Brunswick, N.J.: Transaction, 1988), 118–19; M. I. Finley, *Ancient Slavery and Modern Ideology* (New York: Viking Press, 1980), 31–35.

[50] Wallon, *Histoire de l'esclavage*, 1: xxxvii; David Brion Davis, *The Problem of Slavery in Western Culture* (1966; reprint, New York: Oxford University Press, 1988), 17–19.

freedom," citing Wallon as his source.[51] As a result, Allard became the most popular spokesman for the idea that the early church was opposed to slavery and that it single-handedly caused the decline and eventual end of the ancient institution.[52] The intellectual tradition of Allard and Wallon developed from Montesquieu, who was one of the first philosophers to place slavery on the agenda of the French Enlightenment. Montesquieu had pioneered the view that the spirit of Christianity within the progress of ideas had eliminated chattel slavery in Europe.[53]

Thanks to the influential works of Wallon, Allard, and others in the last century,[54] the question of slavery and early Christianity was framed almost exclusively in terms of whether or not Christianity caused its end. The interpretation of 1 Cor 7:21 as "slaves, avail yourselves of the opportunity of freedom" became a rallying cry in the abolitionist movement. Concerns over slavery as a contemporary problem dominated the scholarly discussion. It is important to remember that the early anti-slavery movement, especially in the United States and France, coincided with the beginnings of the critical-historical inquiry into the Bible.[55] Biblical critics interpreted Scripture in reaction to and in the context of an international debate over the question of slavery.[56] The meaning of 1 Cor 7:21 had urgent political and social implications in countries torn apart by the politics of slavery, such as the divided United States. Both abolitionists and slave apologists claimed that the Bible and specifically this verse legitimated their position.[57] The biblical debate was never

---

[51] Paul Allard, *Les esclaves chrétiens depuis les premiers temps de l'église jusqu'à la fin de la domination romaine en occident*, 6th ed. (Paris: Victor Lecoffre, 1914), 168–69 n. 5. Allard, however, acknowledges that Adolf von Harnack and Alphons Steinmann hold the opposite interpretation of "use slavery."

[52] Finley, *Ancient Slavery and Modern Ideology*, 15; Garlan, *Slavery in Ancient Greece*, 2.

[53] Davis, *Problem of Slavery in Western Culture*, 402–8, 485; Russell Parsons Jameson, *Montesquieu et l'esclavage: Étude sur les origines de l'opinion antiesclavagiste en France au XVIIIe siècle* (Paris: Hachette, 1911), 106. M. de Secondat Baron de Montesquieu, *The Spirit of the Laws*, ed. David Wallace Carrithers (Berkeley and Los Angeles: University of California Press, 1977), §15.

[54] Eduard Meyer, *Kleine Schriften*, 2d ed. (Halle [Saale]: Max Niemeyer, 1924), 1:169–212; for commentary, see Finley, *Ancient Slavery and Modern Ideology*, 44–47.

[55] David Brion Davis, *The Problem of Slavery in the Age of Revolution, 1770–1823* (Ithaca: Cornell University Press, 1975), 527.

[56] Robert Bruce Mullin, "Biblical Critics and the Battle over Slavery," *Journal of Presbyterian History* 61 (1983): 210–26. For the situation in the Roman Catholic Church, see Madeleine Hooke Rice, *American Catholic Opinion in the Slavery Controversy*, Studies in History, Economics, and Public Law 508 (1944; reprint, Gloucester, Mass.: Peter Smith, 1964).

[57] John Fletcher, *Studies on Slavery, in Easy Lessons* (Natchez, Miss.: Jackson Warner, 1852), 422; Albert Barnes, *An Inquiry into the Scriptural Views of Slavery* (Philadelphia: Parry & McMillan, 1855), 338–75; Thornton Stringfellow, *Scriptural and Statistical Views in Favor*

more intense than in the decades that led up to the American Civil War. An illustration from the apologists' camp is a pro-slavery pamphlet written under the pseudonym "Onesimus Secundus":

> In his first letter to the Christians in Corinth, 1 Cor. vii. 20, where he is addressing the heathen slaves, who had been converted to Christianity by his preaching, Paul tells every man to abide in the same calling wherein he was called; and that if he was called, being a slave (δοῦλος), he is to use it rather (that is, the slavery), even though he might be made free. This is the true rendering of the verse, according to most commentators, ancient and modern, including Chrysostom, Theodoret, Theophylact, Œcumenius, Bengel, De Wette, Conybeare, and Alford.
>
> These are the remarks of Alford, one of our best modern scholars, upon the verse: "'Wert thou called (converted) a slave, let it not be a trouble to thee; but if thou art even able to become free, use it (*i.e.*, remain in slavery) rather.' This rendering is required by the usage of the particles εἰ καί, by which the καί, 'also,' 'even,' does not belong to the εἰ, as in καὶ εἰ, but is spread over the whole contexts of the concessive clause. It is also required by the context; for the burden of the whole passage is, Let each man remain in the state in which he was called."[58]

From the abolitionists' camp, the Unitarian theologian William Ellery Channing (1780–1842), Professor at Harvard Divinity School, came as an important scholar and spokesman.[59] Channing's influence not only touched American biblical scholarship, but also extended across the Atlantic to France, where Allard cited Channing's famous work on slavery as both authoritative and

---

of Slavery, 4th ed. (Richmond, Va.: J. W. Randolf, 1856), 50–53, 75–76, 98–99, 102–3; review of *The Bible and Slavery*, by Charles Elliott, D. D. Whedon, ed., *Methodist Quarterly Review* [New York] 39 (October 1857): 634–44; Philip Schaff, *Slavery and the Bible, a Tract for the Times* (Chambersburg, Pa.: M. Kieffer, 1861), 18–29 (the title page quotes 1 Cor 7:21: "Art thou called being a servant, care not for it; but if thou mayest be free, use it rather"); Josiah Priest, *Bible Defence of Slavery; or, The Origin, History, and Fortunes of the Negro Race*, 6th stereotype ed. (1852; reprint, Louisville, Ky.: Bradley & Gilbert, n.d. [1864]), 410–11; 286–307; Thornton Stringfellow, "A Brief Examination of Scripture Testimony on the Institution of Slavery," in *The Ideology of Slavery: Proslavery Thought in the Antebellum South, 1830–1860*, ed. Drew G. Faust, Library of Southern Civilization (Baton Rouge: Louisiana State University Press, 1981), 157.

[58] Onesimus Secundus [pseud.], *The True Interpretation of the American Civil War and of England's Cotton Difficulty: Slavery, From a Different Point of View, Shewing the Relative Responsibilities of America and Great Britain*, 2d ed. (London: Trübner, 1863), 25. In a refutation of this argument by Henry Alford (*The Greek New Testament*, 6th ed. [Boston and New York: Lee & Shepard, 1874], 2:527–28), I shall discuss the grammar, particularly the particles εἰ καί, later in this chapter.

[59] William E. Channing, *The Works of William E. Channing* (1882; reprint, 2 vols. in 1, New York: Burt Franklin, 1970): 723–25, 887; Mullin, "Biblical Critics," 211; John R. McKivigan, *The War against Proslavery Religion: Abolitionism and the Northern Churches, 1830–1865* (Ithaca: Cornell University Press, 1984), 49, 59–60, 173; Larry E. Tise, *Proslavery: A History of the Defense of Slavery in America, 1701–1840* (Athens: University of Georgia Press, 1987), 267, 277–78, with material in notes. I thank Martin E. Marty for bibliographic advice in American church history.

standard.[60] As a direct result of the victories of the American and French abolitionist movements, the prevailing scholarly and popular interpretation of 1 Cor 7:21 became that Paul exhorts slaves to "use their freedom."

In Germany, a turn in the biblical debate came with Adolf von Harnack. In an important footnote in his *Mission und Ausbreitung des Christentums*, the church historian asserts that "the only possible sense of 1 Cor vii. 20 ff. ... is that the Apostle counsels slaves not even to avail themselves of the chance of freedom."[61] In the pages of his text, Harnack makes his famous and oft-quoted statement, "It is a mistake to suppose that any 'slave question' occupied the early church."[62] This declaration has had a lasting impact upon slavery studies in the field of church history and may be one reason why New Testament scholars have largely overlooked or downplayed the importance of slavery as a serious and real issue in early Christian communities.[63] Yet Harnack's pronouncement swung the biblical debate of 1 Cor 7:21 from favoring "use freedom" (Wallon, Allard) to favoring "use slavery."

In the wake of Harnack, the debate continued to stir intense controversy. At the beginning of this century, two Roman Catholic scholars hotly disputed the two options of 1 Cor 7:21. The first, Alphons Steinmann, published in 1911 an essay responding to those in the Catholic church who were writing at the time that the "take freedom" interpretation was a "post-Reformation error."[64] Recognizing that Luther and Calvin both had been famous advocates of the "take freedom" view, which tainted the interpretation for some Catholics, Steinmann argues that it is nevertheless the best interpretation. The second figure was Francis Xavier Kiefl, another Roman Catholic scholar and dean of Regensburg Cathedral. In 1915, Kiefl published his book upholding the opposite and traditional opinion, the view of the early church fathers.[65] In many ways, Kiefl's book was both a response to Steinmann within

---

[60] Allard, *Les esclaves chrétiens*, 165 n. 1; idem, *Esclaves, serfs et mainmortables* (Paris: Société Générale de Librairie Catholique, 1884), 93.

[61] Adolf von Harnack, *Die Mission und Ausbreitung des Christentums in den ersten drei Jahrhunderten*, 4th ed. (Leipzig: J. C. Hinrichs, 1924), 1:192 n. 4.

[62] Harnack, *Die Mission und Ausbreitung*, 192.

[63] Bartchy, *ΜΑΛΛΟΝ ΧΡΗΣΑΙ*, 30–35, correctly notes the neglect of biblical scholarship to consider the academic study of ancient slavery in the interpretation of 1 Cor 7:21. Bartchy echoes the lament of Edgar Johnson Goodspeed: "Slavery is so disagreeable a subject that it has been almost obliterated from the English New Testament" (*The Meaning of Ephesians* [Chicago: University of Chicago Press, 1933], 7 n. 4).

[64] Alphons Steinmann, *Paulus und die Sklaven zu Korinth: 1. Kor. 7,21 aufs neue untersucht* (Braunsberg: Verlag Hans Grimme, 1911). A year earlier, Steinmann had published an apologetic pamphlet entitled *Sklavenlos und alte Kirche: Eine historisch-exegetische Studie über die soziale Frage im Urchristentum* (4th ed., Apologetische Tagesfragen 8 [Gladbach: Volksvereins Verlag, 1922]).

[65] F. X. Kiefl, *Die Theorien des modernen Sozialismus über den Ursprung des Christentums: Zugleich ein Kommentar zu 1 Kor 7,21* (Munich: J. Kösel, 1915).

the Catholic tradition and a polemical treatise against scholars sympathetic to the growing Marxist movement in Europe (as well as pre-World War I anarchists), who saw in early Christianity the embryonic stages of the continual proletarian revolution against the bourgeoisie and upper class. According to Kiefl, modern socialism was the true antichrist. He considered 1 Cor 7:21 the lethal blow against Hegelian and Marxist interpretation of Christian origins. As the chief expression of Paul's conservatism, the verse ordered slaves to keep their places and not overturn the established social order. Kiefl and Steinmann continued their academic dialogue for several years. Both were immersed in at least two ideological controversies, one over the "antichrist" of Marxism and the other over the "taint" of Protestant biblical interpretation.[66]

After the Steinmann-Kiefl exchange, another attempt to solve the 1 Cor 7:21 exegetical crux came in an intriguing, and unfortunately often overlooked, article by C. H. Dodd.[67] In his study, Dodd furnishes a rather close philological parallel to the crux that he found in a recently published papyrus. It reads:

Oxyrhynchus Papyri xvi, 1865, 4 sqq. καὶ πολλάκις ἐξ[ῆν γράψαι σοι περὶ τοῦ] κεφαλαίου τούτου, καὶ προσδοκον (*leg.* προσδοκῶν) καθ' ἑκάστην καταλαμβά[νειν ἐκεῖσε?], τούτου ἕνεκεν οὐκ ἐχρησάμην ἄλλην γράψαι ἄλλοις γράμμα[σι]ν: *ib.* 12–13 καὶ πρὸς τὸ γνῶναι τὸν ἐμὸν δεσπότην ἐχρησάμην παρακαλῶν διὰ τούτον (*leg.* τούτων) μου τῶν γραμμάτων.

I had many opportunites of writing to you concerning this matter, and, expecting each day to come thither, for that reason did not *avail myself of them* to write another letter over again. ... That my master may know this I *took the opportunity* of exhorting you by this my writing.[68]

Dodd argues that the papyrus fragment "favours the rendering of the Pauline passage – 'If you actually have before you the possibility of becoming free, avail yourself of it by preference.' In effect the object of χρῆσαι is supplied from the sense of δύνασαι exactly as in the papyrus it is supplied from the sense of ἐξῆν."[69] Dodd's proposal delved into the hitherto unexplored territory of texts that serve as syntactical parallels to illumine lexical relationships with the aim of rendering the 1 Cor 7:21 crux soluble. Dodd's methodology offers a promising model to emulate. Unfortunately, his single example, *P. Oxy.* 16.1865, is dated to the sixth or seventh century of our era. Dodd himself admits, "The

---

[66] The debate went back and forth, with each drawing extensively on the history of interpretation but without adding any new substantial arguments: Steinmann, "Zur Geschichte der Auslegung von 1 Kor 7,21," *TRev* 15–16 (1917): 340–48; Kiefl, "Erklärung," *TRev* 15–16 (1917): 469; Steinmann, "Antwort," *TRev* 15–16 (1917): 469–70; Bartchy, *ΜΑΛΛΟΝ ΧΡΗΣΑΙ*, 1–3.

[67] C. H. Dodd, "Notes from Papyri," *JTS* 26 (1924–25): 77–78.

[68] Dodd, "Notes," 77; the translation is that of the *P. Oxy.* editors; the emphasis is Dodd's.

[69] Dodd, "Notes," 77–78.

late date detracts somewhat from the value of the comparison."[70] The later philological portion of this chapter, presenting the findings of a powerful research tool unknown in Dodd's day (computerized access to extant Greek authors, digitally recorded on CD-ROM), will pick up the task where Dodd had left it. The section will provide seventeen examples to place next to Dodd's, which serve as compelling parallels for syntactical comparison. The basic conclusions concur with Dodd's hypothesis: philology favors the "use freedom" interpretation.

Important as Dodd's study is in providing a useful philological interpretive model, it nevertheless made little impact upon the commentary literature. The next major study, which did have an impact, came in 1954 with a dissertation by Joseph Lappas presented to the Roman Catholic Theological Faculty of the University of Vienna.[71] Lappas, like previous commentators, sees only two mutually exclusive options for completing μᾶλλον χρῆσαι: one must supply either δουλείᾳ or ἐλευθερίᾳ.[72] He disagrees with Steinmann's position and sides with Harnack (and "the majority of exegetes"),[73] arguing that the "use slavery" interpretation best fits the context of Paul's social conservatism, which advocated that a believer should stay in one's place.[74] Yet his methodology consists in quoting at length previous works by continental Catholic theologians. Relying on a so-called scholarly consensus and on patristic authority, Lappas fails to articulate a cogent, compelling original thesis that contributes positively to the solution of the crux. He also does not consider the contemporary social context of either the abolitionist controversy or the Marxist debate, against which the opinions of the past biblical interpreters and theologians should be read. Lappas agrees with those previous scholars who assert the "use slavery" interpretation but adds nothing new to the interpretation of the crux.

Following Lappas came a monograph by Gerhard Kehnscherper, an East German ecclesiastical historian.[75] In the preface of his book, Kehnscherper describes his methodology to be Marxist philosophy and his goal to be proving how ideas, such as "freedom," work themselves out in history.[76] He col-

---

[70] Dodd, "Notes," 77.

[71] Joseph Lappas, "Paulus und die Sklavenfrage: Eine exegetische Studie in historischer Schau" (doctoral diss., Vienna, 1954), esp. 109–41.

[72] Lappas, "Paulus," 111.

[73] Lappas, "Paulus," 128. His list (129–40) includes patristic and medieval exegetes who favored the "use slavery" interpretation, from Origen to Thomas Aquinas.

[74] Lappas, "Paulus," 123, 125

[75] Gerhard Kehnscherper, *Die Stellung der Bibel und der alten christlichen Kirche zur Sklaverei: Eine biblische und kirchengeschichtliche Untersuchung von den alttestamentlichen Propheten bis zum Ende des römischen Reiches* (Halle [Saale]: Max Niemeyer, 1957).

[76] Kehnscherper, *Die Stellung der Bibel*, 7–12.

lects references from the pre-Socratics (Sophists) and the Stoics to demonstrate that there was an ancient protest against slavery.[77] Kehnscherper, however, makes claims that the primary sources cannot substantiate. By remaining exclusively on the level of ideas, he mistakes intellectual history for all history. The criticism of an Israeli ancient historian, Zvi Yavetz, is well put:

> If all history were, in essence, intellectual history then the claim that even in antiquity protests were voiced against the institution of slavery would be of great significance. Anyone familiar with the classical authors could easily muster a dozen references to prove this point ... but the meagerness of sources and their fragmentary nature preclude a definitive and satisfying answer. One can only say with certainty that such views were not commonly held.[78]

To Kehnscherper history is intrinsically a movement of "ideas" toward the final philosophy (Marxism); this bias alone should call into question his reconstruction of ancient society. Concerning 1 Cor 7:20–24, Kehnscherper sides with the "use slavery" interpretation, saying that the only way the "take freedom" reading makes sense is to see v. 24 as a later scribal addition. For Kehnscherper, Paul clearly orders slaves to remain slaves.[79] But Kehnscherper's arguments are methodologically problematic. He assumes history is the search for universal ideas that are transcultural entities germinating in the past, growing in determinate patterns, and eventually flowering into Marxism. He also is mistaken in assuming that opposition to manumission determined a "social conservative" in Roman society. However, it is important to point out that Yavetz's observation does not refute the hypothesis that even a dozen scattered protests of slavery by ancient intellectuals strongly influenced later thinkers and leaders and thus contributed to the rise of the abolitionist movement. My objection to Kehnscherper lies in his favoring intellectual history exclusively above all other kinds of history.

After Kehnscherper, E. Neuhäusler produced the next influential study.[80] His article, however, is more a theological response to the passage than a critical investigation into it. He assumes that Scripture conveys an enduring message to every community of believers and that the text speaks directly to the Christian vocation today. He offers no background study of Greco-Roman slavery and uncritically presumes "general textbook knowledge" about the institution and its ideology. He writes mainly for a theological audience and aims to interpret the passage for today's believers. He favors the "use freedom" interpretation of 1 Cor 7:21, addresses some philological issues, and

---

[77] Kehnscherper, *Die Stellung der Bibel*, 45–57.

[78] Yavetz, *Slaves and Slavery*, 115, a criticism also applied to Joseph Vogt.

[79] Kehnscherper, *Die Stellung der Bibel*, 97–104.

[80] E. Neuhäusler, "Ruf Gottes und Stand des Christen: Bemerkungen zu 1 Kor 7," *BZ* n.s. 3 (1959): 43–60.

indicates that this exhortation is optional not obligatory. Paul exhorts that a slave *could* use freedom, not *should* use freedom.[81] One might interpret 1 Cor 7:23 ("You were bought with a price, do not become slaves of people") as a Pauline command for Christians not to sell themselves into slavery. If this were so, then Neuhäusler's argument about using freedom being optional would be called into question. If Paul forbade Christians to choose slavery, then his advice to "use freedom" might also be taken as a command. Yet as we saw in chapter 1, very little evidence exists that people in antiquity regularly sold themselves into slavery, although such a claim is often made by New Testament scholars (following Henneke Gülzow). But even if early Christians had an unusual tendency to sell themselves into slavery, I still am not convinced that 1 Cor 7:23 speaks to that particular issue. However, Neuhäusler's overall approach and uncritical methodology, especially on ancient slavery, ultimately weakens the force of his thesis considerably.

In sharp contrast to previous commentators, whose approach to and interest in this passage stemmed essentially from theological concerns, Heinz Bellen published an extremely important study that nearly all New Testament scholars have discounted or overlooked.[82] Bellen was not a theologian but a Roman historian, who studied ancient slavery with his colleague Joseph Vogt in a research program under the auspices of the Akademie der Wissenschaften und der Literatur (Mainz).[83] This project was launched in 1951, at the height of the Cold War, and arose out of concerns about the intellectual impact of Marxist scholarship.[84] Bellen's goal is to clarify 1 Cor 7:21 in the argumentative context of all chapter 7 and in the social context of Roman slavery. This approach is a noticeable improvement over past attempts. He remarks that Paul often enunciates two courses of action, both of which are acceptable, but one of which is preferable. Bellen concludes that Paul exhorts the slave to

---

[81] Neuhäusler, "Ruf Gottes," 49–50.

[82] Heinz Bellen, "Μᾶλλον χρῆσαι (1 Cor. 7,21): Verzicht auf Freilassung als asketische Leistung?" *JAC* 6 (1963): 177–80; see also idem, *Studien zur Sklavenflucht im römischen Kaiserreich*, Forschungen zur antiken Sklaverei 4 (Wiesbaden: Franz Steiner, 1971), 147–54.

[83] On the work of the Mainz Academy, see Norbert Brockmeyer, *Antike Sklaverei*, Erträge der Forschung 116 (Darmstadt: Wissenschaftliche Buchgesellschaft, 1979), 33–40. Its publications include Joseph Vogt and Heinz Bellen, eds., *Bibliographie zur antiken Sklaverei*, new ed., 2 vols., ed. E. Herrmann with N. Brockmeyer (Bochum: N. Brockmeyer, 1983); the monograph series Forschungen zur antiken Sklaverei, ed. Joseph Vogt and Hans Ulrich Instinsky, 23 vols. to date (Stuttgart: Franz Steiner, 1967–); Übersetzungen ausländischer Arbeiten zur antiken Sklaverei, ed. Joseph Vogt, Heinz Bellen, and Herbert Bräuer, 4 vols. to date (Stuttgart: Franz Steiner, 1966–).

[84] Vogt wrote little on the particular problem under study here. For his comments on early Christianity and slavery, see "Ecce Ancilla Domini: The Social Aspects of the Virgin Mary in Antiquity," in *Ancient Slavery and the Ideal of Man*, trans. Thomas Wiedemann (New York: Oxford University Press, 1974), 145–69.

remain a slave as part of the Apostle's overarching argument that urges all Christians toward ascetic behavior. As a Christian should renounce offers of marriage, so too should the slave renounce offers of manumission.

Bellen argues that the relationship of a slave to manumission ought to be, in Paul's opinion, like the attitude of believers toward marriage. Marriage and manumission present comparable problems for Paul; both could find sanction. The unmarried and widowed believer should control desires for matrimony and view celibacy as the Christian ideal. Likewise, the slave should maintain an ascetic posture toward material gain and inhibit his or her desire for outward, legal freedom. A slave should not grieve, worry, or concern him- or herself about slavery. Although those who favor the "use freedom" interpretation are correct, in Bellen's view, to stress that the aorist imperative χϱῆσαι implies movement toward a new situation, he contends that Paul means a movement not to legal liberation (ἐλευθεϱία), but to ascetic self-restraint (ἐγϰϱάτεια). Bellen concludes that the "use slavery" interpretation best fits the argumentative and social context of the verse.

Bellen's interpretation has been criticized as "unsatisfactory" because it is thought Bellen mistakenly assumes that slaves could reject manumission.[85] In fact the claim that slaves could never refuse manumission has become commonplace in New Testament studies, and so requires detailed comment. To answer the question of whether or not ancient slaves could have refused manumission, we need to consider the fact that slaves could have received offers of freedom from a person other than their personal owner. This possibility of nondomestic manumission was especially acute during times of war. Ancient authors state that a slave can, and indeed in some cases should, refuse such offers of manumission. Strabo, for example, reports that in the effort to seize the throne of Pergamum (133–130 B.C.E.), Aristonicus recruited slaves to join his revolt with the lure of manumission promises: "Now he [Aristonicus] was banished from Smyrna, after being defeated in a naval battle near the Cymaean territory by the Ephesians, but he went up into the interior and quickly assembled a large number of resourceless people, and also of slaves, invited with a promise of freedom [δούλων ἐπ' ἐλευθεϱίᾳ ϰατακεκλημένων], whom he called *Heliopolitae* [citizens of the city of the sun-god Helios]."[86] Greco-Roman authors see such slave recruitment, which became widespread during the civil wars of the Roman late Republic, as detrimental to law and order. If a senator wanted to attack a rival senator, he often promised manumission to his rival's slaves in return for their domestic desertion. Appian describes the climate of servile betrayal: "Cinna sent heralds round the city to offer freedom to slaves who would desert to him [ϰήϱυϰας ἐδίδου τοῖς εἰς αὐτὸν

---

[85] Bartchy, *ΜΑΛΛΟΝ ΧΡΗΣΑΙ*, 11.
[86] Strabo 14.1.38; trans. LCL.

αὐτομολοῦσι θεράπουσιν ἐλευθερίαν], and forthwith a large number did desert."[87] The biographer Plutarch in his *Life of Marius* confirms Appian's description of the slave recruitment efforts among principals in the Roman civil wars: "Octavius damaged his own cause, not so much through lack of skill, as by a too scrupulous observance of the laws, wherein he unwisely neglected the needs of the hour. For though many urged him to call the slaves to arms under promise of freedom [ἐπ' ἐλευθερίᾳ καλεῖν τοὺς οἰκέτας], he said that he would not make slaves members of the state [οὐκ ἔφη δούλοις μεταδώσειν τῆς πατρίδος] from which he was trying to exclude Marius in obedience to laws."[88] Appian in several places lauds slaves in this climate of desertion who remained faithful to their masters by refusing nondomestic offers of freedom.[89] There is additional evidence that weakens the argument that slaves in antiquity could never refuse manumission. Although not from the Roman period, a passage from Exodus nevertheless illustrates the case of a slave allowed to refuse a domestic offer of freedom.

When you buy a male Hebrew slave, he shall serve six years, but in the seventh he shall go out a free person, without debt. If he comes in single, he shall go out single; if he comes in married, then his wife shall go out with him. If his master gives him a wife and she bears him sons or daughters, the wife and her children shall be her master's and he

---

[87] Appian, *BC* 1.69; LCL trans.

[88] Plutarch, *Vit. Mar.* 42.2; trans. modified from LCL.

[89] Bradley, *Slaves and Masters*, 84–85; the passages are the following:

"When these arrangements had been made the Senate summoned Gracchus and Flaccus from their homes to the senate-house to defend themselves. But they ran out armed toward the Aventine hill, hoping that if they could seize it first the Senate would agree to some terms with them. As they ran through the city they offered freedom to the slaves [τοὺς θεράποντας συνεκάλουν ἐπ' ἐλευθερίᾳ], but none listened to them." (Appian, *BC* 1.26; trans. LCL)

"The Senate offered a reward of money to any free citizen, freedom to any slave [ἐλευθέρῳ μὲν ἀργύριον, δούλῳ δὲ ἐλευθερίαν], impunity to any accomplice, who should give testimony leading to the conviction of the murderers of Asellio, but nobody gave any information." (Appian, *BC* 1.54; trans. LCL)

"The followers of Marius fought feebly against these new-comers, and as they feared lest they should be surrounded they called to their aid the other citizens who were still fighting from the houses, and proclaimed freedom to slaves who would share their dangers [συνεκάλουν καὶ τοῖς δούλοις ἐκήρυττον ἐλευθερίαν εἰ ματάσχοιεν τοῦ πόνου]. As nobody came forward, they fell into utter despair and fled at once out of the city together with those of the nobility who had cooperated with them." (Appian, *BC* 1.58; trans. slightly modified from LCL)

"Cinna, who had been emboldened by the numbers of the new citizens to think that he should conquer, seeing the victory won contrary to his expectation by the bravery of the few, hurried through the city calling the slaves to his assistance by an offer of freedom [τοὺς θεράποντας ἐπ' ἐλευθερίᾳ συγκαλῶν]. As none responded he hastened to the towns nearby. ... The Senate decreed that since Cinna had left the city in danger while holding the office of consul, and had offered freedom to slaves [δούλοις ἐλευθερίαν κηρύξαντα], he should no longer be consul, or even a citizen." (Appian, *BC* 1.65; trans. LCL)

shall go out alone. But if the slave declares, "I love my master, my wife, and my children; I will not go out a free person," then his master shall bring him before God [alternative: "to the judges"]. He shall be brought to the door or the doorpost; and his master shall pierce his ear with an awl; and he shall serve him for life. (Exod. 21:2–6; NRSV)

Here we see that slaves might have their own reasons for refusing liberation, such as not breaking up a family. This passage from Exodus does not support the Roman situation, but helps us to envision particular situations when slaves could, and according to ancient slaveholding ideologies should, refuse manumission, even when offered by their own masters. Therefore Bellen's assumption is in fact correct.

After Bellen, the next major treatment of this passage is found in a dissertation by Darrell Doughty, written under the direction of Hans Conzelmann.[90] Doughty does not intend to solve the riddle of 1 Cor 7:21 (although he adopts the "take freedom" side), but seeks to understand 1 Cor 7 as a whole. He concludes that chapter 7 is really an *ad hoc* response to pressing issues within the Corinthian congregation itself. Thus, Paul does not intend to compose an abstract theoretical discussion on slavery as such, but addresses a particular point brought up by the Corinthians about their slaves. Doughty, however, does not address slavery as a social institution and does not make an argument aimed specifically at solving the interpretive crux of 1 Cor 7:21.[91]

Following Doughty's study came a monographic treatment by Henneke Gülzow of Christianity and slavery in the first three centuries.[92] This book attempts to be extensive and exhaustive, beginning with slavery in the pre-Christian Jewish communities and ending with the career of the Christian slave Callistus who became bishop of Rome (d. 222 C.E.) under the brief reign of Elagabalus. Gülzow includes a five-page excursus on the interpretation of 1 Cor 7:21, in which he notes that Paul is addressing not just any slave, but only a specific kind of slave whose manumission involved a potentially unpleasant burden. Gülzow points to the Hellenic and Hellenistic institution of *paramonē*, which required the freedman/woman to "hang around," serving the ex-master often "as a slave" until the master's death. *Paramonē* contracts were common in the Greek East and more binding than *liberti* stipulations of *operae* (specific number of days to work for the ex-master) and *obsequium* (obligation for respectful behavior and attitude).[93] Paul, then, advises the slave

---

[90] Darrell Doughty, "Heiligkeit und Freiheit: Eine exegetische Untersuchung der Anwendung des paulinischen Freiheitsgedankens in I Kor. 7" (doctoral diss., Göttingen, 1965).

[91] Bartchy, *ΜΑΛΛΟΝ ΧΡΗΣΑΙ*, 11–13.

[92] Henneke Gülzow, *Christentum und Sklaverei in den ersten drei Jahrhunderten* (Bonn: Rudolf Habelt, 1969), which is a revision of the dissertation that he presented to the Protestant Theological Faculty in Kiel, under the direction of Professor Heinrich Kraft.

[93] William L. Westermann, "The *paramonē* as General Service Contract," *JJP* 2 (1948): 9–50; Alan E. Samuel, "The Role of *paramonē* Clauses in Ancient Documents," *JJP* 15

facing the prospects of such post-manumission *paramonē* obligations to remain in slavery.[94] It has been rightly pointed out that Gülzow mistakenly thinks that the overwhelming majority of scholars have favored the "take slavery" option and so works from a misguided assumption that all the grammatical and syntactical problems have been solved by previous exegetes. In addition to this valid objection, however, Gülzow like Bellen has been unfairly criticized for his premise that slaves could refuse an offer of manumission.[95] Yet this criticism of Gülzow is mistaken, as we saw earlier. In fact, Gülzow guides scholars in the right direction: toward *paramonē* obligations. However, Gülzow's assumption that manumission brought burdens to the ex-slave so unpleasant that it was in the slave's best interests to avoid liberation is based not on social actuality but on the ideology of ancient slaveholders, who denied that freedom was an unambiguous good for their slaves.

Another theologian, Siegfried Schulz, needs mention.[96] Schulz's book was written under great pressure after the 1968 student revolt in the Federal Republic of Germany. In that uprising, Marxists violently accused the Christian theologians of being "oppressive" because they supported the "repressive hierarchy" of unjust authorities. Calling his work a "position paper,"[97] Schulz states that the fundamental passage of 1 Cor 7:20–24 proves unambiguously that the Apostle indeed held the conviction that slaves must remain slaves and not seek freedom. Paul, in Schulz's view, is attempting to remedy a specific problem in the Corinthian church caused by "enthusiasts" who have taken the Apostle at his literal word (Gal 3:28) that the sociolegal statuses of slave and free are null and void. According to Schulz, Paul's call for a "spiritual" Christian freedom does not involve any kind of ancient Christian "emancipation proclamation." Such an interpretation, he claims, is a "fundamental misunderstanding" of Paul's message.[98] Spiritual freedom and worldly justice have noth-

---

(1965): 256–84; Keith Hopkins, *Conquerors and Slaves*, Sociological Studies in Roman History 1 (New York: Cambridge University Press, 1978), 137 n. 5, 141–58. Note the critical review of Hopkins by Keith R. Bradley, *CP* 76 (1981): 83, 86. Thomas Wiedemann, *Greek and Roman Slavery* (1981; reprint, London: Routledge, 1988), 3, 42–44, 46–49, 105, 120. I shall discuss these issues further in chapter 4.

[94] Gülzow, *Christentum und Sklaverei*, 177–81, who follows Johannes Weiss, *Der erste Korintherbrief*, 2d ed., MeyerK 5 (Göttingen: Vandenhoeck & Ruprecht, 1910), 188. Against this view, see Heinrich Greeven, *Das Hauptproblem der Sozialethik in der neueren Stoa und im Urchristentum*, Neutestamentliche Forschungen 3,4 (Gütersloh: Bertelsmann, 1935), 51 n. 3; Bartchy, *ΜΑΛΛΟΝ ΧΡΗΣΑΙ*, 17 n. 37.

[95] Bartchy, *ΜΑΛΛΟΝ ΧΡΗΣΑΙ*, 11–13, 17–19.

[96] Siegfried Schulz, *Gott ist kein Sklavenhalter: Die Geschichte einer verspäteten Revolution* (Zurich: Flamberg, 1972).

[97] Schulz, *Gott ist kein Sklavenhalter*, 9.

[98] Schulz, *Gott ist kein Sklavenhalter*, 170; Brockmeyer, *Antike Sklaverei*, 192, 346–47 n. 95; Carl W. Weber, *Sklaverei im Altertum: Leben im Schatten der Säulen* (Düsseldorf: Econ,

ing to do with each other; Christian liberty of slaves does not depend upon freedom from their socio-institutional bondage in this material world. Schulz unfortunately cites only H. D. Wendland's commentary to support his interpretation of 1 Cor 7:20–24.[99] Schulz's reader, unless personally knowledgeable of the long and complex history of research on this interpretative crux, would mistakenly believe that a consensus exists among New Testament scholars.

In the preface of his book, Schulz mentions that only in 1963 did slavery end formally in Saudi Arabia.[100] The perennial existence of slavery as a tragic phenomenon in human history poses considerable moral problems for Schulz, problems that he argues every theologian must face. Although he correctly stresses that Paul's eschatological outlook led the Apostle not to attack slavery as a social institution, Schulz nevertheless blames Paul for his inaction and lack of social concern.[101] Because he holds Paul responsible for not abolishing the institution of slavery, he commits what M. I. Finley has termed a "teleological fallacy" found in many studies on ancient slavery. Finley writes:

my immediate concern is with the methodological fallacy that pervades [many accounts of slavery], a common one in the history of ideas, which we may call the "teleological fallacy." It consists in assuming the existence from the beginning of time, so to speak, of the writer's values – in this instance, the moral rejection of slavery as an evil – and in then examining all earlier thought and practice as if they were, or ought to have been, on the road to this realization; as if men in other periods were asking the same questions and facing the same problems as those of the historian and *his* world.[102]

Finley notes elsewhere:

The habit of using the ancient world as a springboard for a larger political polemic is of course not a monopoly of any one camp or school. ... [M]y critique of the moralistic approach [does not] imply an end to moral judgments. ... Slavery is a great evil: there is no reason why a historian should not say that, but to say only that, no matter with how much factual backing, is a cheap way to score a point on a dead society to the advantage of our own: "retrospective indignation is also a way to justify the present" [quoting Pierre Bourdieu]. The present-day moralistic approach has taken a different turn. It starts from the high evaluation of ancient culture and then tries to come to terms with its most troubling feature, slavery. Anyone who clings to the cause of neo-classicism or classical humanism has little room to manoeuvre, except in the way he prefers to abate the

---

1981), 344, 347; John M. G. Barclay, "Paul, Philemon, and the Dilemma of Christian Slave-Ownership," *NTS* 37 (1991): 161–62.

[99] Schulz, *Gott ist kein Sklavenhalter*, 247 n. 76; H. D. Wendland, *Die Briefe an die Korinther*, 12th ed., NTD 7 (Göttingen: Vandenhoeck & Ruprecht, 1968).

[100] Schulz, *Gott ist kein Sklavenhalter*, 7.

[101] Schulz, *Gott ist kein Sklavenhalter*, 79–96; Kehnscherper, *Die Stellung der Bibel*, 79–96; cf. Schulz, "Hat Christus die Sklaven befreit? Sklaverei und Emanzipationsbewegungen im Abendland," *EvK* 5 (1972): 13–17, in which he answers his own question negatively.

[102] Finley, *Ancient Slavery and Modern Ideology*, 17 (emphasis his). Finley specifically criticizes Vogt, *Ideal of Man*.

nuisance of ancient slavery, or, as with Vogt, in the way he tries to "rescue" the record of Christianity.[103]

Finley's criticism of Joseph Vogt also clarifies the methodological problem of Schulz, who follows this moralistic approach to solve the interpretative crux of 1 Cor 7:21. However, I do agree with Schulz that Paul addresses slavery in response to a practical or legal interpretation of Gal 3:28; furthermore, his argument that Paul's notion of freedom was spiritual, not social, has a certain plausibility.

Dieter Lührmann's work critiques Schulz and offers a response.[104] He begins by pointing out that Schulz has a particular social hermeneutic and agenda. Lührmann notes the difference between analysis and judgment, and faults Schulz for judging Paul rather than analyzing him.[105] Lührmann states that moderns ought not to hold Paul accountable for present issues and difficulties; one cannot blame Paul for not solving modern problems. Additionally, Lührmann questions Schulz's assertion that evidence exists for ancient "abolition movements" among the pre-Socratics, the Essenes, and the "enthusiasts" of Corinth. The fact that Schulz can find only three "bright spots" in the history of Western civilization before the eighteenth-century abolitionist movement tells how Schulz pushes his thesis too far.[106] Lührmann argues that the only interpretation of 1 Cor 7:21 that makes sense in the argumentative context is "rather use slavery."[107] In retrospect, Paul's social ethic looks conservative, and so the Pauline ethic of slavery cannot serve as a model for today, Lührmann contends. This point is well taken, yet Lührmann's attempt to solve the interpretive crux has not proven convincing, especially to those scholars who side with S. Scott Bartchy.

From this survey it is clear that no thoroughly convincing case for the interpretation of 1 Cor 7:21 had been made on the basis of grammar and syntax alone.[108] As Bartchy notes, it seems ironic that Heinrich Schlier, writ-

---

[103] Finley, *Ancient Slavery and Modern Ideology*, 63–64.

[104] Dieter Lührmann, "Wo man nicht mehr Sklave oder Freier ist: Überlegungen zur Struktur frühchristlicher Gemeinden," *WD* 13 (1975): 53–83.

[105] Lührmann, "Wo man nicht mehr Sklave," 69.

[106] Lührmann, "Wo man nicht mehr Sklave," 53.

[107] Lührmann, "Wo man nicht mehr Sklave," 62. Although he agrees with S. Scott Bartchy's reconstruction of ancient slavery (i.e., manumission, when offered, was mandatory in antiquity), Lührmann nevertheless argues *contra* Bartchy that the object of χρῆσαι cannot be "calling" (κλῆσις).

[108] Bartchy, *ΜΑΛΛΟΝ ΧΡΗΣΑΙ*, 23. In this regard, several other studies deserve mention: Roland Gayer, *Die Stellung des Sklaven in den paulinischen Gemeinden und bei Paulus: Zugleich ein sozialgeschichtlich vergleichender Beitrag zur Wertung des Sklaven in der Antike*, Europäische Hochschulschriften, 23d ser. 78 (Bern: Herbert Lang, 1976), 173–222, 206–9; Ulf-Rainer Kügler, "Die Paränese an die Sklaven als Modell urchristlicher Sozialethik" (doctoral diss., Erlangen, 1977), 63–106; J. N. Sevenster, *Paul and Seneca*, NovTSup 4

ing on ἐλεύθερος in a volume of G. Kittel's *Theological Dictionary of the New Testament*, supplies τῇ δουλείᾳ to μᾶλλον χρῆσαι while Karl Heinrich Rengstorf, writing on δοῦλος in the same volume, adds τῇ ἐλευθερίᾳ.[109] As will be evident, however, Bartchy's own solution to the puzzle presents problems that need correction. In particular his social reconstruction of first-century slavery demands detailed consideration. His assumption that manumission in all cases was mandatory, which some New Testament scholars claim Bartchy has shown decisively,[110] is mistaken.

Bartchy's study is one of the major attempts of the past two decades to solve the riddle of 1 Cor 7:21. Bartchy states that his explicit goal is to discover "what hindered Paul or Christian slaves and Christian owners from drawing the kind of social consequences from the Gospel which were drawn by the abolitionists in the nineteenth century."[111] He means "abolitionist" in the technical sense of a political activist who, in the tradition of the Enlightenment, does not tolerate slavery in any form of human society. Paul was not an abolitionist, and this fact deeply troubles Bartchy. In many ways Bartchy hopes to exonerate Paul from an "apparent indifference" to slavery as a thoroughly evil human institution.[112] By framing his question around this modern concern, Bartchy obscures both the historical institution of ancient slavery and the rhetorical intent of 1 Cor 7:21.

His first chapter succinctly sketches the history of research, plotting on a timeline who was on the "take freedom" side and who was on the "use slavery" side. Here he criticizes other scholars, such as Heinz Bellen, whose arguments do not conform to Bartchy's own picture of how slavery operated in first-century Greco-Roman society – in particular, to Bartchy's impression that slaves could not refuse manumission offers. For this reason, his history of the passage's interpretation must be used with care.

Bartchy's second chapter examines slavery as an institution in the first century C.E. Throughout this discussion, the author laments the poverty of New

---

(Leiden: E. J. Brill, 1961), 189–90; Liem Khiem Jang, "Der Philemonbrief im Zusammenhang mit dem theologischen Denken des Apostels Paulus" (doctoral diss., Bonn, 1964), 53–57; Kenneth C. Russell, *Slavery as Reality and Metaphor in the Pauline Letters* (Rome: Catholic Book Agency, 1968); and Dale B. Martin, *Slavery as Salvation: The Metaphor of Slavery in Pauline Christianity* (New Haven: Yale University Press, 1990), 198 n. 16.

[109] Bartchy, *ΜΑΛΛΟΝ ΧΡΗΣΑΙ*, 5 n. 11; H. Schlier, "ἐλεύθερος, κ.τ.λ.," *TDNT* 2 (1964): 501; K. H. Rengstorf, "δοῦλος, κ.τ.λ.," *TDNT* 2 (1964): 272.

[110] Gervase Corcoran, "Slavery in the New Testament II," *Milltown Studies* 6 (1980): 72; Baumert, *Ehelosigkeit*, 134; Fee, *Corinthians*, 317; Stanley E. Porter, *Verbal Aspect in the Greek of the New Testament with Reference to Tense and Mood*, Studies in Biblical Greek 1 (New York: Peter Lang, 1989), 357–58, all wrongly accept as truth Bartchy's assertion that no ancient slave could ever refuse a manumission offer.

[111] Bartchy, *ΜΑΛΛΟΝ ΧΡΗΣΑΙ*, 62.

[112] Ibid.

Testament studies on slavery and tries to correct what he sees as "uncritical assumptions which have distorted modern understanding of ancient slavery and the interpretation of 1 Cor 7:21."[113] One of these "distorted modern assumptions" is that slaves were unhappy with their lot.[114] Manumission, he correctly observes, routinely occurred in Roman (urban) society; this fact, he argues, both humanized the institution and softened the brutalizing effects of bondage. This conclusion, however, does not follow. It ignores another fact, that new slaves were coming into bondage, often by brutal violence, to replace liberated slaves.[115] Another of Bartchy's so-called distorted modern assumptions is that slaves in this period were provided mainly through warfare. Bartchy argues that breeding was the main source; he concludes from this "fact" that slaves were treated well:

> The first century A.D., then, was a time in which the living conditions for those in slavery were improving. Legal action and public opinion supported better treatment of slaves. The chief reason for this improvement in slave-life was the fact that the principal source of slaves was no longer war and piracy (with the hostility these acts involved) but breeding. That is, most slaves in the first century were born in the households of their owners, and were given training for personal and public tasks of increasing importance and sensitivity. They were treated accordingly.[116]

While it is true that breeding replaced warfare in some areas and to a limited extent as a source of slaves under the early Principate, it nevertheless does not follow that breeding led to more humane treatment. In claiming that slaves born and bred at home would naturally receive affectionate treatment, Bartchy constructs a model of slavery as a human phenomenon that appears improbable in the light of comparative study. Indeed, the opposite case appears to be more prevalent. We need only look to the American South as a test case of Bartchy's model: of all the slave societies in the New World, that of the antebellum South alone maintained a slave population that reproduced itself.[117] Yet no serious scholar of American slavery claims that just because most African-American slaves were born on southern plantations or farms, they somehow received humane treatment from white slaveholders.[118] One can-

---

[113] Bartchy, *ΜΑΛΛΟΝ ΧΡΗΣΑΙ*, 118.

[114] Bartchy, *ΜΑΛΛΟΝ ΧΡΗΣΑΙ*, 85.

[115] I owe this observation to conversations with Keith R. Bradley.

[116] Bartchy, *ΜΑΛΛΟΝ ΧΡΗΣΑΙ*, 71.

[117] Eugene D. Genovese, *Roll, Jordan, Roll: The World the Slaves Made* (New York: Vintage Books, 1976), 5. The total number of African slaves imported to the United States was less than 400,000, yet by 1860 the American slave population had swelled to more than 4,000,000. For the statistical data, see the standard work by Philip D. Curtin, *The Atlantic Slave Trade: A Census* (Madison: University of Wisconsin Press, 1969).

[118] Kenneth M. Stampp, *The Peculiar Institution: Slavery in the Ante-Bellum South* (New York: Vintage Books, 1956); Stanley Elkins, *Slavery: A Problem in American Institutional and Intellectual Life* (Chicago: University of Chicago Press, 1959); Winthrop D. Jordan, *White*

not emphasize too much that Roman slavery in all times and places was a brutal institution, which held human chattel in an inherently vulnerable position by violence and robbed them of any sense of honor.[119] For example, the ruling from the Christian Emperor Constantine that slaveowners were not liable for beating their slaves to death should be sufficient refutation of this belief in the humane development of slavery.[120] As Keith Bradley appropriately maintains, the "growth of humanitarian concern for slaves ... is beyond proof and inconsistent with what can be determined of actual practice."[121] Bartchy's picture of ancient slavery as somehow a relatively humane practice is unlikely. Violence was endemic to and an essential element of the institution.

Bartchy makes three other questionable assertions.

1. The lack of slave revolts proves slave "contentment":

This lively expectation of manumission must have been a major factor in the relative "contentment" among those in slavery in the first century A.D. Indeed the ease and frequency of manumission during this period relieved any pressures which might have led to slave-revolts. ... Without examining the evidence, some Biblical scholars have assumed that a general climate of "unrest" within the slave population in the first century A.D. was the background and occasion for 1 Cor 7:21. Therefore, against this assumption, it must be stressed that the last serious slave-revolt in the Greco-Roman world occurred at least 120 years before Paul wrote to the Corinthian Christians.[122]

2. Numerous persons sold themselves into slavery in order to better their lives:

Contrary to the supposition that first-century slavery was a way of life which was to be avoided if possible, many persons sold themselves into slavery in order to climb socially, to secure a specific job open only to slaves, and to find greater security than they had experienced as free men. The chief advantage of living as a slave was personal and job security.[123]

---

over Black: American Attitudes toward the Negro, 1550–1812 (Baltimore: Penguin Books, 1969); Carl N. Degler, *Neither Black nor White: Slavery and Race Relations in Brazil and the United States* (New York: Macmillan, 1971); Genovese, *Roll, Jordan, Roll*; James Oakes, *The Ruling Race: A History of American Slaveholders* (New York: Vintage Books, 1983); Elizabeth Fox-Genovese, *Within the Plantation Household: Black and White Women of the Old South*, Gender and American Culture (Chapel Hill: University of North Carolina Press, 1988), 146–91; Orlando Patterson, *Slavery and Social Death: A Comparative Study* (Cambridge: Harvard University Press, 1982), 132–47; Bradley, *Slaves and Masters*, 123. Of course, Robert W. Fogel and Stanley L. Engerman do argue that slaves were not beaten as often as previously thought, but that does not make slavery humane (*Time on the Cross: The Economics of American Negro Slavery*, 2 vols. [Boston: Little, Brown, 1974]).

[119] Bradley, *Slaves and Masters*; Patterson, *Slavery and Social Death*.

[120] *Cod. Theod.* 9.12.1; Bradley, *Slaves and Masters*, 126.

[121] Bradley, *Slaves and Masters*, 127.

[122] Bartchy, *ΜΑΛΛΟΝ ΧΡΗΣΑΙ*, 85.

[123] Bartchy, *ΜΑΛΛΟΝ ΧΡΗΣΑΙ*, 116.

3. Slaveowners treated their slaves like children:

A person's experience as a slave depended primarily upon the character, customs, business and social class of the owner. Most slaves were treated well. An owner's control over his slaves was very similar to his control over his children, and the owner who treated his children well usually gave the same treatment to his slaves. Warm friendly relationships developed between slaves and their owners.[124]

In his claim that Greco-Roman masters felt as paternal toward their slaves as they did toward their children, Bartchy is open to criticism. As we saw in chapter 1, the ancient slaveholding ideology was far from paternalistic. In the Roman family, in particular, the two roles of "parent" to children and "master" to slaves were clearly defined and distanced from one another.[125] This nonpaternal attitude marks an important break between the Greco-Roman slaveholding ideology and that of the American South, where masters saw themselves as parents to their slaves who were their inferiors by race.[126] This distinctly American attitude grew out of response to the anti-slavery movement; southern slaveowners had to justify their roles as master by claiming their motives were purely paternal, the immature savage their "white man's burden." American slaveholders were defensive about slavery, even to the point of acknowledging it as their "peculiar institution." However, Greek and Roman slaveholders saw no need to defend their treatment of slaves as paternalistic; to them slavery was anything but peculiar.

Bartchy's further claim that slaves rebel only under abuse is problematic for at least two reasons. First, Bartchy uncritically accepts the ancient slaveholders' ideology, which presumed that slaves were normally satisfied with their lot and became disgruntled only under abuse. The ancient sources invariably blame every slave revolt on an arrogant master's maltreatment of his slaves, not on the evils of slavery as such.[127] Second, Bartchy misinterprets slave psychol-

---

[124] Bartchy, *ΜΑΛΛΟΝ ΧΡΗΣΑΙ*, 70.

[125] Ter. *Ad.* 70; Cic. *Rep.* 3.25; Richard P. Saller, "Corporal Punishment, Authority, and Obedience in the Roman Household," in *Marriage, Divorce, and Children in Ancient Rome*, ed. Beryl Rawson (Oxford: Clarendon Press, 1991), 144–65; idem, "*Pietas*, Obligation, and Authority in the Roman Family," in *Alte Geschichte und Wissenschaftsgeschichte: Festschrift für Karl Christ zum 65. Geburtstag*, ed. Peter Kneissl and Volker Losemann (Darmstadt: Wissenschaftliche Buchgesellschaft, 1988), 393–410; idem, *Patriarchy, Property, and Death in the Roman Family* (Cambridge: Cambridge University Press, 1994), 133–53. For Greek culture, the two roles of master and parent were also clearly distinguished; Arist. *Pol.* 1.3 (1253b); 1.12–13 (1259b–60b).

[126] For southern paternalism, see Genovese, *Roll, Jordan, Roll*; but cf. criticisms of Genovese's class analysis by Oakes, *Ruling Race*.

[127] Diod. Sic. 34/35.2.33; Plut. *Vit. Crass.* 8.1 (on Spartacus); Posidonius, F 59 (L. Edelstein and I. G. Kidd, *Posidonius*, vol. 1, *The Fragments* [1972; reprint, Cambridge: Cambridge University Press, 1989], 80–81; trans. in Kidd, *Posidonius*, vol. 2, *The Commentary: (i) Testimonia and Fragments 1–149* [Cambridge: Cambridge University Press, 1988], 293).

ogy. The mistake here, as Keith Bradley has demonstrated in his work on slavery and rebellion in the Roman world, is to assume that the scarcity of direct, open revolt proves servile contentment within the system.[128] In the history of slavery, slave revolts are extremely rare occurrences; only four outright "slave wars" are known: one in modern Haiti, two in ancient Sicily, and one led by Spartacus in ancient Italy. The ancient revolts occurred in a very limited time span in the context of massive military expansion and political upheaval under the Roman late Republic. Moreover, when open revolts are recorded, they historically coincide with relaxation – not tightening – of a slave system's control over its slave population.[129] In addition, when we allow for an expanded definition of resistance, which includes truancy, theft, black marketeering, sabotage, random violence, uppity or slovenly behavior, feigned illness, and suicide, we enter into an investigation of how human beings react to enslavement that is far more complex than Bartchy allows. A large-scale slave revolt is not the only way that slaves resist their condition; indeed, slave wars are extremely rare.

Bartchy's reliance upon legal codes as evidence for the improving condition of slaves raises yet another methodological problem. He writes, "Roman legal practice kept pace with this development [of slave breeding] by guaranteeing to those in slavery more humane treatment."[130] Too often he speaks of

---

[128] Keith R. Bradley, *Slavery and Rebellion in the Roman World: 140 B.C.–70 B.C.* (Bloomington: Indiana University Press, 1989), 41.

[129] Such was the case during the Second Sicilian Slave War (104–101 B.C.E.). The Roman Senate passed a decree, at the request of the Bithynian king Nikomedes, that the abducted and enslaved citizens of states allied to Rome should be set free. However, at the urgent request of the Sicilian governor Licinius Nerva, who faced a multitude of slaves all claiming liberation, the Senate repealed its decree, thus causing the outbreak of the rebellion (Diod. Sic. 36.3.3–6). If the Senate had not relaxed control over its slave population by offering large-scale manumission, then slaves would not have had the latitude to mobilize an uprising. The rebellions in Haiti (then called Saint Domingue) (1791), of Gabriel Prosser in Virginia (1800), of Denmark Vesey in South Carolina (1822), those in Barbados (1816) and Demerara (1823), and the famous insurrection of Nat Turner in Virginia (1831) occurred precisely when the institution was becoming less oppressive. The largest slave revolt in the United States took place in Louisiana in 1811 and involved between 300 and 500 slaves. Nat Turner had about 70 slaves; Gabriel Prosser and Demark Vesey apparently expected to raise more but never got the chance. For studies on American slave resistance and revolt, see Gerald W. Mullin, *Flight and Rebellion: Slave-Resistance in Eighteenth-Century Virginia* (New York: Oxford University Press, 1972); Genovese, *Roll, Jordan, Roll*, 587–98; David Brion Davis, *Slavery and Human Progress* (New York: Oxford University Press, 1984), 164; Gary Y. Okihiro, ed., *In Resistance: Studies in African, Caribbean, and Afro-American History* (Amherst: University of Massachusetts Press, 1986); Paul Cartledge, "Rebels and Sambos in Classical Greece: A Comparative View," in *Crux: Essays in Greek History Presented in G. E. M. de Ste. Croix on His 75th Birthday*, ed. P. A. Cartledge and F. D. Harvey (London: Gerald Duckworth, 1985), 16–46.

[130] Bartchy, *ΜΑΛΛΟΝ ΧΡΗΣΑΙ*, 117.

"Greek," "Roman," and "Jewish" law as if they composed monolithic institutions.[131] He continually claims that "in Greek law" this happens, "in Roman law" that happens, and "in Jewish law" the following occurs, as if law codes reflect actual behavior or even themselves "act." As we saw in chapter 1, this method is at best inappropriate given the scattered and fragmentary nature of the primary sources and at worst highly misleading in its use of laws as positive indicators of social practice. Because of his juridical hermeneutic, Bartchy paints a picture of first-century slavery as it was legally defined, not as it was actually practiced. He mistakes legal history for all history.

He states, for example, that "the closer Paul came to Rome [geographically], the more he found the institution of slavery to be an essential part of the economy and a normal part of the life of most families."[132] While we have seen in chapter 1 that of all the areas of the Roman Empire Sicily and peninsular Italy best fit the term "slave society," Bartchy's argument on this point is problematic. He cites M. I. Finley in support of this claim, but he misapplies the findings of Finley's work.[133] In his article on slave labor in Greece, Finley describes slavery in fourth-century B.C.E. Athens and Sparta, not the first-century C.E. Roman province of Achaia of Paul's day. Bartchy wants to argue that slavery permeated Roman society more than Greek, yet he footnotes secondary literature that describes the institution in the classical, not Roman, periods. As with his use of rabbinic material for the "Jewish law" of Paul's day, Bartchy is not comparing contemporary sources. What can Thucydides and Plato say about the Roman Corinth of the first century C.E.? The information is four centuries out of date. Bartchy constantly reminds his reader of his specific goal, "to define with some precision what it meant to be a slave in Corinth in the middle of the first century A.D."[134] Yet he never does this. Except in noting that the city may have replaced Delos as "the eastern 'clearing house' for the slave trade ... as the name 'Corinthus' seems to indicate,"[135] Bartchy nowhere uses evidence specific to Corinth beyond Paul's Corinthian correspondence. Indeed, he cannot, for the primary evidence necessary to document a detailed and comprehensive urban history of slavery in Roman Corinth does not survive.[136]

---

[131] On this mistake, see the sober remarks of M. I. Finley, "The Problem of the Unity of Greek Law," in *The Use and Abuse of History* (1975; reprint, New York: Penguin Books, 1987), 134–52.

[132] Bartchy, *ΜΑΛΛΟΝ ΧΡΗΣΑΙ*, 51.

[133] M. I. Finley, "Was Greek Civilization Based on Slave Labour?" in *Slavery in Classical Antiquity: Views and Controversies*, ed. idem (Cambridge: W. Heffer & Sons, 1960), 33–72.

[134] Bartchy, *ΜΑΛΛΟΝ ΧΡΗΣΑΙ*, 37.

[135] Bartchy, *ΜΑΛΛΟΝ ΧΡΗΣΑΙ*, 58 n. 185.

[136] On the methodological problems of writing an urban history of any particular ancient city, see M. I. Finley, "The Ancient City: From Fustel de Coulanges to Max Weber and Beyond," *CSSH* 19 (1977): 305–27.

However, the most questionable assumption in Bartchy's study is that slaves could never refuse manumission. Furthermore, as we saw in chapter 1, manumission took many forms, formal and informal, and occurred in many contexts, Roman and non-Roman. The ancient sources show that in some cases, especially in times of personal need or political upheaval, slaves did not always accept offers of freedom, notably when a nondomestic party proposed to put up the cost. Of all the critical reviewers of Bartchy, only C. K. Barrett found the mandatory manumission argument unconvincing. He writes, "In some cases, but not all, it is (or so at least Paul thinks) within the power of the Corinthian slave to secure his manumission. Shall he do so or not? This is the question, and the answer will be either Yes or No. I think it is No."[137] Barrett does not cite any ancient sources to refute Bartchy's assumption and to argue that slaves sometimes had a choice when faced with liberation prospects, but he could have.

However, Bartchy offers valuable treatments of some other issues. His third chapter investigates the question of Corinthian enthusiasts, the so-called *pneumatikoi* who oppose (or misunderstand) Paul. Bartchy then examines the possibility that Paul is addressing a specific case of slave resistance at Corinth, which the *pneumatikoi* have incited, as a social context for understanding the Apostle's statements about slavery, marriage, and celibacy. Bartchy concludes that no specific slave problem existed in Corinth for Paul or his community. There is no evidence in the passage, he says, that these enthusiasts were flaming the fires of rebellious sentiment among the Christian slaves in Corinth. Paul introduces questions of marriage, circumcision, and slavery not because these were burning issues at Corinth but because all three themes were customarily connected with baptism. In 1 Cor 7:20–24, Paul expresses not his opinions about the social-legal-political aspects of slavery and freedom (in fact he seems to have none, at least none articulated publicly), but his view that God's calling, in the spiritual sense, is available to all people, irrespective of social class, order, or status. I am not in complete agreement with Bartchy's argument about the *pneumatikoi*: surely the association of the three themes with baptism cannot be so neatly separated from social, legal, and political issues. Nonetheless, what is helpful is his drawing our attention to this possibility.

Bartchy's final chapter includes a rhetorical analysis of the passage, using the "thought pattern" of Gal 3:28 as a guide. Paul thinks in contrasting pairs – circumcised with uncircumcised, male with female, slave with free – and these dichotomies play a role in Paul's "theology of calling." The basic point is that one's earthly status makes no difference in one's calling to become a

---

[137] C. K. Barrett, review of *ΜΑΛΛΟΝ ΧΡΗΣΑΙ*, by S. Scott Bartchy, *JTS* 26 (1975): 174.

"saint" (Paul's word for a "Christian"). Paul is, therefore, addressing two types of people in 1 Cor 7:21: present slaves and future freedmen/women. In both cases, one must "use one's calling" irrespective of present or future position in society. Bartchy favors the third possibility for interpreting the passage.[138] The Greek clause μᾶλλον χρῆσαι refers neither to τῇ ἐλευθερίᾳ nor to τῇ δουλείᾳ, but to τῇ κλήσει ("the calling"). Bartchy reaches this conclusion via a comparative philological examination of how Josephus and a few other writers apply the verb χράομαι to mean "to live according to."[139] Bartchy's translation of the verse is as follows: "Were you a slave when you were called? Don't worry about it. But if, indeed, you become manumitted, by all means (as a freedman[/woman]) live according to (God's calling)."[140]

Paul, then, is not talking about the social institution of slavery at all, but his view of one's calling to God's service. God calls all "saints" irrespective of marital status, gender, ethnicity, or place within the social order. Surely Bartchy is correct in this exposition of Paul's theology, yet for all his praiseworthy exegetical skill, Bartchy's sweeping generalizations about slavery in the Hellenistic and Roman East weaken the force of his thesis. His problematic conclusions about the "humane" implications of manumission, his view that slaves and children were treated in the same way, his belief that breeding mitigated the violence of slavery, his reading of legal materials as descriptive of social reality, his speculative conclusions concerning the nature of human behavior in resistance, and his argument that slaves in antiquity could never refuse manumission all cast doubts upon his work.

Finally, Bartchy's proposed translation of 1 Cor 7:21 is not persuasive. He reaches back and completes the brachylogical expression (μᾶλλον χρῆσαι) with a word (κλῆσις) that occurs four clauses earlier. In addition, Bartchy takes the verb χράομαι out of its Pauline context and translates the verb as an isolated lexical unit according its usage in (mostly) a single author, Josephus. His elliptical translation, bending the clause back to supply "calling" as the object of the verb, is doubtful.[141] By assuming the priority of words over sentences, he

---

[138] Following F. W. Grosheide, *Commentary to the First Epistle to the Corinthians*, NICNT (Grand Rapids, Mich.: William B. Eerdmans, 1953), 170; J. S. Ruef, *Paul's First Letter to Corinth*, Pelican New Testament Commentaries (New York: Penguin Books, 1971), 60. See Fee, *Corinthians*, 308 n. 8.

[139] Bartchy, *ΜΑΛΛΟΝ ΧΡΗΣΑΙ*, 156–57, citing Josephus, *Ant.* 4.6.11 §145; 4.8.41 §295; 11.6.12 §281; 12.3.2 §126; 13.9.1 §257; 14.7.2 §116; 15.10.1 §371; *Herm. Sim.* 1.3; 1.6 (GCS 48.1.47); 1 Tim 1:8.

[140] Bartchy, *ΜΑΛΛΟΝ ΧΡΗΣΑΙ*, 183.

[141] So Barrett in his critical review of Bartchy, 174, notes that Bartchy ignores the force of δύνασαι in the verse "if you are able …" The use of the verb implies that Paul at least considered the slave had a choice. Fee, *Corinthians*, 316 n. 42. Gregory W. Dawes, "'But If You Can Gain Your Freedom' (1 Corinthians 7:17–24)," *CBQ* 54 (1990): 693–94, stresses that the ellipsis should be taken from the immediate context (thus either "slavery"

overlooks that, in the words of Jonathan Z. Smith, "It is, after all, the sentence, rather than the individual word which makes translation possible."[142] Syntactical relations convey just as much, if not more, linguistic information for determining the meaning as the pure linguistic aspects of the individual word. The sentence, unlike the word, is unique and nonrecurrent. The interpretation of 1 Cor 7:21 must be solved not by studying a word in isolation from the specific sentence in which the author penned it, but in terms of syntax and other philological, contextual considerations. On these linguistic grounds, Bartchy's argument is open to criticism.

In sum, Bartchy's overall reconstruction of ancient slavery needs correction because of its major methodological problems. As he states at the outset of his investigation, Bartchy hopes to "save" the phenomenon under study by certain concessions: In an effort to rescue Paul from his modern critics, Bartchy argues that "[s]lavery was by no means an ideal situation, but it was often much better than modern men are inclined to think."[143] Bartchy formulates his main query in moralistic language. "What hindered Paul," he asks, "... from drawing the kind of social consequences from the Gospel which were drawn by the abolitionists in the nineteenth century?"[144] Bartchy's study contains the same problem as that of Schulz, for its goal is to explain why Paul was not an enlightened abolitionist by showing that ancient slavery was not so bad, even humane.

Recent Investigations

Bartchy's findings have informed the work of scholars such as Peter Stuhlmacher, Friedrich Lang, Gordon Fee, Norbert Baumert, Stanley Porter, F. Stanley Jones, Klaus Schäfer, and Franz Laub.[145] Five studies subsequent to

---

or "freedom") rather than a word not already suggested by the immediate context ("call"); Vincent L. Wimbush, *Paul, the Worldly Ascetic: Response to the World and Self-Understanding according to 1 Corinthians 7* (Macon, Ga.: Mercer University Press, 1987), 15–16 n. 12; and Baumert, *Ehelosigkeit*, 128 n. 255, also find Bartchy's exegetical argument unconvincing.

[142] Jonathan Z. Smith, *Drudgery Divine: On the Comparison of Early Christianities and the Religions of Late Antiquity*, Chicago Studies in the History of Judaism (Chicago: University of Chicago Press, 1990), 77–78. This point is not original to Smith, of course, since lexicographers do pay attention to context in their determination of the correct definition of a word.

[143] Bartchy, *ΜΑΛΛΟΝ ΧΡΗΣΑΙ*, 46.

[144] Bartchy, *ΜΑΛΛΟΝ ΧΡΗΣΑΙ*, 62.

[145] Peter Stuhlmacher, *Der Brief an Philemon*, 2d ed., EKKNT 18 (Zurich: Benziger, 1981), 44–49 (see also his extensive review of Bartchy, *TLZ* 101 [1976]: 837–39); Friedrich Lang, *Die Briefe an die Korinther*, NTD 7 (Göttingen: Vandenhoeck & Ruprecht, 1986), 95–98; Fee, *Corinthians*, 306–22; Baumert, *Ehelosigkeit*, 114–60; Porter, *Verbal As-*

Bartchy, however, raise substantial issues concerning our crux, and so they deserve detailed mention.

In an appendix to his 1975 article, Peter Trummer discusses Bartchy's 1971 dissertation.[146] Trummer finds some of Bartchy's findings unconvincing, but concludes that Bartchy's detailed representation of ancient slavery as a whole makes a great contribution to the field of New Testament studies.[147] Trummer evaluates Bartchy's work as complementing his own findings. Like many commentators before him, Trummer sees the issue hinging on Paul's "social conservatism" on slavery.[148] If Paul thought that slaves ought not to be manumitted and ought to remain slaves, then 1 Cor 7:21 illustrates his deliberately conservative attitudes toward the institution. Yet this view, as I hope has become apparent, is wholly inaccurate. Trummer argues for the "textual unity"[149] of vv. 17–24, identifying its epistolary style (*Stichwortartige*) and locating the catchwords upon which Paul connected his paragraphs. According to Trummer, Paul chose to include a diatribe on slavery within his larger discourse of marriage because of the *Stichwort* "bound" in v. 15 (οὐ δεδούλωται ὁ ἀδελφὸς ἢ ἡ ἀδελφὴ ἐν τοῖς τοιούτοις). Trummer takes Heinz Bellen to task, asserting that Bellen overstates his thesis and that the whole context does not persuade him of Paul's so-called exaggerated sense of asceticism.[150] Trummer contends the weight of argumentation suggests instead that the chance of social freedom, to Paul's mind, was a new possibility for the slave's realization of his or her Christian call.[151] The Apostle does not close out the possibility of freedom. Trummer, then, congratulates Paul for starting a "quiet revolution of conviction" (*eine stille Revolution der Gesinnung*), which led not only to a new

---

pect, 357–58; F. Stanley Jones, *"Freiheit" in den Briefen des Apostles Paulus: Eine historische, exegetische und religionsgeschichtliche Studie*, GTA 34 (Göttingen: Vandenhoeck & Ruprecht, 1987), 155 n. 87; 159 n. 6; 160–61 n. 15; 162 nn. 22, 25, 30; 164 n. 43; 165 n. 59; Klaus Schäfer, *Gemeinde als "Bruderschaft": Ein Beitrag zum Kirchenverständnis des Paulus*, Europäische Hochschulschriften, 23d ser. 333 (Frankfurt: P. Lang, 1989), 283–90; Franz Laub, *Die Begegnung des frühen Christentums mit der antiken Sklaverei*, SBS 107 (Stuttgart: Verlag Katholisches Bibelwerk, 1982), 63–67. Conzelmann, *Erste Brief*, 160 n. 26a, notes Bartchy without questioning Bartchy's basic conclusions; Margaret M. Mitchell, *Paul and the Rhetoric of Reconciliation*, HUTh 28 (Tübingen: J.C.B. Mohr [Paul Siebeck], 1991), 124 n. 357, leaves the question open without disputing Bartchy's reconstruction of ancient slavery. See also the discussion in Samuel Vollenweider, *Freiheit als neue Schöpfung: Eine Untersuchung zur Eleutheria bei Paulus und in seiner Umwelt*, FRLANT 147 (Göttingen: Vandenhoeck & Ruprecht, 1989), 233–46.

[146] Peter Trummer, "Die Chance der Freiheit: Zur Interpretation des μᾶλλον χρῆσαι in 1 Kor 7,21," *Biblica* 56 (1975): 367–68.

[147] Trummer, "Chance der Freiheit," 367.

[148] Trummer, "Chance der Freiheit," 344–45.

[149] Trummer, "Chance der Freiheit," 346–48.

[150] Trummer, "Chance der Freiheit," 355.

[151] Trummer, "Chance der Freiheit," 364.

form of humane behavior of masters toward slaves, but also to visible socio-legal consequences (more manumissions).[152] Yet Trummer criticizes modern commentators who favor the "use slavery" interpretation for their misunderstanding of the Pauline message, which they see as on principle a preservation of the ancient structure of oppression. Paul quietly opposed slavery, claims Trummer; the completion of μᾶλλον χρῆσαι as "use freedom" proves that. Although I agree with Trummer's basic exegesis that 1 Cor 7:21 means "use freedom," I disagree with his theological assertion that Paul opposed slavery in the sense of wishing to abolish the institution. As we shall see in the contextual analysis below, no evidence in Paul's argumentative structure or train of thought supports such a contention. The passage cannot be used as proof of emancipation drives within Christian congregations. It is one thing to say that Paul thought that the social institution of slavery should be abolished (emancipation); it is quite another to say that he viewed the status of a slave as undesirable and degraded, and enfranchisement within the rules of society as beneficial (manumission). The two pieces of advice μή σοι μελέτω (v. 21) and μὴ γίνεσθε δοῦλοι ἀνθρώπων (v. 23) seem to imply that the latter statement is accurate. Trummer conflates emancipation and manumission.

A second study is a monograph on 1 Corinthians 7, a revised *Habilitations-schrift*, by Norbert Baumert.[153] Baumert agrees with Bartchy that ancient slavery was, in many cases, not very oppressive, since slaves expected that their manumission would eventually occur.[154] He begins his exegesis of 7:21 by pointing out that one of its earliest commentators, John Chrysostom, rejected the "use freedom" interpretation not on linguistic but on contextual grounds. Such an interpretation, argued Chrysostom, stands in contradiction to Paul's mode of thought and is no consolation to those who did not have the opportunity for freedom. Baumert then runs through a history of interpretation, showing how Chrysostom's "use slavery" view prevailed nearly universally up to the Reformation, when Luther, who saw the Apostle making a rigorous appeal for freedom, challenged established exegetical orthodoxy. One crucial aspect of Baumert's survey lies in his suggestion that the καί may have been omitted in witness G in order to support the "use freedom" interpretation.[155] Yet Baumert, like Trummer before him, accepts uncritically Bartchy's reconstruction of ancient slavery and understands Bartchy's "background information" to be of great value to New Testament commentators.[156] Building upon Bartchy's basic conclusions, Baumert reviews the many different contextual arguments for and against the competing interpretations of the verse.

---

[152] Ibid.
[153] Baumert, *Ehelosigkeit.*
[154] Baumert, *Ehelosigkeit*, 115.
[155] Ibid.
[156] Baumert, *Ehelosigkeit*, 120 n. 237; 134.

Baumert argues for the "use freedom" interpretation, and thus finds Paul pleading for the possibility of manumission.[157] He, however, takes issue (following Trummer) with Bartchy's translation of "by all means [as a freedman/woman] live according to [God's calling]," concluding that the contextual and lexical evidence prohibits Bartchy's solution. Bartchy ignores, Baumert rightly argues, the force of δύνασθαι, which must signify a clear opportunity placed before the slave.[158] He determines the verse to be a Pauline call to "remain in one's calling" that does not hinder enslaved believers from seizing the opportunity for freedom.[159] This interpretation, in Baumert's opinion, shatters the belief held dear by many commentators – notably Siegfried Schulz, with his moralistic censure of Paul – that Paul was a "social conservative" on slavery. Thus some of Baumert's exegesis is correct, although he misinterprets ancient slaveholding ideology.

A third significant study is a 1990 article by Gregory Dawes.[160] By siding with Chrysostom and other patristic commentators who favored the "use slavery" interpretation, the New Zealander scholar disagrees with Trummer and Baumert.[161] Dawes analyzes 7:17–24 as a *digressio* in the classical sense that Quintilian enunciated in his handbook on rhetoric. The Greco-Latin rhetorical technique of *digressio* (known alternatively as *egressio*, *egressus*, or παρέκβασις) involves the handling of some theme, which must have some bearing on the case argued, in a passage that detours from the logical order of the speech (Quint. *Inst.* 4.3.14). Dawes remarks that Johannes Weiss long ago and W. Wuellner recently noted that Paul uses this technique in 1 Corinthians.[162] He correctly shows that the recurring refrain of verses 17–24 is the injunction, "remain in one's baptismal calling," first found in v. 17. He observes, "In other words, in vv. 17–24 a rule is given, a general principle (vv. 17, 20, and 24), which is then illustrated [in a *digressio*] by the two cases cited, that of circumcision and that of slavery."[163] These two illustrations apply the general rule to "remain" and are not exceptions, according to Dawes. Slaves must remain slaves; the circumcised must remain circumcised (and vice versa). Dawes notes that those commentators who favor (as he does) the "use slavery" interpretation do so because the immediate context requires it. "They there-

---

[157] Baumert, *Ehelosigkeit*, 120.
[158] Baumert, *Ehelosigkeit*, 131–32 n. 266; 141 n. 278.
[159] Baumert, *Ehelosigkeit*, 154.
[160] Dawes, "'But If You Can Gain.'"
[161] Dawes, "'But If You Can Gain,'" 682 n. 9.
[162] Dawes, "'But If You Can Gain,'" 683; Weiss, *Erste Korintherbrief*, xliii; W. Wuellner, "Greek Rhetoric and Pauline Argumentation," in *Early Christian Literature and the Classical Tradition: in honorem Robert M. Grant*, ed. W. R. Schoedel and R. L. Wilken, Théologie historique 53 (Paris: Beauches, 1979), 177–88.
[163] Dawes, "'But If You Can Gain,'" 685.

fore feel compelled to choose this reading of the verse, even if on lexical and syntactical grounds … it lacks support."[164] Although he considers the arguments of commentators (e.g., Gordon Fee) who respond that 7:21 can be read as an exception, Dawes concludes that nothing in its context compels us to so understand the passage. According to Dawes, Paul chose to digress on circumcision and slavery within his argumentation on marriage because all three were viewed negatively by the Corinthian congregation as incompatible with the Christian life. Ultimately, the slave should remain being a slave and not worry about his or her social station.[165] Although he offers substantial insights, Dawes's main problem lies in his uncritical acceptance of Bartchy's social reconstruction of ancient slavery.[166] He also too quickly discounts the lexical evidence.

Allen Callahan presents a fourth recent study.[167] Unlike other commentators, Callahan is well versed in the secondary literature of ancient slavery, having read such scholars as Orlando Patterson and M. I. Finley. He argues in favor of the "use freedom" interpretation and points to Ignatius, *Ad Polycarp.* 4.3. Ignatius describes what Callahan terms "ecclesial manumission," churches' funding of the manumission of slaves out of the common chest. Paul, Callahan contends, addresses a similar situation in 7:21:

> I would suggest, therefore, that behind this text lies the Corinthian practice of ecclesial manumission, by which the change in status from *doulos* to *apeleutheros* was effected. The church at Corinth would have been in the practice of obtaining the freedom of enslaved members by marshalling their collective funds to pay the price of said member's manumission. … This explains Paul's financial language in v. 23a, which I would read as a rhetorical question akin to v. 21 and on the pattern of rhetorical questions in v. 18. "You were bought with a price, weren't you? Do not become slaves to human beings." Paul forbids those *apeleutheroi* who were *douloi* before their calling (i.e., previous to *klesis*) to relapse into considering themselves or allowing others to consider them as still in some way slaves, no doubt an important interdiction in a society which never allowed the freedman to forget his origins.[168]

Callahan states that although the sentence "you were bought with a price … do not become slaves of human beings" refers to enfranchisement of slaves, in 1 Cor 6:20 Paul uses this language in a clearly metaphorical sense. Paul describes the situation of every Christian, whether freeborn or slave. Therefore, when Paul writes, "you were bought with a price," he is not necessarily making a specific reference to legal manumission.

---

[164] Dawes, "'But If You Can Gain,'" 689.

[165] Dawes, "'But If You Can Gain,'" 696–97.

[166] Dawes, "'But If You Can Gain,'" 694.

[167] Allen Callahan, "A Note on 1 Corinthians 7:21," *Journal of the Interdenominational Theological Center* 17 (1989–90): 110–14.

[168] Callahan, "Note," 113.

There are two problems with Callahan's proposal. First, taking a second-century document (Ign. *Ad Polycarp.* 4.3) and projecting back the social situation reflected in it into 1 Corinthians is problematic. Second, when one realizes the nascent nature of the Corinthian congregation's common chest, additional problems appear. It is very telling that Paul, in 1 Cor 16:1–4, must give directions concerning the formation of a common fund. Paul writes, "On the first day of every week, each of you is to put aside and save whatever extra you earn, so that collections need not be taken when I come" (16:2).[169] Evidently, the Corinthian congregation did not already have an operating common chest in place at the writing of 1 Corinthians. Although the lack of a permanent chest need not preclude the possibility that a sum of money was raised for a specific occasion, to argue, as Callahan does, that 1 Cor 7:21 refers exclusively to permanent, institutional corporate funding collected by the Corinthian congregation to redeem its slave members goes too far. Callahan's ideas, although interesting for understanding Ignatius's advice in *Pol.* 4.3, do not prove relevant to Paul's advice in 1 Cor 7:21. Chapter 3 will discuss the common chest in antiquity in detail, and chapter 4 will clarify Ignatius's specific concerns regarding the danger of ecclesiastical corporate manumission.

A fifth recent study is by S. R. Llewelyn, who, after discussing a second-century C.E. deed of manumission from Oxyrhynchos, considers the ellipsis in 1 Cor 7:21.[170] Because it draws syntactical parallels, Llewelyn's investigation offers important insights into the grammatical structure of our crux. He argues for a solution from an analysis of other New Testament Greek ellipses in conditional sentences using εἰ. He finds that every example in the New Testament follows the same rule of thumb: an ellipsis in an apodosis is to be inferred from "the immediately preceding clause, i.e. its protasis."[171] The ellipsis of 1 Cor 7:21, according to Llewelyn, may be best classed with 2 Cor 5:16b, which reads: "even though we once knew Christ from a human point of view, we no longer know him [from a human point of view]" (εἰ καὶ ἐγνώκαμεν κατὰ σάρκα Χριστόν, ἀλλὰ νῦν οὐκέτι γινώσκομεν). Based on this rule of thumb, Llewelyn argues, against Bartchy, that the logical completion of the "rather use …" (μᾶλλον χρῆσαι …) ellipsis is "freedom" (τῇ ἐλευθερίᾳ). If Paul had meant to have his ellipsis completed by anything else (namely, by "slavery" or "one's calling in Christ," words not located in the clause imme-

---

[169] Unless, of course, Paul refers *only* to the "collection of the saints" and *not* to the Corinthian's own common chest, which they might have already institutionally established.

[170] S. R. Llewelyn, "'If You Can Gain Your Freedom': Manumission and 1 Cor. 7:21," in *New Documents Illustrating Early Christianity*, ed. S. R. Llewelyn et al. (Sydney, Australia: The Ancient History Documentary Research Centre [Macquarie University], 1992), 6:63–70.

[171] Llewelyn, "'If You Can Gain,'" 68.

diately preceding μᾶλλον χρῆσαι), he "would have needed to say so explicitly."[172] Llewelyn then examines the Greek word pair εἰ καί and the claim that it always carries a strong contrastive sense. He contends that "since the pleonastic reading of the apodosis is μᾶλλον χρῆσαι τῇ ἐλευθερίᾳ, there is no semantic contrast between it and its protasis and consequently there is no need to translate εἰ καί by 'even though' or 'even if.'"[173] Lastly, he compares 1 Cor 7:21 to two Pauline passages, 1 Cor 9:12 and Phil 3:4, which contain ellipsis and a usage of μᾶλλον that "cannot be translated by the contrastive 'rather.'"[174] He concludes: "A better translation is 'all the more,' i.e. 'But if you are able to become free, avail yourself of it all the more.'"[175] Llewelyn rightly takes grammatical structure as the key to the crux's solution. His procedure of drawing syntactical parallels from the Koine Greek of the New Testament is a fruitful one; this is especially seen in his comparison of 1 Cor 7:21 to 2 Cor 5:16b: it suggests that much can be learned by casting our net more widely and seeking such parallels outside the New Testament. It is to this task that the next section turns.

The correct translation of 1 Cor 7:21 remains to this day an open question. Even the NRSV, while reversing the decision of the RSV, acknowledges the continuing lack of scholarly consensus. The three solutions proposed in the commentary literature are that μᾶλλον χρῆσαι means (1) "rather use freedom," (2) "indeed use slavery," or (3) "by all means [as a freedman/woman] live according to [God's calling]." In the commentary literature, a major problem has been in understanding the problems, debates, and controversies over the essential elements of ancient slavery. Additionally, commentators, in their proposed translations of 1 Cor 7:21, have understood the context and syntax of the verse to favor contradictory readings. The next step is to analyze the text itself.

Philological Analysis:
Examples of μᾶλλον + χράομαι in Ancient Greek Literature

Having outlined the history of interpretation, we proceed to exegete the grammar of the crux.[176] This section begins, as the work of other exegetes such as Llewelyn has, with a consideration of philology. We pick up the task

---

[172] Llewelyn, "'If You Can Gain,'" 69.

[173] Ibid.

[174] Llewelyn, "'If You Can Gain,'" 70.

[175] Ibid.

[176] Unless otherwise noted, all translations in this section are my own. For Greek authors, this monograph follows the standard citation systems of *Thesaurus Linguae Graecae* (*TLG*) listed in Luci Berkowitz and Karl A. Squitier, *Thesaurus Linguae Graecae: Canon of*

where C. H. Dodd left it back in 1924, following his exegesis of *P. Oxy.* 16.1865. The purpose of this section is to provide additional texts for syntactical comparison with 1 Cor 7:21. This section collects seventeen examples, from at least fourteen different authors, reflecting a wide range of genres and periods, in order to accumulate sources with which to compare and so to interpret the syntax of μᾶλλον χρῆσαι in 1 Cor 7:21.[177] These texts demonstrate one major philological point. The force of the adverb μᾶλλον, when used with the deponent verb χράομαι, is usually adversative, but occasionally appears intensive. Yet since the two grammatical functions of contrast and intensification are related and merge into each other, they are not always mutually exclusive. In the cases below in which there is division between the two uses, the context shows that μᾶλλον is used mostly in the sense of "instead" (or "preferably") rather than conveying the sense of "more" (or "intensely").[178] This opposition is sometimes implicit, at other times explicit. In sum, the texts below lend support to the argument that in 1 Cor 7:21b Paul is contrasting two possible courses of action for Christian slaves facing two different situations. While I recognize the inherent ambiguity in the clause for Greek readers or hearers, as Chrysostom clearly shows, this evidence tips the scales in one direction ("use instead freedom") rather than another ("use slavery more").

The seventeen examples can be divided into four categories. The first three illustrate the adversative use of μᾶλλον; the fourth shows the strictly intensive use.

A. *Adversative with Explicit Opposition. 8 Cases.* In these examples, the author sets up two different situations in which two different courses of action are necessary and contrasts these courses of action with μᾶλλον. Translation: "use *X* instead/rather."

B. *Adversative with Implicit Opposition. 3 Cases.* These examples differ from those in category A only in that the opposition between the two situations is implicit. Translation: "use *X* instead/rather."

Greek Authors and Works, 3d ed. (New York: Oxford University Press, 1990), 439–71 (appendix 4). I thank Elizabeth Asmis and Margaret M. Mitchell for their criticism and suggestions on the texts translated in this section.

[177] A full corpus search of *TLG* on CD-ROM yielded 18 instances of μᾶλλον + χράομαι (admittedly, much of ancient literature is lost and not on *TLG*). I do not count the 3 instances found in the work of the sixth-century Christian grammarian John Philoponus, because the author's date falls outside the bounds of the present study; John Philoponus, *In libros de generatione animalium commentaria* (M. Hayduck, ed., *Ioannis Philoponi [Michaelis Ephesii], in libros de generatione animalium commentaria*, Commentaria in Aristotelem Graeca 14.3 [Berlin: Reimer, 1903] 42.3.237.10–12): τὰ γὰρ δηλοῦντα διὰ λόγου τὰ βουλήματα αὐτῶν ἀλλήλοις *μᾶλλον χρῆται* τῷ φθέγγεσθαι, τὸ <δὲ> *μᾶλλον χρώμενον* τῷ φθέγγεσθαι *μᾶλλον χρῆται* τῷ ὀξεῖ καὶ βαρεῖ. ἐπὶ δὲ τοῦ *μᾶλλον χρωμένου* τῷ ὀξεῖ καὶ βαρεῖ μᾶλλον δῆλόν ἐστι ποίων ὀξυφωνότερα.

[178] The adverb μᾶλλον has the core meaning of "rather" (more or less), which then diverges in various directions as pulled by context.

C. *Comparative with Intensity. 3 Cases.* This category represents an intermediate, quantitative meaning. The construction expresses intent to use one sort of thing more than another sort of thing: that is, to use both, but to use this more than that. In these examples, the author sets up two different situations and presents several possible courses of action (*X* or *Y* or *Z*). In one situation, you should use *X*, but can also use *Y* or *Z*; in the other, using *X* is even more preferable to using either *Y* or *Z*. Translation: "use *X* more (preferably)."

D. *Intensive. 3 Cases.* In these examples, the author uses μᾶλλον not to contrast two opposing courses of action, but to urge that a single course of action be done more intensely in a similar but more urgent situation. This category is not completely distinct from the first three in that, even in its intensive use, μᾶλλον still contrasts two ways of carrying out the same course of action. Translation: "use *X* more."

At an initial glance, it is apparent that all but three of the seventeen cases fall into categories A, B, and C. The following discussion presents these examples in Greek with English translations; only the ones in categories B, C, and D requre additional commentary.[179]

A. *Adversative with Explicit Opposition.*

1. Aretaeus of Cappadocia, medical author (ca. 150–200 C.E.), *De curatione diuturnorum morborum libri duo* 1.3.8.5–9.1.

ἀναφωνέειν χρή, τοῖσι βαρέσι φθόγγοισι *μᾶλλον χρεόμενον* ἠχεῖν. ὀξέες γὰρ κεφαλῆς διατάσιες, κροτάφων παλμοί, ἐγκεφάλου διασφύξιες, ὀφθαλμῶν πρήσιες, ἤχων ἀκοή. μετρίη ὀξυφωνίη κεφαλῇ ὀνηϊστόν.

[To cure vertigo, after a regimen of moderate sleep, friction of the limbs by means of rough towels, walking routines, and breathing exercises] it is necessary to exercise the voice, *using* low notes *instead*[180] to make sounds. For high notes are distensions of the head, vibrations of the temples, pulsations of the brain, fullness (or "burning") of the eyes, noise in the ears. A note of medium intensity is beneficial to the head.[181]

2. Ps.-Hippocrates, medical author (Hellenistic period), *De diaeta I–IV* 35.19–22.

εἰ δὲ ὀρθῶς διαιτῶντο, καὶ φρονιμώτεροι καὶ ὀξύτεροι γένοιντο παρὰ τὴν φύσιν. ξυμφέρει δὲ τοῖσι τοιούτοισι τοῖσι πρὸς πυρὸς διαιτήμασι *μᾶλλον χρέεσθαι* καὶ μὴ πλησμονῇσι μήτε σιτίων μήτε πομάτων.

---

[179] Because it is being used merely as a comparative between two nouns, one case of μᾶλλον and χρῆσθαι appearing together does not fit my typology. Flavius Josephus, Jewish historian (b. 37/38 C.E.), *Ant.* 18.7.1 §243: μηδὲ πενίαν ἀποφήνῃς τὴν ἐκείνου τῆς ἡμετέρας εὐπορίας ἀρετῇ *μᾶλλον χρῆσθαι* δυναμένην. "Do not broadcast that his poverty *can make use of* virtue *more than* our riches can."

[180] One witness adds ἢ ὀξέσι: "using low notes rather than high notes." Aretaeus does seem to set up an opposition between low and high notes.

[181] Aretaeus, *De curatione diuturnorum morborum libri duo* (*Aretaeus*, ed. Carolus Hude, CMG 2, 2d ed. [Berlin: Akademie-Verlag, 1958], 1.3.8.5–9.1); my translation is a correc-

And if they diet properly, they would become wiser and sharper beyond their nature. Also, it is beneficial for such patients *to use* a regimen (or "diet") from heat *rather* than to indulge in a surfeit of food or drink.[182]

3. Ps.-Hippocrates, *De diaeta I–IV* 59.8–11.

ὁκόταν μὲν οὖν στῆσαι βούλῃ, τὴν ταχίστην φαγόντα χρὴ ἐξεμέειν, πρὶν ἂν διυγρανθῆναι τὸν σῖτον καὶ κατασπασθῆναι κάτω, καὶ τοῖσι στρυφνοῖσι καὶ τοῖσιν αὐστηροῖσι σιτίοισι *μᾶλλον χρέεσθαι·*

So when you want to stop [the flux of the stomach], it is necessary to vomit as soon as you have eaten, before the food has been soaked thoroughly and swallowed down, and *to use rather* sour and bitter food.[183]

4. Vettius Valens of Antioch, professional astrologer (fl. 2d cent. c.e.) *Anthologiae* 5.6.38–39.

οὗτος μὲν ὁ ἀριθμὸς ἀναγκαστικὸς καὶ ἐπιδιπλούμενος διὰ τὴν φύσιν τῆς ὀργανοθεσίας, ἐπὶ δὲ πολλῶν φυσικώτερος δοκεῖ καὶ κυριώτερος ὁ διὰ τῆς δωδεκαετίας <ὅς> ἐν δευτέρῳ μέρει κείσεται. δεῖ οὖν πρότερον ἐκείνῳ προσέχειν καὶ ἀπολύειν τὰς δωδεκάδας καὶ τὸν ἐπίλοιπον ζητεῖν· καὶ ἐὰν μὲν εὑρεθῇ ἔχων παράδοσιν, ἐκείνῳ *μᾶλλον χρῆσθαι,* εἰ δὲ μὴ εὑρεθῇ, ἐξ ἀνάγκης ἐπὶ τοῦτον κατελευσόμεθα.

This number is a fixed one[184] and is doubled according to the nature of the table [of astrological calculations]. In many cases the number that seems more natural and more ruling is the one throughout the twelve year period, which will lie in the second part [of the decan]. Therefore, we must first pay attention to the number, begin to count the number of zodiacal signs [from one planet A], and to find the remainder. If it is found having a "yielding" [that is, if it is found that the influence of planet A is "yielded" to planet B],[185] then we *must use* that number *instead*; but if a "yielding" is not found, then out of necessity we shall resort to this number.[186]

---

tion of *The Extant Works of Aretaeus, the Cappadocian,* trans. Francis Adams (London: The Syndenham Society, 1856), 466.

[182] Hippocrates et Corpus Hippocraticum, *De diaeta I–IV* (Littré, *Oeuvres complètes d'Hippocrate* [Paris: J.-B. Baillière, 1849], 6:35.19–22).

[183] Hippocrates et Corpus Hippocraticum, *De diaeta I–IV* (Littrè, *Oeuvres d'Hippocrate,* 6:59.8–11).

[184] "Having the fixity of law," a technical term in ancient astrology; LSJ, s.v. II.3 (astrol.).

[185] *Paradosis,* a technical term in ancient astrology, which indicates that the influence of planet A is "yielded" to planet B. The term means "chronocratorship," or "the transmission of rulership from one planet to another according to the sequence of periods of life"; O. Neugebauer and H. B. Van Hoesen, *Greek Horoscopes,* Memoirs of the American Philosophical Society 48 (Philadelphia: The Society, 1959), 10. See also A. Bouché-Leclercq, *L'Astrologie grecque* (Paris: Leroux, 1899), 493–94; LSJ, s.v. II.2. (astrol.); *Vettii Valentis anthologiarum libri,* ed. W. Kroll (Berlin: Weidmann, 1908), 382 (Index II: Vocabulorum astrologicorum, s.v.). Ancient astrology was calculated, not observed.

[186] Vettius Valens, *Anthologiae* 5.6.38–39 (*Vettii Valentis Antiocheni anthologiarum libri novem,* ed. David Pingree, Bibliotheca scriptorum Graecorum et Romanorum Teubneriana [Berlin: B. G. Teubner, 1986], 212.31–213.2) (= Kroll, *Vettii Valentis anthologiarum libri IX* 5.9, 223.35–224.3).

5. Galen of Pergamum, Greek physician (ca. 129–199 C.E.), *In Hippocratis librum de articulis et Galeni in eum commentarii* 18a.577.11–13.

τῇ δὲ ἐπιδέσει, ἔστ᾿ ἂν μὲν ἰσχναίνῃς, ἐρηρεισμένῃ *μᾶλλον χρέεσθαι*, ὁκόταν δὲ ἐς τὸν ἀπαλυσμὸν ἄγῃς, ἐπιχαλαρωτέρῃ·

With respect to the bandage, so long as you are reducing [a swelling], [you are] *to use instead* a tightened one; but whenever you cause [the area] to swell up, [rather use] a looser one.[187]

6. Origen, Christian theologian (ca. 185/6–254/5 C.E.), *Philocalia* 27.8.34–39.

ταῦτα δὲ ἡμῖν ἐπὶ τοῦ παρόντος, ὡς ὑπέπεσεν, εἰρήσθω περὶ τοῦ, ᾿Εσκλήρυνε Κύριος τὴν καρδίαν Φαραώ. ἐὰν δέ τις τὸ πρὸς τὸν Θεὸν εὐσεβὲς τηρῶν, κρείττονα, καὶ μηδαμῶς ἀσεβείας ἐφαπτόμενα εὑρίσκῃ, μετὰ μαρτυριῶν τῶν ἀπὸ τῶν θείων Γραφῶν, ἐκείνοις *μᾶλλον χρηστέον*.

For the present let the foregoing, which we put down as it came into our head, suffice for the words, "The Lord hardened Pharaoh's heart" [Exod 9:12; 10:20; 10:27; 11:10; 14:8]. But if anyone with due regard to God's glory should discover better arguments, and such as have no tincture of impiety, and can support them with the evidence of the divine Scriptures, those *must be used instead*.[188]

7. Ps.-John Chrysostom, Christian author (ca. 4th/5th cent. C.E.), *De paenitentia* (*PG* 59.759.1–9).

λέγεις, ποιήσω τὴν ἁμαρτίαν σήμερον, καὶ αὔριον μετανοήσω. κύριος εἶ τῆς αὔριον; τίς σοι τῆς αὔριόν ἐστιν ἐγγυητής; ἐὰν ἀκριβῶς ἀκούσῃς, οὐδὲ ἡ σήμερον ὅλη σή· καὶ τῆς σήμερον τὸ μὲν παρελήλυθε, τὸ δὲ μέλλει· τὸ μὲν οὐκ ἔστι σόν, τὸ δὲ οὔπω σόν. λέγεις· σήμερον ποιήσω τὴν ἡδονήν, καὶ μετανοήσω τῇ αὔριον. ὃ ἔχεις, τῇ ἡδονῇ, τὸ ἀλλότριον, τῇ μετανοίᾳ; ἐμοὶ *μᾶλλον χρῆσαι* συμβούλῳ, τὸ σήμερον τῇ μετανοίᾳ, τῇ δὲ ἁμαρτίᾳ μηδὲ τὸ αὔριον.

You say, "I shall commit sin today, and tomorrow I shall repent." Are you the master of tomorrow? Who is guaranteeing tomorrow for you? If you will listen precisely, all of today does not belong to you. Part of today has come, and part is yet to come. The former does not belong to you, and the latter is not yet yours. You say, "I shall make pleasure today, and repent tomorrow." Do you have one in pleasure and another in repentance? *Instead use* me as a counselor: have today in repentance, and tomorrow have not in sin.

---

[187] Galen, *In Hippocratis librum de articulis et Galeni in eum commentarii* (Kühn, *Claudii Galeni*, 18a.577.11–13) = Hippocrates et Corpus Hippocraticum, *De articulis* (É. Littre, ed., *Oeuvres complètes d'Hippocrates* [Paris: J.-B. Baillière, 1844], 4:50.29–33).

[188] Origen, *Fragmenta ex commentariis in Exodum* (*PG* 12.276.44–46) = Origen, *Philocalia* (Éric Junod, ed., *Origène, Philocalie 21–27: Sur le libre arbitre*, SC 226 [Paris: Cerf, 1976], 27.8.34–39); trans. modified from George Lewis, *The Philocalia of Origen: A Compilation of Selected Passages from Origen's Works Made by St. Gregory of Nazianzus and St. Basil of Caesarea* (Edinburgh: T. & T. Clark, 1911), 233.

8. Eusebius of Caesarea, church historian (ca. 260–340 C.E.), *De ecclesiastica theologia* 2.17.3–4.

διό φησιν καὶ θεὸς ἦν ὁ λόγος, ἵν' ἴδωμεν θεὸν τὸν ἐπὶ πάντων πρὸς ὃν ἦν ὁ λόγος. καὶ θεὸν αὐτὸν τὸν λόγον ἄκουε, ὡς εἰκόνα τοῦ θεοῦ, καὶ εἰκόνα οὐχ ὡς ἐν ἀψύχῳ ὕλῃ, ἀλλ' ὡς ἐν υἱῷ ζῶντι καὶ ἀκριβέστατα πρὸς τὴν ἀρχέτυπον θεότητα τοῦ πατρὸς ἀφωμοιωμένῳ. ἐπεὶ δὲ τῷ ἀνθρωπίνῳ λόγῳ τὸν τοῦ θεοῦ παραβάλλειν ἐδόκει Μαρκέλλῳ, καὶ πόσῳ βελτίω εἶναι φήσομεν, εἰκόνι χρώμενον τῷ ἀνθρωπίνῳ λόγῳ, τούτῳ *μᾶλλον χρήσασθαι* τῷ παραδείγματι καὶ φάναι τοῦ παρ' ἡμῖν λόγου πατέρα εἶναι τὸν νοῦν, ἕτερον ὄντα παρὰ τὸν λόγον.

Therefore he says, "And the *logos* was God" [John 1:1], so that we might understand God to be who is over all, with whom the *logos* was. Listen also to God himself, the *Logos*, as an image of God, and an image not as on lifeless wood, but as in a living son, also most exact with the divine nature, an archetype of the Father by virtue of having been copied. But since it seemed good to Marcellus to compare the *Logos* of God with human *logos*, we indeed say that it is much better for one using human *logos* as an image [of the real *Logos*] *to use* this example *instead*, and to say that the mind [*Nous*] is the Father of the *logos* among us, but that the other one [the real *Logos*] exists beyond the [human] *logos*.[189]

B. *Adversative with Implicit Opposition*

9. Anonyma in ethica Nicomachea commentaria, Aristotelian commentator/compiler (various dates up to the sixth century C.E.), *Heliodori in Ethica Nicomachea paraphrasis* 140.26–29.

ἦν γάρ τις εἰδῇ, ὅτι τοῖς ξηροῖς χρηστέον, μὴ εἰδῇ δὲ ὅτι τάδε ξηρά, οὐδὲν *μᾶλλον χρήσεται* τοῖς ξηροῖς· οὕτω δὴ καὶ ἐπὶ τούτων ἔχει· ἄν τις τῇ καθόλου χρῆται καὶ θεωρῇ, τῇ μερικῇ δὲ οὐ χρῆται, οὐδὲν τῆς ἐπιστήμης ἀπώνατο.

But if someone knows that dry things must be used, but does not know that these are dry things, he *will* not on that account *use* dry things *instead* [of wet things]. Also in these cases it holds: if someone makes use of and has an understanding of the whole, but does not make use of knowledge of the part, then he derives no benefit from his knowledge.[190]

The issue at hand appears to be that the ethical person must know the particular (e.g., such-and-such is a just action; a particular just action ought to be done) as well as the universal (all just actions are to be done). The language is medical. A physician may know the universal (e.g., every dry food is digestible), but not the particular (e.g., this item is dry food, or that item is digestible). The negative οὐδὲν μᾶλλον differs from simply using μᾶλλον: he will not "on that account" or "any more for that" use dry food instead of wet (moist) food. The μᾶλλον χρήσεται grammatical structure creates an implicit opposition.

---

[189] Eusebius, *De ecclesiastica theologia* 2.17.3–4 (E. Klostermann and G. C. Hanson, eds., *Eusebius Werke*, vol. 4, *Gegen Marcell. Über die kirchliche Theologie. Die Fragmente Marcells*, 2d ed., GCS 14 [Berlin: Akademie-Verlag, 1972], 120–21).

[190] Gustavus Heylbut, ed., *Heliodori in ethica Nicomachea paraphrasis*, Commentaria in Aristotelem Graeca 19.2 (Berlin: G. Reimer, 1909), 140.26–29.

10. Galen, *De compositione medicamentorum secundum locos libri X* 13.232.3–6.

ἔνθα δὲ ὅλως οὐδὲν προστίθησιν, ἐπὶ τῶν ἀπυρέτων ἐστὶ μᾶλλον χρηστέον, ὥσπερ γε κἀπειδὰν δι' οἴνου μόνου τὴν χρῆσιν ἢ δι' οἰνομέλιτος ἀξιώσαμεν γενέσθαι, τὰ γὰρ τοιαῦτα τοῖς ἀπυρέτοις ἁρμόττει.

When he [a physician] contributes nothing at all, it is necessary *to use [it] instead* upon nonfeverish people, just as whenever we deem it right to do the application through wine alone or through honeyed wine, for such things are fitting for those who are nonfeverish.[191]

In the sentence structure, the verbal adjective χρηστέον grants the case that precedes it. Galen argues that one medical procedure is to be used more than another in cases of patients free from high fever. This implies hidden opposition: another medical procedure is to be used in cases of feverish patients.

11. Galen, *De compositione medicamentorum per genera libri VII* 13.389.5–9.

εἰ δὲ πλέον ἤδη κατεψυγμένον ἐρυσίπελας ὑπὸ τῶν ἀμέτρως ψυχόντων ἰατρῶν παραλάβοιμεν, ὡς ἤδη καὶ μελαίνεσθαι, τῇ τε καταντλήσει καὶ τῇ ἀποχαράξει *μᾶλλον χρησόμεθα*.

If by this time we should receive from excessively cooling physicians a cooled [patient] and there is still a great deal of erysipelas [reddish eruption on the skin], so that [the area] is already blackened, we *shall use instead* both a douche and an incision.[192]

The "if" clause sets up a condition: If we do all these treatments and the infected area of skin still turns darker, then we use another treatment instead (of continuing with the same procedure). The "if" clause sets up a new condition and instructs to do something new. The sequence of events is (1) sickness, (2) patient gets worse, and (3) new course of treatment.

C. *Comparative with Intensity*

12. Anonyma in Aristotelis artem rhetoricam commentaria, *In Aristotelis artem rhetoricam commentarium* (1418a1), Aristotelian commentator/compiler (various dates).

εἰ καὶ ἐν τοῖς δημηγορικοῖς χρώμεθα τοῖς ἐνθυμήμασιν, ἀλλὰ *μᾶλλον χρώμεθα* τοῖς παραδείγμασι, διότι τῇ δημηγορικῇ οἰκειότερα *μᾶλλον* τὰ παραδείγματα·

Although in our public speaking we make use of enthymemes, we nevertheless *use* paradigms *more (by preference)*, because paradigms are more suited to public speaking.[193]

---

[191] Galen, *De compositione medicamentorum secundum locos libri X* (in *Claudii Galeni opera omnia*, ed. Carolus Gottlob Kühn [Leipzig: Knobloch, 1827], 13.232.3–6).

[192] Galen, *De compositione medicamentorum per genera libri VII* (Kühn, *Claudii Galeni*, 13.389.5–9).

[193] *In Aristotelis artem rhetoricam commentarium* 1418a1 (Hugo Rabe, ed., *Anonymi et Stephani in artem rhetoricam commentaria*, Commentaria in Aristotelem Graeca 21.2 [Berlin: G. Reimer, 1896], 250.14–16).

This case illustrates an adversative use merging into the intensive. The meaning is: "we should use paradigms more than enthymenes." This use differs from the straightforward adversative use in that it does not exclude the alternative — it is not "instead of" — but allows some small use of the alternative (i.e., it means "rather" nonexclusively; "more" than). The ἀλλά goes with the course of action, not with the situation.

13. Aelius Theon of Alexandria, rhetor (ca. 2d cent. C.E.), *Progymnasmata* 178–182 ("On the Fable").

γένοιντο δ' ἂν καὶ ἑνὸς μύθου πλείονες ἐπίλογοι, ἐξ ἑκάστου τῶν ἐν τῷ μύθῳ πραγμάτων τὰς ἀφορμὰς ἡμῶν λαμβανόντων, καὶ ἀνάπαλιν ἑνὸς ἐπιλόγου πάμπολλοι μῦθοι ἀπεικασμένοι αὐτῷ. τὴν γὰρ τοῦ ἐπιλόγου δύναμιν ἁπλῆν προτείναντες προστάξομεν τοῖς νέοις μῦθόν τινα πλάσαι τῷ προτεθέντι πράγματι οἰκεῖον· προχείρως δὲ τοῦτο ποιεῖν δυνήσονται πολλῶν ἐμπλησθέντες μύθων, τοὺς μὲν ἐκ τῶν παλαιῶν συγγραμμάτων ἀνειληφότες, τοὺς δὲ καὶ αὐτοὶ μόνον ἀκούσαντες, τοὺς δὲ καὶ παρ' ἑαυτῶν ἀναπλάσαντες. ἀνασκευάσομεν δὲ καὶ κατασκευάσομεν τοῦτον τὸν τρόπον...

καὶ μὴν καί ὁ ἐκ τοῦ ἀσυμφόρου τόπος σαφής ἐστιν, ᾧ καὶ *μᾶλλον χρησόμεθα* εἰς ἀνασκευὴν τοῦ ἐπιλόγου. οἱ δὲ ἐκ τοῦ ἀνομοίου καὶ τοῦ ψευδοῦς μόνον εἰσὶ τοῦ ἐπιλόγου ἀνασκευαστικοί· ἐκ μὲν οὖν τοῦ ἀνομοίου, ἐπειδὰν τὰ ἐν τῷ μύθῳ κατὰ μηδὲν ἢ μὴ πάντη τῷ ἐπιλόγῳ προσεοικότα ὑπάρχῃ· ἐκ δὲ τοῦ ψευδοῦς, ὅταν μὴ κατὰ πᾶν συμβαίνῃ, ὥς φησιν ὁ μυθογράφος, ὅτι οἱ τῶν πλειόνων ὀρεγόμενοι καὶ τῶν ὄντων στερίσκονται· οὐ γὰρ ἀεὶ τοῦτο ἀληθές ἐστιν.

And there can be several epilogues [or "punch lines"] for one fable, since we take our starting points from individual points in the fable. And vice versa: there can be for one epilogue numerous fables that fit it, for after we have provided the simple meaning of the epilogue, we shall instruct the young students to fashion a fable that is suitable to the proposed subject. And they will be able to do this exercise easily since they have been crammed with many fables, having taken some from ancient writings, having themselves only heard others, and having fashioned still others on their own. We shall "refute" and "confirm" in this way. ...

Now then, the commonplace argument made on the basis of "disadvantageousness" is clear. This commonplace we *shall use* even *more (preferably)* in refutation of the epilogue. But the refutative commonplaces based on "dissimilarity" and "falsehood" relate only to the epilogue. So then, "dissimilarity" is when the details in the fable are totally irrelevant to the epilogue, or whenever they do not fit in the epilogue as a whole. "Falsity" is when the epilogue is not universally applicable, as when the fable writer says, "Those who yearn for more things lose even what they have"; for this statement is not always true.[194]

Aelius teaches that in the refutation of a fable a rhetorician can use the commonplace arguments based on its "disadvantageousness," "dissimilarity," and/

---

[194] Aelius Theon, *Progymnasmata* 178–82 (Leondari Spengel, ed., *Rhetores Graeci* [Leipzig: B. G. Teubner, 1854], 2:75.27–76.6 and 77.27–78.3); trans. modified from James R. Butts, "The Progymnasmata of Theon: A New Text with Translation and Commentary" (Ph.D. diss., Claremont Graduate School, 1986), 269, 275–76. Butts translates the μᾶλλον χρησόμεθα clause into "we will use particularly" (275).

or "falsehood." Yet in the particular case of refuting the epilogue, one should use the "disadvantageous" commonplace argument more preferably than using either the "dissimilarity" or "falsehood" commonplace arguments. This passage, like example 12, illustrates how the adversative merges into the intensive, with opposition remaining in the lexical environment. In this instance, the conjunction καί goes with the course of action, not with the situation.

14. Ps.-Herodianus, Atticist author (ca. 2d cent. C.E.), *Philetaerus* 88.1–5.

τὸ ἀρέσκει ῥῆμα οὐ μόνον τῇ αἰτιατικῇ πτώσει συντάττουσιν, οἷον ἀρέσκει με τόδε καὶ οὐκ ἀρέσκει με, ἀλλὰ καὶ τῇ δοτικῇ. καὶ ὁ Δημοσθένης· "εἰ μὲν ἤρεσκέ τί μοι τῶν ὑπὸ τούτων ῥηθέντων." ὧι καὶ *μᾶλλον χρηστέον*.

They construct a pleasing phrase not only in the accusative case, the sort that is both pleasing and not pleasing to me, but also in the dative case. So Demosthenes said, "If I were pleased by any of the things that were said by them" [Dem. 4.1 (*First Philippic*), in LCL 1:68], which is *to be used* even *more (preferably)*.[195]

The author argues that the rhetorician can construct a "pleasing phrase" either in the accusative or dative cases. Yet if a certain Greek construction is naturally pleasing in the dative, then it is more preferable to use the dative and less preferable to use the accusative. As in the previous two examples, the adversative use here merges into the intensive. Again, the καί goes with the course of action, not with the situation.

D. *Intensive*

15. Dionysius of Halicarnassus, Roman rhetor (fl. 7 B.C.E.), 11.41.3.1–4.1.

ἔπειτ' ἐκεῖνοι μὲν ἑνὸς οὐκ ἤνεγκαν ἀκολάστου μειρακίου τυραννικὴν ὕβριν εἰς ἓν σῶμα ἐλεύθερον γενομένην, ὑμεῖς δὲ πολυκέφαλον τυραννίδα πάσῃ παρανομίᾳ τε καὶ ἀσελγείᾳ χρωμένην καὶ ἔτι *μᾶλλον χρησομένην*, ἐὰν νῦν ἀνάσχησθε, ὑπομενεῖτε;

Then, when they refused to bear the tyrannical outrage committed by one licentious youth upon one free person, will you tolerate a many-headed tyranny that indulges in every sort of crime and licentiousness and *will indulge* still *more* in it if you now submit to it?[196]

Dionysius uses an *a fortiore* argument, drawing a conclusion that is inferred to be even more certain than another. The rhetor demonstrates his point with a moral *exemplum* from a past golden age, recalling a time when citizens refused to tolerate the licentiousness of even one delinquent, a juvenile at that. Dionysius argues that if citizens nowadays continue their toleration of a "many-headed" tyranny, then their suffering under tyranny is even more (μᾶλλον) certain to increase than to decrease.

---

[195] Ps.-Herodianus, *Philetaerus* (A. Dain, ed., *Le "Philétaeros" attribué à Hérodien* [Paris: Les Belles Lettres, 1954], 88.1–5).

[196] Dion. Hal. 11.41.3.1–4.1; I have slightly changed the LCL translation.

16. Aspasius, Peripatetic philosopher (ca. 100–150 C.E.), *In ethica Nicomachea commentaria* 123.21–23.

ὁ γὰρ ἐν οἷς μηδὲν διαφέρει ἀληθεύων, δῆλον ὅτι ἐν οἷς διαφέρει *μᾶλλον* χρήσεται τῇ ἀληθείᾳ.

For who speaks the truth in things that do not matter clearly *will use* the truth *more* in things when it matters.[197]

Aspasius, like Dionysius, uses an *a fortiori* argument. The philosopher argues that if someone tells the truth in mundane matters, then it is even more certain that he or she will tell the truth in critical matters. If one situation (everyday speech) calls for a particular action (telling the truth), then that same situation heightened (crucial speech) calls for the same action (telling the truth) only more so (μᾶλλον).

17. Iamblichus, Neoplatonist philosopher (ca. 250–325 C.E.), *Protrepticus* 11.

οὐκοῦν τό γε χρῆσθαι παντὶ τοῦτ' ἐστίν, ὅταν εἰ μὲν ἑνὸς ἡ δύναμίς ἐστι, τοῦτο αὐτὸ πράττῃ τις, εἰ δὲ πλειόνων τὸν ἀριθμόν, ὃ ἂν τούτων τὸ βέλτιστον, οἷον αὐλοῖς, ἤτοι μόνον ὅταν αὐλῇ χρῆταί τις ἢ μάλιστα· ἴσως γὰρ τοῦτο καὶ ἐπὶ τῶν ἄλλων. οὐκοῦν καὶ *μᾶλλον* χρῆσθαι τὸν ὀρθῶς χρώμενον φατέον· τὸ γὰρ ἐφ' ὃ καὶ ὡς πέφυκεν ὑπάρχειν τῷ χρωμένῳ καλῶς καὶ ἀκριβῶς.

Wherefore "use" or "the useful" is predicated of anything when, the capacity existing, someone brings it into activity; but if he deals with many things he will use the best of them as, for instance, if one uses flutes, he will play only or at least mostly with the best. Moreover, to this other things are similar. Therefore, it must be said that he or she *uses* rightly, who uses it *more or to greater degree*. For he or she who uses anything rightly and accurately knows how to use it in the manner and for the purpose to which it is naturally adapted.[198]

The μᾶλλον intensifies χρῆσθαι: "He or she who uses a thing rightly and accurately uses it to a greater degree." The Neoplatonist's discussion of "right use" has relevance to Paul's concept of *chrēsis*, or "proper use" of situations as Christians.[199]

---

[197] Aspasius, *In ethica Nichomachea commentaria* (*Aspasii in ethica Nicomachea quae supersunt commentaria*, ed. Gustavus Heylbut, Commentaria in Aristotelem Graeca 19.1 [Berlin: G. Reimer, 1889], 123.21–23).

[198] Iambl. *Protr.* 11 (*Jamblique: Protreptique*, ed. Édouard Des Places, Collection des Universités de France [Paris: Les Belles Lettres, 1989], 87.15–21, which slightly alters the previous critical edition of H. Pistelli, ed., *Iamblichi protrepticus ad fidem codicis Florentini* [Leipzig: B. G. Teubner, 1888], 57.23–58.3); see *Iamblichus: The Exhortation to Philosophy*, trans. Thomas Moore Johnson, ed. Stephen Neuville (Grand Rapids, Mich.: Phanes Press, 1988), 58.

[199] On *chrēsis* as a *topos* in ancient literature, see G. Redard, "Recherches sur XPH, XPHΣΘAI: Étude sémantique," in *Bibliothèque: Sciences historiques et philologiques*, fasc. 303, ed. L'École practique des hautes études (Paris: Librarie Ancienne Honoré Champion, 1953), 11–47; Christian Gnilka, *XPHΣIΣ: Die Methode der Kirchenväter im Umgang mit der antiken Kultur. I. Der Begriff des "rechten Gebrauchs,"* Westfälische Wilhelms-Universität, Münster Institut für Missionswissenschaft (Stuttgart: Schwabe, 1984), esp. 29–43, 102–121.

Application of Results

The results of this philological study demonstrate the adversative use of the adverb μᾶλλον with the deponent verb χράομαι. Categories A, B, and C are more prevalent and expected. In A, B, and C, two different, or opposing, situations are described. The μᾶλλον is adversative ("instead" or "preferably"), directing a new course (A and B) or a new mode (C) of action now that the situation has changed. Category D differs from A, B, or C in that there the authors describe two *similar* situations, only the second is more intense. The μᾶλλον, then, is intensive ("even more"), directing the same course of action as before, with greater forcefulness.

These findings can now be applied to our crux: δοῦλος ἐκλήθης, μή σοι μελέτω· ἀλλ' εἰ καὶ δύνασαι ἐλεύθερος γενέσθαι, μᾶλλον χρῆσαι, which I translate as "You were called as a slave. Do not worry about it. But if you can indeed become free, *use instead* [freedom]." Because Paul sets up a contrast, I argue that the construction in 1 Cor 7:21b is most like category A (adversative with explicit opposition). Yet Paul contrasts *μᾶλλον χρῆσαι* not with the situation ("if also you can indeed become free"), but with another course of action ("do not worry about it"). In the first sentence, the protasis is δοῦλος ἐκλήθης, and the apodosis is μή σοι μελέτω. In the second sentence, the protasis is ἀλλ' εἰ καὶ δύνασαι ἐλεύθερος γενέσθαι, and the apodosis is *μᾶλλον χρῆσαι*. The adverb *μᾶλλον* is adversative not to its protasis ("if you can indeed become free"), but to the previous apodosis ("do not worry about it"). A different situation calls for a different course of action. If manumission *is* offered, then the slave *should* be concerned. Manumission places new responsibilities upon the Christian slave. In the first situation, being a slave, Paul directs one course of action and tells the slave *not* to be concerned and to "use slavery instead" (of worrying about becoming free). In the second situation, becoming free through manumission, Paul directs a different course of action and orders the slave *to be concerned* and to "use freedom instead" (of remaining a slave). The "if" clause of 7:21 sets up the second situation. Paul directs the person in the second situation to a different course of action ("use your becoming free instead").

One might argue, however, that the contrast is not with μή σοι μελέτω but rather with ἐν ταύτῃ μενέτω (v. 20); according to this alternative interpretation, the μή σοι μελέτω prepares for v. 22a, with the latter sentence giving the reason why the slave need not be concerned. In support of this reading, an exegete disagreeing with my thesis could point to how the exception of v. 15 refers back to vv. 12–13. In response, I argue that no compelling reason exists in the text for us to look beyond the verse to find the clause contrasted. The burden of proof lies with those who object to solutions found within 1 Cor 7:21 itself.

The closest parallel to 1 Cor 7:21 is example 4, from the second-century professional astrologer from Antioch, Vettius Valens. In his work, Vettius also sets up two situations: one having a successfully calculated astrological *paradosis*, and the other not. Vettius then presents his reader two different courses of action, depending on which situation is applicable. If a particular calculation works, then use it; if it fails to work, then do not use it and resort to another number. Vettius's first protasis is καὶ ἐὰν μὲν εὐρεθῇ ἔχων παράδοσιν ("and if it is found having a 'yielding' [*paradosis*]"), and his first apodosis is ἐκείνῳ μᾶλλον χρῆσθαι ("we must use that number instead"). His second protasis is εἰ δὲ μὴ εὐρεθῇ ("but if [a *paradosis*] is not found"), and his second apodosis is ἐξ ἀνάγκης ἐπὶ τοῦτον κατελευσόμεθα ("out of necessity we shall resort to this number"). The μᾶλλον is adversative not to the first protasis, but to the second apodosis. A different situation calls for a different course of action.

We have seen three solutions that commentators offer to complete the μᾶλλον χρῆσαι brachylogy of 1 Cor 7:21: (1) "use your becoming free," (2) "use your being a slave," or (3) "use your calling (in Christ)." Of these, only the first has philological support. The μᾶλλον contrasts not with the present situation ("if you can indeed become free"), but with another stated course of action (different from "do not worry about it"). At first glance, the καί presents the only possible textual support for the "use slavery" interpretation. Curiously, the only element of the passage without universal textual support is this καί, which is lacking in three witnesses (F G a). If Paul wrote καί in his autograph (admittedly, a supposition that may not necessarily hold), these witnesses perhaps reflect scribal redaction to favor the "use freedom" interpretation by intentional omission. Yet it is unlikely that scribes omitted the καί deliberately to support an interpretation that was, at best, a minority reading at the time. It is much more likely that the word was omitted by accident.

The lexical problem is as follows. If used as an adverb, καί appears to make the sentence read: "but *even* [καί] if you can become free, rather use your being a slave."[200] Although there are instances where Paul combines εἰ and καί to mean "although" or "even if" (e.g., 2 Cor 7:8a; 4:3, 16), there are also counterexamples in which Paul uses the same combination to mean "if indeed," with καί serving not as an adverb, but an emphatic particle.[201] Gordon Fee argues that "[t]he normal Pauline sense of the combination *ei kai* is not 'even though,' but 'if indeed.'"[202] He points to three examples.

---

[200] Baumert, *Ehelosigkeit*, 123; *pace* Bartchy, *ΜΑΛΛΟΝ ΧΡΗΣΑΙ*, 3 n. 8, who argues that the καί is grammatically insignificant.

[201] Thrall, *Greek Particles*, 79–81. On this emphatic particle usage, see J. D. Denniston, *The Greek Particles*, 2d ed. (Oxford: Clarendon Press, 1954), 303–5.

[202] Fee, *Corinthians*, 317.

τί δὲ ἔχεις ὃ οὐκ ἔλαβες; εἰ δὲ καὶ ἔλαβες, τί καυχᾶσαι ὡς μὴ λαβών;
What do you have that you did not receive? And *if indeed* you have received it, why do you boast as if it were not a gift? (1 Cor 4:7)

ἐὰν δὲ καὶ χωρισθῇ, μενέτω ἄγαμος ἢ τῷ ἀνδρὶ καταλλαγήτω.
But *if indeed* she does separate, let her remain unmarried or else be reconciled to her husband. (1 Cor 7:11)

δέδεσαι γυναικί, μὴ ζήτει λύσιν· λέλυσαι ἀπὸ γυναικός, μὴ ζήτει γυναῖκα. ἐὰν δὲ καὶ γαμήσῃς, οὐχ ἥμαρτες.
You are bound to a wife, do not seek to be released. You are released from a wife, do not seek a wife. But *if indeed* you marry, you do not sin. (1 Cor 7:27–28)

Fee, I believe, is correct. Nevertheless, he could have presented a more compelling argument if he had also demonstrated, as Norbert Baumert has done, that in the other instances where Paul combines εἰ and καί to mean "although" (2 Cor 7:8a; 4:3, 16), the construction remains adversative. Pauline usage of εἰ plus καί is always in opposition to what was said before.[203] We should also note the proximity of two of Fee's examples (1 Cor 7:11; 7:27–28) to my text.

In addition, Sophocles offers two informative parallels. In different tragedies, he writes:

εἰ καὶ δυνήσει γ'· ἀλλ' ἀμηχάνων ἐρᾷς.
If you shall also be able; but you desire impossibilities. (*Antigone* 90)

δεινόν γ' εἶπας, εἰ καὶ ζῆς θανών.
A strange thing have you uttered, if, though slain, you indeed live. (*Ajax* 1127)

In both examples, the καί of εἰ καί goes closely with the following word.[204] The meaning is either *also* (as in the first instance) or *indeed* (as in the second). Note that *Antigone* 90 contains εἰ καὶ δυνήσει, a protasis remarkably similar to Paul's in 7:21b.

Thus, the presence of καί in 1 Cor 7:21 strengthens, not weakens, my philological argument, which is that μᾶλλον with χράομαι carries the adversative sense. Yet it is important to remember that the μᾶλλον is adversative not with respect to its protasis ("if you can *indeed* become free"), but with respect to the previous apodosis ("do not worry about it"). Paul exhorts the slave facing this different situation to be concerned and take a different option ("use *instead* [freedom]").

---

[203] Baumert, *Ehelosigkeit*, 123–24; Denniston, *Greek Particles*, 303–5; and Thrall, *Greek Particles*, 78–82, 86–91. However, Thrall, 80–81, writes that because, unlike in 1 Cor 4:7; 7:11, 28, the connecting particle in 1 Cor 7:21 is not δέ but ἀλλά, "the alternative interpretation of εἰ καί as 'although' is to be preferred." I side with Baumert.

[204] Richard Jebb, *Sophocles: Plays and Fragments*, part 3, *The Antigone*, 3d ed. (1900; reprint, Amsterdam: Adolf M. Hakkert, 1962), 26 n. 90; Smyth, *Greek Grammar*, 538 §2377. I thank Margaret M. Mitchell for drawing my attention to this important paragraph in Smyth.

The seventeen philological examples illustrate the tendency of the adverb μᾶλλον to have an adversative meaning (categories A, B, and C), when an author describes two *different* situations. The strictly intensive meaning of μᾶλλον (category D) occurs only when an author describes two *similar* situations. In 7:21b Paul presents two different situations: slavery and manumission. These examples of μᾶλλον + χράομαι in ancient Greek literature, therefore, help us understand what Paul means. The Apostle tells the slave facing a different situation (specifically, an offer of manumission) to "*use* freedom *instead.*" When these texts are laid alongside *P. Oxy.* 16.1865 furnished by C. H. Dodd, who argued that in effect supplying the object of χρῆσαι from the sense of δύνασαι exactly parallels supplying it from the sense of ἐξῆν, we confront an accumulation of compelling arguments heavily favoring the "use freedom" interpretation.[205]

Contextual Analysis

The philological conclusion above leaves a further question: whether the overriding force of Paul's blanket statement for each Christian "to remain" excludes the reading of "use freedom instead." Does the context clearly mandate a reading that goes contrary to these lexical findings?

To be sure, the constant refrain of 7:17–24 is indeed the imperative, styled as diatribe, to let each walk or live (v. 17; περιπατείτω) as the Lord has assigned, and to let each remain (v. 20; μενέτω) in the calling in which each was called (ἐν τῇ κλήσει, ᾗ ἐκλήθη). Because it contradicts Paul's overarching concern that every Christian abide in his or her original, baptized calling, many commentators consider the reading "use freedom" implausible.[206] According to their argument, Paul exhorts converted slaves to remain forever slaves; even if faced with liberation prospects, slaves must rather "use slavery." To a society in which social conservatives practiced and favored selective manumission on an individual basis to deserving slaves, such an admonition would have been exceedingly radical, unparalleled in extant ancient literature.[207] If his inten-

---

[205] Dodd, "Notes," 77–78. See also the New Testament parallels in Llewelyn, "'If You Can Gain,'" 63–70.

[206] Heinrici, *Erste Brief an die Korinther*, 231–33; Barrett, *First Epistle to the Corinthians*, 170–71; Conzelmann, *Erste Brief an die Korinther*, 160–61; Grant, *Early Christianity and Society*, 90; idem, *Augustus to Constantine*, 56, 269; Meeks, *Writings of St. Paul*, 33 n. 4.

[207] The only possible parallel would be Sen. *Ep.* 47.18, where Seneca anticipates criticism of his exhortation for humane treatment of slaves: "Some may maintain that I am now offering the liberty-cap [*pileus*] to slaves in general and am toppling down masters from their high rank [*fastigium*]." While he clearly does not advocate emancipation or even large-scale manumission, Seneca is not saying that all slaves must remain slaves. He like all

tion was to halt the manumission of baptized slaves, Paul would have been an oddball in his own cultural milieu. While it is true that Paul does indeed say radical things (in keeping with his eschatological outlook that the parousia was imminent), it seems unlikely that he is saying baptized slaves should never be manumitted. Although one might agree here with Heinz Bellen that Paul espouses an ascetic principle, there is no evidence that self-denial of opportunities for manumission was considered an ascetic act. Indeed, seizing such opportunities for liberation would have enabled a slave to escape a master's violent coercion and, as a freedman/woman, to secure more control over his or her own body and daily activities to pursue asceticism. A contextual exegesis strengthens the clear philological-lexical comparative evidence that the correct translation of the verse is: "if indeed you can become free, then use instead (of your slavery) your freedom."

The first step in such an exegesis is to delineate the text. Bracketed by similar clauses in 1 Cor 7:20 and 24, an *inclusio* is immediately apparent:

> 20. ἕκαστος ἐν τῇ κλήσει ᾗ ἐκλήθη, ἐν ταύτῃ μενέτω.
> 21. δοῦλος ἐκλήθης, μή σοι μελέτω·
> ἀλλ' εἰ καὶ δύνασαι ἐλεύθερος γενέσθαι,
> μᾶλλον χρῆσαι [ἐλευθερίᾳ].
> 22. ὁ γὰρ ἐν κυρίῳ κληθεὶς δοῦλος ἀπελεύθερος κυρίου ἐστίν,
> ὁμοίως ὁ ἐλεύθερος κληθεὶς δοῦλός ἐστιν Χριστοῦ.
> 23. τιμῆς ἠγοράσθητε·
> μὴ γίνεσθε δοῦλοι ἀνθρώπων.
> 24. ἕκαστος ἐν ᾧ ἐκλήθη, ἀδελφοί, ἐν τούτῳ μενέτω παρὰ θεῷ.

> 20. Let each of you remain in the condition in which you were called.
> 21. You were called as a *slave*. Do not worry about it.
> But if you can indeed become *free*,
> use instead [freedom].
> 22. For whoever is called in the Lord as a *slave* is a freedman/woman of the Lord, just as whoever was *free* when called is a slave of Christ.
> 23. You were bought with a price;
> Do not become slaves of human masters.
> 24. In whatever condition you were called, brothers and sisters, there remain with God. (NRSV, slightly altered and emphasis added)

Roman social conservatives believed that manumission was efficacious. *Humanitas* of slaveholders in both the treatment and manumission of their slaves served to reinforce the institution itself, not to weaken it. Finley, *Ancient Slavery and Modern Ideology*, 121; Keith R. Bradley, "Seneca and Slavery," *C & M* 37 (1986): 166; Miriam T. Griffin, *Seneca, a Philosopher in Politics* (Oxford: Clarendon Press, 1976), 278 (called an "overstatement" by Bradley, "Seneca and Slavery," 166 n. 8); William Watts, "Seneca on Slavery," *Downside Review* 90 (1972): 184; Will Richter, "Seneca und die Sklaven," *Gymnasium* 65 (1958): 211 n. 42 (Richter soft-pedals the evidence at times, dancing around the main point that Seneca never attacked slavery itself, only corrupt masters). I discuss the Augustan legislation (*lex Fulfia Caninia, lex Aelia Sentia, lex Junia*), which restricted (N.B., not prohibited) manumission, in chapter 4.

Κλῆσις ("calling") refers to the situation and circumstances in which one was called at the time of baptism. Although Paul does use κλῆσις in other places to mean the general Christian "vocation" to belong to Christ (1 Cor 1:26; Phil 3:14) or God's "calling" of Israel (Rom 11:29), the specific examples chosen in chapter 7 – marriage, circumcision, slavery – make the alternative, setting-in-life meaning of κλῆσις clear in this *inclusio*.[208] Paul must have written this paragraph to be read as a unit, whose principal target audience was any (and all) slave member(s) of the Corinthian congregation. The indentations in the above schematic diagram of 1 Cor 7:20–24 show my view of ἀλλ᾽ εἰ καὶ δύνασαι ἐλεύθερος γενέσθαι, μᾶλλον χρῆσαι as an exception to Paul's general rule to remain in one's baptismal κλῆσις.

Within the larger context (1 Cor 6:20–7:40), marriage serves as Paul's principal theme. Commentators have often wondered why Paul chose to voice advice on slavery in the midst of his wider discussion of marriage. A partial answer may lie in the social position of slaves in antiquity: they could not legally marry. Paul's entire response to the Corinthian congregation on marriage, therefore, has little relevance to slaves, unless Paul recognized that full enfranchisement enabled them to contract a legal marriage. It is no accident, then, that Paul placed the question of manumission in his larger discussion of marriage. Because manumission was the institutional practice in Roman urban society (and Paul mainly visited Romanized cities), the Apostle must have been well aware of its effects. Paul has three kinds of auditors in mind: (1) the unmarried and widows (οἱ ἄγαμοι καὶ αἱ χῆραι; 1 Cor 7:8); (2) the married and separated (οἱ γεγαμηκότες, χωρισθῇ; 7:10, 11); and (3) the "rest" (λοιποί; 1 Cor 7:12), which includes both those married to an unbeliever (7:12–16) and those not empowered to marry at all unless enfranchised (7:21–23).

Understanding the composition of Paul's three target groups helps answer an objection to the "use freedom" reading that many commentators often raise. Why, they ask, would Paul grant an exception for slaves? Yet one can immediately see that Paul grants other exceptions. For example,

7:10. Τοῖς δὲ γεγαμηκόσιν παραγγέλλω, οὐκ ἐγὼ ἀλλὰ ὁ κύριος, γυναῖκα ἀπὸ ἀνδρὸς μὴ χωρισθῆναι,
    11. – ἐὰν δὲ καὶ χωρισθῇ, μενέτω ἄγαμος ἢ τῷ ἀνδρὶ καταλλαγήτω, –
καὶ ἄνδρα γυναῖκα μὴ ἀφιέναι.

7:10. To married I give this command – not I but the Lord – that the wife should not separate from her husband
    11. (*but if* she does separate, *let her remain* unmarried *or else be reconciled* to her husband),
and that the husband should not divorce his wife. (NRSV, emphasis added)

---

[208] Dawes, "'But If You Can Gain,'" 684 n. 17; *pace* Bartchy, *ΜΑΛΛΟΝ ΧΡΗΣΑΙ*, 135–37. See also Lightfoot, *Notes*, 228–29; Fee, *Corinthians*, 314; Wimbush, *Paul*, 15–16 n. 12; Callahan, "Note," 111.

Paul grants an exception for women who separate from their husbands, despite his general principle, backed up by a dominical saying (7:10), of remaining married. Another exception is found in 1 Cor 7:15:

12. Τοῖς δὲ λοιποῖς λέγω ἐγώ οὐχ ὁ κύριος· εἴ τις ἀδελφὸς γυναῖκα ἔχει ἄπιστον καὶ αὕτη συνευδοκεῖ οἰκεῖν μετ' αὐτοῦ, μὴ ἀφιέτω αὐτήν·
13. καὶ γυνὴ εἴ τις ἔχει ἄνδρα ἄπιστον καὶ οὗτος συνευδοκεῖ οἰκεῖν μετ' αὐτῆς, μὴ ἀφιέτω τὸν ἄνδρα.
14. ἡγίασται γὰρ ὁ ἀνὴρ ὁ ἄπιστος ἐν τῇ γυναικὶ καὶ ἡγίασται ἡ γυνὴ ἡ ἄπιστος ἐν τῷ ἀδελφῷ· ἐπεὶ ἄρα τὰ τέκνα ὑμῶν ἀκάθαρτά ἐστιν, νῦν δὲ ἅγιά ἐστιν.
15. *εἰ δὲ ὁ ἄπιστος χωρίζεται,*
χωριζέσθω·
οὐ δεδούλωται ὁ ἀδελφὸς ἢ ἡ ἀδελφὴ ἐν τοῖς τοιούτοις·
ἐν δὲ εἰρήνῃ κέκληκεν ὑμᾶς ὁ θεός.
16. τί γὰρ οἶδας, γύναι, εἰ τὸν ἄνδρα σώσεις; ἢ τί οἶδας, ἄνερ, εἰ τὴν γυναῖκα σώσεις;

12. To the rest I say – I and not the Lord – that if any believer has a wife who is an unbeliever, and she consents to live with him, he should not divorce her.
13. And if any woman has a husband who is an unbeliever, and he consents to live with her, she should not divorce him.
14. For the unbelieving husband is made holy through his wife, and the unbelieving wife is made holy through her husband. Otherwise, your children would be unclean, but as it is, they are holy.
15. *But if* the unbelieving partner separates,
let it be so;
in such a case the brother or sister is not bound.
It is to peace that God has called you.
16. Wife, for all you know, you might save your husband. Husband, for all you know, you might save your wife. (NRSV, emphasis added)

The Christian spouse should not separate from an unbelieving spouse. Yet Paul concedes cases where separation is permissible: "In such cases, the brother or sister is not bound." Then the Apostle returns to his general principle, stating that if the marriage survives, the possibility remains that the Christian spouse may convert the unbelieving partner.

In 1 Cor 7:28 and 36 we encounter additional Pauline exceptions to a general rule. Paul writes:

27. δέδεσαι γυναικί, μὴ ζήτει λύσιν· λέλυσαι ἀπὸ γυναικός, μὴ ζήτει γυναῖκα.
28. *ἐὰν δὲ καὶ γαμήσῃς, οὐχ ἥμαρτες,*
καὶ ἐὰν γήμῃ ἡ παρθένος, οὐχ ἥμαρτεν·
θλῖψιν δὲ τῇ σαρκὶ ἕξουσιν οἱ τοιοῦτοι, ἐγὼ δὲ ὑμῶν φείδομαι.
29. Τοῦτο δέ φημι, ἀδελφοί, ὁ καιρὸς συνεσταλμένος ἐστίν· τὸ λοιπόν, ἵνα καὶ οἱ ἔχοντες γυναῖκας ὡς μὴ ἔχοντες ὦσιν ...

36. *Εἰ δέ τις ἀσχημονεῖν ἐπὶ τὴν παρθένον αὐτοῦ νομίζει,*
ἐὰν ᾖ ὑπέρακμος καὶ οὕτως ὀφείλει γίνεσθαι,
ὃ θέλει *ποιείτω,*
οὐχ ἁμαρτάνει, γαμείτωσαν.
37. ὃς δὲ ἕστηκεν ἐν τῇ καρδίᾳ αὐτοῦ ἑδραῖος μὴ ἔχων

ἀνάγκην, ἐξουσίαν δὲ ἔχει περὶ τοῦ ἰδίου θελήματος καὶ τοῦτο κέκρικεν ἐν τῇ ἰδίᾳ καρδίᾳ, τηρεῖν τὴν ἑαυτοῦ παρθένον, καλῶς ποιήσει.

38. ὥστε καὶ ὁ γαμίζων τὴν ἑαυτοῦ παρθένον καλῶς ποιεῖ καὶ ὁ μὴ γαμίζων κρεῖσσον ποιήσει.

27. Are you bound to a wife? Do not seek to be free. Are you free from a wife? Do not seek a wife.
    28. *But if* you marry, you do not sin,
    and if a virgin marries, she does not sin.
    Yet those who marry will experience distress in this life, and I would spare you that.
    29. I mean, brothers and sisters, the appointed time has grown short; from now on, let even those who have wives be as though they had none. …

    36. *If* anyone thinks that he is not behaving properly toward his financée,
    if his passions are strong, and so it has to be,
    let him marry as he wishes;
    it is no sin. Let them marry.
    37. But if someone stands firm in his resolve, being under no necessity but having his own desire under control, and has determined in his own mind to keep her as his financée, he will do well.
    38. So then, he who marries his financée does well; and he who refrains from marriage will do better. (NRSV, emphasis added)

Christian virgins are to remain virgins (unmarried). Yet Paul offers an exception to the virgins who marry: they "do not sin." Christian fiancés are to restrain their erotic impulses and not marry. Yet, again, Paul grants an exception to the fiancé who has strong passions: "let him marry as he wishes." The Apostle then returns to his general principle that one does best to refrain from marriage.

Paul continues with a further exception, this time for widows:

39. Γυνὴ δέδεται ἐφ' ὅσον χρόνον ζῇ ὁ ἀνὴρ αὐτῆς·
    ἐὰν δὲ κοιμηθῇ ὁ ἀνήρ,
    ἐλευθέρα ἐστὶν ᾧ θέλει *γαμηθῆναι*,
        μόνον ἐν κυρίῳ.
40. μακαριωτέρα δέ ἐστιν ἐὰν οὕτως μείνῃ, κατὰ τὴν ἐμὴν γνώμην· δοκῶ δὲ κἀγὼ πνεῦμα θεοῦ ἔχειν.

39. A wife is bound as long as her husband lives.
    But if the husband dies,
    she is free *to marry* anyone she wishes,
        only in the Lord.
40. But in my judgment she is more blessed if she remains as she is. And I think that I too have the Spirit of God. (NRSV, emphasis added)

A Christian wife is bound to her husband. Paul, however, grants an exception in the case of the husband's death, acknowledging the social reality that Roman wives often outlived their husbands, since marriage for women was in their early teens and for men in their early twenties.[209] Yet, after granting this exception, he returns to his general rule, holding that Christian widows *should*, but not *must*, remain unmarried. This exhortation is similar to Roman praise of an aristocratic woman who lived *univira* (a one-husband woman).[210]

Summation

In all the examples, the protases, or εἰ (ἐάν) clauses, imitate the rhetorical style found in the second protasis of 7:21 (ἀλλ᾽ εἰ καί). Likewise, their apodoses use imperatives – μενέτω, καταλλαγήτω and χωριζέσθω, ποιείτω (and, by extension, of the infinitive γαμηθῆναι) – paralleling the use of the imperative χρῆσαι in 7:21. Indeed, 7:11, 15, 21, 28, 36, and 39 share common rhetorical elements of a Pauline exception clause, each with an analogous protasis (if *X*) and apodosis (then *Y*). The protasis sets up a new situation; the apodosis calls for a new course of action, given this new situation. In sum, the context does not exclude the "use freedom" interpretation. To the contrary, this reading naturally fits Paul's argumentative and rhetorical structure in 1 Cor 7 of granting particular exceptions to general principles.

One might still object that the immediate context, 7:17–24, mentions slavery as a parallel to circumcision and that Paul grants no exception in the latter case. The logic follows, one might argue, that slavery likewise brings no exception; every Christian slave must remain a slave, even if capable of becom-

---

[209] Keith Hopkins, "The Age of Roman Girls at Marriage," *Population Studies* 18 (1965): 309–27; Ronald Syme, "Marriage Ages for Roman Senators," *Historia* 36 (1987): 318–32; Richard Saller, "Men's Age at Marriage and Its Consequences in the Roman Family," *CP* 82 (1987): 21–34 (aristocratic men married in their early twenties); Brent D. Shaw, "The Age of Girls at Marriage: Some Reconsiderations," *JRS* 77 (1987): 30–46. Although the marrying ages of people below the senatorial and equestrian orders were older (nonaristocratic men commonly married in their late twenties or thirties), the evidence still suggests a significant age differential between spouses: namely, younger women wedded much older men. For the marrying ages of Jews, see P. W. van der Horst, *Ancient Jewish Epitaphs: An Introductory Survey of a Millennium of Jewish Funerary Epigraphy (300 B.C.E.–700 C.E.*, Contributions to Biblical Exegesis 2 (Kampen, The Netherlands: Kok Pharos, 1991), 103–5.

[210] Erik Wistrand, *The So-Called Laudatio Turiae: Introduction, Text, Translation, and Commentary*, Studia Graeca et Latina Gothoburgensia 24 (Gothenburg: Acta Universitatis Gothoburgensis, 1976), 19–31. *CIL* 13.2056 (for Hadrian's mother-in-law Matidia) and 14.3579.23 (for a certain Asmilia Valeria) both mention continuance in a widowed state as particularly praiseworthy, as the women commemorated were each young and attractive when their husbands died; Susan Treggiari, *Roman Marriage: Iusti Coniuges from the Time of Cicero to the Time of Ulpian* (Oxford: Clarendon Press, 1991), 499; Keith R. Bradley, *Discovering the Roman Family: Studies in Roman Social History* (New York: Oxford University Press, 1991), 129, 156–76.

ing free. Yet Paul himself understands differences between circumcision and slavery. The two are not precisely parallel cases. To the circumcised at the time of the baptismal call, Paul enjoins, "*Let him not seek* to remove the marks of circumcision" (7:18); to the uncircumcised at the time of the baptismal call, Paul similarly forbids, "*Let him not seek* circumcision." But to one called as slave at the time of baptism, Paul advises, "*if you are able* to become free, μᾶλλον χρῆσαι" (7:21). The difference is one of activity over against passivity. Circumcision (and, to a lesser degree, marriage) reflects active effort on the part of the agent to change.[211] Slavery, however, does not imply active effort. The slave facing manumission *is able*, not *seeking*, to become free. The hypothetical slave addressed in Paul's diatribe is given ability or power (δύναμις) to become free (ἐλεύθερος). The δύναμις at issue is, presumably, an offer of manumission bestowed by the slave's owner, although Paul does not limit his diatribe to this condition only. At any rate, Paul's basic meaning is clear. In becoming circumcised or undoing its marks, active, premeditated effort to change one's status is at issue; by contrast, becoming free is a passive response to an offer of new status. To the slave with δύναμις to become ἐλεύθερος, Paul grants an exception: indeed to be concerned and use freedom.

One final question lingers: why would Paul have made an exception for slaves? A partial answer lies in Roman manumission practices. Unlike slaveholders in classical Greece (specifically, Athens, Sparta, and Gortyn) and in the ancient Near East (Pharaonic Egypt, Mesopotamia, Babylonia, Assyria, and Persia), Romans saw manumission as *the* regular reward for their deserving urban slaves. Because the city of Corinth was Roman, it is therefore valid to apply Roman norms of manumission to 1 Cor 7:21. By permitting the manumission exception within his wider discussion of marriage, Paul makes room in his theology for the institutionalized exercise of manumission. In 1 Cor 7:21, the Apostle exhorts slaves who are offered manumission *indeed* to avail themselves of the opportunity and to *use freedom*.[212]

Given Paul's advice to Christian slaves to accept offers of manumission, one might ask why Ignatius of Antioch, in *Ad Polycarp.* 4.3, seemingly condemns the efforts of Christians to manumit their fellow Christians who were slaves.

---

[211] "Lesser" because Paul admits that one's passions may be so overwhelmingly strong as to negate one's volition in the matter.

[212] Paul (perhaps) argues an analogous case in Rom 14:5. Here, Paul presents a problem ("Some judge one day to be better than another, while others judge all days to be alike"), and provides an ambiguous solution (ἕκαστος ἐν τῷ ἰδίῳ νοῖ πληροφορείσθω: "Let each be fully convinced in one's own mind"), suggesting that both things can be done for the Lord. Similarly, 1 Cor 7:21 presents a problem ("You were called as a slave"), and provides two possible personal responses to solve this problem: either (1) "do not worry about it" (if you cannot become free), or (2) "use instead freedom" (if you can become free), both of which can be done for the Lord.

However, a closer reading of the passage tells that the bishop addresses a specified economic procedure only. He censors practices that lead slaves to expect the church will draw funds out of its common chest and will purchase their freedom. Therefore, the issue is corporately funded, not privately funded, manumission; the crux of the passage is correctly understanding the phrase "out of the common chest." Therefore, before investigating Ignatius's passage in detail, it will be necessary to examine the social functions and meanings the common chest had in the Greco-Roman world.

Chapter 3

The Common Chest in Antiquity

Far from being a trivial matter of administration, a group's common fund had significant social meanings and functions in the ancient world.[1] To insiders, it made cultic activities possible; contributions to the fund demonstrated loyalty to the group and showed where one placed his or her values. The size of the contribution, often recorded in inscriptions, established certain members as sponsors, and the disbursement of funds from the chest defined others as dependents. Contributions and disbursements made explicit and reinforced a hierarchy of group members, and hence made possible competing sources of authority. Donors provided funds to help poorer members, and in this way the common treasury bound members together across social orders. To outsiders, the chest defined a group as a legitimate association, not only legally, but also socially. It enabled the group to own corporate property, and to exercise the rights (especially in Roman private law) to meet and to make contracts. Jewish and Christian apologists would point to their common chests in order to show Roman authorities that their respective associations were legitimate.

Yet having a chest could also be seen as dangerous. This chapter explores the significant social functions and meanings of the common chest in antiquity by focusing upon voluntary associations or "corporations." It discusses two Greek associations, *orgeōnes* and *thiasoi* (*eranoi* will be reserved for chapter 4), and then turns to a study of Roman *collegia*. The chapter examines slaves who belonged to these Greek and Roman groups, "belonged" in the sense both of being members of the group and of being owned by the group. The goal is to establish that these associations sometimes liberated their slaves by an economic practice that I term "corporate" manumission. The final part of the chapter includes commentary on a recently discovered charter of a Roman town in Spain that provides rare detailed testimony of municipal manumission, and argues that municipal manumission served as a model for corporate

---

[1] On how seemingly trivial transactions of everyday life become imbued with profound significance, see Peter L. Berger and Thomas Luckmann, *The Social Construction of Reality: A Treatise in the Sociology of Knowledge* (Garden City, N.Y.: Doubleday, 1966), 99 et passim.

manumission. We begin our inquiry with an elucidation of assorted Greek, Latin, and Hebrew technical terms specific to ancient commerce, banking, and the common fund.

Terms and Definitions

The economic practice of collecting wealth into a common chest is attested far back into the earliest periods of antiquity, even before the invention of coined money. One of the oldest known Greek poets, Hesiod, mentions such a practice when he writes: "Do not be rude at a meal where there are many guests; / Shared in common [ἐκ κοινοῦ] the delight is greatest and the expense is least."[2] M. L. West considers the phrase "the expense is least" (δαπάνη τ' ὀλιγίστη) to reflect the loan (ἔρανος) that each participant contributed to a common fund to pay for the meal.[3] This activity does not seem to evince a permanently instituted common "chest," but rather occasional potluck activity of a common "fund," perhaps similar to the Spartan *syssitia*.[4] At any rate, in this passage Hesiod not only emphasizes the practical and ethical value of cost sharing at a communal meal, but also underlines the advantage or "delight" that was gained from the creation of such fraternity. At first sight, the practice of collecting money for a common feast or any other purpose may seem mundane. Yet when one considers the corporate statement of identity and belonging such activity implied, the action appears socially significant, for it bound participants together.

Aside from those who renounced wealth altogether, most people in the ancient world cared deeply, even religiously, about the proper and safe deposit of their money. The treasure chamber, cash box, chest, coffer, and purse were prominent features in public and private life. Herodotus speaks of treasure boxes and caskets of money captured from Persian vessels, and the Gospel of Matthew describes similar oriental chests in its story of the magi visitation of the infant Jesus. Varro speaks of deposits into temple treasuries and the etymologies of the related financial terms. Catullus notes a certain Furius who was so poor that he had neither a slave nor a money box. Horace satirizes a rich miser who, upon gazing at the money in his chest, applauds himself. Juvenal mocks the avarice of his age when men come to the gambling table

---

[2] Hes. *Op.* 723.

[3] M. L. West, ed., *Hesiod, Works and Days* (Oxford: Clarendon Press, 1974), 333.

[4] On *syssitia*, the Laconian practice of gathering potluck to bibulate in *symposia* fashion, see N. R. E. Fisher, "Drink, *Hybris*, and the Promotion of Harmony in Sparta," in *Classical Sparta: Techniques behind Her Success*, ed. Anton Powell, Oklahoma Series in Classical Culture (Norman: University of Oklahoma Press, 1988), 26–50.

not with wallets but whole treasure chests.[5] All these sources demonstrate the extensive use of cash chests in the practical business of daily life.[6] These chests were also part and parcel of imaginative literature, particularly fables of hidden treasure troves,[7] which even caught the attention of the Roman jurists.[8]

Chests used for storing money and other valuables tended to be of wood or metal construction, with iron or brass fasteners, bindings, and locks. In the aristocratic Roman house, access to the money chest was controlled, guarded, and under the care of the *dispensator arcae*, who was a trusted and ranking domestic slave.[9] The chests' sizes varied, but Appian and Dio Cassius relate an episode of a certain Titus Vinius hiding from Augustan proscription and living for several days in his freedman Philopoemen's money chest.[10] A constellation of metaphors surrounded the money chest and treasure storehouse, ranging from the idea of a beehive with its buzz of acquisitive activity, to a temple with its religious sanctity and divine protection, to a prison with its physical strength and security.[11] Even the gods had money pouches and chests; the purse of Hermes was represented in Greek and Roman art, and Minerva's coin box was proverbial.[12] Lucian of Samosata even personifies Treasure (Thesaurus) as the attendant and obedient slave of Wealth (Plutus).[13] Yet not all considered money chests a good thing, especially when full of idle cash. As a civic benefactor, Herodes Atticus (ca. 101–77 c.e.) took a dim view of safe-deposit boxes. Philostratus describes the generosity of the wealthy Athenian:

---

[5] Herod. 7.190; 9.106; Matt 2:11; Varr. *Ling.* 5.180–83; Catull. 23; Hor. *Sat.* 1.1.61–68; Juv. *Sat.* 1.89–91. See Juv. *Sat.* 11.23–27, for the difference between a purse and an iron-bound money box; 14.259–60 for brass-bound treasure chests and a description of cash deposits into the Temple of Castor in the Roman forum.

[6] On coin hoards and the general use of coined money in the practical business of daily life, see Michael Crawford, "Money and Exchange in the Roman World," *JRS* 60 (1970): 40–48. Fergus G. B. Millar, "The World of the Golden Ass," *JRS* 71 (1981): 73–74, argues that cash exchanges for produce went right down to the lowest levels of society.

[7] Herbert Newell Couch, *The Treasuries of the Greeks and Romans* (Menasha, Wis.: George Banta, 1929), 94–96.

[8] *Digest* 41.1.31.1 (*thesauri inventio*); W. W. Buckland, *A Textbook of Roman Law from Augustus to Justinian*, 3d ed., rev. Peter Stein (Cambridge: Cambridge University Press, 1966), 218–21; Barry Nicholas, *An Introduction to Roman Law*, 3d ed., Clarendon Law Series (Oxford: Clarendon Press, 1987), 140; J. A. Crook, *Law and Life of Rome, 90 b.c.– a.d. 121*, Aspects of Greek and Roman Life (Ithaca: Cornell University Press, 1967), 142.

[9] Andrew Wallace-Hadrill, "The Social Structure of the Roman House," *PBSR* 56 (1988): 78.

[10] Appian, *BC* 4.44; Dio Cassius 47.7.4.; cf. Suet. *Aug.* 27.

[11] Couch, *Treasuries*, 43–68.

[12] Couch, *Treasuries*, 97–98 (on the purse of Hermes); Mart. 1.76. (on Minerva's box).

[13] Lucian, *Tim.* 29, 39, 40, 41; Couch, *Treasuries*, 67. The text does not explicitly state that Thesaurus is a δοῦλος owned by Plutus. Yet the context shows that Thesaurus is a slave; he is ordered about by and under the sole authority of Plutus (not Hermes or any other god).

He [Herodes Atticus] used to call riches that did not circulate and were tied up in parsimony "dead cash" [νεκρὸν πλοῦτον], and the treasure chambers [θησαυροὺς] in which some people hoard their money "detention centers of cash" [πλούτου δεσμωτήρια], and those who thought that they must actually offer sacrifices to their hoarded money he nicknamed "Aloadae," for they sacrificed to Ares after they had imprisoned him.[14]

The rhetoric voices the ancient concept of benefaction.[15] Wealthy patrons must not jail their coins, but let them circulate publicly. Thus prison imagery for repositories can have negative as well as positive associations.

A number of different terms were used to describe repositories of wealth.[16] Θησαυρός, which Lucian personified, is the Greek word customarily rendered by "treasure" or "treasury." It can refer to a number of different things, such as a vault in a particular building, a physical container, or the contents inside a building or container. Koine usage of this word is found in the New Testament, for example in Matt 2:11; 6:20–21; 12:35; 13:44, 52; 19:21; Mark 10:21; Luke 6:45; 12:33–34; 18:22; Heb 11:26; 2 Cor 4:7; Col 2:3.[17] This usage shows in a general sense that these terms belonged to common language. Related terms for repositories of wealth include γαζοφυλάκιον (Mark 12:41, 43; Luke 21:1), ταμεῖον (Luke 12:24), κοινόν (Ign. Pol. 4.3), χρῆμα in the sense of "a fund or sum of money" (Acts 4:37; 8:18, 20; 24:26), and simply οἶκος (Acts 7:10). Buildings, public and private, often had an ὀμφαλός ("vault"), an ἀνάγαιον ("raised storage area" or "upper room" for grain and other valuables: Mark 14:15; Luke 22:12), as well as various types of coffers, chests, or boxes for depositing wealth called θήκη, λάρναξ, κιβωτός (Heb 9:4; Rev 11:19), κυψέλη, γλωσσόκομον (John 12:6; 13:29), ἄρκη, and κίστη (the last two are Latin loan words).[18] A stored-up or hidden treasure was designated the ἀπόθετον or κειμήλιον. Individuals often carried a βαλλάντιον ("bag, pouch,

---

[14] Philostr. VS 2.1 (547). The nickname "Aloadae" alludes to the story of Otos and Ephialtes, the sons of Aloeus (hence, "the Aloadae"), who kept the god Ares chained in a brazen cauldron for thirteen months; Hermes effected his escape (Iliad 5.384).

[15] Frederick W. Danker, Benefactor: Epigraphic Study of a Graeco-Roman and New Testament Semantic Field (St. Louis, Mo.: Clayton Publishing, 1982), 375; idem, II Corinthians, ACNT (Minneapolis: Augsburg Publishing, 1989), 120.

[16] For the terms that follow, I consulted Couch, Treasuries; G. Humbert, "Arca," in Dictionnaire des antiquités greques et romains, ed. C. Daremberg and E. Saglio, 1 (1877; reprint, Graz, Austria: Akademische Druck–U. Verlagsanstalt, 1966), 364–66; Ettore De Ruggiero, "Arca," in Dizionario epigrafico di antichità romana 1 (1895; reprint, Rome: "L'Erma" di Bretschneider, 1961), 626–32; Gerhard Beseler, "Corpus, fiscus, arca, deus," ZRG 46 (1926): 83–89; E. Kornemann, "κοινόν," PWSup 4 (1924): 916–41; Adolf Berger, Encyclopedic Dictionary of Roman Law, TAPhS 42.2 (Philadelphia: The Society, 1953), s.v. arca (p. 366); J. Kollwitz, "Arca," RAC 1 (1950): 595–96.

[17] BAGD, s.v. θησαυρός. All the New Testament references that follow were found with the aid of BAGD.

[18] Hugh J. Mason, Greek Terms for Roman Institutions: A Lexicon and Analysis, American Studies in Papyrology 13 (Toronto: A. M. Hakkert, 1974), s.v. ἄρκη (pp. 5, 143).

purse": Luke 10:4; 12:33; 22:35–36; cf. Matt 10:8–10) or ἀργύριον (Matt 25:18, 27; 28:12, 15; Mark 14:11; Luke 9:3; 19:15, 23; 22:5; Acts 7:16; 8:20). Rom 15:28 uses the expression σφραγισάμενος αὐτοῖς τὸν καρπὸν τοῦτον ("having sealed to them this fruit"), employing an administrative *terminus technicus* for the sealing of sacks of money for delivery.[19]

In Latin *arca* served as a broad term and identified a place for keeping anything of value, ranging from the large vaults of institutions to the little money boxes of individuals. The term *arca* so pervaded the general vocabulary of Roman society that it came to mean "cash on hand," an important idiom in daily economic discourse. In a letter to Atticus, Cicero writes that he could easily afford the cost of an awaited shipment of Megaric marble statues, and that his *arca* (or amount of "ready cash") could buy even more statues if Atticus could find them. In a letter to a friend, Pliny mentions his intention to buy some property that adjoined his estate in Tifernum Tiberinum, adding that although he himself did not have the money in cash, he could have readily gotten the cash from the *arca* ("cash assets") of his mother-in-law.[20] In addition, the expression *ex arca solvere* became colloquial to mean "to pay one's debts."[21] Besides *arca*, another economic term for a fund of money was *fiscus*, which could simply refer to a "(money) basket," or more generally to the public treasury of a city or state. Related terms include *aerarium, thesaurus* (a Greek loan word), *pecunia communis* (which the Senate expressly prohibited Bacchanalian cults to have after the Bacchanalian "conspiracy" of 186 B.C.E.),[22] *pecunia publica, favissae* ("treasury crypt," as under a temple), *cista* ("wooden box"), *locellus* ("chest"), and *corbona*[23] ("treasure chamber": κορβᾶν, Mark 7:11; κορβανᾶς, Matt 27:6). Expressions for "wallet" or "money pouch" include *loculus* and *crumena*. At Herculaneum and Pompeii, the skeletons of victims who were trying to escape a mud flow by boat include that of a soldier

---

[19] Hans Dieter Betz, *2 Corinthians 8 and 9: A Commentary on Two Administrative Letters of the Apostle Paul*, ed. George W. MacRae, Hermeneia (Philadelphia: Fortress Press, 1985), 141.

[20] Cic. *Att.* 1.9.2; Pliny, *Ep.* 3.19.9: *accipiam a socru, cuius arca non secus ac mea utor.* Suet. *Tib.* 49 also mentions "ready cash."

[21] Donat. *Ad Terent. Adelph.* 2.4.13; *Ad Phorm.* 5.8.27.

[22] Livy 39.18.9; *Senatus Consultum de Bacchanalibus*, most recent publication in Attilio Degrassi, *Inscriptiones Latinae Liberae Rei Publicae*, Biblioteca di studi superiori 40 (Florence: La Nuova Italia, 1963), no. 511 (= *CIL* 1².581); recent bibliog. in Arthur E. Gordon, *Illustrated Introduction to Latin Epigraphy* (Berkeley and Los Angeles: University of California Press, 1983), 83–85. J. A. North, "Religious Toleration in Republican Rome," *PCPhS* n.s. 25 (1979): 92–93, argues that the institution of the *collegium* provided a model for the development of the Bacchic *thiasoi* in Italy.

[23] Cypr. *De opere et eleemosynis* 15 (CCSL 3A.64) used *corbona* to describe church money funds; G. Uhlhorn, *Christian Charity in the Ancient Church*, trans. Sophia Taylor (Edinburgh: T. & T. Clark, 1883), 142. Tert. *Apol.* 39 (CCSL 1.150–53), with his pagan audience in mind, had applied *arca* with the technical legal sense of *arca collegii*.

with his *crumena* and sword at his side, apparently his two most important personal items.[24] On the frontier, Tacitus reports soldiers were once paid out of the personal wallet of Germanicus himself.[25]

In rabbinic Judaism, the authors of the Mishnah and Talmud mention synagogues having a קוּפָּה (derived from Latin *cupa*),[26] which was a money chest of weekly donations supervised by at least two officers of the synagogue.[27] One such officer is called a "commissioner" (φροντιστής) in synagogue inscriptions.[28] In Josephus's writings, we find included among the list of the specific exemptions granted to the Jews the right to collect money and to have common meals.[29] The permission to collect money, with the aim of sending some to Jerusalem, underscores the sense of identity and belonging that a common chest implied. Having such a chest and the right to send the "sacred funds" to Jerusalem enabled a certain degree of autonomy, status, recognition, and respect from outsiders.[30] It advertised the hierarchy (or, in some cases, commonality) within the internal organization of Jewish communities and demonstrated their loyalty to Jerusalem. In biblical Hebrew, the term אָרוֹן

---

[24] Victims of the great eruption of the volcano Vesuvius in 79 C.E.; see Colin Wells, *The Roman Empire* (Stanford: Stanford University Press, 1984), 206, 332 with material in notes.

[25] Tac. *Ann.* 1.37.

[26] Samuel Krauss, *Griechische und lateinische Lehnwörter in Talmud, Midrasch und Targum*, (1899; reprint, Hildesheim: Georg Olms, 1964), 2:516.

[27] *m. Pe'a* 8.7; *b. B. Bat.* 8a–9a; *b. B. Meṣ.* 38a; *t. B. Meṣ.* 3.9 (Zuck. 376); *b. Sanh.* 17b; David Seccombe, "Was there Organized Charity in Jerusalem before the Christians?" *JTS* 29 (1978): 140–41; Emil Schürer, *The History of the Jewish People in the Age of Jesus Christ (175 B.C.–A.D. 135)*, rev. and ed. Geza Vermes, Fergus Millar, and Matthew Black (Edinburgh: T. & T. Clark, 1979), 2:437; Gildas Hamel, *Poverty and Charity in Roman Palestine, First Three Centuries C.E.*, Near Eastern Studies 23 (Berkeley: University of California Press, 1990), 218.

[28] P. W. van der Horst, *Ancient Jewish Epitaphs: An Introductory Survey of a Millennium of Jewish Funerary Epigraphy (300 B.C.E.–700 C.E.)*, Contributions to Biblical Exegesis 2 (Kampen, The Netherlands: Kok Pharos, 1991) 94–95; James T. Burtchaell, *From Synagogue to Church: Public Services and Offices in the Earliest Christian Communities* (Cambridge: Cambridge University Press, 1992), 257.

[29] Josephus, *Ant.* 14.10.8 §213–216; 14.10.20–24 §241–261.

[30] George LaPiana, "Foreign Groups at Rome during the First Centuries of the Empire," *HTR* 20 (1927): 350–51; Victor Tcherikover, *Hellenistic Civilization and the Jews*, trans. S. Applebaum (New York: Athanaum, 1977), 308; E. Mary Smallwood, *The Jews under Roman Rule: From Pompey to Diocletian*, SJLA 20 (Leiden: E. J. Brill, 1976), 134–35; Tessa Rajak, "Was There a Roman Charter for the Jews?" *JRS* 74 (1984): 116; Paul R. Trebilco, *Jewish Communities in Asia Minor*, SNTSMS 69 (Cambridge: Cambridge University Press, 1991), 15. On the importance of the weekly "money chest" (קוּפָה), "plate" for alms (תמחוי) and the synagogal office of the "receiver of alms" (גבאי צדקה) in later rabbinic Judaism, see Krauss, *Griechische und lateinische Lehnwörter* 2:516–17 (s.v. קוּפָה), 590–91 (s.v. תמחוי); Str-B 1:387–91 (on the ἐλεημοσύνη from Matt 6:4), 2:547–48 (on τὸ γλωσσόκομον from John 12:6); Schürer, *History of the Jewish People* 3.1:116; see 2:437 and 577 for the communal chest of the Essenes.

designates (among other things) the ark of the covenant, which served as a locus of identity for ancient Israelite society. Its primary function was as a repository for the Mosaic law tablets, and it constituted a kind of common chest for the Israelites.[31] We also find אָרוֹן to describe the offertory chest that King Joash (Jehoash) of Judah set up in the Jerusalem Temple to collect funds for the building's repair.[32]

Like the offertory chest of King Joash, many Greek and Roman temples had a thesaurus for storing the votive gifts that pilgrims brought. Some temples, such as the Pythian oracle at Delphi or the Asklepieion at Epidauros (with its famed healing powers), became quite rich. One of the inscriptional testimonies from Epidauros records the story of a certain Echedorus, who once tried to cheat the god out of payment by not contributing to the offertory chest:

> Echedorus received the marks [στίγματα] of Pandarus [a Thessalian and a fellow pilgrim at the Asklepieion] in addition to those he already had. He had received money from Pandarus to offer to the god at Epidaurus in his name, but he failed to deliver it. In his sleep he saw a vision. It seemed to him that the god stood by him and asked if he had received any money from Pandarus to set up as an offering to Athena in the Temple. He answered that he had received no such thing from him.[33]

After lying about not having the money to offer, Echedorus asked the god to make him well. In the morning, he found his face covered with marks in addition to the στίγματα of Pandaros as a punishment for trying to cheat the god out of his due fees. The moral of the aretalogy: Asclepius deserved an *honorarium* too, and a full money chest. Offering up money was serious business and a solemn duty in cultic worship.

Given this story and the understanding that temples in general often housed depositories of wealth, we are not surprised to find temples serving as the earliest banks. While most Greeks and Romans preferred to keep their money hidden safely at home, the use of banks is attested in ancient society, although their importance is difficult to judge.[34] The only temple in ancient Greece for

---

[31] Exod 25:10–22; Num 10:33–36; Deut 10:1–9; Josh 3:6–16; 1 Sam 3:3; 4:3–7.

[32] 2 Kgs 12:9–16; 2 Chr 24:8–11; for the Temple treasury in general, see Schürer, *History of the Jewish People* 2:279–84.

[33] *IG* 4².1.121–22 (ca. 2d half of the 4th cent. B.C.E.); trans. in Emma J. Edelstein and Ludwig Edelstein, *Asclepius: A Collection and Interpretation of the Testimonies*, Ancient Religion and Mythology (1975; reprint, Salem, N.H.: Ayer, 1988), 1:231. On the Greek healer gods and their cultic offertory chests, see R. Herzog, "Arzthonorar," *RAC* 1 (1950): 725. On στίγματα, see C. P. Jones, "*Stigma*: Tatooing and Branding in Greco-Roman Antiquity," *JRS* 77 (1987): 139–55.

[34] Millar, "World of the Golden Ass," 70, 72. The standard monograph on Greek banks remains Raymond Bogaert, *Banques et banquiers dans les cités grecques* (Leiden: A. W. Sijthoff, 1968); see also idem, "Geld (Geldwirtschaft)," *RAC* 9 (1976): esp. 862–907. Nothing of its scope has been written for the Roman world; but still useful is William Linn Westermann, "Warehousing and Trapezite Banking in Antiquity," *Journal of Economic and*

which sufficient evidence exists to reconstruct its finances over time is the Temple of Apollo at Delos, which derived revenues from investments, real estate rentals, and loans.[35] Temples provided the guardianship of the gods and a safe haven from robbers. The Roman institution of *depositum* into temple banks was a sacred and binding contract.[36] We shall see this type of legal obligation again in the discussion below on the church chest as a depository of Christian wealth.[37] Depositing money was a deep expression of trust and loyalty.

Related to private temple banks were state treasuries. Before its destruction during the Persian invasion of 480 B.C.E., the ὀπισθόδομος ("back chamber") of the old temple of Athena on the Acropolis stored the public money and tribute for Athens. Afterward, Pericles commissioned the building of the Parthenon, which among other things housed the city treasury.[38] The treasury demonstrated in practical terms the city's power, in ideological terms its glory.[39] It housed not only minted coins, but also treaties, laws, and official records. Like Athens, other ancient cities had treasuries; otherwise they could not govern or function in politics in any practical way.[40] Tacitus reports that the senatorial decrees, the *acta senatus*, were registered in the imperial treasury.[41] The state treasury under Republican Rome was the *aerarium populi Romani*, also called the *aerarium Saturni* because of its location in the Temple of Saturn on the capitol. As with the civic treasuries of the Greek East, the

---

Business History 3 (1930–31): 30–54; and now Wesley E. Thompson, "Insurance and Banking," in *Civilization of the Ancient Mediterranean: Greece and Rome*, ed. Michael Grant and Rachel Kitzinger (New York: Charles Scribner's Sons, 1988), 2:829–36.

[35] John Harvey Kent, "The Temple Estates of Delos, Rheneia, and Mykonos," *Hesperia* 17 (1948): 243–338; Roger S. Bagnall and Peter Derow, *Greek Historical Documents: The Hellenistic Period*, SBLSBS 16 (Chico, Calif.: Scholars Press, 1981), 210–15; see Bogaert, *Banques et banquiers*, 279–304, for the financial operations of temple banks in general.

[36] Berger, *Encyclopedic Dictionary*, 432; J. Ranft, "Depositum," *RAC* 3 (1957): 778–84.

[37] Cf. Reinhart Staats, "Deposita pietatis – Die Alte Kirche und ihr Geld," *ZTK* 76 (1979): 1–29. For the institution of deposit in rabbinic Judaism, see Daniel Sperber, *A Dictionary of Greek and Latin Legal Terms in Rabbinic Literature*, Dictionaries of Talmud, Midrash, and Targum 1 (Jerusalem: Bar-Ilan University Press, 1984), s.v. נוטי נוטומי (p. 112).

[38] Couch, *Treasuries*, 62–64.

[39] M. M. Austin and P. Vidal-Naquet, *Economic and Social History of Ancient Greece: An Introduction*, trans. and rev. M. M. Austin (Berkeley and Los Angeles: University of California Press, 1977), 297.

[40] Erastus, mentioned in Rom 16:23, evidently had duties pertaining to the municipal treasury of Corinth, perhaps as an aedile (there was no quaestor at Corinth); Anita Bagdikian, "The Civic Officials of Roman Corinth" (master's thesis, University of Vermont, 1953), 17–18. See also Henry J. Cadbury, "Erastus of Corinth," *JBL* 50 (1931): 59–70; Gerd Theissen, *The Social Setting of Pauline Christianity: Essays on Corinth*, ed. and trans. John H. Schütz (Philadelphia: Fortress Press, 1982), 75–83.

[41] Tac. *Ann.* 3.51.

aerarium Saturni not only housed coined money, but also archived official and other important documents. In the Principate, this state treasury became distinct from the personal *fiscus Caesaris* of the emperor.[42] Yet the intimate connection between the institutions of temple and treasury remained a constant feature in Rome and other cities and towns throughout the ancient Mediterranean world.[43] The functions and meanings of these civic treasuries were the models for how common funds operated in Greek associations, Roman *collegia*, Jewish synagogues, and Christian congregations.

The Common Fund in Greek Associations

As we saw above with the passage from Hesiod, the Greek idea that a gathering of companions required some form of common fund was very ancient, although shared banqueting does not necessarily presume a permanent, institutional common chest. In the Homeric world, ceremonial eating together reinforced existing social relationships and inaugurated new friendships. When the heroes were not engaged in the pursuits of combat, they were supposed to occupy their time with heroic feasting, which had its own ethics. The suitors in the halls of Odysseus, for example, were blameworthy not because of the idleness and luxury of their daily banqueting: that constituted ordinary and quite proper behavior for nobles not at war. Instead, it was considered unethical to expect the banqueting cost and provisions to be at one man's expense, and it was deemed worse that the suitors took the wealth from the chest of an absent man.[44] All ought to share in the cost of the feast. As an integral part of the heroic meals, the common fund established ties of shared responsibility and honorable friendship.

After the Homeric poems, the evidence for common funds in Greek voluntary associations falls into five main categories: epigraphic evidence from official notices and personal epitaphs, ancient lexicographical definitions of specific corporate terms (such as ἑταιρίαι, ὀργεῶνες, γεννῆται, φρατρίαι, θίασοι, ἔρανοι, συμπόσια, and σύσσιτοι), law codes, casual references in classical literature, and the datable votive offerings found in cultic shrines.[45] Literary sources

---

[42] Berger, *Encyclopedic Dictionary*, s.vv. *aerarium populi Romani* (p. 355), *fiscus* (p. 473). On the vexed question of the difference between the *aerarium* and *fiscus*, see H. H. Scullard, *From the Gracchi to Nero: A History of Rome, 133 B.C. to A.D. 68*, 5th ed. (London: Methuen, 1982), 221, and the literature cited in 456 n. 20.

[43] Couch, *Treasuries*, 51–68.

[44] M. I. Finley, *The World of Odysseus*, 2d ed., rev. (New York: Penguin Books, 1979), 124.

[45] William Scott Ferguson, "The Attic Orgeones," *HTR* 37 (1944): 121, speaking about *orgeōnes* but applicable also to Greek associations in general.

make surprisingly few references to associations and their common funds. The lexicographers, when not manifestly incorrect, are not very informative.[46] By far the largest body of evidence is epigraphic, which exists in a scattered and fragmentary state and, in the main, is particular to Athens and Attica. This section will address two major manifestations of Greek association: the *orgeōnes* and the *thiasoi*.[47] By using these two terms, however, I do not mean to imply that these groups embodied monolithic institutions. I know that not every *thiasos*, for example, was the same, and that differences did exist according to the peculiar constituency of a particular *thiasos*, the locality involved, and the specific time period under study. These terms represent two broadly defined types of Greek association and function in this section as heuristic categories.

The term ὀργεῶνες is difficult to translate, but "sacrificing associates" comes nearer to the meaning than "priestly colleges."[48] *Orgeōnes*, so named because the members were designated ὀργεῶνες, formed some of the oldest manifestations of Greek associations. The *orgeōnes* met for mainly religious purposes, with most maintaining local shrines to particular divine personages. Many corporately owned buildings and real estate, and operated the business of the cult out of the capital funds that came from votive offerings, dues payments, or other forms of revenue. Membership consisted of adult males and appears to have been based on kinship, although some associations of *orgeōnes* seem to have opened their ranks to others than descendants (ἔκγονοι). The epigraphic evidence for these groups is thin and spread unevenly from around 450 B.C.E. to about 70 B.C.E., with most of it dating to between 340 and 170 B.C.E. *Orgeōnes* seem to have been mainly of two types: one including devotees who sacrificed together as a cult of one or more heroes or heroines, and the other consisting of those initiates who sacrificed to higher deities, mostly of foreign origin.[49] From both types, examples can be found of specific *orgeōnes* possessing a common fund as a necessary part of the daily operation and maintenance of their cults.

---

[46] Ferguson, "Attic Orgeones," 62–63; A. Andrews, "Philochoros on Phratries," *JHS* 81 (1961): 1 n. 4.

[47] In his classic study of Greek associations, Erich Ziebarth, *Das griechische Vereinswesen* (Leipzig: S. Hirzel, 1896), 134–35, affirmed that the distinction between *orgeōnes*, *thiasotai*, and *eranistai* eventually wholly disappeared. I follow Ferguson, "Attic Orgeones," 127 et passim, who challenges Ziebarth's claim with a careful reading of the inscriptions and argues that distinctiveness among the three terms was indeed recognized in later Athenian society. Ferguson also takes issue with Ziebarth's claim that the old Attic *orgeōnes* were composed of only *kleine Leute*, and shows that their social and economic status was much more complicated than Ziebarth thought.

[48] Ferguson, "Attic Orgeones," 62, 82–83 n. 4.

[49] Ferguson, "Attic Orgeones," 73.

A rental lease written by the *orgeōnes* of the hero Egretes, found in Athens at the foot of the Hill of the Nymphs, serves as one example.[50] According to the lease, the *orgeōnes* rented out their sacred precinct to a certain Diognetos for a ten-year period. The terms of the agreement were that Diognetos paid 200 drachmas per year to the association's treasurer in return for the right to use the sacred precinct and to live in its buildings. Diognetos was obligated to keep the walls stuccoed and to prune the olive trees, but was allowed to construct a rooftop and doors to make the place more livable, on the provision that he would remove the roof and doors once the ten-year rental period had expired. During this tenure, the *orgeōnes* retained usufruct (the right to enjoy property and take its produce) of their precinct in the month of Boedromion (September) for their annual sacrifices to Egretes. At this time the initiates would use the dwelling house and its cookshop to roast the communal barbecue, which would follow the cultic sacrifices.

The importance of this inscription for the study at hand lies in the explicit transaction recorded and the implicit assumption behind it. The text explicitly documents a transaction involving money going from an individual (Diognetos) to the common fund of a group (*orgeōnes*) to pay rent on group-held property (dwelling house, cookshop, a sacred plot of sylvan land). Implicit is the assumption that the *orgeōnes* owned, or had similar proprietary rights to rent out, the property. Such collective, not individual, proprietorship implies a form of corporation, which must have been recognized in or at least have been intelligible by Athenian private law at the time. Otherwise, such a rental agreement between a corporation and an individual would not have been binding and would have made little sense. Although it is uncertain whether Athenian corporations at this time had the legal capacity of title ownership of real estate, they certainly had title ownership of common funds, as this rental lease proves.

Two mortgage inscriptions from the village of Kome (on the island of Lemnos) provide further evidence of Attic *orgeōnes* owning common funds, and not necessarily small ones.[51] These *orgeōnes* were sacrifice associates to the divine Heracles. Archaeological excavations at Kome (modern Komi) have uncovered the association's shrine to Heracles and the substantial accompanying temple. Although admittedly no evidence survives that positively proves the *orgeōnes* collectively owned the shrine, the *orgeōnes* were nevertheless con-

---

[50] For the text of the inscription, see *IG* 2².2499 (Athens, 306/305 B.C.E.); discussion in Ferguson, "Attic Orgeones," 80, 95 n. 38.

[51] *IG* 12.8.19 (314/313 B.C.E.), and 21. Kome was one of the many villages on the Aegean isle of Lemnos where Athenian cleruchs lived. Ferguson, "Attic Orgeones," 92, postulates that the *orgeōnes* were outright owners of the temple and Heraclean shrine. I am aware that there is some debate among legal scholars over whether ownership in the Greek world was absolute ownership (*dominium*) as the Roman jurists defined it.

stantly associated with it, possibly as owners but certainly as officiants. Whether or not they owned the actual real estate, the *orgeōnes* nevertheless did possess collectively a large enough monetary fund to lend 1,000 drachmas on the mortgage of one farm and 400 drachmas on security of another. Evidently, the association operated as a kind of village bank and lending company.[52]

A third group of inscriptions emanated from another type of *orgeōnes* group, one of the Magna Mater, which exhibited a remarkable degree of corporate identity. These groups had a hierarchical organization with several *epimeletai* (curators of sacred matters) and one treasurer, secretary, and priestess.[53] These formal signs of articulated authority enabled the association to conduct business with outsiders. The association owned private structures, such as Magna Mater sanctuaries, edifices, and cookshops. Such ownership demonstrated in a physical way the group's corporate identity to those both inside and outside the cult. The inscriptions also show how the common fund was an integral and indispensable component of cultic activity: their collection box held votive offerings, membership dues, and fees. From this evidence, one can see how the common fund (and common property) had significant social meanings and functions.

Another inscription of a Magna Mater association illustrates how the common fund functioned within the group to bind members across social levels.[54] This inscription provided for burial expenses of the poorer members to be paid out of the common treasury, or out of the treasurer's personal funds when the treasury was empty. Associations of *orgeōnes* did not normally distribute burial funds, and this particular case may reflect the cult's connection with *thiasotai*, members of another kind of Greek association known to have provided for burial of poorer members.[55] The possession of a burial fund does not necessarily imply that this association of *orgeōnes* was a cult of the dead, but seems instead to denote financial charity to persons within its own membership who otherwise would not have been able to belong. In this instance, the common fund functioned not only to maintain the business of the cult, but also to establish certain members as patrons and others as dependents, further reinforcing hierarchy.

---

[52] For lending by corporate institutions in general, see now Paul Millett, *Lending and Borrowing in Ancient Athens* (Cambridge: Cambridge University Press, 1991), 171–78.

[53] For a discussion of the various inscriptions, see Ferguson, "Attic Orgeones," 107–15, 125.

[54] *IG* 2².1327 (178/177 B.C.E.). The association's burial fund is mentioned in lines 10 and following; see commentary in Ferguson, "Attic Orgeones," 115.

[55] Ferguson, "Attic Orgeones," 115: "This is the only association [of *orgeōnes*] for which anything of this sort is attested."

Responsibility for a person's burial signified a bond and, according to a document preserved in the writings of Ps.-Demosthenes, a legally recognized relationship.[56] This document clearly states that Athenian law placed the duty of the burial or cremation of free persons upon heirs and kin. For slaves, kinless people by definition, funeral expenses according to this law were the responsibility of their masters. The law empowered the demarchs to collect the costs in cases of default. Yet there is a presupposition in this law, which becomes important in the light of the inscription discussed here: namely, that all free people would either have financial resources or kin. Such might have been the case for most citizens, their families, and well-connected metics, but not necessarily for all resident aliens. With the burial funds, this group of *orgeōnes* could have been assisting a specific segment of its membership, which probably included not only kinless resident aliens, but also a number of others too poor to bear the cost of their own funerals.[57] The necrological fund bonded socially diverse members together.

Although rare among the *orgeōnes*, such a burial fund was common among other Greek associations, in particular *thiasoi*. Using this fund meant that the deceased would be buried in a common grave, or ashes kept in urns, regardless of family relationships. Such practice was long-standing in the ancient world. The earliest extant example is provided by a necrological notice from Campanian Cyme of a Dionysian cult (ca. before 450 B.C.E.). It reads: οὐ θέμις ἐν / τοῦθα κεῖσθ/αι ἰ μὲ τὸν βεβαχχευμένον ("None has the right to be buried here save the initiated [of Dionysus])."[58] The practice of common burial may have originated from the theophoric cult of the chthonic Dionysus, whose initiates were called βάκχοι; early Christian cemeteries are comparable.[59] This cultic funerary tradition continued in Athens and Boeotia until well into the later second century of the common era and spread to other *koina* (private associations) of a more commercial nature, such as the associations of traders, mer-

---

[56] Ps.-Dem. 43.57–58 (*Against Macartatus*), in LCL 5:98–101.

[57] Ferguson, "Attic Orgeones," 140 (commenting on *IG* 2².1316), argues that because the Athenian burial law required relatives of the deceased (and masters of dead slaves) to bear the financial burden of cremation or interment, it follows that an association of *orgeōnes*, without *thiasotai* (especially the kinless resident aliens), did not need a common funeral fund. All *orgeōnes*, after all, had kin in Athenian society. I question whether Ferguson can make this assumption, given that the Athenian law codes enjoyed at best varying degrees of compliance, and that, in any case, we cannot assume that the laws reflect actual social practice.

[58] *DGE* 792; P. M. Fraser, *Rhodian Funerary Monuments* (Oxford: Clarendon Press, 1977), 58–59; additional commentary on Fraser in G. H. R. Horsley et al., eds., *New Documents Illustrating Early Christianity*, vol. 2, *A Review of the Greek Inscriptions and Papyri Published in 1977* (Marrickville, Australia: The Ancient History Documentary Research Centre [Macquarie University], 1982), 48–52.

[59] Georg Klingenberg, "Grabrecht (Grabmulta, Grabschändung)," *RAC* 12 (1982): 624–32.

chant-ship owners, and the like, throughout the Greek world.[60] It must be stressed, however, that the practice of *koina* accepting responsibility for the burial of its members must be distinguished from the practice of forming Roman *collegia funeraticia* expressly and exclusively for the purposes of burial.[61] Related evidence of similar theophoric cult activity includes the Orphic-Dionysiac *lamellae* or so-called Gold Leaves, which are thin metal plates found in tombs in Italy, Thessaly, and Crete (dating from around 400 B.C.E. on) that contain instructions in verse on the procedure to be followed in the underworld in order to achieve heroic or divine status.[62] Whether commercial or cultic, these *koina* recognized burial as a duty of one "brother" (ἀδελφός, as initiates of Dionysus called each other) to another.[63] The island of Rhodes provides remarkable evidence for reconstructing the whole process, from the purchase of grounds for a cemetery plot by the *koinon* to the burial and commemoration of individual members. This process further strengthens the argument that Greek associations could own property corporately.

Two documents emanating from the theophoric *koinon* of *Aphrodisiastai Hermogeneioi* at Rhodes and dated to the second century B.C.E. illustrate this corporate ownership. Both were inscribed on the front and back of a placard erected within the burial precinct. The first consisted of a decree of the *koinon* and reads:

> In order that the documents relating to the survey of the land [or perhaps "title deeds": ἀμφουριασμοί] of the real estate belonging to the *koinon*, and of the burial plots [ταφίαι], may be accessible, as far as is possible, to all members of the *koinon* [ἐρανισταί] forever, and that no injustice may be done to any member, it has been decreed by the *koinon* ...[64]

In what follows, the inscription outlined provisions to the magistrates of the *koinon* to compensate an inscriber for his work on the stele. The second docu-

---

[60] The κοινά or σύνοδοι ἐμπόρων καὶ ναυκλήρων, which made contact and spread from port to port in the Hellenistic world. See J. K. Davies, "Cultural, Social, and Economic Features of the Hellenistic World," in *CAH*, 2d ed., vol. 7.1: *The Hellenistic World*, ed. F. W. Walbank et al. (Cambridge: Cambridge University Press, 1984), 283.

[61] Fraser, *Rhodian Funerary Monuments*, 59–60; cf. Peter Herrmann et al., "Gnossenschaft," *RAC* 10 (1978): esp. 146–50, for comparison with early Christian congregations.

[62] Günther Zuntz, *Persephone: Three Essays on Religion and Thought in Magna Graeca* (Oxford: Clarendon Press, 1971), 277–413; M. L. West, *The Orphic Poems* (Oxford: Clarendon Press, 1983), 22–23, 25–26, 171, 265; Wolfgang Luppe, "Zu den neuen Goldblättchen aus Thessalien," *ZPE* 76 (1989): 13–14; R. Merkelbach, "Zwei neue orphisch-dionysische Totenpässe," *ZPE* 76 (1989): 15–16; Susan Guettel Cole, "Voices from beyond the Grave: Dionysus and the Dead," in *Masks of Dionysus*, ed. Thomas H. Carpenter and Christopher A. Faraone, Myth and Poetics (Ithaca: Cornell University Press, 1993), 276–95.

[63] Fraser, *Rhodian Funerary Monuments*, 150 n. 340.

[64] The docments, found in the eastern necropolis (Dermen-dere in Rhodes), can be found in *SEG* 3.674, with translation and commentary in Fraser, *Rhodian Funerary Monuments*, 60–61. The second-century dating is from orthography.

ment, on the back of the stele, was a copy of the *koinon's* deeds of ownership.[65] Both illustrate the sense of belonging that corporate ownership, and a common fund, implied.

From these examples, we can see that corporate ownership was feasible and central for associations in the Greek world. However, a comment on methodology is warranted, especially when we move to identifying slaves in such documents. Determining slave status in epigraphic sources presents notorious difficulties and raises the very difficult methodological question of how slaves are to be recognized. We must be sensitive to three major but highly speculative considerations in examining Greek material: the type of name (although presuppositions of what a "slave name" is can result in erroneous conclusions), the absence of patronymic (last name), and the person's ethnicity. Yet even these three criteria can at best only create a presumption.[66] As we saw in the excursus of chapter 1, any serious onomastic study of ancient names and other pieces of biographic information requires awareness of and sensitivity to the guiding methodological assumptions that lie behind such a study. On the Roman side, P. R. C. Weaver has challenged the belief that the distinction between slaves and Junian Latins can be made solely on the basis of personal cognomen, especially when of Latin derivation. Weaver's work has shown how arbitrary and subjective such distinctions often are, and how the statistics based on them are valueless. In addition, a Greek cognomen in a Roman setting does not necessarily denote slave status (or even Greek origin); similarly, a *tria nomina* does not necessarily designate a Roman citizen (especially in the case of Junian Latins).[67]

A good example of how this methodology works is provided by an inscription from the eastern necropolis at Knidos. It was a roster advertising to insiders and outsiders alike the subscriptions made for the founding of a *thiasos*. Some scholars claim to have identified some names as belonging to slaves and thus conclude that this inscription proves that slaves were indeed admitted to this and perhaps similar *thiasoi*. The original inscription, however, contains no clear attestation that any of the names belonged to slaves. Scholars have based

---

[65] Fraser, *Rhodian Funerary Monuments*, 61 and 151 n. 348; see Fritz Pringsheim, *The Greek Law of Sale* (Weimar: Mermann Böhlaus, 1950), 151–54, for the technical legal terms involved.

[66] Fraser, *Rhodian Funerary Monuments*, 144–45 n. 308.

[67] P. R. C. Weaver, "Cognomina Ingenua: A Note," *CQ* n.s. 14 (1964): 311–15; idem, "Where Have All the Junian Latins Gone? Nomenclature and Status in the Early Empire," *Chiron* 20 (1990): 275–305; idem, "Children of Freedmen (and Freedwomen)," in *Marriage, Divorce, and Children in Ancient Rome*, ed. Beryl Rawson (Oxford: Clarendon Press, 1991), 166–90. Note Pliny, *Ep.* 10.104, where Junian Latins already have the *tria nomina* before becoming full Roman citizens. Weaver's work has direct applicability to New Testament scholarship that tries to recognize slaves in the various New Testament name lists (such as Rom 16:12).

their conclusion on a questionable triadic methodological rule of thumb, namely that the omission of a patronymic, the designation of ethnicity, or the absence of any descriptive information denoted a slave.[68] This methodology, as argued above, foists a spurious rigidity upon ancient Greek nomenclature, constructing an ideal but wrong model of how names functioned in the Greek (or Roman) environment. Conclusions based on such unexamined presuppositions about names supply a false sense of scientific exactitude.

Whereas the inscription from Rhodes furnishes little exact information about the presence of slaves in this particular *thiasos*, it does provide other data. This inscription, we should remember, recorded the founding of a cult. The principal activity involved in the cult's foundation was the collection of a financial endowment, a common fund. Such an endowment was one key element in the founding of any association, religious or secular. The heading of the inscription reads: οἵ δὲ συντάξειν προαιρούμενοι / τὸν θίασον ἐπαγγείλαντο καθὼς ἔδω-/καν ("Those who chose to organize / the *thiasos* are listed in accordance with how / they have given").[69] The individual names, with the amount in drachmas that each contributed to the newly formed common fund, follow.

This inscription is telling because it recorded the collecting of funds not as just one element in the cult's foundation, but as the basic one. It is true that the genre of the inscription, a commemorative plaque recording monetary donors and their donations, dictated to some degree its contents. Nevertheless, in the ancient business of cult founding, fund solicitation and collection played a prominent and essential role. The common fund established certain members as patrons within the group and thus formed a hierarchy. Yet one could envisage an association based on equal contributions, so that the hierarchy based on contribution amount would be diminished. Where an individual placed his or her wealth indicated where he or she placed loyalty and trust. The common fund functioned as one way to display publicly a member's loyalty to insiders, demonstrating to outsiders community affiliation.

---

[68] The inscription, dated to the second century B.C.E., is found in Gustav Hirschfeld, ed., *The Collection of Ancient Greek Inscriptions in the British Museum*, pt. 4, sec. 1, *Knidos, Halikarnassos, and Branchidae* (Oxford: Clarendon Press, 1893), no. 795 (p. 12). I side with Hirschfeld, who challenged Paul François Foucart's conclusion (based upon nomenclature alone) that there is evidence in the inscription that slaves were admitted to this particular *thiasos* (*Des associations religieuses chez les Grecs: Thiases, éranes, orgéons* [1873; reprint, New York: Arno Press, 1975], 7–9).

[69] Hirschfeld, *Ancient Greek Inscriptions*, pt. 4, sec. 1, 12.

The Common Chest in Roman Collegia

No English word adequately translates the Latin term *collegium*. Both "guild" and "college" suit the medieval period better than the Greco-Roman era. Wholly unlike medieval guilds, Roman *collegia* were not organized solely around a trade, the preservation of monopolies, or the training of apprentices.[70] The Roman associations had several varieties but customarily were groups of neighborhood and work associates organized around patron deities or professional trades. They were generally small, with average memberships under fifty, although a few had several hundred members. For the purposes of this monograph, *collegia* will remain untranslated and will serve as an umbrella term for all professional and religious corporate bodies in the time of the late Republic and early Empire, including *sodalicium, sodalitas, universitas, ordo, contubernium, commune,* and (in some cases) *corpus*[71] (συνεργασία, συντεχνία, σύνοδος, κοινόν, and a variety of other Greek terms, in the Roman East).[72]

Wherever their location, most *collegia* seem to have shared similarly articulated organizational structures. The epigraphic evidence reveals that *collegia* advertised themselves as democratic bodies, which held general meetings of members to lay down the statutes, adopt patrons, and elect officers. The chief officers, the presidents, varied in number from two to six and generally were called *magistri* (or *quinquennales,* after the tenure of their office). Under the presidents stood the *curatores* and *quaestores* (treasurers). Larger *collegia* divided themselves into *centuriones* and *decuriones,* and in some of these sizable *collegia,*

---

[70] J.-P. Waltzing, *Étude historique sur les corporations professionnelles chez les romains depuis origines jusqu'á la chute de l'empire d'occident,* (1895–1900; reprint, Bologna: Forni, 1968), 1:182; recently, M. I. Finley, *The Ancient Economy,* 2d ed., Sather Classical Lectures 43 (Berkeley and Los Angeles: University of California Press, 1985), 81.

[71] Waltzing, *Corporations,* 2:140, argues that from the second century onward, the word *corpus* occurs more frequently than *collegium* in inscriptions, and that the former appears to have supplanted the latter in nonjuridical usage as a technical term for associations. For juridical usage, the fundamental text is *Digest* 3.4.1, which seems to use *corpus* synonymously with *collegium* (the traditional scholarly opinion), although not all Roman legal scholars are in agreement on this issue; Karl Olivecrona, "'Corpus' and 'Collegium' in D. 3.4.1," *Iura* 5 (1954): 181–90, argues for textual interpolation. In my discussion, I shall concentrate more on the inscriptions as evidence for reconstructing social practice, and less on the nuances of the debate in Roman legal history.

[72] Waltzing, *Corporations,* 4:236–42; Francesco M. de Robertis, *Il fenomeno associativo nel mondo romano: Dai collegi della Repubblica alle corporazioni del basso impero* (Naples: Libreria Scientifica, 1955), 9–17; Susan Treggiari, *Roman Freedmen during the Late Republic* (Oxford: Clarendon Press, 1969), 169 n. 4; Frank M. Ausbüttel, *Untersuchungen zu den Vereinen im Westen des römischen Reiches,* Frankfurter althistorische Studien 11 (Frankfurt: Michael Laßleben, 1982), 16–33; Halsey L. Royden, *The Magistrates of the Professional Collegia in Italy from the First to the Third Century* A.D. Biblioteca di studi antichi 61 (Pisa: Giardini, 1988), 2–3; F. Poland, "σύνοδος," PWSup 4 (1934): 1415–34.

a committee of *decuriones* was the effective governing body. The democratic nature of the organization seems to have been rather limited, for magistrates upon election by the *collegia* had to pay a substantial contribution to the common fund, the *summa honoraria*, and were expected to finance out of their own pockets lavish entertainment, the *sportulae*. Only the richer members, therefore, could in practice afford to hold elected office.[73]

No matter how large or small, each *collegium* had a common chest (*arca collegii, arca communis, arca publica, ratio publica, respublica collegii*), which one or more elected officers managed.[74] In addition to the legal texts, inscriptional evidence shows how *collegia* patterned themselves after municipal models. For example, in one inscription a certain Gaius Atius Tertullinus from Mediolanum (a municipality in Cisalpine Gaul) is called "the guardian of the common chest of the association [*curator arcae collegii*] of patchwork makers."[75] The title *curator* belonged to the language of municipal administration. Further inscriptions follow this pattern of employing the technical term *curator arcae* to indicate the financial officer of *collegia*.[76] In addition, other inscriptions used *arca decuriae* in the technical municipal sense[77] and recorded that *collegia* also had the office of a *dispensator arcae* in the technical domestic sense.[78] This testimony confirms that *collegia* modelled the titles of their magistracies after the titles of municipal authorities and the titles within the hierarchy of the aristocratic house. The second-century C.E. jurist Gaius provides for the establishment of a common chest by corporate bodies:

---

[73] A. H. M. Jones, *The Roman Economy*, ed. P. A. Brunt (Oxford: Basil Blackwell, 1974), 172; Waltzing, *Corporations*, 1:357–453; E. Kornemann, "Collegium," PW 7 (1900): 415–28; Francesco M. de Robertis, *Storia delle corporazioni e del regime associativo nel mondo romano* (Bari: Adriatica, 1971), 2:26–40.

[74] Waltzing, *Corporations*, 1:449 and 4:624–25; P. Habel, "Arca," PW 3 (1895): 426; De Ruggiero, "Arca," 629–31; Kornemann, "Collegium," 429–31. For the common chest (ταμεῖον) in the East, see Kornemann, "κοινόν," 938–40; Foucart, *Associations*, 140–46; Franz Poland, *Geschichte des griechischen Vereinswesens* (Leipzig: B. G. Teubner, 1909), 380–83, although Poland confused the *eranos*-loan and *eranos*-club, as will become evident below in chapter 4.

[75] *CIL* 5.5738, trans. mine; Waltzing, *Corporations*, 3:154; 4:330.

[76] *CIL* 5.5612: *curatores ar[k(ae) T]i[t(ianae)] coll[egii] fabr[um] et centon c[oloniae] ... M[ediolaniensis] ann[i] CXXXVII*; 5.5869: *curator[is] ark[ae] Titianae coll[egii] s[upra] s[cripti] anni CLI colon[iae]*; 10.6675: *D[is] [M(anibus)]. L[ucio] Afinio H ... seviro Augus[tali cur(atori)?] arkae col[legii] fab[rum], L[ucius] Afinius proc[urator], patri optimo*; Waltzing, *Corporations*, 4:330. Each inscription is reprinted with critical apparatus in 3:153, 155, 469.

[77] Waltzing, *Corporations*, 4:625–26.

[78] W. Liebenam, *Zur Geschichte und Organisation römischen Vereinswesens: Drei Untersuchungen* (Leipzig: B. G. Teubner, 1890), 208, referring to *CIL* 5.7372, which is fragmented but reads: *[A]rruntiu[s] ... collegae et a[micro] ... rectori in c ... [dis]pensator co[llegii] ... Dert[onensium], coll[egium] bene ... C[aius] Arruntius H ... [Arruntia] ...fili ipsi[us] ... ob memoriam be[ne merenti]*; Waltzing, *Corporations*, 3:161.

Those permitted to form a corporate body [*corpus*] consisting of a *collegium* or a partnership [*societatis*] or specifically one or the other of these have the right on the pattern of the state [*res publica*] to have common property [*res communes*], a common treasury [*arcam communem*], and an authorized agent [*actorem, syndicum*] through whom, as in a state, what should be transacted and done in common is transacted and done.[79]

Gaius stresses that the internal organization and operation of corporate bodies should be on the model of a *res publica*.[80] Like a municipal treasury, the *arca communis* established political and legal legitimacy and symbolized the wealth and power of the group, both to insiders and outsiders. This excerpt shows members of *collegia* consciously employing the model of *municipia*.

This common chest consisted of contributions from the officers (*summa honoraria*), dues from the members (*stips menstrua*), penalties and fines levied against members for misconduct, and endowments from patrons inside and outside the group.[81] Often *collegia* used these endowments to commemorate festivals and feasts important to the *collegium*'s deity and to distribute cash, grain, or other *sportulae*.[82] In this way the common chest functioned to publicize the *collegia* and strengthen its authority and legitimacy in the eyes of outsiders who lived in the local community. The membership dues acted as signs of loyalty within the group. Within this hierarchy, even the lowest orders of society had a place.

Slaves as Members in Collegia

The admission of slaves to *collegia* is presumed in many texts of the *Digest*. One important text is illustrative. Preserved from the *Public Prosecutions* of the jurist Marcian (active in the period after Caracalla), it is quoted in the *Digest*:

Slaves, too, with the consent of their masters, may be admitted to the associations of the lower orders [*in collegio tenuiorum*]; those in charge of such associations should know that if they admit slaves to such associations without the master's knowledge or consent, they will henceforth be liable to a penalty of a hundred gold pieces per slave.[83]

---

[79] *Digest* 3.4.1.1; trans. slightly altered from that in *The Digest of Justinian*, ed. Theodor Mommsen with Paul Krueger, trans. Alan Watson (Philadelphia: University of Pennsylvania Press, 1985), 1:96. For commentary, see de Robertis, *Storia delle corporazioni*, 2:274–75, 298–300; Ausbüttel, *Untersuchungen zu den Vereinen*, 16–17.

[80] Waltzing, *Corporations*, 1:513.

[81] Guido Clemente, "Il patronato nei collegia dell'impero romano," *SCO* 21 (1972): 142–229.

[82] Waltzing, *Corporations*, 1:449–515 ("Finances des collèges"), 4:685–99 ("Banquets et sportules"); Jones, *Roman Economy*, 44; A. R. Hands, *Charities and Social Aid in Greece and Rome*, Aspects of Greek and Roman Life (Ithaca: Cornell University Press, 1968), 92.

[83] *Digest* 47.22.3.2; Mommsen-Krueger-Watson, *Digest*, 4:793.

In his *Roman Law of Slavery*, W. W. Buckland discusses this law as if it applied uniformly to all *collegia tenuiorum* in every part of the Empire for all periods.[84] Yet anyone attempting to move from law codes to social practice must remember that Roman law was no monochrome institution. The Roman world was ruled by the legal principle of self-help (e.g., it was your, not the state's, responsibility to bring the defendant to court) and lacked a standard system of law enforcement. Especially in the provinces, the "law" was really a mixed bag of local, foreign, and Roman procedures that varied with the goals of the individual litigants and the arbitrary whims of the individual magistrate hearing the case.[85] In practice, the imposition of a unified legal system across the Empire was unfeasible, even had this been the aim of the imperial provincial administration.[86]

With that said, we return to the admission of slaves to Roman voluntary associations. In this vein, M. I. Finley claims, "satisfactory evidence from the western Empire indicates that masters were reluctant to give the necessary approval except in the case of cult associations."[87] However, there is not much evidence to support Finley's claim, although an analogy can be found in early Christianity. In his *Apostolic Tradition*, the Roman bishop Hippolytus (ca. 170–236 C.E.) describes how a slave in his kind of church required the master's permission to be admitted as catechumen.[88] This requirement of gaining the master's approval draws one point of connection between *collegium tenuiorum* and early churches, a connection that we shall consider below in greater detail.

---

[84] W. W. Buckland, *The Roman Law of Slavery: The Condition of the Slave in Private Law from Augustus to Justinian* (1908; reprint, New York: AMS Press, 1969), 75.

[85] Millar, "World of the Golden Ass," 71.

[86] Peter Garnsey and Richard Saller, *The Roman Empire: Economy, Society, and Culture* (Berkeley and Los Angeles: University of California Press, 1987), 110.

[87] Finley, *Ancient Economy*, 187; citing Ausbüttel, *Untersuchungen zu den Vereinen*, 40–42, and Poland, *Griechischen Vereinswesen*, 328–29 (to show that the eastern part of the Empire indicates a similar pattern).

[88] Hippol. *Ap. Trad.* 15.4–5 (Dom Bernard Botte, ed., *La Tradition Apostolique de Saint Hippolyte*, 2d ed., Liturgiewissenschaftliche Quellen und Forschungen 39 [Münster: Aschendorffsche Verlagsbuchhandlung, 1963], 32–33): "If he be the slave of a believer and his master permit him, let him hear. If his master does not bear witness to him, let him be rejected. If his master be a heathen [ἐθνικός] let him be taught 'to please his master' that there be no scandal [βλασφημία]"; trans. in Gregory Dix, *The Treatise on the Apostolic Tradition of St. Hippolytus of Rome* (1937; corr. reprint with bibliog. by Henry Chadwick, London: S.P.C.K., 1968), 23–24. On this passage, see Peter Lampe, *Die stadtrömischen Christen in den ersten beiden Jahrhunderten*, 2d expanded ed., WUNT 18, 2d ser. (Tübingen: J. C. B. Mohr [Paul Siebeck], 1989), 105. It is not certain that the *Apostolic Tradition* was actually written by Hippolytus. For a summary of research and bibliography, see Paul F. Bradshaw, *The Search for the Origins of Christian Worship: Sources and Methods for the Study of Early Liturgy* (New York: Oxford University Press, 1992), 89–92.

Moving from the legal to the literary sources, we hear a somewhat hostile tone concerning *collegia*. The most vicious attacks against *collegia* were directed at the neighborhood street gangs that terrorized the unpoliced city of Rome under the late Republic. In 58 B.C.E., the populist tribune P. Clodius Pulcher legalized *collegia*, which a *senatus consultum* had suppressed six years before, and he mustered these bands of thugs ("thugs" in Cicero's view) in his campaign to undermine the authority of Roman magistrates by violence. Cicero provides the most detailed evidence for these groups.[89] Although Cicero saw the *collegia* as a threat, both he and M. Licinius Crassus were not above mobilizing rival gangs of their own, under the leadership of T. Annius Milo. Cicero describes Clodius's *collegia* in military language to accentuate their threat to the safety of the Republic. He further colors his description with the claim that these *collegia* were filled with "plebs and slaves," a standard rhetorical device or *topos* used in slandering.[90] Similar charges were levied against both the Bacchanalian (186 B.C.E.) and Catilinarian (?67–66 and 63–62 B.C.E.) conspiracies.[91] Clodius did recruit slaves in his paramilitary gangs, but we should also be sensitive to the level of rhetoric in our (hostile) literary sources when making claims about the actual number and importance of slaves in these paramilitary *collegia*.

In contrast to the hostility toward *collegia* found in the writings of the upper equestrian and senatorial orders, the epigraphic sources provide rich positive testimony of their widespread popularity. Both high and low in society participated in them, as we find in a marble stele dating to the first century B.C.E., which a private cultic association erected in Philadelphia. It reads in part:

---

[89] Cic. *Pis.* 9; 11; *Mil.* 23; 36; 37; 73; *Dom.* 54; *Att.* 3.15; *Red. Quir.* 13; *Red. in Sen.* 33; *Sest.* 34.

[90] As even Cicero admits, the term "slaves" often included freedmen/women. Ausbüttel, *Untersuchungen zu den Vereinen*, 90 n. 29, correctly notes that H. Kühne, "Die stadtrömischen Sklaven in den collegia des Clodius," *Helikon* 6 (1966): 95–113, takes this rhetoric too literally and overemphasizes the importance of slaves in these *collegia*; see now Jean-Marc Flambard, "Clodius, les collèges, la plèbe, et les esclaves: Recherches sur la politique populaire au milieu sur la politique populaire au milieu de Ier siècle," *MEFRA* 89 (1977): 123; Treggiari, *Freedmen*, 174; P. A. Brunt, "The Roman Mob," in *Studies in Ancient Society: Past and Present Series*, ed. M. I. Finley (London: Routedge & Kegan Paul, 1974), 98.

[91] Livy (39.8.3) slandered the Bacchanalia, among using other rhetorical tactics, by claiming that a *Graecus ignobilis* first introduced the cult to Italy; both Cicero (*Cat.* 1.27; 3.8; 4.4, 13) and Sallust (*Cat.* 24.2; 30.2; 46.3; 50.1, 2; 56.5) repeatedly tried to discredit Catiline with the taint of servile association; Keith R. Bradley, "Slaves and the Conspiracy of Catiline," *CP* 73 (1978): 330. Details about the so-called first Catilinarian conspiracy are extremely uncertain; some scholars deny the existence of any supposed plot (it seems to be more a figment of Cicero's rhetoric than a real event). However, the second conspiracy was a real event planned by Catiline. See Scullard, *Gracchi to Nero*, 105–10; 423 n. 2; 424–25 n. 8.

The commandments given to Dionysius [the owner of the house] [by Zeus], granting access in sleep to his own house both to free men and women, and to household slaves. ... These commandments were placed [here] by Agdistis, the most holy Guardian and Mistress of this house, that she might show her good will [or intentions] to men and women, slave and free, so that they might follow [the rules] written here and take part in the sacrifices which [are offered] month by month and year by year.[92]

In its membership and access to religious participation, this cultic association disregarded the ordinary, hierarchical social roles of male and female, slave and free. This text serves as a counterexample to the documents emanating from the voluntary associations mentioned above,[93] which had reiterated the hierarchy found in wider Greco-Roman society. Unlike the previous examples, in the Philadelphian association both slave and freeborn apparently took part in the sacrifices and other cultic activities, which the common chest maintained. The homeowner Dionysius, who may have been a Pythagorean of sorts, even donated space in his house for cultic meetings, hence establishing (and advertising) himself as a patron. As patron, he had the authority to post regulations for conduct, the power to enforce rules, and the duty to protect the rights of less powerful members, including kinless and marginalized people such as slaves.[94]

Two further inscriptions prove that slaves contributed to and received aid from the common chests of *collegia*. The inscriptions offer glimpses of a specific type of *collegium* that is often compared to Christian churches, the *collegium tenuiorum* ("of lower ranking persons"). The first inscription (ca. 12 B.C.E.) from the Campanian town of Nola (twenty miles east of Naples) recorded the membership of one such *collegium tenuiorum* consisting, interestingly enough, mostly of freedmen. Evidently to serve as a public notice, like the Greek horos-inscriptions, the marble plaque listed the *liberti* members and the contribution of each to the common chest for their burial (ranging from 20 sesterces to 200 sesterces). These sums, their monthly subscription dues (*stips*), advertised publicly the hierarchy of the group, since poorer members contributed less to the common chest than more wealthy ones. The inscription most likely reflects a *senatus consultum* that granted permission for *collegia tenuiorum* to exist, provided they met only once a month for payment of the *stips* men-

---

[92] W. Dittenberger, *SIG*[3] 985; trans. in *Hellenistic Religions: The Age of Syncretism*, ed. Frederick C. Grant (Indianapolis: Bobbs-Merrill, 1953), 28–29; text and commentary also in Franciszek Sokołowski, *Lois sacrées de l'Asie Mineure*, École Française d'Athènes: Travaux et mémoires, fasc. 9 (Paris: Boccard, 1955), no. 20 (pp. 53–58).

[93] The Greek associations that erected *IG* 2[2].1327 and 2499; *IG* 12.8.19 and 21.

[94] On this cult association, see Otto Weinreich, *Stiftung und Kultsatzungen eines Privatheiligtums in Philadelphia in Lydien*, SHAW 1919.8 (Heidelberg: Carl Winter, 1919); Wayne A. Meeks, "The Image of the Androgyne: Some Uses of a Symbol in Earliest Christianity," *HR* 13 (1974): 169; S. C. Barton and G. H. R. Horsley, "A Hellenistic Cult Group and the New Testament Churches," *JAC* 24 (1981): 7–41.

strua.[95] The *stips* into the common chest served not only to differentiate high and low within the group, but also to bind the members across social statuses.

The second inscription, from another Italian town, Lanuvium (southeast of Rome), and dated to 136 C.E., furnishes a remarkably detailed picture of the daily life of another *collegium tenuiorum*. Set up by the *Collegium Dianae et Antinoi*, the inscription recorded the bylaws of the group with the regulations, duties, and privileges for both freeborn and servile members.[96] The opening statement included an admonition to the general membership concerning the common chest: "We must all agree to contribute faithfully, so that our *collegium* may be able to continue in existence a long time." The bylaws continue with the fee structure: "It was voted unanimously that whoever desires to enter this *collegium* shall pay an initiation fee of 100 sesterces and an amphora of good wine, and shall pay monthly dues of 5 asses." Slaves joined the membership, as the following excerpt shows: "It was voted that if a slave member of this *collegium* dies, and his master or mistress unreasonably refuses to relinquish his body for burial, and that he has not left written instructions, a token funeral ceremony will be held." This "token funeral," and the cenotaph that could have been erected, functioned not only as an observance of a lost member, but was also a rite to bind together those present at the funeral. It was a time for one member to look upon another and to reaffirm ties of fraternity, ties that even death would not sever. Contributions to the common chest would have ensured such continued support and ritual observance.

A further reference to slaves in the Lanuvium bylaws concerned another rite of passage, manumission: "It was voted that if any slave member of this *collegium* becomes free, he is required to donate an amphora of good wine."[97] Why was the amphora of wine required? Because it indicated that the person's status in the *collegium* had changed with his or her manumission. Here, the presence of slave members alongside free members further strengthens the view that slaves in not insignificant numbers participated in Roman associations alongside freeborns.

Slaves and freedmen were even magistrates of *collegia*.[98] The abbreviations *s.* (*ser.*) or *l.* (*lib.*) for *servus* and *libertus* respectively offer the most secure guide to servile origin. However, use of this status indication outside the *familia*

---

[95] R. Donceel, "Une inscription inédite de Nole et la date du sénatus-consulte 'de collegiis tenuiorum,'" *BIBR* 42 (1972): 27–71.

[96] H. Dessau, *ILS* 7212; trans. in Robert L. Wilken, *The Christians as the Romans Saw Them* (New Haven: Yale University Press, 1984), 36–39; the importance of this inscription was noticed as early as Theodor Mommsen, *De collegiis et sodaliciis romanorum* (Kiel: Libraria Schwersiana, 1843), 98–116.

[97] Wilken, *Christians as the Romans*, 37–38.

[98] *CIL* 6.168; 11.4771; 14.2874, 2875, 2877, 2878; Waltzing, *Corporations*, 3:170, 501–2, 657–58.

Caesaris was in decline by the second century C.E., which might partially account for its absence in many grave-inscriptions from Rome and elsewhere.[99] As we saw above, many onomastic studies identify slaves in name lists simply by the presence of a Greek cognomen or lack of a patronymic.[100] Such conclusions rest on unsure methodological grounds. Granting this skepticism, we still find plenty of evidence for slaves participating in *collegia* and especially cult associations.[101] This participation would not have been possible without contributions to the common funds. Some of these slaves, therefore, must have been quite wealthy, especially the ones who served as magistrates and who would themselves have had to pay the *summa honoraria* and *sportulae*.[102]

Slaves Owned by Collegia *and Municipalities*

By the time of classical law, many Roman *collegia* and municipalities began not only to have servile members, as in the Lanuvium *collegium*, but also actually to employ and own slaves. As a result, these *collegia* can be called "juristic personalities" or corporations (*universitates* in juridical Latin). They could have a common chest, receive inheritances, and own and manumit slaves.[103] According to the *Digest*, this corporate form of ownership and manumission of slaves gained formal recognition in law from the emperor Marcus Aurelius in the latter half of the second century C.E.

The text in the *Digest* concerning the manumission of slaves owned by a *collegium* is short, with three entries:

Manumissions of Slaves Owned by a Corporation
1. ULPIAN, *Sabinus*, book 5: The Deified Marcus gave to all *collegia* which have the right to meet the power to manumit,
2. ULPIAN, *Sabinus*, book 14: in consequence of which they will claim the lawful inheritance of the freedman [or freedwoman].

---

[99] Lily Ross Taylor, "Freedmen and Freeborn in the Epitaphs of Imperial Rome," *AJP* 82 (1961): 121; P. R. C. Weaver, "The Status Nomenclature of Imperial Freedmen," *CQ* 13 (1963): 277; idem, *Familia Caesaris*, 43, 80–86; idem, "Children of Freedmen (and Freedwomen)," 174, 188.

[100] See the problematic claims in Tenney Frank, *An Economic Survey of Ancient Rome* (Baltimore: Johns Hopkins University Press, 1940), 5:247, 271.

[101] Waltzing, *Corporations*, 4:251–54; de Robertis, *Storia delle corporazioni*, 2:52–53; Franz Bömer, *Untersuchungen über die Religion der Sklaven in Griechenland und Rom*, pt. 1, *Die wichtigsten Kulte und Religionen in Rom und im lateinischen Westen*, 2d ed., rev. Peter Herz, Forschungen zur antiken Sklaverei 14.1 (Wiesbaden: Franz Steiner, 1982); Carl Schneider, *Kulturgeschichte des Hellenismus* (Munich: C. H. Beck, 1969), 2:180–81.

[102] However, since the slave's personal funds (*peculium*) belonged in law to the master, a slave normally could not legally have spent money on the *collegium* without his or her master's consent.

[103] Crook, *Law and Life of Rome*, 235; Waltzing, *Corporations*, 2:455–56.

3. PAPINIAN, *Replies*, book 14: The slave of a *civitas* lawfully manumitted retains *peculium*, if not expressly deprived of it, and so a debtor is released on paying the debt to him [or her].[104]

The first two entries were from Ulpian (Domitius Ulpianus), one of the last Roman jurists of the classical period. The quotations were extracted from Ulpian's work *Ad Sabinum*, a commentary on the civil law textbook of the first-century C.E. jurist Sabinus. The third entry came from Papinian (Aemilius Papinianus), another prominent jurist of the third century, and was taken from his work *Responsae*. These three excerpts fell under the title *De manumissionibus quae servis ad universitatem pertinentibus imponuntur.* In juridical Latin, the term *universitas* referred to a corporate body, and it appears in many other titles in the legal evidence with this technical usage.[105] Two out of the three entries concerned themselves with financial matters. Manumission placed the slave in a financially vulnerable position; it was a time when a slave needed protection.

This imperial edict by Marcus Aurelius has provoked considerable controversy among modern scholars. Although some argue that the reference proves that no *collegia* were legally empowered to manumit slaves until this time,[106] others insist that the precise wording (*omnibus collegiis quibus coeundi ius est*) does not exclude the possibility that some may have obtained this right earlier,[107] for Marcus Aurelius might be officially recognizing a practice that had been going on unofficially for some time.[108] The emperors were very hesitant to declare blanket rules, as the Pliny–Trajan correspondence shows. Their role was more passive, making constitutions based upon *libelli*.[109] It is, therefore, highly doubtful that Marcus Aurelius would have created in a single act a universal rule giving a right to all *collegia*. Some *collegia* could have already had this right, prompting other *collegia* to request similar rights. In fact, several inscriptions, predating the reign of Marcus Aurelius, do mention slaves freed

---

[104] *Digest* 40.3.1–3; trans. altered from Mommsen-Krueger-Watson, *Digest* 3:428.

[105] *Digest* 1.8.6; 3.4.2; Gaius, *Inst.* 2.11.

[106] A. M. Duff, *Freedmen in the Early Roman Empire*, 2d ed., rev. (Cambridge: Cambridge University Press, 1958), 34; Treggiari, *Roman Freedmen*, 18.

[107] R. H. Barrow, *Slavery in the Roman Empire* (London: Methuen, 1928), 188–89; S. Scott Bartchy, *ΜΑΛΛΟΝ ΧΡΗΣΑΙ: First-Century Slavery and the Interpretation of First Corinthians 7:21*, SBLDS 11 (1973; reprint, Atlanta: Scholars Press, 1985), 102.

[108] See Purcell, review of *Magistrates* by Royden, 179. Some argue that *collegia* did not have this power before Hadrian based on the lack of references in the *Digest* from that period, but the Justinianic compilers of the *Corpus Iuris Civilis* normally did not include material earlier than the reign of Hadrian. It is therefore by the very nature of our source material that we have few imperial edicts before the second century C.E. For example, the terms *humiliores/honestiores* first appear in a rescript of Hadrian, but that does not mean Hadrian created the distinction.

[109] Fergus B. G. Millar, *The Emperor in the Roman World* (London: Gerald Duckworth, 1977), 6 et passim.

by *collegia*. Often, in such inscriptions, the freed slave's new gentile name was derived from the name of the *collegium*.[110] In his discussion of servile names, Varro reported a similar nomenclature involved in municipal manumission.[111] As will be argued below, municipalities, with their legally recognized civic treasuries and property that included slaves, furnished a ready model for *collegia* to structure their own hierarchies with corresponding common funds, property, and slaves.[112]

Because of this similarity between municipalities and *collegia*, we can reconstruct how corporate manumission worked. Municipal manumission occurred by a *decretum* of the local town senate, the *ordo* or *curia*, with the consent of the *praeses* or *rector*, who was in most cases the provincial governor.[113] Such manumissions were *inter vivos*, and the freedman or freedwoman of a town could keep his or her *peculium* unless it was expressly taken away.[114] Public slaves, *servi populi Romani*, obtained freedom in a similar fashion by a decree of a magistrate, upon authorization of the Roman Senate, or later, the emperor.[115] *Collegia* patterned their hierarchical structures after the municipal model. Under this hierarchy, manumission would have been a matter for the magistrates to decide, with or without consultation from the *collegium* as a whole, depending on its size and bylaws.[116] During this manumission proce-

---

[110] Max Radin *The Legislation of the Greeks and Romans on Corporations* (New York: Tuttle, Morehouse, & Taylor, 1909), 144–45; he follows Kornemann, "Collegium," 433–35, who follows Waltzing *Corporations*, 1:455–56. Examples include *Quinta Centonia, Fabricius, Collegius Fabricius, Fabricius Centonius collegiorum lib[ertus] Cresimus* and the feminine form *Fabricia Centonia Arethusa, Q. Navicularius Victorinus, Quaestorius, Symphonius, T. Velatius accensorum velatorum l[ibertus] Ganymedes*. Waltzing compares this nomenclature practice to the use of *Publicus* as a gentile name for slaves of the state.

[111] Varr. *Ling.* 8.83. Patrick William Duff, *Personality in Roman Private Law* (Cambridge: Cambridge University Press, 1938), 86, calls this reference in Varro "our earliest record of such manumission" by municipalities, but cautions that the text "is obscure and corrupt." The reference also mentions *societates*, which were not corporate bodies in later Roman law, but partnerships of individuals. Their legal position became entirely different from *collegia*, because each *socius* owned a share of the slave. Theodor Mommsen, however, had argued (*De collegiis*, 117) that for the Republic *societas* and *collegium* were indistinguishable in law and could serve as equivalent legal concepts. *Contra* Mommsen, see Radin, *Legislation*, 138–40; P. W. Duff, *Personality*, 144. The LCL rendering of *societatum* as "of guilds" in the Varro passage is an interpretation siding with Mommsen.

[112] P. W. Duff, *Personality*; review of Duff by David Daube, *JRS* 33 (1943), 88–90; Royden, *Magistrates*, 12–17; review of Royden by Nicholas Purcell, *CP* 87 (1992): 178–82, esp. 181.

[113] *Just. C.* 7.9.1–2; *Just. C.* 11.37.1.

[114] *Digest* 40.3.3.

[115] Walter Eder, *Servitus Publica*, Forschungen zur antiken Sklaverei 13 (Wiesbaden: Franz Steiner, 1980), 114–25.

[116] See Buckland, *Roman Law of Slavery*, 588–89 esp. n. 14, although he admits "the form of manumission by a *collegium* is not known" (588). He goes on to describe how

dure, the slave became highly vulnerable to struggles over what the liberated slave's new position in society would be.

A newly discovered charter from a previously unknown town in Roman Spain, the *Municipium Flavium Irnitanum*, provides documentary evidence of legal rules for, and remarkably detailed information concerning, the manumission of public slaves by a *municipium*.[117] Prior to this discovery, the scholarly discussion had hinged on an obscure passage in Justinian's *Code*.[118] With this Spanish charter, we can now reconstruct with some degree of confidence the procedure a municipality used to manumit its public slaves. The relevant statute reads in part:

Concerning the Manumission of Public Slaves

If any [*duumvir*] wishes to manumit a male or female public slave, he is to raise with the *decuriones* or *conscripti* when not less than two-thirds of the *decuriones* or *conscripti* are present, concerning him or her, whether they believe that he or she should be manumitted. If not less than two-thirds of those who are present decide that the manumission should take place and if he or she [i.e., the slave] gives and pays to the public account[119] for the *municipes* of the *Municipium Flavium Irnitanum* the sum which the *decuriones* decide should be received from him or her or gives security for it, then that *duumvir* in charge of the administration of justice is to manumit that male or female slave and order him or her to be free.[120] Whatever man or woman has been manumitted and ordered to be free in this way is to be free and a Latin and they are to be *municipes* of the *Municipium Flavium Irnitanum*, nor is anyone to receive from them for their freedom more than the *decuriones* decide nor act in such a way that anyone receives anything for this reason or on this account; and the rights of the *Municipium Flavium Irnitanum* in claiming the inheritance or the possession of the goods of the man or woman who has been manumitted in this way or over their *operae* or gifts or services are to be the same as if he or she were a freedman or freedwoman of a *municipium* of Italy.[121]

The section continues with a final sentence concerning the monetary penalty for whoever violated this statute. As a whole, the statute shows no hesitation

anyone could give a *fideicommissum* of freedom to the slave of a town. Perhaps the same was true of *collegia*. See also idem, *Textbook*, 81; P. W. Duff, *Personality*, 86.

[117] Julián González, "The Lex Irnitana: A New Copy of the Flavian Municipal Law," *JRS* 76 (1986): 171 for Latin text, 192–3 for English translation, 222 for commentary and bibliography. Gary Forsythe directed my attention to this reference.

[118] González, "Lex Irnitana," 222–23; in *Just. C.* 7.9.2–3, Diocletian mentions a law authorizing or in some way (the text is corrupt at the crucial point) regulating manumission by towns in Italy and refers to a *senatus consultum*, which extended this right to the provinces in 129 c.e. As González notes, T. Giménez-Candela, "Una contribucción al estudio de la ley Irnitana: La manumisión de esclavos municipales," *Iura* 37 (1984): 37, offers one possible emendation in the light of the newly discovered Spanish charter. For older discussions of this text in *Just. C.* and municipal manumission, see Buckland, *Roman Law of Slavery*, 588 n. 12; P. W. Duff, *Personality*, 86; Waltzing, *Corporations*, 2:455.

[119] See González, "Lex Irnitana," 192, for the common funds of the *municipium*.

[120] See González, "Lex Irnitana," 184 and 206, for the procedure, which suggests that this Spanish *municipium* used a mixture of various Roman and native manumission forms.

[121] González, "Lex Irnitana," 192–93.

whatever in ascribing the power to manumit to a *municipium*.[122] The law outlines how a slave must have a *duumvir* to sponsor his or her manumission and must pay, or give security for, the price decided by the *decuriones* as compensation for the slave's release. This monetary transaction accompanied all municipal manumissions, it seems, and was payment to instead of from the common chest. The freedman or freedwoman attained full Latin (not Junian Latin) status,[123] was enrolled in the citizenry as one of the *municipes*, and was protected from extortion by others who might have demanded additional and unauthorized manumission payments. In return, the municipality claimed the enfranchised slave's "*operae* or gifts or services" and reserved the right of intestate succession.[124]

Having outlined *how* corporate bodies manumitted slaves, we move to tackle the reasonable question of *why*: what motivated corporate bodies to free their slaves? The second entry in the *Digest* section quoted above provides one answer. This second excerpt, from Ulpian's commentary "On Sabinus" reads: "in consequence of [manumission] they [the *collegia*] will claim the lawful inheritance of the freedmen/women." The *collegium*, then, obtained not only intestacy rights, but also became effectively the freedmen's or freedwomen's *patronus*. With this edict, Marcus Aurelius took an important step in legitimating the legal power of corporate bodies to control the property of their deceased freedmen/women. Such practical concerns on the part of *collegia* to protect their interests, not hypothetical or unreal problems fabricated by the jurists, may have occasioned this edict.[125]

Summation

The common chest of collected funds had various meanings and functions in the ancient world. Far from being a trivial matter of administration, the establishment of a common fund was often the first step in the foundation of a religious cult, Greek association, or Roman *collegium*. Contributions expressed individual loyalty, announced personal trust, and indicated one's sense

---

[122] González, "Lex Irnitana," 223, correcting earlier claims by Roman legal scholars that cities could not properly manumit before the second century C.E. González argues that the legislation laying down testate succession rules for municipia in Italy, cited in this charter, goes back at least to the period after the Social War; see David Johnston, "Munificence and *Municipia*: Bequests to Towns in Classical Roman Law," *JRS* 75 (1985): 105.

[123] González, "Lex Irnitana," 223, notes the phrasing: the freedman's or freedwoman's estate reverted to their patrons not as *peculium* (as one would expect for Junian Latins), but as *hereditas*.

[124] González, "Lex Irnitana," 149, 206, 222–23.

[125] P. W. Duff, *Personality*, 151–52; Radin, *Legislation*, 144–45.

of values. Having a chest partially defined the group to outsiders and insiders not only legally, but also socially as a "corporation." In this vein, early Christian congregations can be termed corporations, even though they do not qualify as such according to modern textbook definitions of a juridical person.[126]

Possession of a common fund enabled corporate ownership of property as well as the rights (especially in Roman private law) to enter into contracts, to have an articulated hierarchy that may or may not have reflected larger Greco-Roman society, and to meet. A common chest made cultic activities possible. Roman *collegia* could advertise and legitimate themselves through use of their funds in building projects, *sportulae*, and other forms of euergetism. The fund also defined certain members as patrons and established an administrative structure on the model of a *municipium*. This administration permitted help to particular people within the association. Such help would have looked very attractive as an alternative source of patronage to kinless people, the most vulnerable members of society such as widows, orphans, and slaves. Christian churches in particular may have used the common chest as a conscious tool of mission to these marginalized groups.

This chapter has drawn various sources together from many different periods and places to demonstrate that corporate manumission was a known and widespread practice throughout the Greco-Roman world. We have seen that a voluntary association's common fund had serious social meanings and functions in the personal lives of slaves and masters, and in the lives of liberated slaves and their patrons. These associations provided alternative means of patronage and thus were models for ancient synagogues and early Christian congregations to follow. This finding leads us to the next chapter and the earliest known Christian document that mentions the intriguing practice of corporate manumission paid from the common chest of local house churches: Ignatius, *Ad Polycarp.* 4.3.

---

[126] Cf. the Edict of Milan, where Constantine is reported to describe churches with property "belonging to the legal right of their corporation [σῶμα], that is, of the churches, not of individual persons" (Eus.Hist. *HE* 10.5.11). Earlier, Eusebius refers to the Christian church as "our θίασος" (*HE* 10.1.8). Julian "the Apostate" deprived the church of Edessa of its money as a means of ending its corporation (Julian, *Ep.* 40).

Chapter 4

Ignatius, *Ad Polycarp.* 4.3 and
the Corporate Manumission of Christian Slaves

This chapter exegetes the passage in the second-century letter of the bishop Ignatius of Antioch to his fellow bishop Polycarp in Smyrna that concerns the liberation of baptized slaves. It argues that Ignatius does not prohibit private manumissions of Christian slaves by individual slaveowners in general, but seeks in particular to curb abuses of common chest (or corporate) manumissions by local house churches. The study then locates the passage within the context of Greco-Roman rhetorical and literary commonplaces alarming audiences to the dangers of slave recruitment. Ignatius's apprehension about the corporate manumission of Christian slaves reveals his wider apologetic stratagem for social acceptability and internal unity under his own terms as bishop. The argument is that the passage addresses a clearly specified economic procedure and, therefore, cannot be used as a text proving that the early church was generally opposed to the manumission of Christian slaves.

An unusual feature of Roman slavery, compared with the institution in classical Athens, is that the Romans, unlike the Athenians, manumitted their urban slaves with regularity.[1] Consequently, when it attempted to secure converts from the urban *familiae* of Roman citizens, the early Christian movement had to deal with the concrete expectations of slaves that manumission was a realistic, albeit fragile, prospect in their daily lives.[2] Likewise, when they

---

[1] I want to be clear that I do not believe that every slave, or even most slaves, in Roman urban society were manumitted. I am only saying that many urban slaves were (over time) set free, and that urban slaves probably had relatively better chances of manumission than rural slaves. Roman slaveholding ideology, unlike the ideology of ancient Athenian or modern American slavery, held manumission to be *the* appropriate reward for deserving slaves, and this ideology often translated into social practice.

[2] On the problem of translating the Latin *familia* into English "family," see M. I. Finley, "The Silent Women of Rome," in *Aspects of Antiquity: Discoveries and Controversies*, 2d ed. (New York: Penguin Books, 1977), 126; Richard P. Saller, "*Familia, Domus,* and the Roman Conception of the Family," *Phoenix* 38 (1984): 336–55; Suzanne Dixon, *The Roman Family*, Ancient Society and History (Baltimore: Johns Hopkins University Press, 1992), 1–3. I use the term "Roman" in the technical sense of Roman citizens, and the term

approached non-Roman households for potential believers, Christian congregations observed local, Hellenistic manumission customs. Early Christian authors write about both situations, and describe the specific economic practice of churches manumitting baptized slaves with funds drawn from a common chest.[3] In his correspondence with the second-century bishop Polycarp of Smyrna, however, Ignatius of Antioch mentions this particular procedure with distaste, and warns of its dangers to both the church as a group and the slaves themselves.

Although there are excellent studies on Ignatius, this particular piece of his writing (*Pol.* 4.3) has not gained the full attention it deserves.[4] Ignatius offers a rare glimpse into the actual lives of early Christians. My goal is to clarify the significance of this passage for early Christian social history in three ways: first, to provide a working hypothesis of what form this manumission took, whether Roman or non-Roman;[5] second, to look at the extent of this manumission practice in both ancient Judaism and early Christianity; and third, to explain why Ignatius saw it as injurious to his episcopal order. I argue that Ignatius's apprehension about the corporate manumission of slaves by churches reflects his wider concern for unity under his own terms. In short, Ignatius considered manumission pledges by local house churches and their wealthy patrons a threat to his efforts to legitimate his authority as bishop.[6] The social

---

"Hellenistic" in the technical sense of non-Romans influenced mainly by Greek legal customs. I recognize that the two terms are not necessarily mutually exclusive.

[3] These texts will be discussed below.

[4] See Peter Meinhold, *Studien zu Ignatius von Antiochien,* Veröffentlichungen des Instituts für Europäische Geschichte Mainz 97, Abt. für Abendenländ. Religionsgeschichte (Wiesbaden: Franz Steiner, 1979); Walter Bauer, *Die Briefe des Ignatius von Antiochia und der Brief des Polykarp von Smyrna,* 2d ed., rev. Henning Paulsen, HNT 18 (Tübingen: J. C. B. Mohr [Paul Siebeck], 1985); William R. Schoedel, *Ignatius of Antioch: A Commentary on the Letters of Ignatius of Antioch,* Hermeneia (Philadelphia: Fortress Press, 1985), to list only three recent, standard studies.

[5] Because *Pol.* 4.3 provides no detail on how the manumission ceremonial rites were observed, this determination will, of course, be to some degree conjectural. But my endeavor is to build a more plausible context than is currently found in commentary literature for an extremely brief epistolary reference by an ancient Christian author to a particular social practice.

[6] For an excellent discussion of the terminology, see John Howard Schütz, *Paul and the Anatomy of Apostolic Authority,* SNTSMS 26 (Cambridge: Cambridge University Press, 1975) 1–21. See also Hans von Campenhausen, *Ecclesiastical Authority and Spiritual Power in the Church of the First Three Centuries,* trans. J. A. Baker (Stanford: Stanford University Press, 1959), 97–106; Robert F. Stoops Jr., "'If I Suffer ...': Epistolary Authority in Ignatius of Antioch," *HTR* 80 (1987): 176 n. 69; Helmut Koester, "Writings and the Spirit: Authority and Politics in Ancient Christianity," *HTR* 84 (1991): 355, 360–61; Harry O. Maier, *The Social Setting of the Ministry as Reflected in the Writings of Hermas, Clement, and Ignatius,* Dissertations SR 1 (Waterloo, Ontario: Wilfrid Laurier University Press, 1991), 163–70, 182–87.

situation envisioned in Smyrna is a metropolitan center with multiple house (or tenement) churches, each holding distinct attitudes toward Ignatian episcopal authority and each with its own common chest.[7] Ignatius was advising Polycarp to unite several of these house churches together under one administrative ecclesiastical umbrella, with one common chest. Indeed, unity, with the imagery of musical harmony, resonates as a key theme throughout the Ignatian correspondence. One might, however, interpret the statements in *Pol.* 4.3 as an expression of personal interest in the overall spiritual well-being of baptized slaves. I would agree that the passage is a general comment on how all baptized slaves should not desire to be manumitted, *if* the phrase ἀπὸ τοῦ κοινοῦ were absent. But since it stands securely in the text, we as interpreters must explain this qualification that Ignatius placed upon his exhortation. It is the crux of the passage. Ignatius addressed in this letter a specific concern about a particular economic practice. Here, the bishop shows care not about the *general* manumission of slaves, only the *corporate* manumission of slaves.

The passage under study occurs in a list of exhortations, through which Ignatius outlines in detail how Polycarp was to carry out the task of bishop. It reads:

> Let widows not be uncared for [financially]; after the Lord, you [singular] be their trustee. Let nothing happen without your decree [ἄνευ γνώμης σου]. And, you, do not do anything without God, which indeed you do not. Stand firm. Let meetings occur more frequently; seek out all by name. Do not behave arrogantly towards slaves, either male or female. But let them not be puffed up. Rather, let them be enslaved all the more to the glory of God, so that they may happen upon a greater freedom from God. Let them not desire [μὴ ἐράτωσαν] to be manumitted out of the money in the [church's] common chest [ἀπὸ τοῦ κοινοῦ], so that they may not be found slaves of [their] greed [ἵνα μὴ δοῦλοι εὑρεθῶσιν ἐπιθυμίας].[8]

Four initial considerations come to bear upon this passage. First, the use of the phrase "without your decree" (ἄνευ γνώμης σου) echoes state language of political authority, especially of Roman governors. This political parlance under-

---

[7] Floyd V. Filson, "The Significance of the Early House Churches," *JBL* 58 (1939): 110, 112; Virginia Corwin, *St. Ignatius and Christianity in Antioch*, Yale Publications in Religion 1 (New Haven: Yale University Press, 1960), 44–45, 65, 85; Hans-Josef Klauck, *Hausgemeinde und Hauskirche im frühen Christentum*, SBS 103 (Stuttgart: Katholisches Bibelwerk, 1981), 62–63; Stoops, "'If I Suffer,'" 163 n. 13; Maier, *Social Setting*, 4–5, 147–56; Robert Jewett, "Tenement Churches and Communal Meals in the Early Church: The Implications of a Form-Critical Analysis of 2 Thessalonians 3:10," *Biblical Research* 38 (1993): 23–43. I disagree with Jewett's claim that the physical structure of tenement churches (in multistory buildings called *insulae*) necessarily indicates an "egalitarian ethos" without patrons.

[8] Ign. *Pol.* 4.1–3 (SAQ 2.1.1.111–12 = SC 10.148–50). There are no significant alternative readings in the MSS for this text. My translation differs markedly from that of Schoedel, *Ignatius*, 269. By avoiding the translation "slaves of lust" for the phrase δοῦλοι ἐπιθυμίας, I hope to bring greater clarity to its meaning.

scores the civil authority of the bishop in administrative matters, which is the overarching concern of *Pol. 4.*[9] Second, to give widows money corporately is entirely acceptable, even encouraged, but to do the same for slaves for the purpose of manumission is considered dangerous. Third, the expression "out of the common chest" (ἀπὸ τοῦ κοινοῦ) appears in pagan contexts to designate public expenditures of a city or the disbursements of Hellenistic private associations. Both public and private models seem to be at work here.[10] Fourth, the phrase "slaves of greed" (δοῦλοι ἐπιθυμίας) has a peculiar accent. Based upon its usage in *Pol.* 5.2, William Schoedel argues that the metaphor has sexual significance. He contends that "freedmen [and freedwomen] frequently had little choice but to take up low trades and often became associated with prostitution in particular."[11] Because liberated slaves often found "themselves in morally questionable positions" forced upon them by poverty (according to Schoedel), Ignatius warns Polycarp not to encourage manumission.[12] Furthermore, Schoedel connects the first sentence of the next section,

---

[9] In *Pol.* 4, Ignatius addresses financial disbursements to widows, law and order in the churches, meeting schedules, and treatment of slaves. Schoedel, *Ignatius,* 109, 269 n. 3; cf. *OGI* 669.53–54: there is to be no transfer of title "without the permission of the prefect" (χωρὶς τῆ[ς ἀδείας τοῦ] ἐπάρχου).

[10] Schoedel, *Ignatius,* 14 and 271; cf. the image of the ship of state in *Pol.* 2.3 (SAQ 2.1.1.111 = SC 10.148); the characterization of Ignatian church solidarity as a σωματεῖον, "corporation," in *Smyrn.* 11.2 (SAQ 2.1.1.109 = SC 10.140–42); the expression "ambassadorship befitting the community" (τὴν διακονίαν τὴν εἰς τὸ κοινόν) in *Phil.* 1.1 (SAQ 2.1.1.102 = SC 10.120).

[11] Schoedel, *Ignatius,* 271. On the erotic vocabulary, see Edward N. O'Neil, "De cupiditate divitiarum (Moralia 523c–528b)," in *Plutarch's Ethical Writings and Early Christian Literature,* ed. Hans Dieter Betz, SCHNT 4 (Leiden: E. J. Brill, 1978), 333; Hubert Martin Jr., "Amatorius (Moralia 748e–771e)," in Betz, *Plutarch's Ethical Writings,* 450, 530.

[12] Schoedel, *Ignatius,* 271 and n. 15. The evidence Schoedel adduces to "prove" that freedmen/women frequently fell into prostitution is the following: first, he cites two sources, Isaeus, *De Philoct. hered.* 19–20, and Ps.-Dem. 59.18–20 (*Against Neaera*), in LCL 3:364, which only mention ex-slaves who happened also to be prostitutes (the sources in any case reflect slavery in fourth-century B.C.E. Athens and cannot be used as evidence for the Roman period); and, second, he cites Arr. *Epict. diss.* 4.1.35, which is a highly rhetorical passage and cannot be taken literally. The philosophers were given to paradox by exaggeration, and this statement by Epictetus must be weighed against the mass of epigraphic evidence that freedmen/women were quite proud of their status as artisans and other workers and not (as if they constituted some homogeneous economic class) often forced by poverty to become associated particularly with prostitution; Keith R. Bradley, *Slaves and Masters in the Roman Empire: A Study in Social Control* (1984; reprint with suppl. bibliog., New York: Oxford University Press, 1987), 82. Epictetus espouses ideology. To take the passage literally accepts uncritically ancient slaveholding ideology, which held that slavery was not, after all, a bad thing for slaves, and confuses that ideology for social description. I know of no recent scholar from the standard modern works who takes this passage as descriptive of the socio-economic condition of the entire freedman/woman

"flee the evil arts,"[13] to *Pol.* 4.3 as continuing the bishop's exhortation that slaves should avoid prostitution by avoiding manumission.[14] Yet Schoedel's claim that Roman freedmen/women frequently had little choice but to take up prostitution – presumably, because they were homeless and thus destitute – is mistaken, and his reading of δοῦλοι ἐπιθυμίας as referring exclusively to such freedmen/women is doubtful.

To interpret "slaves of greed" as exclusively referring to destitute freedmen/women prostitutes overlooks a fundamental element of both Hellenistic and Roman slavery. As Keith Bradley writes, when slaves were manumitted by Romans, "they did not find themselves absolved of all responsibilities toward their former owners, now patrons."[15] Liberated slaves often owed public displays of respect, remaining with their former masters for stipulated duties and periods of time in return for the slaveholder's grant of manumission. For the eastern Mediterranean and other regions influenced by Hellenistic norms, ex-slaves were regularly bound to their former masters by *paramonē* contracts. *Paramonē* obligated the ex-slave to "hang around" (παραμένω) the former master for a specified period, frequently "as a slave," before the manumission contract became valid.[16] For Roman citizens and people living in urban areas

population of the Roman empire (*pace* Aristide Calderini, *La manomissione e la condizione dei liberti in Grecia* [Milan: Ulrico Hoepli, 1908], 369): M. I. Finley, *Ancient Slavery and Modern Ideology* (New York: Viking Press, 1980), esp. 117; A. M. Duff, *Freedmen in the Early Roman Empire,* 2d ed. (Cambridge: W. Heffer & Sons, 1958); Susan Treggiari, *Roman Freedmen during the Late Republic* (Oxford: Clarendon Press, 1969); P. R. C. Weaver, *Familia Caesaris: A Social Study of the Emperor's Freedmen and Slaves* (Cambridge: Cambridge University Press, 1972); Georges Fabre, *Libertus: Recherches sur les rapports patron-affranchi à la fin de la république romaine,* Collection de l'École Française de Rome 50 (Paris: École Française de Rome, 1981); Wolfgang Waldstein, *Operae Libertorum: Untersuchungen zur Dienstpflicht freigelassener Sklaven,* Forschungen zur antiken Sklaverei 19 (Stuttgart: Franz Steiner, 1986). Furthermore, the main evidence for servile prostitution involves sources that report the sexual exploitation of slaves by their masters and their masters' family and friends, not homeless and impoverished freedmen/women "walking the streets"; see Finley, *Ancient Slavery and Modern Ideology,* 95–96.

[13] *Pol.* 5.1 (SAQ 2.1.1.122 = SC 10.150).

[14] Yet as Schoedel, *Ignatius,* 269 n. 17, himself admits, the term κακοτεχνία has a very wide range of possible meanings. To which I would add Athenag. *Leg.* 11.3 (Schoedel, OECT, 24), which calls the art of oratory (τέχνη λόγων) an evil (κακόν) when used to replace the display of deeds (ἐπίδειξις ἔργων).

[15] Bradley, *Slaves and Masters,* 81.

[16] William L. Westermann, "The *Paramonē* as General Service Contract," *JJP* 2 (1948): 9–50. Alan E. Samuel, "The Role of *Paramonē* Clauses in Ancient Documents," *JJP* 15 (1965): 256–84, is the fullest account of *paramonē* clauses in English, but makes legalistic claims without considering how the law operated in social practice; see also Keith Hopkins, *Conquerors and Slaves,* Sociological Studies in Roman History 1 (New York: Cambridge University Press, 1978), 137 n. 5, 141–58. Note the critical review of Hopkins by Keith R. Bradley, *CP* 76 (1981): 83, 86; and E. Badian, "Figuring Out Roman Slavery," *JRS* 72 (1982): 164–69. Yvon Garlan, *Slavery in Ancient Greece,* rev. and expanded ed.,

governed by Roman private law, manumission was customarily understood in the language and ideology of patronage as the most important *beneficium* a master could bestow upon a slave.[17] This *beneficium* placed the freedman/woman under a heavy moral as well as legal obligation.[18] Such obligations included the freedman/woman's stipulation of deference (*obsequium*) and specific chores (*operae*), both falling under the Roman ethic of reciprocity for personal patronage given by a social better.[19]

The traditional Roman means of support for freedmen/women and other social dependents would have entailed enduring the humiliating ritual of the morning *salutatio*: freedmen/women and other protégés of a patron would, at the crack of dawn, line up (often by social rank) outside a patron's house, hoping for handouts of money or food leftovers. Morning callers presented a daily theater of social hierarchy. The experience for those performing *salutatio* was thought degrading. Later European society would develop no similar customs that articulated and reinforced status so rehearsed on a daily basis as the Roman salutation.[20] This coerced dependence upon a patron is a more plausible model of the social and economic position of freedmen/women than Schoedel's vision of destitute freedmen/women forced to prostitute themselves. The fate of *liberti*, of course, varied according to individual circumstances. Nevertheless, because Romans associated sexual violation with slavery more than with freed status, manumission would not have been regarded as likely to degrade sexual conduct.

There has been considerable debate in recent years among ancient historians over how much autonomy from their former masters Roman freedmen/

---

trans. Janet Lloyd (Ithaca: Cornell University Press, 1988), 78–80; for Egypt, see Lienhard Delekat, *Katoche, Hierodulie, und Adoptionsfreilassung,* Münchener Beiträge zur Papyrusforschung und antiken Rechtsgeschichte 47 (Munich: C. H. Beck, 1964), 107–12. Examples of *paramonē* contracts are found in the useful sourcebook by Thomas E. J. Wiedemann, *Greek and Roman Slavery* (1981; reprint, London: Routledge, 1988), 3, 42–44, 46–49, 105, 120.

[17] For the uneven and opportunistic use of either Roman private law or local legal customs (whichever best suited a litigant's interests) in the hodgepodge that was provincial jurisprudence, see now Y. Yadin, *The Documents from the Bar Kokhba Period in the Cave of Letters: Greek Papyri,* ed. N. Lewis, *Aramaic and Nabatean Signatures and Subscriptions,* ed. Y. Yadin and J. C. Greenfield, JDS 11 (Jerusalem: Israel Exploration Society, 1989); and the critical review by Martin Goodman, "Babatha's Story," *JRS* 81 (1991): 169–75.

[18] Richard P. Saller, *Personal Patronage under the Early Empire* (Cambridge: Cambridge University Press, 1982), 24.

[19] Saller, *Personal Patronage,* 24; Waldstein, *Operae Libertorum*; Philo, *Quod Deus immut. sit.* 48; Tac. *Ann.* 13.26–27; Suet. *Aug.* 67. See also the critical review of Waldstein by Thomas E. J. Wiedemann, "Duties of Freedmen," *CR* n.s. 38 (1988): 331–33.

[20] Saller, *Personal Patronage,* 11, 61–62, 128–29; Peter Garnsey and Richard Saller, *The Roman Empire: Economy, Society, and Culture* (Berkeley and Los Angeles: University of California Press, 1987), 122, 151, 153.

women actually enjoyed. The issue hinges on a disputed legal rule: whether or not a manumission payment out of a slave's business funds (*peculium*) absolved the ex-slave of *operae*.[21] Many historians go so far as to claim that freedmen/women for the most part remained virtual slaves to their patrons, their new status being merely "a modified form of slavery."[22] Peter Garnsey, however, maintains that a significant number of freedmen/women worked with greater self-reliance than Roman historians generally recognize in the urban economy and society of Rome and other major Italian cities, such as Ostia and Pompeii.[23] His argument is based on the legal rule that slaves freed following payment of their value did not owe *operae,* and it assumes that this rule applied to slaves who paid for their freedom out of their own *peculium.*[24] Garnsey contends that, working independently in business as agents, some urban slaves accumulated enough money in their *peculium* to purchase their freedom. These manumission payments involved "an aspect of 'deals' made between masters and enterprising slaves," deals that gave masters the replacement cost of a new slave and thus earned ex-slaves a social and economic position of autonomy, away from the influence of their former masters.[25]

Garnsey's argument is impressive, but not wholly without problems. His conclusion that manumission payments out of their *peculium* enabled ex-slaves to claim social and economic independence from their former masters has not convinced all Roman historians. To be sure, slaves and masters may not have seen eye to eye on which one of them actually owned the *peculium,* although in law the master certainly did. Yet Garnsey's working model of and overall approach to the social and economic position of Roman freedmen/women have useful applications for studying Ignatius and the particular question of corporate manumission. If local house churches practiced charity to redeem and support Christian slaves, then this charity would have liberated ex-slaves from dependence upon a former master for daily support, from the humiliating morning salutation, and from other formalized duties of *operae.* I want to

---

[21] Even if such a freedman/woman did not owe *operae* to his or her patron, he or she would still have owed *obsequium,* which (unlike *operae*) was never closely defined in law and thus was less a controlled Roman legal institution; Peter Garnsey, "Independent Freedmen and the Economy of Roman Italy under the Principate," *Klio* 63 (1981): 366.

[22] Géza Alföldy, "Die Freilassung von Sklaven und die Struktur der Sklaverei in der römischen Kaiserzeit," *RSA* 2 (1972): 119–22; cited in Garnsey, "Independent Freedmen," 361. Barry Nicholas, *An Introduction to Roman Law,* 3d ed., Clarendon Law Series (Oxford: Clarendon Press, 1987), 75–76. Note also the servility of Sabinianus's groveling freedman in Pliny, *Ep.* 9.21 (which is often cited, erroneously, as a parallel to Philemon; it deals with a freedman and not a slave, and Pliny's tone is entirely different from Paul's in Philemon); *Ep.* 9.24; A. N. Sherwin-White, *The Letters of Pliny: A Historical and Social Commentary* (1966; corr. reprint, Oxford: Clarendon Press, 1985), 505, 507.

[23] Garnsey, "Independent Freedmen," 359–71.

[24] Garnsey, "Independent Freedmen," 364.

[25] Ibid.

be clear that my argument for independent freedmen/women does not suffer from the same uncertainty as Garnsey's above. In Roman private law, the *peculium* belonged to the master, and so a purchase of freedom from the *peculium* was not legally comparable to the purchase of freedom by a third party, which would have entailed independence and exemption from *operae*. But a house church or a synagogue undoubtedly qualified as a third party, so its provision of the purchase price gave the freedman/woman considerable independence in law from his or her former master.

With this model of both Hellenistic and Roman slavery in view, I propose a new interpretation for Ignatius's use of "slaves of greed."[26] From the time of Plato, the phrase acquired a distinctive sense in Greek philosophy, especially in the Stoics, as an important philosophical and ethical concept. It became a rhetorical stock term of derision for those who lacked self-control (ἐγκράτεια).[27] Socrates, as the archetypal free person, reportedly claimed to be less a slave to his bodily appetites (δουλεύοντα ταῖς τοῦ σώματος ἐπιθυμίαις) than anyone else because he refused financial gifts, including those offered to ransom his way out of prison.[28] Classical authors from Isocrates to Plutarch employ the "slave of greed" metaphor as a common *topos* of derision against the utterly unfree person, who is anxiously self-seeking.[29] Early Christian writers from the author of Titus to composers of the apocryphal acts appropriated this philosophical concept.[30] These examples illustrate how Ignatius's

---

[26] ἐπιθυμία occurs only three times in Ignatius, and always in a negative sense: verbal form in *Rom.* 4.3 (SAQ 2.1.1.99 = SC 10.112); and 7.1 (SAQ 2.1.1.100 = SC 10.114); nominal form in *Pol.* 5.2 (SAQ 2.1.1.112 = SC 10.150); Robert M. Grant, ed., *The Apostolic Fathers: A New Translation and Commentary,* vol. 4, idem, *Ignatius of Antioch* (London: Thomas Nelson & Sons, 1966), 133.

[27] Friedrich Büchsel, "θυμός, κ.τ.λ.," *TDNT* 3 (1965): 168.

[28] Xen. *Ap.* 16.

[29] The following citations are not to be thought of as parallels to *Pol.* 4.3, but as illustrations to prove that the expression δοῦλοι ἐπιθυμίας occurs in literature as a generic rhetorical commonplace and need not refer exclusively or even remotely to destitute freedmen/women forced by poverty into prostitution: Isoc. *Ad Nic.* 29.5; *Ad Dem.* 21.11; Xen. *Mem.* 4.4.24–5.12; Pl. *Phdr.* 238e.3; *Resp.* 554a.7; *Leg.* 838d.4; Arist. *Rhet.* 2.13.13–14 (1390a.15); Polyb. 18.15.16.2; Dion. Hal. 2.3.5.9; Plut. *Mor. con. praecepta* 142e.9; *Vit. Agis* 1.3.6; Diog. Laert. 6.66.11; Arr. *Epict. diss.* 4.1.35–37; Philo, *Quod omn. prob. lib. sit.* 156–57; 159–60; *De cherub.* 71.6; *Spec. leg.* 4.113.9; *De praem. et poen.* 124.3; Josephus, *Ant.* 4.18.23 §244.1; 15.4.1 §91.2; 15.7.4 §219.3; Lucian, *Hermot.* 8.10; Galen, *De placitis Hippocratis et Platonis* 3.7.12.4 (De Lacy, CMG 5.4.1.2.1.214); Ps.-Hippoc. *Ep.* 12.20 (Wesley D. Smith, ed., *Hippocrates: Pseudepigraphic Writings,* Studies in Ancient Medicine 2 [Leiden: E. J. Brill, 1990], 62); Achilles Tatius, *Leucippe et Clitophon* 6.19.4.4; Aristid. *Or.* 2.44–46 (Charles A. Behr, ed., *P. Aelius Aristides* [Leiden: E. J. Brill, 1986], 1:105–6 §§191, 195, 197); *Or.* 3.119 (Behr, 153 §17); 3.123 (Behr, 155 §28); 3.281 (Behr, 256 §556); *Or.* 4.387 (Behr, 309 §42).

[30] Titus 3:3; Eph 2:3; 1 Pet 4:3; 2 Pet 3:3; *Herm. Man.* 8.5.2 (GCS 48.1.35); Just. *2 Apol.* 5.4.5 (Goodspeed, 82); *Dial.* 134.1 (Goodspeed, 256); Athenag. *Leg.* 21.4.9 (Schoedel,

rhetoric was shaped as much by Greco-Roman commonplaces and models as by early Christian tradition.[31] Because in *Pol.* 4.3 Ignatius speaks of slaves "attaining a better freedom from God," we may assume that slaves were seeking their manumission in addition to their baptism. Baptisms based upon self-seeking ἐπιθυμία, baptisms only for the manumission money, brought (to Ignatius's mind) undesirable converts to Christianity. In this manner, *Pol.* 4.3 reflects concerns comparable to those of other Roman and Hellenistic religions, such as the Isis cult, which preached against hollow conversions of believers who had impure thoughts about, and selfish motivations for, joining the cult.[32] Similar concerns are documented in ancient Judaism.[33] Moreover, the literary and moral *topos* of the slave attempting to break out of bondage by questionable means and of his or her vanity (τῦφος) as a recently liberated slave is present. In Lucian of Samosata, for example, there are passages ridiculing the rich because they tolerated former slaves getting hold of their wealth and squandering it.[34]

Yet it must be admitted that desiring freedom does not always connote negative images in ancient authors. Literary sources sometimes sound quite the opposite tone, and call desire (ἐπιθυμία) for liberty (ἐλευθερία), particu-

---

OECT, 46); 31.4.3 (Schoedel, OECT, 76); Clem. Alex. *Paed.* 2.2.34.2.1 (SC 108.72); 3.1–2 (SC 158.12–16); *Str.* 3.12.90.3.1 (GCS 52[15].2.237); 6.16.136.2.2 (GCS 52[15].2.500) quoting LXX Exod 20:17 (= Deut 5:21) N.B., connection with slaves (cf. Sirach 5:2 [ed. J. Ziegler]); *A. Jo.* 35.11 (LB 2.1.169); Burton S. Easton, *The Pastoral Epistles* (New York: Charles Scribner's Sons, 1947), 186–88. Cf. Paul's discussion throughout Romans 7.

[31] A point made in several contexts in Schoedel, *Ignatius.*

[32] H. S. Versnel, *Inconsistencies in Greek and Roman Religion,* vol. 1, *Ter Unus: Isis, Dionysos, Hermes. Three Studies in Henotheism,* Studies in Greek and Roman Religion 6 (Leiden: E. J. Brill, 1990), 91; although Versnel, 91 n. 180, overstates that Ignatius "firmly opposed" the concept of corporate manumission. Ignatius only wanted to curb its abuse. His exhortation is that slaves should not join the church in order to gain access to the church's money, since the Christian ideal (like the Stoic) was to desire nothing of the material world; see *Rom.* 4.3 (SAQ 2.1.1.99 = SC 10.112); 7.1 (SAQ 2.1.1.103 = SC 10.114).

[33] The *Community Rule* from Qumran speaks about the convert who outwardly performs the rituals of the group, but keeps his or her heart stubborn; 1QS 2.25–3.12 (Eduard Lohse, ed., *Die Texte aus Qumran: Hebräisch und Deutsch,* 4th ed. [Munich: Kösel-Verlag, 1986], 8–11). The Talmud records rabbinic discussions about caution in accepting untrue proselytes (*b. Yebam.* 47a–b).

[34] Hans Dieter Betz, *Lukian von Samosata und das Neue Testament: Religionsgeschichtliche und paränetische Parallelen,* TU 76 (Berlin: Akademie-Verlag, 1961), 191 n. 1. On the *topos* of the τῦφος of (liberated) slaves, see Betz, *Lukian,* 194–99, esp. 196 with the material in notes; Ernst Meyer, *Der Emporkömmling: Ein Beitrag zur antiken Ethologie* (Giessen: Otto Kindt, 1913), 14, 43, 47–62, 73, 78–82, 85, who provides examples of individual slaves and freedmen as social types for the character of the upstart "social climber." Ethically, the phenomenon falls under "hypocrisy"; see Ulrich Wilckens, Alois Kehl, and Karl Hoheisel, "Heuchelei," *RAC* 14 (1988): 1205–31.

larly in the political sense, an instinctive passion of human nature.[35] In this context, servile desires for personal freedom were quite natural emotions, intelligible to both Hellenistic and Roman slaveholders. Ignatius responded to these emotions. In *Pol.* 4.3, the expression δοῦλοι ἐπιθυμίας refers not to an enslaving desire for liberty, but to an enslaving desire for what they do not have (e.g., access to the church's money). Despite attempts to link it with prostitution, δοῦλοι ἐπιθυμίας is a rhetorical commonplace found in various literary contexts generally to characterize a person enslaved to his or her material wants. But unlike δοῦλοι ἐπιθυμίας, the phrase ἀπὸ τοῦ κοινοῦ refers not to a vague psychological state, but to a specific institution: corporate manumission. The bishop was concerned not with manumission of Christian slaves *in general*, but with abuse of corporate manumission paid out of the church's common chest *in particular*. Understanding how common chest manumission operated in the ancient world, not finding some so-called social practice behind the metaphor "slaves of desire," is the key to the puzzle.

Corporate Manumission

The economic practice of group-sponsored manumission supplies a promising model against which to read Ignatius. Known from Athens and many other parts of the Greek-speaking world, this procedure enabled a slave to purchase his or her freedom through sums borrowed from an *ad hoc* group in a loan called an *eranos*.[36] In Athenian sources, *eranos*-loans are regularly distinguished from other kinds of lending. Typically, the loan operation involved a temporary meeting of individual lenders, who together gave large or small sums, depending on the group's means and the borrower's requirements. *Eranos*-loans were by their very nature non-interest-bearing. They served a variety of purposes, though personal emergency – ransom, tax or liturgy payments, and manumission of a slave – was the underlying need in most cases.[37] The particular financial arrangement stressed reciprocity and ἀνταπόδοσις, or "giving back in return."[38]

---

[35] Josephus, *JW* 4.3.10 §175; Diod. Sic. 11.36.5; Caes. *BGall.* 3.10; C. Wirszubski, *Libertas as a Political Idea at Rome during the Late Republic and Early Principate* (1950; reprint, Cambridge: Cambridge University Press, 1960); see also the critical review of Wirszubski by Arnaldo Momigliano, *JRS* 41 (1951): 146–53; Keith R. Bradley, "*Servus Onerosus*: Roman Law and the Troublesome Slave," *Slavery and Abolition* 11 (1990): 135.

[36] M. I. Finley, *Studies in Land and Credit in Ancient Athens, 500–200 B.C.: The Horos Inscriptions*, Social Science Classics Series (1951; corr. reprint with introd. by Paul Millett, New Brunswick, N.J.: Rutgers University Press, 1985), 105.

[37] Finley, *Studies*, 100.

[38] Paul Millett, *Lending and Borrowing in Ancient Athens* (Cambridge: Cambridge University Press, 1991), 153–55.

We learn about *eranos*-loans for Athenian manumissions from a set of inscriptions, commonly called the "Attic manumission lists," which date to the reign of Alexander the Great.[39] The inscriptions served as public notices in a bulletin board fashion and registered payments, in the form of 100-drachma silver bowls, which ex-slaves remitted to the city of Athens upon acquittal in a special legal procedure called a fictitious "trial of abandonment." Inscribing the procedure guaranteed the validity of an ex-slave's oral claim to freedom.[40] The precise legal details are difficult to reconstruct given the abbreviated and fragmentary nature of the inscriptions.[41] Yet these documents occasionally cite a provisional group (κοινόν) of creditors (ἐρανισταί), who together put up the cost of the manumission.[42] These texts provide significant evidence that group or "corporate" manumission, paid from a common fund, developed at Athens at the beginning of the Hellenistic period.[43] I use the term common "fund" and not "chest" to stress that I understand these groups were not permanent associations but *ad hoc* groups.

This custom of corporate manumission continued to be practiced throughout Attica and the Hellenistic East. Another group of Hellenistic texts, the so-called Delphic manumissions, provides additional evidence for this practice.[44]

---

[39] *IG* 2².1553–78. Dale B. Martin, *Slavery as Salvation: The Metaphor of Slavery in Pauline Christianity* (New Haven: Yale University Press, 1990), 186 n. 52, doubts that these lists are in fact manumission records, and posits an alternative hypothesis that they describe metics acquitted of some legal responsibility to Athenian citizens. I, however, agree with Finley, *Studies*, 100–106, that these inscriptions certainly reflect manumission activity. The word ΠΑΙΔΙΟΝ does occur, and the context clearly indicates that the word refers to chattel slaves.

[40] William V. Harris, *Ancient Literacy* (Cambridge: Harvard University Press, 1989), 71.

[41] Marcus N. Tod, "Some Unpublished 'Catalogi Paterarum Argentearum,'" *ABSA* 8 (1901–2): 197–202; William L. Westermann, "Two Studies in Athenian Manumissions," *JNES* 5 (1946): 94–99; David M. Lewis, "Attic Manumissions," *Hesperia* 28 (1959): 237–38; idem, "Dedications of Phialai at Athens," *Hesperia* 37 (1968): 368–80; Arnold Kränzlein, "Die attischen Aufzeichnungen über die Einlieferung von φιᾶλαι ἐξελευθερικαί," in *Symposion 1971: Vorträge zur griechischen und hellenistischen Rechtsgeschichte*, ed. Hans Julius Wolff, AGR 1 (Cologne: Böhlau, 1975), 255–64.

[42] J. Vondeling, *Eranos*, Historische Studies 17 (Groningen: J. B. Wolters, 1961), 117–50, 259–61, contends (*contra* Finley) that the inscriptions emanate not from *ad hoc* groups, but permanent Hellenistic charity associations. See, however, recent criticism of Vondeling in Millett, *Lending and Borrowing*, 14–15, 155–56.

[43] Finley, *Studies*, 291 n. 71, notes that because all the evidence is crowded around a short time span of a few years before and after the death of Alexander the Great, the whole procedure may not have been a normal one in Athens, and may have been created to meet the peculiar needs of the moment. If this is true, then corporate manumission appears not routine at Athens, but exceptional. As to the specific circumstances around the time of Alexander the Great that gave rise to this procedure, one can only speculate. Macedonian conquest and occupation may have changed Athenian society and economy in many and significant ways; but cf. Harris, *Ancient Literacy*, 117.

[44] *GDI* 1772, 1791, 1804, 1878, 1909, 2317.

These documents date from 200 B.C.E. to 70 C.E. and record manumissions transacted in the Apollonian sacred precinct. Some of the sales indicate that the slave was legally freed through an *eranos*-loan, but nevertheless still owed *paramonē* obligations to the individual responsible for the loan, usually the former master.[45] As in the Attic manumission documents, a few Delphic inscriptions registered a sum of money – a friendly, interest-free *eranos*-type loan – given by a group to liberate a slave.[46] For this study of early Christian manumission, it is significant that pagan temples provided the settings for the manumission ceremonies. Indeed, temple altars often served as religious sanctuaries for slaves.[47] This evidence shows that the economic practice of corporate manumission paid from a common fund was accepted in the Hellenistic East, in both civic and cultic contexts. Such practice provided a model for early Christian congregations to follow, such as the ones in Asia Minor that so concerned Ignatius.[48] Unlike the Greek *ad hoc* groups, however, Christian house churches were permanent associations. Roman *collegia* and municipalities provided further models of corporate manumission.

This model raises a further question of motivation. Why would groups of creditors have wanted to fund a slave's manumission? Because the institution of *eranos* constituted friendly, non-interest bearing loans, an enticement other than money must have been at issue. The Greek institution of *paramonē*, which was an integral part of slavery in the East, provides a partial answer. As we saw above, *paramonē* contracts were widespread in Hellenistic areas of the Mediterranean and were a more demanding agreement than the stipulation under Roman private law of *operae* from *liberti* to a patron. These *paramonē* obliga-

---

[45] Herbert Rädle, "Selbsthilfeorganisationen der Sklaven und Freigelassenen in Delphi," *Gymnasium* 77 (1970): 1–5; Westermann, "Two Studies," 94; Franz Bömer, *Untersuchungen über die Religion der Sklaven in Griechenland und Rom*, pt. 2, *Die sogenannte sakrale Freilassung in Griechenland und die (δοῦλοι) ἱεροί*, AAWM (Wiesbaden: Franz Steiner, 1960), 35.

[46] S. Scott Bartchy, *ΜΑΛΛΟΝ ΧΡΗΣΑΙ: First-Century Slavery and the Interpretation of First Corinthians 7:21*, SBLDS 11 (1973; reprint, Atlanta: Scholars Press, 1985), 103; he follows Rädle, "Selbsthilfeorganisationen," 2–4, who follows Erich Ziebarth, *Das griechische Vereinswesen* (Leipzig: S. Hirzel, 1896). Yet these works must be read cautiously in the light of Finley, *Studies*, 101–2, who correctly argues that the word *eranos* here almost invariably refers to the loan (or the *ad hoc* lending group) and not to a permanent club. Finley, esp. 275 n. 5 and 289 n. 59, is sharply critical of Ziebarth and those who follow his anachronistic assumptions about ancient Athenian law recognizing juridical personalities.

[47] Suet. *Claud.* 25.2; William L. Westermann, *The Slave Systems of Greek and Roman Antiquity*, Memoirs of the American Philosophical Society 40 (Philadelphia: The Society, 1955), 17–18, 40–41, 108. Micheline Fasciato, "Note sur l'affranchissement des esclaves abandonnés dans l'île d'Esculape," *RD* 27 (1949): 454–64, lists references in the primary sources. However, I disagree with Fasciato's claim that the Stoic so-called humanitarianism alleviated the brutality of Roman slavery.

[48] Schoedel, *Ignatius*, 270; Bartchy, *ΜΑΛΛΟΝ ΧΡΗΣΑΙ*, 103.

tions would have supplied a group with an incentive to fund a slave's manumission. The very act of giving itself established all kinds of obligations of receiver to giver. Especially when gifts were exchanged between persons of unequal order, status, or class, the act of giving was done for the sake of a return.[49] Members of Athenian and Hellenistic *ad hoc* partnerships, which lent *eranos*-loans for manumission purposes, would have been well aware of the heavy moral and legal obligations placed upon freedmen/women. I argue that these *eranos*-loans were paid out in order to obtain *paramonē* services.

It is difficult to enumerate what specific tasks and services *eranos* groups expected the slaves they freed to perform for them. By their very nature, Hellenistic *paramonē* contracts were drafted in rather general terms; indeed, such contracts were intentionally vague. William Westermann characterizes the position of someone bound under *paramonē* as a kind of "handyman."[50] The indeterminate nature of a freedman's or freedwoman's duties and obligations makes *paramonē* wholly unlike other Hellenistic labor contracts, which often spelled out concrete job descriptions. In the Delphic manumissions that contain *paramonē* clauses, this lack of specificity is evident. The ex-slave agreed to "do what is necessary," or in another formulation, to "do what is ordered," or in longer statements to "do whatever [or] everything he [or she] is ordered to do as far as possible."[51] To the group making an *eranos*-loan, obtaining a *paramonē* contract might prove more valuable than either hiring a leased slave or a freeborn laborer, since avoidance of precise statements placed these freedmen/women in a particularly vulnerable legal position.[52]

But if the group wanted to secure someone in a vulnerable legal position, why did it not simply buy a slave of its own outright? An initial answer includes avoiding the added cost of clothing, feeding, and maintaining a slave. This explanation, however, goes only so far. A variety of reasons existed for manumission in both the Hellenistic and Roman ideologies of slavery. Often slaves were of more practical use after manumission. We must keep in mind that these lending groups were temporary, *ad hoc* partnerships. The outright purchasing of a slave, which groups certainly did in the Hellenistic period, might have proved less desirable to the *eranos*-lenders attested in these particu-

---

[49] A. R. Hands, *Charities and Social Aid in Greece and Rome,* Aspects of Greek and Roman Life (Ithaca: Cornell University Press, 1968), 26–48; Orlando Patterson, *Slavery and Social Death: A Comparative Study* (Cambridge: Harvard University Press, 1982), 211–14, applying the anthropological theories of Marcel Mauss, *The Gift: Forms and Functions of Exchange in Archaic Societies,* trans. Ian Cullison (London: Cohen & West, 1954), 3–5.

[50] Westermann, "*Paramonē*," 24.

[51] E.g., *GDI* 2060.7–10 (183–182 B.C.E.): παραμεινάτω δὲ Εὐάνδρα τὸ δέον ποιοῦσα Νίκωνι ἕως κα ζῇ Νίκων, ἀνέγκλητος οὖσα καὶ ποιοῦσα τὸ δέον.

[52] Westermann, "*Paramonē*," 25–26. On renting a slave, see Jo-Ann Shelton, *As the Romans Did: A Source Book of Roman Social History* (New York: Oxford University Press, 1988), 169–70.

lar inscriptions because these groups lacked permanence; there might have been complications over who would keep the slave once the group was dissolved.

During the Roman period, from which many of these documents date, factors other than *paramonē* contracts come into play.[53] Besides the hope of gaining more loyalty, a group of lenders might have wanted an enfranchised slave because of the freedman/woman's usefulness as a Roman citizen. Formal manumission by a Roman citizen master normally gave citizenship to the ex-slave.[54] Citizenship carried the three legal rights of *ius commercii* (the right to be a party to *mancipatio*, in form a conveyance on sale, and other specifically Roman methods of acquiring property and making contracts), *ius conubii* (the right to contract with a Roman citizen a marriage recognized by civil law), and *testamenti factio* (the right to take under and make a Roman will), and increased one's status generally.[55] Not infrequently slaves were freed to serve their patrons as citizen freedmen/women *procuratores*, personal business managers who could legally make contracts.[56] These domestic officials were charged with supervising the household slave staff and representing their patrons in commercial affairs. In addition, lenders might have wanted freedmen/women dependents in order to swell their train of clients and protégés. In the Roman understanding of aristocratic virtue, greater *dignitas* came to the householder surrounded by many protégés and clients, since there was no special honor in having a large train of slaves who were forced by violence to be there. A Roman master might free her or his slaves, as Susan Treggiari writes, so she or "he might enjoy the prospect of a fine funeral, his corpse attended by grateful freedmen [/women] with caps of liberty on their heads, witness to their patron's munificence."[57] Manumission brought the slave-holder *dignitas*. Manumission was a regular feature of Roman slavery because it suited the master's interests. Another reason why lenders might have wanted a freedman/woman instead of a slave might be that they had hoped to avoid examination by torture of their dependents, which was *required* – not just permitted – in the court testimony of slaves.[58] All these motivations partially explain why Romans viewed manumission as a regular, even desirable, feature

---

[53] If a slave was freed by a group of Roman citizens and received citizenship, he or she would have been subject not to *paramonē*, but to *obsequium* and *operae*.

[54] W. W. Buckland, *The Roman Law of Slavery: The Condition of the Slave in Private Law from Augustus to Justinian* (1908; reprint, New York: AMS Press, 1969), 439.

[55] Nicholas, *Roman Law*, 64–65.

[56] *Digest* 40.2.13; Gaius, *Inst.* 1.19; Duff, *Freedmen*, 20.

[57] Treggiari, *Roman Freedmen*, 14; Dion. Hal. 4.24; Petron. *Cena* 71.

[58] P. A. Brunt, "Evidence Given under Torture in the Principate," *ZRG* 97 (1980): 256–65; Page duBois, *Torture and Truth* (London: Routledge, 1991), 63–68, discusses Aristotle and classical Athens.

of slavery, and why purchasing a slave's freedom was sometimes more attractive to *eranos*-investors than acquiring a slave.[59]

In early Christianity, motivations for manumission similar to those described above could have been at work. In addition, some congregations might have interpreted the early baptismal formula of Gal 3:28, "neither slave nor free," literally.[60] To these house churches, baptism created a new person, spiritually free and legally manumitted. But before we engage the question of corporate manumission in early Christian congregations, the situation among Jewish synagogues deserves attention.

Similar Manumission Forms in Jewish Synagogues

Jews practiced corporate manumission in forms similar to the *eranos*-loans reflected in the Attic and Delphic documents. Evidence of this economic activity is found among Jewish communities all over the ancient world, from Egypt to the northern shores of the Black Sea. Jewish synagogues had common chests.[61] These chests functioned institutionally in ways similar to those in a Roman *collegium* (*arca collegii, arca communis, arca publica, ratio publica, respublica collegii*), which one or more elected officers of the association managed.[62] Hellenistic private associations also operated a common fund (ταμεῖον, κοινόν).[63] Several pieces of evidence suggest that synagogues used their common chests to redeem their enslaved coreligionists.

One source is a vellum fragment from the Egyptian nome of Oxyrhynchos, which contains a legal instrument of manumission of a Jewish maid and her

---

[59] Duff, *Freedmen,* 18–19; Treggiari, *Roman Freedmen,* 11–20.

[60] See Wayne A. Meeks, "The Image of the Androgyne: Some Uses of a Symbol in Earliest Christianity," *HR* 13 (1974): 165–208.

[61] David Seccombe, "Was There Organized Charity in Jerusalem before the Christians?" *JTS* 29 (1978): 140–41; Emil Schürer, *The History of the Jewish People in the Age of Jesus Christ (175 B.C.–A.D. 135),* rev. and ed. Geza Vermes, Fergus Millar, and Matthew Black (Edinburgh: T. & T. Clark, 1979), 2:437; Gildas Hamel, *Poverty and Charity in Roman Palestine, First Three Centuries C.E.,* Near Eastern Studies 23 (Berkeley and Los Angeles: University of California Press, 1990), 218; *m. Pe'a* 8.7; *b. B. Bat.* 8a–9a; *b. B. Meṣ.* 38a; *t. B. Meṣ.* 3.9 (Zuck. 376); *b. Sanh.* 17b; Samuel Krauss, *Griechische und lateinische Lehnwörter in Talmud, Midrasch und Targum* (1899; reprint, Hildesheim: Georg Olms, 1964), 2:516.

[62] J.-P. Waltzing, *Étude historique sur les corporations professionnelles chez les romains depuis origines jusqu'á la chute de l'empire d'occident,* (1895–1900; reprint, Bologna: Forni, 1968), 1:449 and 4:624–25; P. Habel, "Arca," *PW* 3 (1895): 426; Ettore De Ruggiero, "Arca," *Dizionario epigrafico di antichità romane,* 1 (1895; reprint, Rome: "L'Erma" di Bretschneider, 1961): 629–31; E. Kornemann, "Collegium," *PW* 7 (1900): 429–31.

[63] E. Kornemann, "κοινόν," *PWSup* 4 (1924): 938–40; Franz Poland, *Geschichte des griechischen Vereinswesens* (Leipzig: B. G. Teubner, 1909), 380–83, although Poland confuses the *eranos*-loan with *eranos*-club, as Finley points out.

two (or three) children.[64] The ransom was paid collectively by the Jewish community of Oxyrhynchos. It is unclear whether the common chest referred to belonged to a single synagogue or to an association of synagogues in the nome. The deed reads:

Translation of manumission. We, Aurelius [...] of the illustrious and most illustrious city of Oxyrhynchos, and his sister by the same mother Aurelia [...] daughter of [...] the former *exegetes* and senator of the same city, with her guardian [...] the admirable [...], have manumitted and discharged *inter amicos* our house-born slave Paramone, aged forty years, and her children [...] with a scar on the neck, aged ten years, and Jakob, aged four years, [...] from all the rights and powers of the owner: fourteen talents of silver having been paid to us for manumission and discharge by the community of the Jews [παρὰ τῆς συναγω(γ)ῆς τῶν Ἰουδαίων] through Aurelius Dioskoros [...] and Aurelius Justus, senator of Ono in Syrian Palestine, father of the community [...]. And, the question being put, we have acknowledged that we have manumitted and discharged them, and that for the said manumission and discharge of them we have been paid the above-mentioned sum, and that we have no rights at all and no powers over them from the present day, because we have been paid and have received for them the above-mentioned money, once and for all, through Aurelius Dioskoros and Aurelius Justus. Transacted in the illustrious and most illustrious city of Oxyrhynchos [...], in the second consulship of Tiberianus and the first of Dion, year seven of Imperator Caesar Gaius Aurelius Valerius Diocletianus and year six of Imperator Caesar Marcus Aurelius Valerius Maximianus, Germanici, Maximi, Pii, Felices, Augusti: Pharmouthi [...] nineteenth day,

[second hand] [...] Paramone and her children [...] and Jakob [...] [I witness] the agreement as stated above. I, Aurelius [...] [wrote for him] as he is illiterate.

[third hand] Aurelius Theon also called [...] of the money [...] piety [Eusebia?] [...] rights [...] of Dioskoros [...] Justus [...] the [talents] of silver [...] manumit [...] illiterate.[65]

As the first line indicated, the Greek was a translation of the original Latin document, conforming to the requirement that all Roman legal contracts must be in Latin, even in the Greek-speaking East. The maid had no name; she was called Paramone, a nickname resembling the English pet-name "Fido," which indicates her fidelity to her masters, or simply mocks her. Using a nickname, or refusing to give a real name to chattel, as a tool for the humiliation, dishonor, and – to use the term Orlando Patterson has coined – "social death" of a slave is found in nearly all slave societies, both ancient and modern.[66]

---

[64] P. Oxy. 1205 (ed. A. S. Hunt) = *CPJ* 3.473, dating to 291 C.E.; the late date is admittedly problematic for comparison with earlier periods, but the Bosporus inscriptions (discussed below), dating to the first century C.E., provide a control; but cf. Dale B. Martin, "Slavery and the Ancient Jewish Family," in *The Jewish Family in Antiquity*, ed. Shaye J. D. Cohen, BJS 289 (Atlanta: Scholars Press, 1993), 120–21 n. 24.

[65] P. Oxy. 1205 (text, trans., and commentary in *CPJ* 3.473); Ross Kraemer, ed., *Maenads, Martyrs, Matrons, Monastics: A Sourcebook on Women's Religions in the Greco-Roman World* (Philadelphia: Fortress Press, 1988), 93.

[66] Patterson, *Slavery and Social Death*, 54–58. The name Paramone itself is an interesting example of the intermingling of Hellenistic manumission terminology in what is clearly a Roman legal document.

Two siblings, Aurelius and his sister Aurelia, have manumitted the forty-year-old maid Paramone, along with her two children (there may have been a third child whose mention was lost because of lacunae in the text). The manumission was *inter amicos,* a formless procedure by the declaration of the master "before friends" who served as witnesses.[67] A third party was involved, namely Aurelius Dioskoros and Aurelius Justus, both of whom would have been prominent and powerful patrons (Justus was the son of a decurion from the Syrian-Palestinian town of Ono). These patrons acted as middlemen who handled the financial transaction of fourteen silver talents. That the two sibling owners explicitly in the deed renounce their claim to any of the normal rights and powers over the maid Paramone is significant not only from a legal but also a sociological perspective. Aurelius and Aurelia forfeited their normal rights to the freedwoman's body and labor. The synagogue gained the maid Paramone without any strings attached to her former masters.

In this way, the common chest enabled the synagogue to ransom an enslaved Jewish maid and to integrate her and her family into the synagogue community. Whether she was originally Jewish or was converted as a result of the manumission is unclear.[68] But whether or not there was religious recruitment, the function of the common chest remains socially significant: this function is unitive, joining the maid Paramone and her family to the synagogue at Oxyrhynchos. The release from duties of *operae* enabled the maid Paramone to have formal, legal independence from her former (pagan) master. She became legally an independent freedwoman.[69]

A related situation is reflected in the so-called Bosporus inscriptions, which record Hellenistic manumission activities of organized Jewish communities in the Cimmerian Bosporus on the north shore of the Black Sea, and date to the first century C.E.[70] One fragment concerning the synagogue in Panticapaeum

---

[67] Adolf Berger, *Encyclopedic Dictionary of Roman Law,* TAPhS 43.2 (Philadelphia: The Society, 1953), 576; W. W. Buckland, *A Textbook of Roman Law from Augustus to Justinian,* 3d ed., rev. Peter Stein (Cambridge: Cambridge University Press, 1975), 77, 82; Wiedemann, "Regularity of Manumission," 174.

[68] Although it is interesting that whereas the adult female slave Paramone was not given a proper name, at least one of her children, Jakob, was (and a Jewish name at that). If the name "Jakob" is in fact a Jewish name, it is unlikely that recruitment was involved since the family had already identified itself with Judaism.

[69] However, the document says nothing about the maid Paramone's responsibility to the synagogue. A separate Jewish private contract could have been drawn up about that, if she was Jewish already, as suggested by the son's name, Jakob. In this case, she would not have been an independent freedwoman. I owe this observation to Lyn Osiek.

[70] The texts are from several cities in the Bosporus Kingdom: Panticapaeum (Kertch), *CII* 683 (80 C.E.), 683a (s. II p.), 683b (s. II p.); Gorgippia, *CII* 690 (41 C.E.), 690a (67/68 C.E.), 690b (59 C.E.); Phanagoria, *CII* 691 (16 C.E.?); in most cases, the inscriptions record a calendric date in Bosporanic eras; Laurence H. Kant, "Jewish Inscriptions in Greek and

(Kertch) is illustrative of the formulae in the texts. It contains the final clause of a *paramonē* contract. In this deed, a (perhaps) Jewish widow named Chreste declared the manumission of her foster slave Heracles under the coguardianship of the Jewish community:

In the reign of King Tiberius Julius Rhescuporis, the Pious, friend of the Emperor and the Romans, in the year 377,[71] on the twelfth day of the month of Peritios, I, Chreste, formerly the wife of Drusus, declare in the prayer-house [(προ)σευχή] that my foster slave [θρεπτός] Heracles is free once [for all], in accordance with my vow, so that he may not be captured or annoyed by my heirs, and may move about wherever he chooses, without let or hindrance, except for [the obligations toward] the prayer-house regarding subservience [θωπεία; literally "flattery," perhaps in the sense of *obsequium*] and remaining in attendance [προσκαρτέρησις; literally "perseverance, patience," referring to *paramonē* service, as in *CII* 683a below]. [Done] with the approval of my heirs Heracleides and Heliconias, and with the participation of the community of the Jews in guardianship [συνε(πιτ)ροπεούσης δὲ καὶ τῆ(ς) συναγωγῆ(ς) τῶν Ἰουδαίων].[72]

That Chreste was a woman, and a widow, placed her in a vulnerable legal position. She needed witnesses to support her will. The *paramonē* clause obligated her freedman Heracles to remain at the prayer-house for θωπείας τε καὶ προσκα[ρτερ]ήσεω[ς], perhaps a reference to work as a handyman.[73] The synagogue obtained the privilege of Heracles's services apparently in return for helping Chreste institute her will. If Heracles was Jewish, the ceremony might reflect the synagogue's role in aiding Chreste (who may have bought this slave in order to manumit him) to fulfill the biblical injunction that mandated Jewish masters to liberate their Jewish slaves in the seventh year of servitude (Exod 21:2–6; Deut 15:12–18).[74] If Heracles was not Jewish, then related biblical commandments may have been at issue, ones that enjoined Jewish

---

Latin," *ANRW* 2.20.2 (1987): 675–76; and they reflect patterns of *paramonē* obligations similar to the Delphic manumission inscriptions; Westermann, *Slave Systems*, 125. The stones themselves are housed in museums in Russia and were published there under the title *Corpus Inscriptionum Regni Bosporani* (= *CIRB*), ed. V. V. Struve et al. (Moscow and Leningrad: Institute of Archaeology of the Academy of Sciences of the USSR, 1965).

[71] Ca. 80/81 C.E.; Emil Schürer, "Die Juden im bosporanischen Reiche und die Gnossenschaften der σεβόμενοι θεὸν ὕψιστον," *SPAW* 12–13 (1897): 201.

[72] *CII* 683 (= *CIRB* 70). Baruch Lifshitz, prolegomenon to *Corpus of Jewish Inscriptions: Jewish Inscriptions from the Third Century B.C. to the Seventh Century A.D.*, vol. 1, *Europe*, ed. P. Jean-Baptiste Frey, Library of Biblical Studies (New York: Ktav, 1975), 64, corrects the misprinted "εαί" for "καί" in line 14 of Frey's first edition.

[73] See commentary in Lifshitz, prolegomenon to *Corpus*, 64–65. Benjamin Nadel, "Slavery and Related Forms of Labor on the North Shore of the Euxine in Antiquity," in *Actes du colloque 1973 sur l'esclavage*, Annales littéraires de l'Université de Besançon 182, Centre de recherches d'histoire ancienne 18 (Paris: Les Belles Lettres, 1976), 214–15, translates θωπείας τε καὶ προσκα[ρτερ]ήσεω[ς] of lines 14–15 as "worship and constant attendance," which apparently is a misreading, based upon the erratum εαί in line 14 of Frey's first edition.

[74] Julia Ustinovo, "The *Thiasoi* of Theos Hypsistos in Tanais," *HR* 31 (1991): 163.

masters to circumcise their male, and otherwise convert their female, non-Jewish slaves (e.g., Gen 17:12, 23–27; Exod 12:44).[75] (Under the late Empire, such proselytizing prompted imperial legislation aimed at stopping Jews from converting their non-Jewish slaves.)[76] That Heracles is called a "foster slave" (θρεπτός; equivalent of Latin *alumnus*) implies some privileged status within Chreste's household. In Roman private law, *alumnus* is a conveniently ambiguous term, often referring to either an enslaved foundling infant or a domestic slave subsequently adopted as a "foster child" by his or her owner.[77] In either case, the legal sources clearly reveal that close bonds of affections could be assumed between "foster parent" and *alumnus,* and that such attachments resulted in preferential status.[78] In this document, Heracles receives from Chreste special treatment similar to a Roman *alumnus.*[79]

In his discussion of this text, Benjamin Nadel suggests that the synagogue paid for Heracles's manumission.[80] William Westermann concludes from this *paramonē* clause that the slave must have been a Gentile who was converted to Judaism as part of the manumission procedure, although Franz Bömer expresses doubts as to whether we can know this for sure.[81] If Westermann is

---

[75] Bernard J. Bamberger, *Proselytism in the Talmudic Period* (Cincinnati: Hebrew Union College Press, 1939), 124–32; Joachim Jeremias, *Infant Baptism in the First Four Centuries,* trans. David Cairns, Library of History and Doctrine (London: S.C.M. Press, 1960), 37–38; Paula Fredriksen, "Judaism, the Circumcision of Gentiles, and Apocalyptic Hope: Another Look at Galatians 1 and 2," *JTS* 42 (1991): 560 n. 72.

[76] *Pauli Sententiae* 5.22.3–4 (ca. 300 C.E.); *Cod. Theod.* 16.8.6 and 16.9.2 (Constantine II, 339 C.E.); Amnon Linder, *The Jews in Roman Imperial Legislation* (Detroit: Wayne State University Press; Jerusalem: The Israel Academy of Sciences and Humanities, 1987), 82–85, 117–20, 138–51, 174–77, 272–74, 277–80, 370–71, 375–81; Louis H. Feldman, *Jew and Gentile in the Ancient World: Attitudes and Interactions from Alexander to Justinian* (Princeton: Princeton University Press, 1993), 391–95.

[77] I say "often" because an *alumnus* need not be a slave at all.

[78] Beryl Rawson, "Children in the Roman *Familia,*" in *The Family in Ancient Rome: New Perspectives,* ed. idem (Ithaca: Cornell University Press, 1986), 173–86; Hanne S. Nielsen, "*Alumnus:* A Term of Relation Denoting Quasi-Adoption," *C & M* 38 (1987): 141–88; John Boswell, *The Kindness of Strangers: The Abandonment of Children in Western Europe from Late Antiquity to the Renaissance* (New York: Pantheon Books, 1988), 116–21. Boswell, however, is too positive in his claim for the generally kind treatment of *alumni.*

[79] The text does not state that the ceremony itself made Heracles Chreste's "foster child," but that he was her θρεπτός before the manumission act (Χρήστη γυνὴ πρότερον Δρούσου ἀφείημι ἐπὶ τῆς [προ]σευχῆς θρεπτόν μου Ἡρακλᾶν ἐλεύθερον καθάπαξ κατὰ εὐχή[ν] μου). Therefore, the Hellenistic use of θρεπτός meaning a "fictive adoption" in Attic (and Delphic) manumission texts (C. Bradford Welles, "Manumission and Adoption," *RIDA* 2d ser. 3 [1949]: 507–20) does not seem to be at issue here.

[80] Benjamin Nadel, "Actes d'affranchissement des esclaves du royaume de Bosphore et les origines de la *manumissio in ecclesia,*" in Wolff, *Symposion 1971,* 284–85.

[81] Westermann, *Slave Systems,* 126 n. 100; see also Schürer, "Juden im bosporanischen Reiche," 201–3; Erwin R. Goodenough, "The Bosporus Inscriptions to the Most High God," *JQR* 47 (1957): 221; Adolf Deissmann, *Light from the Ancient Near East: The New*

correct, then here is an example of religious recruitment, manumission paid from a common chest operating as a conscious tool of mission. I, however, agree, with Bömer that the evidence is too meager to prove this hypothesis. In any event, the *paramonē* obligations do seem to be part of some sort of financial and/or legal arrangement by which Jews redeemed fellow Jews.[82] For these services, the Jewish synagogue in Panticapaeum obtained a share of the *paramonē* rights – the freedman would "remain in attendance" – thus granting Heracles an alternative source of patronage. Group patronage from the synagogal common chest freed Heracles from formal, legal dependence upon his former master Chreste and protected him from any *paramonē* claims by her heirs, Heracleides and Heliconias.

Another Jewish inscription discovered in the Euxine city of Panticapaeum provides additional evidence. It records the liberation of a certain slave named Elpia and was drafted with the same *paramonē* formula that occurs in other Bosporan manumission deeds. The document reads:

> I release in the synagogue Elpia the son(?) of my slave, bred in my house [θρεπτός]; he shall remain undisturbed and unassailable by any of my heirs, except for [his duty] to visit regularly the synagogue [χωρὶς τοῦ προσκαρτερεῖν τῇ προσευχῇ]; the community of the Jews and the God-fearers(?) will be [together with me] guardian [of the enfranchised] [ἐπιτροπευούσης τῆς συναγωγῆς τῶν Ἰουδαίων καὶ θεὸν σέβων].[83]

This deed is similar to the other Panticapaeum deed, concerning Chreste and her slave Heracles. Elpia, another θρεπτός, is manumitted without *paramonē* obligations to either his former master or any of his former master's heirs. The freedman Elpia, however, must remain with the synagogue, observing the requirement "to visit [it] regularly" (προσκαρτερεῖν; as we saw above, the nominal form of the same word appears in the manumission deed of Heracles). This "visitation" refers to the *paramonē* services that were given in return for the synagogue's active involvement in the manumission ceremony and its corporate patronage of the freedman.[84]

Testament Illustrated by Recently Discovered Texts of the Graeco-Roman World, 2d ed., trans. R. M. Strachan (London: Hodder & Stoughton, 1927), 321–22. Bömer, *Untersuchungen*, 104–5.

[82] Nadel, "Slavery on the North Shore," 217; idem, "Actes d'affranchissement," 270–76; see Shim'on Applebaum, *Jews and Greeks in Ancient Cyrene*, SJLA 28 (Leiden: E. J. Brill, 1979), 158, for a suggestion of similar practices in North Africa; but cf. Martin, "Slavery in the Ancient Jewish Family," 120–21 n. 24, 125.

[83] *CII* 683a (= *CIRB* 71); trans. and commentary in Lifshitz, prolegomenon to *Corpus*, 65–67. The editors of *CIRB* date the inscription to the second century C.E.

[84] One might argue that the inscription seems rather to suggest a benefaction to the synagogue and that *paramonē* services were given in return for nothing. Yet one must remember that a heavy moral and legal obligation toward the one responsible for manumission was routinely placed upon a freedman/woman in the ancient world. It is, therefore, more plausible to suppose that the stipulated obligation of *paramonē* services to the

Redemption of captured, enslaved Jews by synagogues continued into Rabbinic times. The Talmud calls it a *mitzvah*.[85] The Jewish evidence of the vellum fragment from Oxyrhynchos and the Bosporan inscriptions, together with the Hellenistic evidence of the Attic and Delphic manumission documents, supports the argument that corporate manumission was practiced throughout the East. This material provides background and a social context against which to read Ignatius.[86]

The Corporate Manumission of Slaves in Ancient Christianity

Ad Polycarp. 4.3 is not an isolated example treating corporate manumission as practiced by early Christian congregations. Many other Christian sources discuss such public displays of generosity from ecclesiastical common chests. In these sources, the three categories of slave, captive, and prisoner become blurred, with all sharing the imagery of chains, shackles, bondage, and need for redemption.[87] This early Christian paraenesis includes calls to both individual and corporate acts of charity.

One example, found in the *Shepherd of Hermas*, presents the "proper way" for individual Christians to spend their personal funds.[88] In the third part of

---

synagogue implies that the synagogue had some important role in effecting Elpia's manumission.

[85] *b. Giṭ.* 46b; also, *m. Giṭ.* 4.9; *m. Šegal.* 2.5; *t. Giṭ.* 3.4 (Lieberman, 255); *t. Šegal.* 1.12 (Lieberman, 204); cf. Josephus, *Vit.* 75 §419; Boaz Cohen, "Civil Bondage in Jewish and Roman Law," in *Louis Ginzberg Jubilee Volume,* Eng. ed. (New York: American Academy for Jewish Research, 1945), 127; Solomon Zeitlin, "Slavery during the Second Commonwealth and the Tannaitic Period," in *Solomon Zeitlin's Studies in the Early History of Judaism,* vol. 4, *History of Early Talmudic Law* (New York: Ktav Publishing House, 1978), 209; G. Fuks, "Where Have All the Freedmen Gone? On an Anomaly in the Jewish Grave-Inscriptions from Rome," *JJS* 36 (1985): 30.

[86] Nadel, "Actes d'affranchissement," 284–85. However, we should recognize that the reverse case may be the more accurate one: namely that Ign. *Ad Polycarp.* 4.3 provides a social context against which to read the two Black Sea documents (*CII* 683 and 683a), since we know more about Ignatius than we do about manumission in the Jewish and non-Jewish communities of the Black Sea region.

[87] Adolf von Harnack, *Die Mission und Ausbreitung des Christentums in den ersten drei Jahrhunderten,* 4th ed. (Leipzig: J. C. Hinrichs, 1924), 1:190.

[88] The *Shepherd of Hermas* is generally considered to be an apocalyptic text written in the early second century at Rome; David Hellholm, *Das Visionenbuch des Hermas als Apokalypse: Formgeschichtliche und texttheoretische Studien zu einer literarischen Gattung,* ConBNT 13.1 (Lund: C. W. K. Gleerup, 1980); Carolyn Osiek, "The Genre and Function of the Shepherd of Hermas," in *Early Christian Apocalypticism: Genre and Social Setting,* ed. Adela Yarbro Collins, Semeia 36 (Decatur, Ga.: Scholars Press, 1986), 113–21; Peter Lampe, *Die stadtrömischen Christen in den ersten beiden Jahrhunderten,* 2d expanded ed., WUNT 18, 2d ser. (Tübingen: J. C. B. Mohr [Paul Siebeck], 1989), 187–88.

the work, the *Similitudes*, the author advises personally affluent Christians: "Therefore instead of lands, purchase afflicted souls as each one is able, and look after widows and orphans."[89] The passage is paraenetic, and connects this purchasing of souls with other duties of Christian charity. The Shepherd additionally encourages corporate charity by the church as a whole: "to minister to widows, to look after orphans and the destitute, to redeem from distress the slaves of God [λυτροῦσθαι τοὺς δούλους τοῦ θεοῦ]."[90] As Carolyn Osiek argues, the most acceptable interpretation of this sentence is that "it refers to the moral tradition and pious praxis of ransoming prisoners."[91] The precise nature of the imprisonment is unclear, partially because the social patterns of slavery, captivity, and detention after arrest were not unambiguously differentiated in early Christian paraenesis.[92]

The *Apostolic Constitutions* provides additional evidence.[93] Using the authority of Solomon, its author exhorts Christian congregations to offer corporate aid to the needy. The passage reads: "Therefore, maintain and clothe those who are in want from the righteous labor of the faithful. And such sums of money as are collected from them in the manner aforesaid, appoint to be laid out in the redemption of the saints, the deliverance of slaves [ῥυόμενοι δούλους], and of captives, and of prisoners, and of those that have been condemned by tyrants to single combat and death in the name of Christ."[94] The *Constitutions* continues, exhorting believers to perform individual acts of personal charity. They are "not to go to any of those public meetings, unless to purchase a slave, and save a soul [or life; ψυχὴν περιποιήσασθαι], and at the same time to buy such other things as suit their necessities."[95] Here is a clear case of individual Christians being advised to visit the urban chattel markets, to approach slave dealers, and to buy slaves, perhaps for conversion.[96] The clause "save a life/soul" is admittedly ambiguous. It may simply have the

---

[89] *Herm. Sim.* 1.8 (GCS 48.1.47); see Norbert Brox, *Der Hirt des Hermas*, Kommentar zu den Apostolischen Väter 7 (Göttingen: Vandenhoeck & Ruprecht, 1991), 288.

[90] *Herm. Mand.* 8.10 (GCS 48.1.35); see Brox, *Hirt des Hermas*, 234–35.

[91] Carolyn Osiek, "The Ransom of Captives: Evolution of a Tradition," *HTR* 74 (1981): 372; arguing correctly against Bartchy, *ΜΑΛΛΟΝ ΧΡΗΣΑΙ*, 101, who places exclusive emphasis on slavery at the expense of the broader metaphor of imprisonment generally.

[92] Osiek, "Ransom," 373.

[93] The *Const. App.* is a composite work dated to around 380; Marcel Metzger, *Les Constitutions Apostoliques*, SC 320 (Paris: Cerf, 1985), 1:54–62.

[94] *Const. App.* 4.9.2 (SC 329.186); cf. 5.1–2 (SC 329.202–4). The author(s) of the *Didascalia Apostolorum*, which was compiled in the third century and served as a source for the *Const. App.*, retains the meaning "to redeem," translating Greek ῥυόμαι into Syriac *prq*; *Didasc. Ap.* 19 (CSCO 407.184). I thank David Brakke for translating the Syriac for me.

[95] *Const. App.* 2.62.4 (SC 320.336).

[96] Harnack, *Mission und Ausbreitung*, 1:189–90.

ordinary sense of bodily safety and survival – the slave would be spared death.[97] Yet the clause may also reflect traditions similar to those behind Jas 5:20, which interpret "saving a life" (σώσει ψυχήν) in its technical, theological Christian sense of rescuing (and converting) a sinner's soul – the slave would become a Christian. I find the latter interpretation more plausible, and argue for the translation "save a soul" in the technical sense of conversion.[98]

In his *Social Structure of the Early Christian Communities,* the Marxist scholar Dimitris Kyrtatas denies that the "purchasing" in this passage implies manumission, or that it has anything to do with slavery. He argues, instead, that the author of the *Constitutions* refers to "illegally captured free[born] Christians."[99] Yet Kyrtatas's overarching agenda aims to deny an old thesis, chiefly expressed and made popular within and outside academic circles by the French ecclesiastical historian Paul Allard, that ancient Christianity advocated all-out emancipation (N.B., not manumission) of every slave and abolition of the entire institution of slavery.[100] This thesis has largely been abandoned by scholars of ancient slavery, in part because Westermann so successfully refuted it in his *Slave Systems of Greek and Roman Antiquity.*[101] Ancient Christians did not hold abolitionist tendencies, but considered slavery a natural, integral part of human civilization; they used slavery as a fundamental metaphor for the believer's proper relation to God. Here as in chapter 1, "abolition" refers exclusively to the moral and political conviction (originating out of the Enlightenment) that slavery, both as an institution and an ideology, is repugnant to the aims of all civilized and just societies of human beings.[102] Rather than serving as an example of early Christian abolitionist activity (Allard's thesis) or having nothing at all to do with manumission (Kyrtatas's position), the situation in the *Constitutions* appears more analogous to that of the Jewish maid at Oxy-

---

[97] Cf. Luke 17:33. The Evangelist, however, plays upon the ambiguity between the ordinary, everyday meaning and the technical, Christian interpretation of ψυχή.

[98] This interpretation is also advanced in *ANF* 7:424 n. 9; M. Metzger, *Constitutions Apostoliques,* 337, translates Greek ψυχή into French *vie,* not *âme.*

[99] Dimitris J. Kyrtatas, *The Social Structure of the Early Christian Communities* (New York: Verso Press, 1987), 68.

[100] Paul Allard, *Les esclaves chrétiens, depuis les premiers temps de l'eglise jusqu'à la fin de la domination romaine en occident,* 6th ed. (Paris: Victor Lecoffre, 1914), xiii et passim; he, in turn, was influenced by Henri Wallon (*Histoire de l'esclavage dans l'antiquité,* 2d ed. [Paris: Hachette, 1879], esp. 3:1–46, 296–444), whose monograph and personal legislative efforts pressed the abolition of slavery in the French colonies during the period that led up to the 1848 revolution.

[101] Westermann, *Slave Systems,* 152–53; Finley, *Ancient Slavery and Modern Ideology,* 14–15. See also Ramsay MacMullen, *Changes in the Roman Empire: Essays in the Ordinary* (Princeton: Princeton University Press, 1990), 142–55.

[102] David Brion Davis, *The Problem of Slavery in Western Culture* (1966; reprint, New York: Oxford University Press, 1988), 422–45; idem, *Slavery and Human Progress* (New York: Oxford University Press, 1984), 107–16.

rhynchos and what Ignatius found threatening in Asia Minor churches. Thus, it provides further testimony that Christians ransomed slaves as a conscious tool of mission.

Justin Martyr provides a third illustration. In his first *Apology*, a petition (τὸ βιβλίδιον, corresponding to Latin *libellus*) addressed to the Roman Emperor Antoninus Pius and his sons Marcus Aurelius and Lucius Verus,[103] Justin sketches the institution of a common chest and the use of its funds for corporate charity. He writes: "And they who are wealthy, and willing, give what each thinks fit; and the collection is deposited with the president, who supports [ἐπικουρεῖ] the orphans and widows, and those who are in want, through sickness or any other cause, and those who are in chains [τοῖς ἐν δεσμοῖς], and the stranger sojourning among us, and, in a word, takes care of all who are in need."[104] Justin describes churches performing corporate acts of charity, using their common chests to support "those in chains." Whether "those in chains" refers to prisoners, captives, or slaves is unclear. Most likely Justin follows common early Christian paraenesis by blending together all three categories of shackled persons in his description of church support of the imprisoned.[105]

These examples show that exhortations to and descriptions of both corporate and individual public displays of generosity to the imprisoned are common in early Christian literature. These particular calls to and acts of public charity differ from the practices of Athenian, Hellenistic, or Roman private associations, which seem more commonly to give mutual aid to their own than to offer unsolicited help to widows, orphans, slaves, and other kinless people.[106] The manumission of slaves operated for these Christians as a conscious tool of mission to gain converts. It was still practiced in the time of Augustine.[107] Further examples of Christians ransoming "those imprisoned"

---

[103] Fergus G. B. Millar, *The Emperor in the Roman World, 31 B.C.–A.D. 337* (London: Duckworth, 1977), 563; Robert M. Grant, *Greek Apologists of the Second Century* (Philadelphia: Westminster Press, 1988), 54–55.

[104] Just. *1 Apol.* 67.6 (Goodspeed, 75–76).

[105] Cf. Osiek, "Ransom," 374–75.

[106] G. Uhlhorn, *Christian Charity in the Ancient Church*, trans. Sophia Taylor (Edinburgh: T. & T. Clark, 1883), 8 et passim, argues for a fundamental distinction between Greco-Roman *liberalitas* and Christian *caritas*; Harnack, *Mission und Ausbreitung*, 1:170–220, calls Uhlhorn "unfair to paganism" (170–71 n. 3). Harnack, nonetheless, still agrees with the pagan/Christian distinction; as does Hamel, *Poverty*, 219–20, who follows Hands, *Charities*, 35–61. See also the earlier work by Hendrick Bolkestein, *Wohltätigkeit und Armenpflege im vorchristlichen Altertum: Ein Beitrag zum Problem "Moral und Gesellschaft"* (Utrecht: A. Oosthoek, 1939).

[107] Henry Chadwick, "New Letters of St. Augustine," *JTS* 34 (1983): 432–33. On Augustine and slavery, see now Richard Klein, *Die Sklaverei in der Sicht der Bischöfe Ambrosius und Augustinus*, Forschungen zur antiken Sklaverei 20 (Stuttgart: F. Steiner, 1988), and the recent critical review by Andrew Lenox-Conyingham, *JTS* 43 (1992): 255–58.

include the work known as the martyr-acts of Pionius (ca. 300 C.E.), which describes Christians in Smyrna sneaking supplies to the runaway (or banished) slave Sabina, and offering funds to buy her freedom from her pagan mistress.[108] Even critics of Christianity noticed its ransoming of the imprisoned. Lucian of Samosata satirizes such Christian charitable contributions to redeem a prisoner, depicting how a charlatan like Peregrinus could easily bamboozle these stupid Christians out of their money.[109] Ignatius stands alone among Christian authors in his criticism of ransoming taken too far.

The Greco-Roman Rhetoric on the Dangers of Slave Recruitment

Why was Ignatius against this practice? Perhaps he was concerned that congregations might offer ransom money for himself, releasing him from his chains and thereby denying his opportunity to "attain God" through the mouths of the beasts in the Roman arena. Yet, given that Ignatius in *Smyrn.* 6.2 attacks his opponents on the grounds that they show no concern for the widowed, orphaned, distressed, or imprisoned, the issue demands further consideration.[110] When compared to similar Christian charity lists, this type of exhortation would normally include, not exclude, financial help to ransom those enslaved, especially since the association between prisoners and slaves was common in early Christian paraenesis. Ignatius's restriction of the corporate manumission of slaves differs significantly from other Christian authors, and seems odd in the light of what he writes about the importance of charity to "those imprisoned" in his correspondence with Polycarp's Smyrnaean congregations.[111] Ignatius does not condemn corporate manumission by

---

[108] *Mart. Pion.* 9.3–4 (Musurillo, 138); Robert M. Grant, *Early Christianity and Society: Seven Studies* (San Francisco: Harper & Row, 1977), 93; Kyrtatas, *Social Structure,* 67. The passage suggests that Sabina was already a Christian when she was cast out on the mountains and when other Christians offered her help. Thus the eventual manumission was not for the purpose of mission in this case, but to save a fellow Christian. For the dating of *Mart. Pion.,* see Arthur J. Droge and James D. Tabor, *A Noble Death: Suicide and Martyrdom among Jews and Christians in Antiquity* (New York: HarperCollins, 1992), 164–65 n. 124.

[109] Lucian, *Peregr.* 12–13; Osiek, "Ransom," 375–76. For Lucian's knowledge of Ignatius's letter to Polycarp, and his possible parody of the letter in *Peregrinus,* see Schoedel, *Ignatius,* 279. On the verbal parallels between Lucian and Ignatius, see Betz, *Lukian,* 109 n. 9; C. P. Jones, *Culture and Society in Lucian* (Cambridge: Harvard University Press, 1986), 122.

[110] Maier, *Social Setting,* 154–55.

[111] *Pace* Martin, *Slavery as Salvation,* 8; Lawrence P. Jones, "A Case Study in 'Gnosticism': Religious Responses to Slavery in the Second Century C.E." (Ph.D. diss., Columbia University, 1988), 132; and Davis, *Problem of Slavery,* 87, who all view Ign. *Pol.* 4.3 incorrectly as an example of some "normative" early Christian attitude against the manumission of slaves.

churches outright, but instead aims to control what he perceives as its abuse. Why were slaves a special case for Ignatius? One might surmise that the issue was simply that common chest manumission should be at the initiative of the bishop or those with wealth as a freely chosen benefaction rather than at the initiative of the slave, which was considered improper and self-centered. I, however, propose that further explanation lies in the Greco-Roman commonplace of slave recruitment.

As we saw in chapter 2, classical authors often warned that groups recruiting slaves by nondomestic offers of manumission presented dangers to unity, especially in times of war and political upheaval. In the Roman late Republic, Cicero had warned of slaves being recruited into the violent gangs (or *collegia*) under the leadership of the populist tribune Clodius. Cicero's language uses a commonplace in Greco-Roman rhetoric: the polarities of the faithful slave and the unfaithful slave.[112] Clodius, Cicero writes, enlists (*conscribo*) slaves as a military commander enlists soldiers.[113] He claims that Clodius "would have made our slaves his own freedmen/women."[114] These charges against Clodius echo similar charges brought against another threat to order in Rome – Catiline and his conspiracy. Plutarch reports that many had "urged Catiline to set the slaves free and to march them on Rome." The Greek biographer further writes that the evening of the attack was fixed to coincide with "one of the nights of the Saturnalia," when slaves typically enjoyed an extraordinary degree of license.[115] Roman historians differ on the historical accuracy of this passage.[116] Whatever its historicity, the rhetoric of the passage nevertheless worked because it played upon Roman slaveholders' very real fears of slave recruitment.

---

[112] On the faithful slave *topos*, see Val. Max. 6.8; Vell. Pat. 2.67.2; Joseph Vogt, *Ancient Slavery and the Ideal of Man*, trans. Thomas Wiedemann (Cambridge: Harvard University Press, 1975), 129–45.

[113] Cic. *Dom.* 54; *Red. in Sen.* 33.

[114] Cic. *Mil.* 89: *servos nostros libertos suos fecisset.*

[115] Plut. *Vit. Cic.* 18.3; Zvi Yavetz, "The Failure of Catiline's Conspiracy," *Historia* 12 (1963): 494.

[116] J. Annequin, "Esclaves et affranchis dans la conjuration de Catilina," in *Actes du colloque 1971 sur l'esclavage*, Annales littéraires de l'Université de Besançon 40, Centre de recherches d'histoire ancienne 6 (Paris: Les Belles Lettres, 1972), 206; Keith R. Bradley, "Slaves and the Conspiracy of Catiline," *CP* 73 (1978): 329 n. 5. Bradley claims that slaves did not need manumission promises because "in their own eyes, slaves automatically became 'free' as soon as they escaped" ("Slaves and the Conspiracy," 335). I disagree with this evaluation of slave psychology, especially in the light of Epictetus, who describes the slave runaway and his or her fear of discovery precisely to exemplify the unfree person. Runaways constantly glance around and "if someone mentions the word 'master' they are instantly all in a flutter and upset" (Arr. *Epict. diss.* 1.29.59–60; see also 2.1.9–11; but cf. 1.9.8–10).

Other ancient authors exploited this rhetorical *topos* to point to the dangers, especially during violent times of political upheaval, of slaves being lured away from their masters by manumission offers from opposing factions.[117] Plutarch reports that after Sulla's capture of Rome, many urged Cinna "to call the slaves to arms under the promise of manumission."[118] Strabo says that Aristonicus "assembled a large number of resourceless people, and also of slaves, invited with the promise of manumission" in his revolt to seize the throne of Pergamum.[119] Appian narrates how aristocratic Romans from the senatorial and equestrian orders recruited slaves, especially slaves of their political enemies, to take their respective sides in factional violence of the Roman Republican civil wars. Some slaves, however, did not accept such manumission offers.[120] These few remained loyal and received praise in the narrative for being moral *exempla* of "faithful slaves."[121]

From these examples, a rhetorical pattern emerges. Resorting to recruitment of followers by promising to manumit slaves, who then owed *operae* to someone other than their master, revealed a city and state turned upside down and in great danger of collapse. In his slandering of Clodius and the Clodian *collegia,* Cicero skillfully crafted his language to exploit the fear of slave recruitment by manumission offers. This language would have had a stunning effect, especially to senators who had fresh memories of Spartacus, who only thirteen years previously had ravaged Italy in a war that took three years and ten consular legions to suppress.[122] Understanding this rhetorical commonplace in the enduring legacy of Spartacus makes the negative tone of Ignatius against the abuse of corporate manumission in house churches more intelligible.

---

[117] The *topos* of slave recruitment belongs to a wider rhetoric of accusation entrenched in Greco-Roman political vocabulary, namely, to brand political enemies, particularly aristocratic competitors, as recruiters of bandits, slaves, and other social inferiors so they might gain power by illegitimate means. See the excellent discussion by Brent D. Shaw, "Bandits in the Roman Empire," *P & P* 105 (1984): 23, 33.

[118] Plut. *Vit. Mar.* 42.2; cf. 35.5; 41.2; 43.3; Kathleen O'Brien Wicker, "Mulierum virtutes (Moralia 242e–263c)," in Betz, *Plutarch's Ethical Writings,* 125.

[119] Strabo 14.1.38; for further examples, see F. W. Walbank, *The Hellenistic World* (Cambridge: Harvard University Press, 1982), 167–68, 170, 173.

[120] *Pace* Bartchy, *ΜΑΛΛΟΝ ΧΡΗΣΑΙ,* 110–11; idem, "Slavery (Greco-Roman)," *ABD* 6 (1992): 71 (stated less strongly), who argues incorrectly that it was impossible for a slave to refuse manumission. One needs to separate an offer of manumission from the master, who had the legal right to manumit, and an offer from a third party. One also needs to distinguish between third parties who legally purchased a slave's freedom and third parties who violently disrupted the master/slave or *patronus/libertus* bond.

[121] Appian, *BC* 1.26; 1.54; 1.58; 1.65; Bradley, *Slaves and Masters,* 85.

[122] On Spartacus, see now Keith R. Bradley, *Slavery and Rebellion in the Roman World, 140 B.C.–70 B.C.* (Bloomington: Indiana University Press, 1989), 83–101.

I argue that Ignatius wanted the Christian slave to imitate the model of the faithful slave in both the Christian and pagan sense. Such calls to loyalty may also reflect Ignatius's own interpretation of 1 Cor 7:21, the final clause of which is both a brachylogy and ambiguous in Greek (μᾶλλον χρῆσαι). The Antiochene bishop possibly understood Paul as exhorting Christian slaves to refuse tempting liberation offers and to remain in their servile positions for the duration of the present eschatological turmoil. Ignatius was a Paulinist, who had clear knowledge of 1 Corinthians; Ign. *Rom.* 4.3 has direct verbal parallels to 1 Cor 7:22. In *Pol.* 4.3, the bishop sought to clarify and interpret 1 Cor 7:21 for Polycarp and his Smyrnaean congregations.[123] In Ign. *Rom.* 4.3, Ignatius sought to clarify and interpret Paul's passage for himself and the Roman congregations. The bishop writes, "I am a convict; those ones [i.e., the apostles Peter and Paul] were free, but I am a slave even up to now. But if I suffer, I will become the freedman of Jesus Christ, and will arise free in him. Now as one bound I am learning to desire nothing [μηδὲν ἐπιθυμεῖν]."[124] Ignatius calls himself an enslaved "convict" (κατάκριτος), using the legal imagery of a *servus poenae* (penal slave), a free person who became a slave and thus lost any citizenship through condemnation with capital punishment, typically sentenced to labor in the public works, the mines, or the gladiatorial troops. But by exhibiting loyalty to his true, divine master, the bishop hoped to gain "spiritual" manumission as a reward. Ignatius aspired not to break out of his imprisonment by questionable means and faced his capital punishment as a "faithful slave." He learned "as one bound [by chains, being a penal slave] to desire [ἐπιθυμεῖν] nothing" worldly, even potential ransom money that might set him free (similar to Socrates' refusal to let his associates ransom him out of prison). Ign. *Rom.* 4.3 uses metaphorical language based upon a social actuality and makes apparent what the bishop's concerns in *Pol.* 4.3 were. He did not want Christian slaves to desire to be freed out of the common chest, a policy that he extended even to his own situation as a *servus poenae*.

Although the corporate manumission of slaves was a common practice in early Christianity, Ignatius could have seen it posing three dangers to his episcopal authority. The first danger was the intrusion of self-seeking initiates into congregations. Freeborn Christians could have rejected baptized freedmen/women, who sought conversion only for the money, as unwelcomed "slaves of greed." The resultant internal strife would have threatened the unity for which Ignatius so passionately strove, as his letters reveal. The second danger was pagan slander against Christianity and its gospel.[125] Even the

---

[123] Meinhold, "Die Ethik des Ignatius von Antiochien," in *Studien zu Ignatius*, 75–77.
[124] *Rom.* 4.3 (SAQ 2.1.1.99 = SC 10.112).
[125] Cf. *Trall.* 8.2 (SAQ 2.1.1.95 = SC 10.100): "Do not give a pretext to the Gentiles, so that the congregation in God may not be slandered because of a few fools. For woe be it to the one through whom my name is slandered among some by foolishness."

rumor that churches corporately sponsored the manumissions of slaves for recruitment purposes could have been seen as subversive by society. Ignatius exploited the *topos* of slave recruitment as an apologetic stratagem to deflect potential criticism by non-Christians that churches institutionally lured slaves away from pagan masters. Pagan slaves may have been attracted to wealthy congregations in the hope that they would (later) be manumitted.[126] The third danger was competition for members among house churches. Without unity and episcopal control over the common chest, only rich – or worse, "heretical" – house churches could have afforded to buy members through corporate manumission.[127] In addition, Ignatius may be saying that the support of widows and orphans is more important than manumission if house churches were limited in funds.

Ignatius writes of the dangers caused by desertion in times of crises with another, related image, which concerns army loyalty. He exhorts:

> Listen to the bishop, so that God may also listen to you. I am the expiation of those subordinate to the bishop, presbyters, and deacons; and may I obtain my lot with them in God. Toil together with one another. Compete together. Race together. Suffer together. Bunk together. Rise together as God's managerial slaves, attendants, and servants. Be pleasing to whom you are enlisted as a soldier, from whom you also receive your wages; let none of you be found a deserter.[128]

The military metaphors reinforce Ignatius's wider theme of unity.[129] Soldiers must remain loyal to their army commander, from whom they receive their military pay. Slaves, likewise, must display fidelity to the bishop's house church and not be lured away by cash offers of liberation by other unauthorized, and to Ignatius's mind "heretical," house churches.[130]

---

[126] There is some evidence that the churches to which Ignatius wrote were relatively wealthy. They had common chests large enough to make charity to widows, the distressed, and imprisoned (and slaves) a key issue. A further indication of comparative wealth is that the Philadelphian congregations even had archives (τὰ ἀρχεῖα); *Phil* 8.2 (SAQ 2.1.1.104 = SC 10.126); W. R. Schoedel, "Ignatius and the Archives," *HTR* 71 (1978): 97–106. On the relative affluence of Polycarp and his Smyrnaean association of house churches, see Maier, *Social Setting*, 156.

[127] I use the admittedly anachronistic term "heretical" only as a heuristic marker to point out second-century Christian believers considered errant by Ignatius, without making a theological value judgment over whether Ignatius or his opponents expressed a more genuine expression of Christian piety.

[128] *Pol.* 6.1–2 (SAQ 2.1.1.112 = SC 10.150–52).

[129] Cf. 4 Macc 9:23; Adolf Harnack, *Militia Christi: The Christian Religion and the Military in the First Three Centuries*, trans. David M. Gracie (Philadelphia: Fortress Press, 1981), 41–42; Barbara Ellen Bowe, *A Church in Crisis: Ecclesiology and Paraenesis in Clement of Rome*, HDR 23 (Minneapolis: Fortress Press, 1988), 92.

[130] Also, there may have been wealthy "heretical" Christians vying for power within house churches loyal to the bishop.

According to Ignatius, the ultimate authority over the metropolitan common chest was the bishop, together with the colleges of both presbyters and deacons. The social setting involved many individual house churches, each with their own particular common chests, liturgical assemblies, and ecclesiastical leaders.[131] Ignatius's goal was to consolidate control over these various house churches and to create one common chest. The Antiochene bishop assumed an adversarial relationship between himself and errant congregations (and their leaders), whom he declined to mention even by name.[132] This rhetorical tactic of no-naming plays an important role also in Cicero to indicate his hostility and distance from opponents.[133] No-naming enemies denies them legitimacy. The bishop's concern was to increase control and solidarity among house churches that constituted the Christian metropolitan community.[134] By controlling the purse strings, and by denying his opponents' legitimacy to authority, Ignatius attempted to pull individual house church operations in the city of Antioch under his own administrative umbrella. He instructs Polycarp to do likewise in Smyrna.

There are other examples of Ignatius trying to consolidate financial and other matters under his own authority as bishop, lessening the purview of local house churches. Ignatius demands control over liturgical rituals and views only those sacraments (such as the Eucharist, baptism, and *agapē*) valid that are administered by the bishop or by someone he appoints.[135] He also asserts, perhaps with a stern eye cast toward ascetics, that the license to marry belongs only to the bishop.[136] Ignatius exclaims that vows of celibacy must be revealed only to the bishop, and must not become a source of boasting.[137] He dictates that corporate generosity in the name of the church, such as common chest payments to widows and orphans – and slaves, I argue – must go exclusively through the bishop. Financial matters must be administered out of the

---

[131] See note 7 above (p. 160).

[132] *Smyrn.* 5.3 (SAQ 2.1.1.107 = SC 10.136).

[133] J. N. Adams, "Conventions of Naming in Cicero," *CQ* 28 (1978): 163–64. The Apostle Paul also employs this tactic; Victor Paul Furnish, *II Corinthians*, AB 32A (New York: Doubleday, 1984), 49.

[134] Maier, *Social Setting*, 154.

[135] Ign. *Eph.* 20.2 (SAQ 2.1.1.88 = SC 10.76); *Phld.* 4 (SAQ 2.1.1.103 = SC 10.122); *Smyrn.* 7 and 8 (SAQ 2.1.1.108 = SC 10.138–40); and probably *Eph.* 13.1 (SAQ 2.1.1.86 = SC 10.68); cited in Cyril C. Richardson, "The Church in Ignatius of Antioch," *JR* 17 (1937): 434–35. Eric G. Jay, "From Presbyter-Bishops to Bishops and Presbyters: Christian Ministry in the Second Century," *SecCent* 1 (1981): 137–38; Maier, *Social Setting*, 148, 154.

[136] *Pol.* 5.2 (SAQ 2.1.1.112 = SC 10.150); Hermann J. Vogt, "Ignatius von Antiochien über den Bischof und seine Gemeinde," *TQ* 158 (1978): 24–25.

[137] *Pol.* 5.2 (SAQ 2.1.1.112 = SC 10.150); Christine Trevett, "Prophecy and Anti-Episcopal Activity: A Third Error Combated by Ignatius?" *JEH* 34 (1983): 7–9, 11.

episcopal, city wide common fund, which presumably was collected into a strongbox and locked safely in a room of the bishop's own house church. Corporate payments should absolutely not come out of other, local house church treasuries without episcopal authorization.[138] Ignatius commands that only the bishop can summon official church councils, employ ecclesiastical letter couriers, sign letters of commendation, and elect authorized ambassadors to visit other churches.[139] He denies anyone liturgical, business, or any other ecclesiastical power without episcopal consent.[140] Ignatius even denies that recalcitrant house churches can claim the holy appellation "church."[141] He curses such unauthorized congregations as "serving the devil."[142] From these examples, one can see that Ignatius attempts to consolidate and legitimate his authority over all areas of Christian life, including prayer, fellowship, creed, organization, correspondence, and titular nomenclature.

But what exactly was going on in the churches where slaves were being freed "out of the common chest"? In answering this question, I am trying to construct a more plausible context than what previous commentators have thus far provided. *Pol.* 4.3 could reflect at least four distinct phenomena, each with differing legal consequences and social implications. In one scenario, churches were buying slaves outright and subsequently manumitting them; church ownership of slaves is attested well into the late antique and Byzantine periods.[143] In this case, freedmen/women obligations would have been owed to the church. In the second scenario, churches were offering payment to individual, private owners as an incentive to manumit particular slaves re-

---

[138] *Pol.* 4.1 (SAQ 2.1.1.111 = SC 10.148); Richardson, "Church in Ignatius," 439.

[139] *Pol.* 7.2 (SAQ 2.1.1.112–13 = SC 10.152); *Smyrn.* 11.2–3 (SAQ 2.1.1.109 = SC 10.140–42); Richardson, "Church in Ignatius," 439. On the letter as a political instrument in ancient Christianity, see the recent discussion in Koester, "Writings and the Spirit," 356–64.

[140] *Smyrn.* 8.1 (SAQ 2.1.1.108 = SC 10.138); Patrick Burke, "The Monarchical Episcopate at the End of the First Century," *JES* 7 (1970): 507–8.

[141] *Trall.* 3.1 (SAQ 2.1.1.93 = SC 10.96); cf. *Magn.* 4 (SAQ 2.1.1.89 = SC 10.82); Maier, *Social Setting,* 165–66. The term "catholic church" (ἡ καθολικὴ ἐκκλησία) appears for the first time in early Christian literature in *Smyrn.* 8.2 (SAQ 2.1.1.108 = SC 10.138), yet it cannot be understood as meaning "orthodox." Rather, Ignatius coins the term to contrast his episcopal churches from other, unauthorized assemblies; Schoedel, *Ignatius,* 243–44; Koester, "Writings and the Spirit," 360 n. 29.

[142] *Smyrn.* 9.1 (SAQ 2.1.1.108 = SC 10.140); Richardson, "Church in Ignatius," 436; Maier, *Social Setting,* 174–75.

[143] Greg.-M. *Ep.* 6.12 (CCSL 140.381 [= PL 77.804], September 595 C.E.); Gervase Corcoran, "The Christian Attitude to Slavery in the Early Church," *Milltown Studies* 13 (1984): 9; Raphael Taubenschlag, *The Law of Greco-Roman Egypt in the Light of the Papyri: 332 B.C.–640 A.D.*, 2d ed. (Warsaw: Państowowe Wydawnictwo Naukowe, 1955), 69 n. 14; cf. P. Oxy. 673 (= Naphtali Lewis and Meyer Reinhold, *Roman Civilization: Selected Readings,* vol. 2, *The Empire,* 3d ed. [New York: Columbia University Press, 1990], 569–70).

cently baptized by the congregation. The freedmen/women, in this case, would still have been held to obligations to their former masters. In the third scenario, churches were ransoming slaves with the guarantee that the former master would have forfeited any future claims upon the freedman/woman's body and labor in legal language similar to the Oxyrhynchos vellum fragment concerning the maid Paramone's manumission. These freedmen/women would have become legally independent of their former masters and would have been indebted to the house church that ransomed them. In the fourth scenario, churches were providing a public assembly with witnessed recognition of some Hellenistic or Roman manumission ceremony, in situations comparable to the Jewish Bosporus inscriptions. The social implications of this fourth hypothetical case are difficult to judge. Although slaves of non-Romans were manumitted according to local customs, the administrative complications for formal manumission by a Roman citizen (that is, *manumissio vindicta* before a magistrate) were great.[144] The formal Roman ceremony was always at the pleasure of the magistrate, normally the provincial governor touring local assize centers in the region. As a consequence, a slave might have had to wait several months after a manumission promise had been given until the governor would have been available to officiate, assuming the magistrate even expressed a willingness to perform the ceremony at all. In addition, Roman slaveowners might not have been inclined to take the added time, effort, and expense of travel to a provincial assize center.[145] Given these difficulties, it is quite understandable why, in the Roman imperial period, informal manumission forms, such as ceremonies "before friends" as witnesses (*manumissio inter amicos*), became more common than those involving formal, magisterial procedures. After Constantine, the church developed its own version of informal Roman manumission, called *manumissio in ecclesia*.[146] Perhaps *Pol.* 4.3 reflects an earlier version of this or some related Hellenistic ceremony.[147] It is difficult to state with precision which one of these four distinct phenomena is reflected in *Pol.* 4.3. Most likely, the passage covers a broad range of activities, including combinations of some or all of the above. What one can say with certainty is that whatever the particulars, corporate manumission became a burning issue for Ignatius. Private, individual forms of manumission do not appear to have concerned him, however, at least not in his extant letters.

---

[144] Buckland, *Textbook of Roman Law*, 73–74; Berger, *Encyclopedic Dictionary*, 577.

[145] Bradley, *Slaves and Masters*, 101–2.

[146] Buckland, *Textbook of Roman Law*, 81–82; Berger, *Encyclopedic Dictionary*, 576; Watson, *Roman Slave Law*, 31; F. Fabbrini, *La manumissio in ecclesia*, Istituto di diritto romano e dei diritti dell'Oriente mediterraneo 40 (Milan: A. Giuffrè, 1965).

[147] Nadel, "Actes d'affranchissement," 284.

This urgent call to restrict corporate manumission belongs to Ignatius's wider concern for unity. Local neighborhood house churches were providing funds out of their common chests to manumit slaves after some Hellenistic or Roman fashion. They did so perhaps with recruitment of additional baptized Christians in mind, but also in the interest of gaining some other tangible return. This return possibly included the *paramonē* obligations that slaves would have owed to the respective house churches. This hypothesis assumes that slave liberation ceremonies were local, following Hellenistic customs, rather than involving Roman manumission procedures, either formal or informal. This assumption is based upon the knowledge that Ignatius's exhortation to Polycarp about slaves was also directed to Christian congregations in Smyrna, a city whose population remained largely non-Roman under the reign of Trajan.[148] Yet even if some Romans were involved, my thesis still holds. In these special cases, the local house church providing for the ceremony would have been after the concrete *operae* work stipulations. What specific *operae* obligations would have been involved? Perhaps the congregation simply wanted a Roman freedman/woman client to increase its public image and respectability (in the technical Roman aristocratic virtue of *dignitas*) before the eyes of either other house churches, its non-Christian neighbors, or a combination of both. Another reason for such recruitment of an enfranchised client could have been that the house church planned to make the Roman citizen its financial *procurator*, an economic officer legally empowered to be a party to *mancipatio*, which later congregations are known to have employed.[149]

But what did a house church hope to gain by claiming Hellenistic *paramonē* rights? Given the unspecific nature of *paramonē* obligations generally, answering this question is difficult. Perhaps the house church wanted a general handyman/woman to hang around the home and serve, in some capacity, the liturgical or custodial needs of the congregation. Or, possibly, the congregation actively recruited slaves by giving them manumission promises in an effort to swell the train of legally free dependents tied to the particular house church. Such a crowded house of protégés would have brought fame, respect, and prominence to the congregation.[150] Additionally, the patron(s) of a house church facing Roman or provincial persecution might have adopted manumission as a legal maneuver to avoid interrogation by torture of its vulnerable servile members. In any case, the giving for the sake of a return is analogous

---

[148] Fergus G. B. Millar, *The Roman Empire and Its Neighbours,* 2d ed. (London: Duckworth, 1981), 85–89, 196–97; idem, *Emperor in the Roman World,* 483–86.

[149] Cypr. *Ep.* 50 (CSEL 3.3.613–14); for commentary, see G. W. Clarke, *The Letters of St. Cyprian of Carthage,* ACW 44 (New York: Newman Press, 1984), 2:280.

[150] See E. Courtney, *A Commentary on the Satires of Juvenal* (London: Athlone Press, 1980), 26.

to the concerns reflected in the Attic, Delphic, and Bosporus inscriptions, as well as in the vellum fragment from Oxyrhynchos. *Paramonē* obligations directly to house congregations would have established a hierarchy of patronage independent of any "monarchical" bishop who claimed authority over the whole metropolitan area.[151] This independence would have fueled the potential for a power struggle between Ignatian clergy and wealthy house church patrons over which group controlled congregational church funds. Indeed, the clergy and the rich were two distinct and sometimes rival sources of authority in early Christianity.[152]

Yet with this said, one might still simply interpret this advice as yet another text proving that Ignatius was a so-called social conservative, like the author of the Pastoral Epistles and other bishops in the second century generally. I contend, however, that such a general reference to "social conservatism" only confuses the issue and ignores the specifics of Ignatius's situation. Personal manumission of individual slaves constituted an ordinary part of Roman life and in itself was not considered a revolutionary act. Favoring or opposing it had nothing at all to do with conservative social, political, or economic attitudes as defined by any ancient standards.[153] Even social conservatives like Cicero freed their slaves and considered the regularity of the act desirable. Ignatius's rhetoric points not to social conservatism on slavery, but rather directs attention to his specific concern about unity and episcopal control over the church funds used for corporate manumission.

Summation

It is notoriously difficult to reconstruct what the actual lives of early Christians were like, since very little evidence survives. Yet the second-century Antiochene bishop Ignatius does provide one important piece of evidence to reconstruct social history. In his letter to Polycarp, he mentions the practice of

---

[151] On the thorny issue of Ignatius as a monarchical bishop, see Allen Brent, "The Relations between Ignatius and the Didascalia," *SecCent* 8 (1991): 130–34, who argues that this term better applies to the *Didasc.* than to the Ignatian letters; idem, "The Ignatian Epistles and the Threefold Ecclesiastical Order," *JRH* 17 (1992): 18–32; Maier, *Social Setting*, 177–78.

[152] L. W. Countryman, "Patrons and Officers in Club and Church," in *SBLSP* 11, ed. Paul J. Achtemeier (Missoula, Mont.: The Society, 1977), 139; cf. Maier, *Social Setting*, 147–48.

[153] As the prime agent of proper Roman social values, the Emperor Augustus certainly allowed for, and approved of, manumission. He directed his manumission legislation (*lex Fulfia Caninia*, *lex Aelia Sentia*, and *lex Junia*) not against manumission *per se*, but against its indiscriminate use by Romans. In this way, Augustus hoped to bar slaves of questionable moral character from access to the Roman citizenship. Bradley, *Slaves and Masters*, 88.

churches manumitting slaves with funds drawn from congregational common chests. This statement becomes quite significant when we consider the serious social meanings and functions that the common chest had in the development of the early church. Like Cicero trying as a senator of consular rank to keep order and unity in the city of Rome under the threat of political upheaval, or a Roman governor trying to maintain control in a province, Ignatius as a second-century Christian leader struggled to maintain church order (under his own terms) in a turbulent period of upheaval and persecution. Trying to wield the authority of a monarchical bishop, he battled to place individual house churches and their liturgical and financial operations under his own control. By attacking what he considered abuses of corporate manumission, Ignatius saw one way to do just that.

Conclusion

From Bondage to Freedom

From the perspective of the science of interpretation, this monograph has explored the problem of how to relate social and economic history to the exegesis of ancient texts. This problem stems from three opposing interpretive methodologies in New Testament studies. The first, the "history of ideas" approach, reads the Christian canon purely for understanding the literary-philosophical development of early Christian intellectual history. The second, the "sociological" (or "social scientific") approach, applies to the ancient sources theoretical models developed from the social sciences in order to augment more traditional modes of exegesis. A third approach, the "social histori-cal," refrains from imposing modern sociological constructs on the ancient data and confines "attention instead to more traditional historiographic ques-tions about the social background and practices of the early Christians."[1] Our hermeneutical task is how best to connect this last approach, also called "social history," to the interpretation of texts. By joining a social historical recon-struction of ancient slavery with an interpretation of 1 Corinthians 7:21 and Ignatius, *Ad Polycarp.* 4.3, this monograph has offered a contribution to solv-ing this hermeneutical problem.

To reconstruct the sociohistorical actuality of ancient slavery, our investiga-tion began with the apothegm, "It is beautiful to die instead of being degraded as a slave," attributed to the freedman Publilius Syrus. Coming from the lips of a liberated slave, these words express the life-giving power of the manu-mission act. The ceremony that effected a move from chattel bondage to legal freedom was a time of celebration in the life of virtually any ancient slave. Early Christianity originated in such a slave culture.

The preceding pages have sought to interpret the earliest extant pieces of Christian literature that deal with the manumission of Christian slaves. Through its exegetical inquiry, the study offers a new interpretation of both 1 Corinthians 7:21 and Ignatius, *Ad Polycarp.* 4.3 that challenges many of the unexamined assumptions behind their traditional readings. It also relocates

---

[1] Susan R. Garrett, "Sociology of Early Christianity," *ABD* 6 (1992): 90.

the issue of slavery in early Christianity from a predominately legal question to one that stems from economic and familial considerations.

The thesis is that neither passage supports the hypothesis, which many scholars in New Testament studies currently hold, that there was early Christian opposition to the liberation of baptized slaves. In fact, the evidence suggests that manumission was of considerable importance in the economic and social affairs of early Christian congregations. Paul allowed for manumission as an exception to his general rule that each should remain in the state in which he or she received the Christian call. Ignatius showed concern only for the abuses of corporate manumission, not private manumission. Perhaps because manumission was an institutional practice in Roman urban slavery, early Christian congregations incorporated its ideology as a tool in their mission to urban areas of the Empire.

Chapter 1 provided a broad map of the terrain under study. It surveyed slavery in the ancient world to clarify how the enslavement process operated in the Greco-Roman milieu of early Christianity. It also exploded a few myths about ancient slavery that unfortunately persist in much of current scholarship. One such myth was that laws reflect social practice; another was that the regularity of manumission in Roman urban society somehow proves that slavery became more humane. Chapter 2 exegeted in detail 1 Corinthians 7:21. After recounting the history of scholarship, the chapter demonstrated through philological and contextual analyses that Paul allows for manumission. I argued on entirely new grounds that the correct translation of the verse is: "You were called as a slave. Do not worry about it. But if you can indeed become free, *use instead* freedom." Essentially, I held that the NRSV wrongly reversed the decision of the previous RSV in its interpretation of 1 Cor 7:21. Additionally, I found nothing in this passage that illustrated Paul's so-called social conservatism on slavery by ancient standards. Like Roman slaveholders, Paul understood that urban slaves might be approached with offers of freedom, and he incorporated the institutional practice of manumission into his theology. My model argues against the common assumption that Paul constructs a systematic ethical position for or against slavery as a social institution in 1 Cor 7:21.

Chapter 3 left the Christian material aside and returned to map out more Greco-Roman territory, this time on the common chest. The common chest was shown to be far more than a trivial matter of administration, as it was a significant issue in the social organization of ancient cities. The argument was that Greek associations (*orgeōnes*, *thiasoi*) and Roman *collegia*, as corporate institutions, followed the model of cities to become actual patrons of freedmen/women. Chapter 4 then took this finding and applied it to Ignatius, *Ad Polycarp.* 4.3. Ignatius, I argued, directed his efforts against a specified economic manumission procedure involving the common chests of local house churches. Because the passage addressed a clearly specified economic proce-dure, it cannot be used as a text proving that the early church was generally opposed to the manumission of Christian slaves. Instead, I directed its com-parison to Greco-Roman commonplaces alarming the audiences to the dan-gers of slave recruitment by associations, a *topos* exemplified by Cicero's rheto-ric against Clodius and Catiline. The thesis was that Ignatius's apprehension about the corporate manumission of baptized slaves revealed his larger apolo-getic stratagem for outside social acceptability and internal ecclesiastical unity under his own terms as a monarchical bishop.

It is my hope that a sophisticated study of how the early forms of Christi-anity related to the ideology and institution of ancient slavery has been pre-sented. Many sources beyond the New Testament came into view and de-manded attention in the effort to see the intellectual undercurrents and presuppositions implicit in the language of Paul and his interpreter Ignatius. These sources required more than just a passing nod to "background," a fate that often befalls the topic of slavery in early Christian studies. Comparative studies were also essential to understanding the fundamental differences be-tween ancient and modern slavery. Yet both institutions share the label "slav-ery," which presumes that they must have some elements in common. I strove to make these similarities and differences clear. The past fifty years have seen an enormous growth of research concerning ancient and modern slavery, the sheer quantity of studies attesting to its continuing fascination. The furious debates over ideologies, Marxist or otherwise, have made this subject more controversial than any other in the study of ancient literature, society, and culture. I cannot claim to have read all of the available secondary literature on every aspect of slavery, but I have made a conscious effort to look at a wide range concerned with the institution and its ideology in antiquity.

Further work to be done includes investigating the role played by slaves and masters in the parables of Jesus, the meaning of the religious language of enslavement and freedom in Pauline theology, the location in Greco-Roman rhetoric of the exhortations to slaves and masters in the New Testament do-mestic codes, and additional patristic literature that provides rich ground for social and cultural history. What this monograph offers is a positive contribu-tion toward the solution of the exegetical problems of 1 Corinthians 7:21 and Ignatius, *Ad Polycarp.* 4.3. It brings an interpretive approach that does not analyze slavery solely in terms of property, but appreciates the dynamic ele-ments of the whole enslavement process, a process that moved for some from bondage to freedom.

Bibliography

Adams, J. N. "Conventions of Naming in Cicero." *CQ* 28 (1978): 145–66.

Adler, Ada, ed. *Suidae Lexicon*. 5 vols. Lexicographi Graeci. Leipzig: B. G. Teubner, 1928–38.

Alföldy, Géza, ed. *Antike Sklaverei: Widersprüche, Sonderformen, Grundstrukturen*. Thyssen-Vorträge 7. Bamberg: C. C. Buchners, 1988.

–. "Die Freilassung von Sklaven und die Struktur der Sklaverei in der römischen Kaiserzeit." *RSA* 2 (1972): 97–129.

Alford, Henry. *The Greek New Testament*. 4 vols. 6th ed. Boston and New York: Lee & Shepard, 1874.

Allard, Paul. *Les esclaves chrétiens, depuis les premiers temps de l'eglise jusqu'à la fin de la domination romaine en occident*. 6th ed. Paris: Victor Lecoffre, 1914.

–. *Esclaves, serfs et mainmortables*. Paris: Société Générale de Librairie Catholique, 1884.

Allioli, Joseph Franz. *Die Heilige Schrift des Alten und Neuen Testaments*. 3 vols. 7th ed. Munich: Vogel, 1851.

Althaus, Paul. *The Ethics of Martin Luther*. Translated by Robert C. Schultz. Philadelphia: Fortress Press, 1972.

Amerasinghe, C. W. "The Part of the Slave in Terence's Drama." *G & R* 19 (1950): 62–72.

Anderson, Graham. *Lucian: Theme and Variation in the Second Sophistic*. Mnemosyne Bibliotheca Classica Batava Supplementum 41. Leiden: E. J. Brill, 1976.

Andreau, Jean. "The Freedman." In Giardina, *The Romans*, 175–98.

Andrews, A. "Philochoros on Phratries." *JHS* 81 (1961): 1–15.

Annequin, J. "Esclaves et affranchis dans la conjuration de Catilina." In *Actes du colloque 1971 sur l'esclavage*, 193–238. Annales littéraires de l'Université de Besançon 40. Centre de recherches d'histoire ancienne 6. Paris: Les Belles Lettres, 1972.

Anshen, Ruth, ed. *Freedom: Its Meaning*. New York: Harcourt, Brace, 1940.

Applebaum, Shim'on. *Jews and Greeks in Ancient Cyrene*. SJLA 28. Leiden: E. J. Brill, 1979.

–. "The Social and Economic Status of the Jews in the Diaspora." In *The Jewish People in the First Century: Historical Geography, Political History, Social, Cultural and Religious Life and Institutions*, edited by S. Safrai and M. Stern, 2:701–27. CRINT 1.2. Amsterdam: Van Gorcum, 1976.

Aretaeus. *Aretaeus*. Edited by Carolus Hude. 2d ed. CMG 2. Berlin: Akademie-Verlag, 1958.

–. *The Extant Works of Aretaeus, the Cappadocian*. Translated by Francis Adams. London: The Syndenham Society, 1856.

Artemidorus. *The Interpretation of Dreams (Oneirocritica)*. Translation and commentary by Robert J. White. Park Ridge, N.J.: Noyes Press, 1975.

Aspasius. *Aspasii in ethica Nicomachea quae supersunt commentaria.* Edited by Gustavus Heylbut. Commentaria in Aristotelem Graeca 19.1. Berlin: G. Reimer, 1889.

Aune, David E., ed. *Greco-Roman Literature and the New Testament.* SBLSBS 21. Atlanta: Scholars Press, 1988.

—. *The New Testament in Its Literary Environment.* Library of Early Christianity. Philadelphia: Westminster Press, 1987.

Ausbüttel, Frank M. *Untersuchungen zu den Vereinen im Westen des römischen Reiches.* Frankfurter althistorische Studien 11. Frankfurt: Michael Laßleben, 1982.

Austin, M. M., and P. Vidal-Naquet. *Economic and Social History of Ancient Greece: An Introduction.* 2d ed. Translated and revised by M. M. Austin. Berkeley and Los Angeles: University of California Press, 1977.

Badian, E. "Figuring Out Roman Slavery." *JRS* 72 (1982): 164–69.

—. *Roman Imperialism in the Late Republic.* Oxford: Basil Blackwell, 1968.

Bagdikian, Anita. "The Civic Officials of Roman Corinth." Master's thesis, University of Vermont, 1953.

Bagnall, Roger S., and Peter Derow. *Greek Historical Documents: The Hellenistic Period.* SBLSBS 16. Chico, Calif.: Scholars Press, 1981.

Bailey, D. R. Shackleton. *Cicero's Letters to Atticus.* Vol. 6. Cambridge: Cambridge University Press, 1967.

Bain, David. *Masters, Servants, and Orders in Greek Tragedy: A Study of Some Aspects of Dramatic Technique and Convention.* Manchester: Manchester University Press, 1981.

Balch, David L. *Let Wives Be Submissive: The Domestic Code in 1 Peter.* SBLMS 26. Chico, Calif.: Scholars Press, 1981.

Bamberger, Bernard J. *Proselytism in the Talmudic Period.* Cincinnati: Hebrew Union College Press, 1939.

Barclay, John M. G. "Paul, Philemon, and the Dilemma of Christian Slave-Ownership." *NTS* 37 (1991): 161–86.

Barnes, Albert. *An Inquiry into the Scriptural Views of Slavery.* Philadelphia: Parry & McMillan, 1855.

Baron, Salo Wittmayer. *A Social and Religious History of the Jews.* Vol. 1. Philadelphia: Jewish Publication Society of America, 1952.

Barrett, C. K. *A Commentary on the First Epistle to the Corinthians.* 2d ed. Black's New Testament Commentaries. London: Adam & Charles Black, 1971.

—. Review of *ΜΑΛΛΟΝ ΧΡΗΣΑΙ,* by S. Scott Bartchy. *JTS* 26 (1975): 173–74.

Barrow, R. H. *Slavery in the Roman Empire.* London: Methuen, 1928.

Bartchy, S. Scott. *ΜΑΛΛΟΝ ΧΡΗΣΑΙ: First-Century Slavery and the Interpretation of First Corinthians 7:21.* SBLDS 11. 1973. Reprint. Atlanta: Scholars Press, 1985.

—. "Philemon, Epistle to." *ABD* 5 (1992): 305–10.

—. "Slavery (Greco-Roman)." *ABD* 6 (1992): 58–73.

Barton, S. C., and G. H. R. Horsley. "A Hellenistic Cult Group and the New Testament Churches." *JAC* 24 (1981): 7–41.

Bauer, Walter. *Die Briefe des Ignatius von Antiochia und der Brief des Polykarp von Smyrna.* 2d ed. Revised by Henning Paulsen. HNT 18. Tübingen: J. C. B. Mohr (Paul Siebeck), 1985.

Baumert, Norbert. *Ehelosigkeit und Ehe im Herrn: Eine Neuinterpretation von 1 Kor 7.* 2d ed. FB 47. Würzburg: Echter, 1986.

Beavis, Mary Ann. "Ancient Slavery as an Interpretive Context for the New Testament Servant Parables with Special Reference to the Unjust Steward (Luke 16:1–8)." *JBL* 111 (1992): 37–54.

Behr, Charles A., ed. *P. Aelius Aristides.* Vol. 1. Leiden: E. J. Brill, 1986.

Bellen, Heinz. "Μᾶλλον χρῆσαι (1 Cor. 7,21): Verzicht auf Freilassung als asketische Leistung?" *JAC* 6 (1963): 177–80.

—. *Studien zur Sklavenflucht im römischen Kaiserreich.* Forschungen zur antiken Sklaverei 4. Wiesbaden: Franz Steiner, 1971.

Berger, Adolf. *Encyclopedic Dictionary of Roman Law.* TAPhS 43.2. Philadelphia: The Society, 1953.

Berger, Peter L., and Thomas Luckmann. *The Social Construction of Reality: A Treatise on the Sociology of Knowledge.* Garden City, N.Y.: Doubleday, 1966.

Berkowitz, Luci, and Karl A. Squitier. *Thesaurus Linguae Graecae: Canon of Greek Authors and Works.* 3d ed. New York: Oxford University Press, 1990.

Berlin, Isaiah. *Four Essays on Liberty.* Chicago: University of Chicago Press, 1960.

Beseler, Gerhard. "Corpus, fiscus, arca, deus." *ZRG* 46 (1926): 83–89.

Betz, Hans Dieter. *Galatians: A Commentary on Paul's Letter to the Churches of Galatia.* Hermeneia. Philadelphia: Fortress Press, 1979.

—. *Lukian von Samosata und das Neue Testament: Religionsgeschichtliche und paränetische Parallelen.* TU 76. Berlin: Akademie-Verlag, 1961.

—. "Paul's Concept of Freedom in the Context of Hellenistic Discussions about the Possibilities of Human Freedom." In *Paulinische Studien: Gesammelte Aufsätze III,* 110–25. Tübingen: J. C. B. Mohr (Paul Siebeck), 1994. First published in The Center for Hermeneutical Studies in Hellenistic and Modern Culture: Protocol of the Twenty-Sixth Colloquy, 9 January 1977, edited by Wilhelm Wuellner, 1–13. Berkeley, Calif.: The Center, 1977.

—, ed. *Plutarch's Ethical Writings and Early Christian Literature.* SCHNT 4. Leiden: E. J. Brill, 1978.

—. *2 Corinthians 8 and 9: A Commentary on Two Administrative Letters of the Apostle Paul.* Edited by George W. MacRae. Hermeneia. Philadelphia: Fortress Press, 1985.

Bieżuńska-Małowist, Iza. "Die Expositio von Kindern als Quelle der Sklavenbeschaffung im griechisch-römischen Ägypten." *JWG* (1971.2): 129–33.

Blass, Friedrich. *Philology of the Gospels.* London: Macmillan, 1898.

Blass, F., and A. Debrunner. *A Greek Grammar of the New Testament and Other Early Christian Literature.* Translated and revised from the 9th–10th German edition by Robert W. Funk. Chicago: University of Chicago Press, 1961.

Bogaert, Raymond. *Banques et banquiers dans les cités grecques.* Leiden: A. W. Sijthoff, 1968.

—. "Geld (Geldwirtschaft)." *RAC* 9 (1976): 797–907.

Bolkestein, Hendrick. "The Exposure of Children at Athens and the ἐγχυτρίστριαι." *CP* 17 (1922): 222–39.

—. *Wohltätigkeit und Armenpflege im vorchristlichen Altertum: Ein Beitrag zum Problem "Moral und Gesellschaft."* Utrecht: A. Oosthoek, 1939.

Bömer, Franz. *Untersuchungen über die Religion der Sklaven in Griechenland und Rom.* 3 Pts. AAWM. Forschungen zur antiken Sklaverei 14, 14.3. Revised by Peter Herz. Wiesbaden/Stuttgart: Franz Steiner, 1982², 1960, 1990².

Booth, Alan D. "The Schooling of Slaves in First-Century Rome." *TAPA* 109 (1979): 11–19.

Bormann, Eugène. "Zu den neuentdeckten Grabschriften jüdischer Katakomben zu Rom." *WS* 34 (1912): 358–69.

Boswell, John E. "*Expositio* and *Oblatio*: The Abandonment of Children and the Ancient and Medieval Family." *AHR* 89 (1984): 10–33.

—. *The Kindness of Strangers: The Abandonment of Children in Western Europe from Late Antiquity to the Renaissance.* New York: Pantheon Books, 1988.

Botte, Dom Bernard, ed. *La Tradition Apostolique de Saint Hippolyte.* 2d ed. Liturgie-wissenschaftliche Quellen und Forschungen 39. Münster: Aschendorffsche Verlags-buchhandlung, 1963.

Bouché-Leclercq, A. *L'Astrologie grecque.* Paris: Leroux, 1899.

Boulvert, Gérard. *Domestique et fonctionnaire sous le Haut-Empire romain: La condition de l'affranchi et de l'esclave du prince.* Annales littéraires de l'Université de Besançon 151. Paris: Belles Lettres, 1974.

–. *Les esclaves et les affranchis impériaux sous le Haut-Empire romain.* 2 vols. in 1. Aix-en-Provence: Centre régional de documentation pédagogique, 1964.

Bourdieu, Pierre. "La production de la croyance: Contribution à une économie des biens symboliques." *Actes de la recherche en sciences sociales* 13 (1977): 3–43.

Bowe, Barbara Ellen. *A Church in Crisis: Ecclesiology and Paraenesis in Clement of Rome.* HDR 23. Minneapolis: Fortress Press, 1988.

Bradley, Keith R. *Discovering the Roman Family: Studies in Roman Social History.* New York: Oxford University Press, 1991.

–. "On the Roman Slave Supply and Slave Breeding." In Finley, *Classical Slavery,* 42–64.

–. Review of *Conquerors and Slaves,* by Keith Hopkins. *CP* 76 (1981): 82–87.

–. "Roman Slavery and Roman Law." *Historical Reflections/Réflexions historiques* 15 (1988): 477–95.

–. "Seneca and Slavery." *C & M* 37 (1986): 161–72.

–. "*Servus Onerosus*: Roman Law and the Troublesome Slave." *Slavery and Abolition* 11 (1990): 135–57.

–. *Slavery and Rebellion in the Roman World: 140 B.C.–70 B.C.* Bloomington: Indiana University Press, 1989.

–. *Slaves and Masters in the Roman Empire: A Study in Social Control.* 1984. Reprint with suppl. bibliog. New York: Oxford University Press, 1987.

–. "Slaves and the Conspiracy of Catiline." *CP* 73 (1978): 329–36.

–. "Social Aspects of the Slave Trade in the Roman World." *MBAH* 5 (1986): 49–58.

–. "Wet-Nursing at Rome: A Study in Social Relations." In *The Family in Ancient Rome: New Perspectives,* edited by Beryl Rawson, 201–29. Ithaca: Cornell University Press, 1986.

Bradshaw, Paul F. *The Search for the Origins of Christian Worship: Sources and Methods for the Study of Early Liturgy.* New York: Oxford University Press, 1992.

Brent, Allen. "The Ignatian Epistles and the Threefold Ecclesiastical Order." *JRH* 17 (1992): 18–32.

–. "The Relations between Ignatius and the Didascalia." *SecCent* 8 (1991): 129–56.

Brockmeyer, Norbert. *Antike Sklaverei.* Erträge der Forschung 116. Darmstadt: Wissenschaftliche Buchgesellschaft, 1979.

Broneer, Oscar. "Colonia Laus Iulia Corinthiensis." *Hesperia* 10 (1941): 388–90.

Brooten, Bernadette J. "'Junia . . . Outstanding among the Apostles' (Rom. 16:7)." In *Women Priests: A Catholic Commentary on the Vatican Declaration,* edited by Leonard Swindler and Arlene Swindler, 141–44. New York: Paulist Press, 1977.

–. *Women Leaders in the Ancient Synagogues.* BJS 36. Chico, Calif.: Scholars Press, 1982.

Brox, Norbert. *Der Hirt des Hermas.* Kommentar zu den Apostolischen Väter 7. Göttingen: Vandenhoeck & Ruprecht, 1991.

Bruce, F. F. *The Acts of the Apostles.* Grand Rapids, Mich.: William B. Eerdmans, 1952.

–. *1 and 2 Corinthians.* NCB. London: Oliphants, 1971.

Brulé, Pierre. *La piraterie Crétoise hellénistique.* Annales littéraires de l'Université de Besançon 223. Centre de recherches d'histoire ancienne 27. Paris: Les Belles Lettres, 1978.

Brunt, P. A. "Aspects of the Social Thought of Dio Chrysostom and the Stoics." *PCPhS* 19 (1973): 9–34.

—. "Evidence Given under Torture in the Principate." *ZRG* 97 (1980): 256–65.

—. "From Epictetus to Arrian." *Athenaeum* 55 (1977): 19–48.

—. *Italian Manpower, 225 B.C.–A.D. 14.* Oxford: Clarendon Press, 1971.

—. "Laus imperii." In *Imperialism in the Ancient World*, edited by P. D. A. Garnsey and C. R. Whittaker, 159–92. Cambridge Classical Studies. Cambridge: Cambridge University Press, 1978.

—. "The Roman Mob." In *Studies in Ancient Society: Past and Present Series*, edited by M. I. Finley, 74–102. London: Routledge & Kegan Paul, 1974. First published in *P & P* 35 (1966): 3–27.

Brunt, P. A., and J. M. Moore, eds. *Res gestae divi Augusti: The Achievements of the Divine Augustus.* New York: Oxford University Press, 1967.

Büchsel, Friedrich. "θυμός, κ.τ.λ." *TDNT* 3 (1965): 167–72.

Buckland, W. W. *The Roman Law of Slavery: The Condition of the Slave in Private Law from Augustus to Justinian.* 1908. Reprint. New York: AMS Press, 1969.

—. *A Textbook of Roman Law from Augustus to Justinian.* 3d ed. Revised by Peter Stein. Cambridge: Cambridge University Press, 1975.

Burdon, Joan. "Slavery as a Punishment in Roman Criminal Law." In *Slavery and Other Forms of Unfree Labour*, edited by Léonie J. Archer, 68–85. History Workshop Series. London: Routledge, 1988.

Burke, Patrick. "The Monarchical Episcopate at the End of the First Century." *JES* 7 (1970): 499–518.

Burtchaell, James T. *From Synagogue to Church: Public Services and Offices in the Earliest Christian Communities.* Cambridge: Cambridge University Press, 1992.

Butts, James R. "The Progymnasmata of Theon: A New Text with Translation and Commentary." Ph.D. diss., Claremont Graduate School, 1986.

Cadbury, Henry J. "Erastus of Corinth." *JBL* 50 (1931): 59–70.

Calderini, Aristide. *La manomissione e la condizione dei liberti in Grecia.* Milan: Ulrico Hoepli, 1908.

Callahan, Allen. "A Note on 1 Corinthians 7:21." *Journal of the Interdenominational Theological Center* 17 (1989–90): 110–14.

Calvin, John. *The Acts of the Apostles, 1–13.* Calvin's Commentaries. Translated by John W. Fraser and W. J. G. McDonald. London: Oliver & Boyd, 1965.

—. *Commentary on the Epistles of Paul the Apostle to the Corinthians.* Calvin's Commentaries. Translated by John Pringle. 1848. Reprint. Grand Rapids, Mich.: Baker Book House, 1984.

Cambiano, Giuseppe. "Aristotle and the Anonymous Opponents of Slavery." In Finley, *Classical Slavery*, 21–42.

Cameron, A. "The Exposure of Children in Greek Ethics." *CR* 46 (1932): 105–14.

—. "ΘΡΕΠΤΟΣ and Related Terms in the Inscriptions of Asia Minor." In *Anatolian Studies Presented to William Hepburn Buckler*, edited by W. M. Calder and J. Keil, 27–62. Manchester: Manchester University Press, 1939.

Campenhausen, Hans von. *Ecclesiastical Authority and Spiritual Power in the Church of the First Three Centuries.* Translated by J. A. Baker. Stanford: Stanford University Press, 1959.

Cartledge, Paul. "Rebels and Sambos in Classical Greece: A Comparative View." In *Crux: Essays in Greek History Presented in G. E. M. de Ste. Croix on His 75th Birthday*, edited by Paul Cartledge and F. D. Harvey, 16–46. London: Gerald Duckworth, 1985.

Case, Shirley Jackson. *The Social Origins of Christianity*. Chicago: University of Chicago Press, 1923.

Casson, Lionel. "Galley Slaves." *TAPA* 97 (1966): 35–44.

Chadwick, Henry. "New Letters of St. Augustine." *JTS* 34 (1983): 425–52.

—. *Origen, Contra Celsum*. 1953. Corr. reprint. Cambridge: Cambridge University Press, 1986.

Channing, William E. *The Works of William E. Channing*. 1882. Reprint, 2 vols. in 1. New York: Burt Franklin, 1970.

Chantraine, Heinrich. "Freigelassene und Sklaven kaiserlicher Frauen." In *Studien zur antiken Sozialgeschichte: Festschrift Friedrich Vittinghof*, edited by Werner Eck, Hartmut Galsterer, and Hartmut Wolff, 389–416. Kölner historische Abhandlungen 28. Cologne: Böhau, 1980.

Chow, John K. *Patronage and Power: A Study of Social Networks in Corinth*. JSNTSup 75. Sheffield: Sheffield Academic Press, 1992.

Ciccotti, Ettore. *Il tramonto della schiavitù nel mondo antico*. 2d ed. Udine: Instituto delle Edizioni Academice, 1940.

Clark, Elizabeth A. "Comment: Chrysostom and Pauline Social Ethics." In *Paul and the Legacies of Paul*, edited by William S. Babcock, 193–99. Dallas: Southern Methodist University Press, 1990.

—. *Jerome, Chrysostom, and Friends: Essays and Translations*. Studies in Women and Religion 1. New York: Edwin Mellen Press, 1979.

—. *Women in the Early Church*. Messages of the Fathers 13. 1983. Reprint. Collegeville, Minn.: Liturgical Press, 1990.

Clarke, G. W. *The Letters of St. Cyprian of Carthage*. Vol. 2. ACW 44. New York: Newman Press, 1984.

Clemente, Guido. "Il patronato nei collegia dell'impero romano." *SCO* 21 (1972): 142–229.

Cohen, Boaz. "Civil Bondage in Jewish and Roman Law." In *Louis Ginzberg Jubilee Volume*, 113–32. Eng. ed. New York: American Academy for Jewish Research, 1945.

Cohen, Naomi G. "Jewish Names as Cultural Indicators in Antiquity." *JSJ* 7 (1976): 99–128.

Cole, Susan Guettel. "Voices from beyond the Grave: Dionysus and the Dead." In *Masks of Dionysus*, edited by Thomas H. Carpenter and Christopher A. Faraone, 276–95. Myth and Poetics. Ithaca: Cornell University Press, 1993.

Coleman-Norton, Paul R. "The Apostle Paul and the Roman Law of Slavery." In *Studies in Roman Economic and Social History in Honor of Allan Chester Johnson*, edited by Paul R. Coleman-Norton, 155–77. Princeton: Princeton University Press, 1951.

Collins, Adela Yarbro. *Crisis and Catharsis: The Power of the Apocalypse*. Philadelphia: Westminster Press, 1984.

Collon, Suzanne. "Remarques sur les quartiers juifs de la Rome antique." *MEFRA* 57 (1940): 72–94.

Conybeare, Fred C. "On the Western Text of the Acts as Evidenced by Chrysostom." *AJP* 17 (1896): 135–71.

Conzelmann, Hans. *Acts of the Apostles: A Commentary on the Acts of the Apostles*. Hermeneia. Translated by James Limburg, A. Thomas Kraabel, and Donald H. Juel. Philadelphia: Fortress Press, 1987.

—. *Der erste Brief an die Korinther*. 2d ed. MeyerK 5. Göttingen: Vandenhoeck & Ruprecht, 1981.

—. "Korinth und die Mädchen der Aphrodite: Zur Religionsgeschichte der Stadt Korinth." *NAWG* 8 (1967–68): 247–61.

Corcoran, Gervase. "The Christian Attitude to Slavery in the Early Church." *Milltown Studies* 13 (1984): 1–16.

—. "Slavery in the New Testament II." *Milltown Studies* 6 (1980): 62–84.

Corwin, Virginia. *St. Ignatius and Christianity in Antioch.* Yale Publications in Religion 1. New Haven: Yale University Press, 1960.

Couch, Herbert Newell. *The Treasuries of the Greeks and Romans.* Menasha, Wis.: George Banta, 1929.

Countryman, L. W. "Patrons and Officers in Club and Church." In *SBLSP* 11, edited by Paul J. Achtemeier, 135–43. Missoula, Mont.: The Society, 1977.

Courtney, E. *A Commentary on the Satires of Juvenal.* London: Athlone Press, 1980.

Cramer, John Anthony, comp. *Catenae Graecorum Patrum in Novum Testamentum.* Vol. 5. 1841. Reprint. Hildesheim: Georg Olms, 1967.

Craton, Michael. "A Cresting Wave? Recent Trends in the Historiography of Slavery, with Special Reference to the British Caribbean." *Historical Reflections/Réflexions historiques* 9 (1982): 403–19.

Crawford, Michael H. "Money and Exchange in the Roman World." *JRS* 60 (1970): 40–48.

—. "Republican Denarii in Romania: The Suppression of Piracy and the Slave Trade." *JRS* 67 (1977): 117–24.

Crocker, Lawrence. *Positive Liberty: An Essay in Normative Political Philosophy.* Melbourne International Philosophy Series 7. The Hague: Martinus Nijhoff, 1980.

Crook, J. A. *Law and Life of Rome, 90 B.C. – A.D. 212.* Aspects of Greek and Roman Life. Ithaca: Cornell University Press, 1967.

Crouch, J. E. *The Origin and Intention of the Colossian Haustafel.* FRLANT 109. Göttingen: Vandenhoeck & Ruprecht, 1972.

Curtin, Philip D. *The Atlantic Slave Trade: A Census.* Madison: University of Wisconsin Press, 1969.

Dain, A., ed. *Le "Philétaeros" attribué à Hérodien.* Paris: Les Belles Lettres, 1954.

Danker, Frederick W. *Benefactor: Epigraphic Study of a Graeco-Roman and New Testament Semantic Field.* St. Louis, Mo.: Clayton Publishing, 1982.

—. *II Corinthians.* ACNT. Minneapolis: Augsburg Publishing, 1989.

Darrow, Fritz S. "The History of Corinth from Mummius to Herodes Atticus." Ph.D. diss., Harvard University, 1906.

Daube, David. Review of *Personality in Roman Private Law,* by P. W. Duff. *JRS* 33 (1943): 86–93.

—. "Slave-Catching." *Juridical Review* 64 (1952): 12–28.

Davies, J. K. "Cultural, Social, and Economic Features of the Hellenistic World." In *CAH,* 2d ed. Vol. 7.1: *The Hellenistic World,* edited by F. W. Walbank et al., 257–320. Cambridge: Cambridge University Press, 1984.

Davis, David Brion. *The Problem of Slavery in the Age of Revolution, 1770–1823.* Ithaca: Cornell University Press, 1975.

—. *The Problem of Slavery in Western Culture.* 1966. Reprint. New York: Oxford University Press, 1988.

—. *Slavery and Human Progress.* New York: Oxford University Press, 1984.

Dawes, Gregory W. "'But If You Can Gain Your Freedom' (1 Corinthians 7:17–24)." *CBQ* 54 (1990): 681–97.

De Bruyn, Theodore. *Pelagius's Commentary on St Paul's Epistle to the Romans: Translated with Introduction and Notes.* OECS. Oxford: Clarendon Press, 1993.

De Robertis, Francesco M. *Il fenomeno associativo nel mondo romano: Dai collegi della Repubblica alle corporazioni del basso impero.* Naples: Libreria Scientifica, 1955.

–. *Storia delle corporazioni e del regime associativo nel mondo romano.* 2 vols. Bari: Adriatica, 1971.

De Ruggiero, Ettore. "Arca." *Dizionario epigrafico di antichità romana* 1: 626–32. 1895. Reprint. Rome: "L'Erma" di Bretschneider, 1961.

De Waele, Ferdinand-Joseph. *Corinthe et Saint Paul. Les hauts lieux de l'histoire.* Paris: Albert Guillot, 1961.

–. "The Roman Market North of the Temple at Corinth." *AJA* 2d ser. 34 (1930): 432–54.

Degler, Carl N. *Neither Black nor White: Slavery and Race Relations in Brazil and the United States.* New York: Macmillan, 1971.

Degrassi, Attilio. *Inscriptiones Latinae Liberae Rei Publicae.* Biblioteca di studi superiori 40. Florence: La Nuova Italia, 1963.

Deininger, F. "Neue Forschungen zur antiken Sklaverei (1970–1975)." *HZ* 222 (1976): 359–74.

Deissmann, Adolf. *Light from the Ancient Near East: The New Testament Illustrated by Recently Discovered Texts of the Graeco-Roman World.* 2d ed. Translated by R. M. Strachan. London: Hodder & Stoughton, 1927.

Del Chiaro, Mario A., and William R. Biers, eds. *Corinthiaca: Studies in Honor of Darrell A. Amyx.* Columbia: University of Missouri Press, 1986.

Delekat, Lienhard. *Katoche, Hierodulie, und Adoptionsfreilassung.* Münchener Beiträge zur Papyrusforschung und antiken Rechtsgeschichte 47. Munich: C. H. Beck, 1964.

Denniston, J. D. *The Greek Particles.* 2d ed. Oxford: Clarendon Press, 1954.

Derrett, J. Duncan M. "The Functions of the Epistle to Philemon." In *Studies in the New Testament.* Vol. 5, *The Sea-Change of the Old Testament in the New,* 196–224. Leiden: E. J. Brill, 1989. First published in *ZNW* 79 (1988): 63–91.

Dieckhoff, Max. *Krieg und Frieden im griechisch-römischen Altertum.* Lebendiges Altertum 10. Berlin: Akademie-Verlag, 1962.

Dindorf, L., ed. *Chronicon Paschale.* Vol. 1. Corpus Scriptorum Historiae Byzantinae. Bonn: Impensis Ed. Weberi, 1832.

Dix, Gregory, ed. *The Treatise on the Apostolic Tradition of St. Hippolytus of Rome.* 1937. Corr. reprint with bibliog. by Henry Chadwick. London: S.P.C.K., 1968.

Dixon, Suzanne. *The Roman Family.* Ancient Society and History. Baltimore: Johns Hopkins University Press, 1992.

Dodd, C. H. "Notes from Papyri." *JTS* 26 (1924–25): 77–78.

Donceel, R. "Une inscription inédite de Nole et la date du sénatus-consulte 'de collegiis tenuiorum.'" *BIBR* 42 (1972): 27–71.

Doughty, Darrell. "Heiligkeit und Freiheit: Eine exegetische Untersuchung der Anwendung des paulinischen Freiheitsgedankens in I Kor. 7." Doctoral diss., Göttingen, 1965.

Droge, Arthur J., and James D. Tabor. *A Noble Death: Suicide and Martyrdom among Jews and Christians in Antiquity.* New York: HarperCollins, 1992.

duBois, Page. *Torture and Truth.* London: Routledge, 1991.

Ducat, J. *Les hilotes.* Bulletin de Correspondance Hellénique Suppl. 20. Paris: École Française d'Athènes, 1990.

Duff, A. M. *Freedmen in the Early Roman Empire.* 2d ed. Cambridge: W. Heffer & Sons, 1958.

Duff, J. W., and A. M. Duff. *Minor Latin Poets.* LCL. Cambridge: Harvard University Press, 1934.

Duff, Patrick William. *Personality in Roman Private Law.* Cambridge: Cambridge University Press, 1938.

Easton, Burton S. *The Pastoral Epistles.* New York: Charles Scribner's Sons, 1947.

Edelstein, Emma J., and Ludwig Edelstein. *Asclepius: A Collection and Interpretation of the Testimonies*. 2 vols. Ancient Religion and Mythology. 1975. Reprint. Salem, N.H.: Ayer, 1988.

Edelstein, L., and I. G. Kidd. *Posidonius*. Vol. 1, *The Fragments*. 1972. Reprint. Cambridge: Cambridge University Press, 1989.

Eder, Walter. *Servitus Publica*. Forschungen zur antiken Sklaverei 13. Wiesbaden: Franz Steiner, 1980.

Elkins, Stanley. *Slavery: A Problem in American Institutional and Intellectual Life*. Chicago: University of Chicago Press, 1959.

Engels, Donald. "The Problem of Female Infanticide in the Greco-Roman World." *CP* 75 (1980): 112–20.

–. *Roman Corinth: An Alternative Model for the Classical City*. Chicago: University of Chicago Press, 1990.

Epictetus. *Epictetus I–II*. LCL. 1925, 1928. Reprint. Cambridge: Harvard University Press, 1989, 1985.

Epp, Erman N. *Servus vicarius: L'esclave de l'esclave romain*. Lausanne: F. Rouge, 1896.

Etienne, Robert. "La conscience médicale antique et la vie des enfants." *Annales de démographie historique* (1973): 15–46.

Eyben, Emil. "Family Planning in Graeco-Roman Antiquity." Translated by Berthold Puchert. *AncSoc* 11–12 (1980–81): 1–82.

Fabbrini, F. *La manumissio in ecclesia*. Istituto di diritto romano e dei diritti dell'Oriente mediterraneo 40. Milan: A. Giuffrè, 1965.

Fabre, Georges. *Libertus: Recherches sur les rapports patron-affranchi à la fin de la république romaine*. Collection de l'École Française de Rome 50. Paris: École Française de Rome, 1981.

Fanning, Buist M. *Verbal Aspect in New Testament Greek*. Oxford Theological Monographs. Oxford: Clarendon Press, 1990.

Fasciato, Micheline. "Note sur l'affranchissement des esclaves abandonnés dans l'île d'Esculape." *RD* 27 (1949): 454–64.

Fee, Gordon D. *The First Epistle to the Corinthians*. NICNT. Grand Rapids, Mich.: William B. Eerdmans, 1987.

Feldman, Louis H. *Jew and Gentile in the Ancient World: Attitudes and Interactions from Alexander to Justinian*. Princeton: Princeton University Press, 1993.

Ferguson, William Scott. "The Attic Orgeones." *HTR* 37 (1944): 61–140.

Ferrua, Antonio. "Addenda et corrigenda ad Corpus Inscriptionum Iudaicarum." *Epigraphica* 3 (1941): 30–46.

–. "Sulla tomba dei Cristiani e su quella degli Ebrei." *Civiltà Cattolica* 87 (1936): 298–311.

Fiedler, Peter. "Haustafel." *RAC* 13 (1986): 1063–73.

Filson, Floyd V. "The Significance of the Early House Churches." *JBL* 58 (1939): 105–12.

Finley, M. I. "The Ancient City: From Fustel de Coulanges to Max Weber and Beyond." *CSSH* 19 (1977): 305–27.

–. *The Ancient Economy*. Sather Classical Lectures 43. 2d ed. Berkeley and Los Angeles: University of California Press, 1985.

–. *Ancient Slavery and Modern Ideology*. New York: Viking Press, 1980.

–. *Aspects of Antiquity: Discoveries and Controversies*. 2d ed. New York: Penguin Books, 1977.

–. "The Black Sea and Danubian Regions and the Slave Trade in Antiquity." *Klio* 40 (1962): 51–59. Reprinted, with reduced annotation to eliminate now outdated debates, in *Economy and Society in Ancient Greece*, 167–75.

–, ed. *Classical Slavery*. Slavery and Abolition Special Issue 8. London: Frank Cass, 1987.

–. *Economy and Society in Ancient Greece*. Edited by Brent D. Shaw and Richard P. Saller. New York: Viking Press, 1982.

–. "Slavery." *International Encyclopedia of the Social Sciences*, edited by David L. Sills, 14 (1968): 307–13.

–, ed. *Slavery in Classical Antiquity: Views and Controversies*. Cambridge: W. Heffer & Sons, 1960.

–. *Studies in Land and Credit in Ancient Athens, 500–200 B.C.: The Horos Inscriptions*. Social Science Classics Series. 1951. Corr. reprint with introd. by Paul Millett. New Brunswick, N.J.: Rutgers University Press, 1985.

–. *The Use and Abuse of History*. 1975. Reprint. New York: Penguin Books, 1987.

–. "Was Greek Civilization Based on Slave Labour?" In *Slavery in Classical Antiquity*, 53–72. Reprinted, with reduced annotation to eliminate now outdated debates, in *Economy and Society in Ancient Greece*, 97–115. First published in *Historia* 8 (1959): 145–64.

–. *The World of Odysseus*. 2d ed., rev. New York: Penguin Books, 1979.

Fischer, Klaus-Dietrich. "Zur Entwicklung des ärztlichen Standes im römischen Kaiserreich." *Medizin-historisches Journal* 14 (1979): 165–75.

Fisher, N. R. E. "Drink, *Hybris*, and the Promotion of Harmony in Sparta." In *Classical Sparta: Techniques behind Her Success*, edited by Anton Powell, 26–50. Oklahoma Series in Classical Culture. Norman: University of Oklahoma Press, 1988.

Flambard, Jean-Marc. "Clodius, les collèges, la plèbe, et les esclaves: Recherches sur la politique populaire au milieu sur la politique populaire au milieu de Ier siècle." *MEFRA* 89 (1977): 115–56.

Flesher, Paul V. M. *Oxen, Women, or Citizens? Slaves in the System of the Mishnah*. BJS 143. Atlanta: Scholars Press, 1988.

Fletcher, John. *Studies on Slavery, in Easy Lessons*. Natchez, Miss.: Jackson Warner, 1852.

Fogel, Robert W., and Stanley L. Engerman. *Time on the Cross: The Economics of American Negro Slavery*. 2 vols. Boston: Little, Brown, 1974.

Forbes, Clarence A. "The Education and Training of Slaves in Antiquity." *TAPA* 86 (1955): 321–60.

Foucart, Paul François. *Des associations religieuses chez les Grecs: Thiases, éranes, orgéons*. 1873. Reprint. New York: Arno Press, 1975.

Fowler, Harold N. "Corinth and the Corinthia." In *Corinth: Results of Excavations Conducted by the American School of Classical Studies at Athens*, edited by Harold N. Fowler and R. Stillwell. Vol. 1, *Introduction, Topography, Architecture*, 18–114. Cambridge: The American School, 1932.

Fox-Genovese, Elizabeth. *Within the Plantation Household: Black and White Women of the Old South*. Gender and American Culture. Chapel Hill: University of North Carolina Press, 1988.

Frank, Tenney. *An Economic Survey of Ancient Rome*. 5 vols. Baltimore: Johns Hopkins University Press, 1940.

Fraser, P. M. *Rhodian Funerary Monuments*. Oxford: Clarendon Press, 1977.

Fraser, P. M., and E. Matthews. *A Lexicon of Greek Personal Names*. Vol. 1, *The Aegean Islands, Cyprus, Cyrenaica*. Oxford: Clarendon Press, 1987.

Fredriksen, Paula. "Judaism, the Circumcision of Gentiles, and Apocalyptic Hope: Another Look at Galatians 1 and 2." *JTS* 42 (1991): 532–64.

Frey, P. Jean-Baptiste, ed. *Corpus of Jewish Inscriptions: Jewish Inscriptions from the Third Century B.C. to the Seventh Century A.D.*. Vol. 1, *Europe*. Library of Biblical Studies. 1936. Reprint with prolegomenon by Baruch Lifshitz. New York: Ktav, 1975.

–. "Les Juifs à Pompéi." *RB* 42 (1933): 365–84.

Friedrich, Carl J., ed. *Liberty.* Nomos 4. 1962. Reprint. New York: Atherton Press, 1964.

Frische, Hartvig. *The Constitution of the Athenians: A Philological-Historical Analysis.* Classica et Mediaevalia Dissertationes 2. Copenhagen: Gyldendalske Boghandel/ Nordisk Forlag, 1942.

Fuks, G. "Where Have All the Freedmen Gone? On an Anomaly in the Jewish Grave-Inscriptions from Rome." *JJS* 36 (1985): 25–32.

Furnish, Victor Paul. *II Corinthians.* AB 32A. New York: Doubleday, 1984.

Gagarin, Michael. "The First Law of the Gortyn Code." *GRBS* 29 (1988): 335–43.

Gaius. *The Institutes of Gaius.* Translated with an introd. by W. M. Gordon and O. F. Robinson. Latin text edited by E. Seckel and B. Kuebler. Texts in Roman Law. Ithaca: Cornell University Press, 1988.

Galen. *Claudii Galeni opera omnia.* 20 vols. Edited by Carolus Gottlob Kühn. Leipzig: Knobloch, 1821–33.

Garlan, Yvon. *Slavery in Ancient Greece.* Rev. and expanded ed. Translated by Janet Lloyd. Ithaca: Cornell University Press, 1988.

–. "War, Piracy, and Slavery in the Greek World." Translated by Marie-Jo Roy. In Finley, *Classical Slavery,* 7–21.

Garland, Andrew. "Cicero's *Familia Urbana.*" *G & R* 39 (1992): 163–72.

Garnsey, Peter. "Child Rearing in Ancient Italy." In *The Family in Italy: From Antiquity to the Present,* edited by David I. Kertzer and Richard P. Saller, 48–65. New Haven: Yale University Press, 1991.

–. "Descendants of Freedmen in Local Politics: Some Criteria." In *The Ancient Historian and His Materials: Essays in Honor of C. E. Stevens on His Seventieth Birthday,* edited by Barbara Levick, 167–80. Westmead, England: D. C. Heath, Gregg International, 1975.

–. *Famine and Food Supply in the Graeco-Roman World: Responses to Risk and Crisis.* Cambridge: Cambridge University Press, 1988.

–. "Independent Freedmen and the Economy of Roman Italy under the Principate." *Klio* 63 (1981): 359–71.

–, ed. *Non-Slave Labour in the Greco-Roman World.* Cambridge Philological Society Suppl. 6. Cambridge: The Society, 1980.

–. *Social Status and Legal Privilege in the Roman Empire.* Oxford: Clarendon Press, 1970.

Garnsey, Peter, and Richard Saller. *The Roman Empire: Economy, Society, and Culture.* Berkeley and Los Angeles: University of California Press, 1987.

Garrett, Susan R. "Sociology of Early Christianity." *ABD* 6 (1992): 89–99.

Garrido-Hory, M. *Martial et l'esclavage.* Annales littéraires de l'Université de Besançon 255. Centre de recherches d'histoire ancienne 40. Paris: Les Belles Lettres, 1981.

Gayer, Roland. *Die Stellung des Sklaven in den paulinischen Gemeinden und bei Paulus: Zugleich ein sozialgeschichtlich vergleichender Beitrag zur Wertung des Sklaven in der Antike.* Europäische Hochschulschriften, 23d ser. 78. Bern: Herbert Lang, 1976.

Genovese, Eugene D. *Roll, Jordan, Roll: The World the Slaves Made.* New York: Vintage Books, 1976.

Geytenbeek, A. C. van. *Musonius Rufus and the Greek Diatribe.* Rev. ed. Translated by B. L. Hijmans. Wijsgerige Teksten en Studies 8. Assen, Netherlands: van Gorcum, 1963.

Giardina, Andrea, ed. *The Romans.* Translated by Lydia G. Cochrane. Chicago: University of Chicago Press, 1993.

Gilula, Dwora. "Did Martial have a Jewish Slave? (7.35)." *CQ* 37 (1987): 532–33.

Giménez-Candela, T. "Una contribucción al estudio de la ley Irnitana: La manumisión de esclavos municipales." *Iura* 37 (1984): 37–56.

Gnilka, Christian. *ΧΡΗΣΙΣ: Die Methode der Kirchenväter im Umgang mit der antiken*

Kultur. I. Der Begriff des "rechten Gebrauchs." Westfälische Wilhelms-Universität Münster, Institut für Missionswissenschaft. Stuttgart: Schwabe, 1984.

Gnilka, Joachim. *Der Philemonbrief.* HTKNT. Freiburg: Herder, 1982.

Goguel, Maurice. *The Primitive Church.* Translated by H. C. Snape. London: George Allen & Unwin, 1964.

Golden, Mark. "Demography and the Exposure of Girls at Athens." *Phoenix* 35 (1981): 316–37.

González, Julián. "The Lex Irnitana: A New Copy of the Flavian Municipal Law." *JRS* 76 (1986): 147–243.

Goodenough, Erwin R. "The Bosporus Inscriptions to the Most High God." *JQR* 47 (1957): 221–44.

Goodman, Martin. "Babatha's Story." Review of *Aramaic and Nabatean Signatures and Subscriptions,* edited by Y. Yadin and J. C. Greenfield. *JRS* 81 (1991): 169–75.

Goodspeed, Edgar Johnson, ed. *Die ältesten Apologeten: Texte mit kurzen Einleitungen.* Göttingen: Vandenhoeck & Ruprecht, 1914.

–. *The Meaning of Ephesians.* Chicago: University of Chicago Press, 1933.

Gordon, Arthur E. *Illustrated Introduction to Latin Epigraphy.* Berkeley and Los Angeles: University of California Press, 1983.

Gordon, Mary L. "The Nationality of Slaves under the Early Roman Empire." In Finley, *Slavery in Classical Antiquity,* 171–90. First published in *JRS* 14 (1924): 93–111.

Grant, Frederick C. *Hellenistic Religions: The Age of Syncretism.* Indianapolis: Bobbs-Merrill, 1953.

Grant, Michael. *A Social History of Greece and Rome.* New York: Charles Scribner's Sons, 1992.

Grant, Robert M., ed. *The Apostolic Fathers: A New Translation and Commentary.* Vol. 4, *Ignatius of Antioch.* London: Thomas Nelson & Sons, 1966.

–. *Augustus to Constantine: The Rise and Triumph of Christianity in the Roman World.* 1970. Reprint. San Francisco: Harper & Row, 1990.

–. *Early Christianity and Society: Seven Studies.* San Francisco: Harper & Row, 1977.

–. *Greek Apologists of the Second Century.* Philadelphia: Westminster Press, 1988.

Greeven, Heinrich. *Das Hauptproblem der Sozialethik in der neueren Stoa und im Urchristentum.* Neutestamentliche Forschungen 3,4. Gütersloh: Bertelsmann, 1935.

–. "Prüfung der Thesen von J. Knox zum Philemonbrief." *TLZ* 79 (1954): 374–78.

Griffin, Miriam T. *Seneca, a Philosopher in Politics.* Oxford: Clarendon Press, 1976.

Grosheide, F. W. *Commentary to the First Epistle to the Corinthians.* NICNT. Grand Rapids, Mich.: William B. Eerdmans, 1953.

Gruen, Erich S. *The Hellenistic World and the Coming of Rome.* 2 vols. Berkeley and Los Angeles: University of California Press, 1984.

Gschnitzer, Fritz. *Studien zur griechischen Terminologie der Sklaverei.* 2 pts. AAWM 13. Forschungen zur antiken Sklaverei 7. Wiesbaden: Franz Steiner, 1964, 1976.

Gülzow, Henneke. *Christentum und Sklaverei in den ersten drei Jahrhunderten.* Bonn: Rudolf Habelt, 1969.

Habel, P. "Arca." PW 3 (1895): 425–28.

Haenchen, Ernst. *The Acts of the Apostles: A Commentary.* Translated by R. M. Wilson. Philadelphia: Westminster Press, 1971.

Hahn, Ferdinand. "Paulus und der Sklave Onesimus: Ein beachtenswerter Kommentar zum Philemonbrief." *EvT* 37 (1977): 179–85.

Hamel, Gildas. *Poverty and Charity in Roman Palestine, First Three Centuries* C.E. Near Eastern Studies 23. Berkeley and Los Angeles: University of California Press, 1990.

Hands, A. R. *Charities and Social Aid in Greece and Rome*. Aspects of Greek and Roman Life. Ithaca: Cornell University Press, 1968.

Hansen, Victor. "Thucydides and the Desertion of Attic Slaves during the Decelean War." *ClAnt* 11 (1992): 210–28.

Harnack, Adolf von. *Militia Christi: The Christian Religion and the Military in the First Three Centuries*. Translated by David M. Gracie. Philadelphia: Fortress Press, 1981.

—. *Die Mission und Ausbreitung des Christentums in den ersten drei Jahrhunderten*. 4th ed. 2 vols. Leipzig: J. C. Hinrichs, 1924.

Harrill, J. Albert. "Ignatius, *Ad Polycarp*. 4.3 and the Corporate Manumission of Christian Slaves." *Journal of Early Christian Studies* 1 (1993): 107–42.

—. "Paul and Slavery: The Problem of 1 Cor 7:21." *Biblical Research* 39 (1994): 5–28.

—. Review of *Pelagius's Commentary on St Paul's Epistle to the Romans*, by Theodore de Bruyn. *EMC* 13 (1994): forthcoming.

—. Review of *Slavery as Salvation*, by Dale B. Martin. *JR* 72 (1992): 426–27.

Harris, J. Rendell. "The History of a Conjectural Emendation." *Expositor* 6 (1902): 378–90.

Harris, William V. *Ancient Literacy*. Cambridge: Harvard University Press, 1989.

—. "The Theoretical Possibility of Extensive Infanticide in the Graeco-Roman World." *CQ* 32 (1984): 114–16.

—. "Towards a Study of the Roman Slave Trade." In *The Seaborne Commerce of Ancient Rome: Studies in Archaeology and History*, edited by J. H. D'Arms and E. C. Kopff, 117–40. Memoirs of the American Academy in Rome 36. Rome: The Academy, 1980.

—. *War and Imperialism in Republican Rome, 327–70 B.C.* Oxford: Clarendon Press, 1979.

Harsh, Philip W. "The Intriguing Slave in Greek Comedy." *TAPA* 86 (1955): 135–42.

Hastings, James, ed. *A Dictionary of the Bible*. Vol. 3. New York: Charles Scribner's Sons, 1923.

Hayduck, M., ed. *Ioannis Philoponi [Michaelis Ephesii]*. In *Libros de generatione animalium commentaria*. Commentaria in Aristotelem Graeca 14.3. Berlin: Reimer, 1903.

Hegel, G. W. F. *Phänomenologie des Geistes*. 5th ed. Revised by J. Hoffmeister. Philosophische Bibliothek 114. Hamburg: Felix Meiner Verlag, 1952.

Heidel, W. A. "Why Were the Jews Banished from Italy in 19 A.D.?" *AJP* 41 (1920): 38–47.

Heinen, Heinz. Review of *Slavery and Social Death*, by Orlando Patterson. *European Sociological Review* 4 (1988): 263–68.

Heinrici, C. F. Georg. *Der erste Brief an die Korinther*. 8th ed. MeyerK 5. Göttingen: Vandenhoeck & Ruprecht, 1896.

Hellholm, David. *Das Visionenbuch des Hermas als Apokalypse: Formgeschichtliche und texttheoretische Studien zu einer literarischen Gattung*. ConBNT 13.1. Lund: C.W.K. Gleerup, 1980.

Hellie, Richard. Review of *Slavery and Social Death*, by Orlando Patterson. *AHR* 89 (1984): 411–12.

—. *Slavery in Russia: 1450–1725*. Chicago: University of Chicago Press, 1982.

Hengstl, Joachim. Review of *Corpus der ptolemäischen Sklaventexte*, edited by Reinhold Scholl. *BASP* 29 (1992): 183–89.

Hense, Otto, ed. *C. Musonii Rufi reliquiae*. Bibliotheca scriptorum Graecorum et Romanorum Teubneriana. Leipzig: B. G. Teubner, 1905.

Herrmann, Peter, et. al. "Gnossenschaft." *RAC* 10 (1978): 83–155.

Herzog, R. "Arzthonorar." *RAC* 1 (1950): 724–25.

Heylbut, Gustavus, ed. *Heliodori in ethica Nicomachea paraphrasis*. Commentaria in Aristotelem Graeca 19.2. Berlin: G. Reimer, 1909.

Hirschfeld, Gustav, ed. *The Collection of Ancient Greek Inscriptions in the British Museum.* Pt. 4, sec. 1, *Knidos, Halikarnassos and Branchidae.* Oxford: Clarendon Press, 1893.

Hobbs, Thomas. *Leviathan.* Edited by Richard Tuck. Cambridge Texts in the History of Social Thought. Cambridge: Cambridge University Press, 1991.

Hobson, J. A. *Imperialism: A Study.* Revised with new introd. by Philip Siegelman. Ann Arbor: University of Michigan Press, 1965.

Hohlfelder, Robert L. "Kenchreai on the Saronic Gulf: Aspects of Imperial History." *CJ* 71 (1976): 217–26.

Hoof, Anton J. L. van. *From Autothanasia to Suicide: Self-Killing in Classical Antiquity.* London: Routledge, 1990.

Hopkins, Keith. "The Age of Roman Girls at Marriage." *Population Studies* 18 (1965): 309–327.

—. *Conquerors and Slaves.* Sociological Studies in Roman History 1. New York: Cambridge University Press, 1978.

—. "Contraception in the Roman Empire." *CSSH* 8 (1965–66): 124–51.

—. "A Textual Emendation in a Fragment of Musonius Rufus." *CQ* 15 (1965): 72–74.

Horsley, G. H. R., et al., eds. *New Documents Illustrating Early Christianity.* Marrickville, Australia: The Ancient History Documentary Research Centre (Macquarie University), 1981– .

Horst, P. W. van der. *Ancient Jewish Epitaphs: An Introductory Survey of a Millennium of Jewish Funerary Epigraphy (300 B.C.E.–700 C.E.)*, Contributions to Biblical Exegesis 2. Kampen, The Netherlands: Kok Pharos, 1991.

—. *The Sentences of Pseudo-Phocylides.* Leiden: E. J. Brill, 1978.

Hudson, John, ed. *Flavii Josephi Opera, quae reperiri potuerunt omnia.* 2 vols. Oxford: Theatre Sheldoniano, 1720.

Humbert, G. "Arca." *Dictionnaire des antiquités greques et romains*, edited by C. Daremberg and E. Saglio, 1: 364–66. 1877. Reprint. Graz, Austria: Akademische Druck–U. Verlagsanstalt, 1966.

Iamblichus. *Iamblichi protrepticus ad fidem codicis Florentini.* Edited by H. Pistelli. Leipzig: B. G. Teubner, 1888.

—. *Iamblichus: The Exhortation to Philosophy.* Translated by Thomas Moore Johnson. Edited by Stephen Neuville. Grand Rapids, Mich.: Phanes Press, 1988.

—. *Jamblique: Protreptique.* Edited by Édouard Des Places. Collection des Universités de France. Paris: Les Belles Lettres, 1989.

Jackson, A. H. "Privateers in the Ancient Greek World." In *War and Society: Historical Essays in Honour and Memory of J. R. Western*, edited by M. R. D. Foot, 241–53. London: Paul Elek, 1973.

—. "Some Recent Work on the Treatment of Prisoners of War in Ancient Greece." *Talanta* 2 (1970): 37–53.

Jackson, F. J. Foakes, and Kirsopp Lake. *The Beginnings of Christianity.* Pt. 1, *The Acts of the Apostles.* Vol. 4. Translation and commentary by Kirsopp Lake and Henry J. Cadbury. London: Macmillan, 1933.

Jacquier, E. *Les Actes des Apôtres.* Ebib. Paris: Gabalda, 1926.

Jaeger, Wulf. "Die Sklaverei bei Johannes Chrysostomus." Doctoral diss., Kiel, 1974.

Jameson, Michael H. "Agriculture and Slavery in Classical Athens." *CJ* 73 (1977–78): 122–45.

Jameson, Russell Parsons. *Montesquieu et l'esclavage: Étude sur les origines de l'opinion antiesclavagiste en France au XVIIIe siècle.* Paris: Hachette, 1911.

Jang, Liem Khiem. "Der Philemonbrief im Zusammenhang mit dem theologischen Denken des Apostels Paulus." Doctoral diss., Bonn, 1964.

Jay, Eric G. "From Presbyter-Bishops to Bishops and Presbyters: Christian Ministry in the Second Century." *SecCent* 1 (1981): 125–72.

–. *New Testament Greek: An Introductory Grammar.* 12th corr. impression. London: S.P.C.K., 1987.

Jebb, Richard. *Sophocles: Plays and Fragments.* Part 3, *The Antigone.* 3d ed. 1900. Reprint. Amsterdam: Adolf M. Hakkert, 1962.

Jeffers, James S. *Conflict at Rome: Social Hierarchy in Early Christianity.* Minneapolis: Fortress Press, 1991.

Jenkins, Claude. "Origen on I Corinthians, III." *JTS* 9 (1908): 499–508.

Jeremias, Joachim. *Infant Baptism in the First Four Centuries.* Translated by David Cairns. Library of History and Doctrine. London: S.C.M. Press, 1960.

Jewett, Robert. "Tenement Churches and Communal Meals in the Early Church: The Implications of a Form-Critical Analysis of 2 Thessalonians 3:10." *Biblical Research* 38 (1993): 23–43.

Johnson, Luke T. *The Writings of the New Testament.* Philadelphia: Fortress Press, 1986.

Johnston, David. "Munificence and *Municipia*: Bequests to Towns in Classical Roman Law." *JRS* 75 (1985): 105–25.

Jones, A. H. M. *The Roman Economy.* Edited by P. A. Brunt. Oxford: Basil Blackwell, 1974.

–. "Slavery in the Ancient World." In Finley, *Slavery in Classical Antiquity,* 1–15. First published in *The Economic History Review* 2d ser. 9 (1956): 185–99.

Jones, C. P. *Culture and Society in Lucian.* Cambridge: Harvard University Press, 1986.

–. "*Stigma*: Tatooing and Branding in Greco–Roman Antiquity." *JRS* 77 (1987): 139–55.

Jones, F. Stanley. *"Freiheit" in den Briefen des Apostels Paulus: Eine historische, exegetische und religionsgeschichtliche Studie.* GTA 34. Göttingen: Vandenhoeck & Ruprecht, 1987.

Jones, Lawrence P. "A Case Study in 'Gnosticism': Religious Responses to Slavery in the Second Century C.E." Ph.D. diss., Columbia University, 1988.

Jordan, Winthrop D. *White over Black: American Attitudes toward the Negro, 1550–1812.* Baltimore: Penguin Books, 1969.

Joshel, Sandra R. "Nurturing the Master's Child: Slavery and the Roman Child-Nurse." *Signs* 12 (1986): 3–22.

Junod, Éric, ed. *Origène, Philocalie 21–27: Sur le libre arbitre.* SC 226. Paris: Cerf, 1976.

Justinian. *The Digest of Justinian.* 4 vols. Latin text edited by Theodor Mommsen with Paul Krueger. Translated by Alan Watson. Philadelphia: University of Pennsylvania Press, 1985.

–. *Justinian's Institutes.* Translated with an introd. by Peter Birks and Grant McLeod. Ithaca, N.Y.: Cornell University Press, 1987.

Kajanto, Iiro. *Onomastic Studies in the Early Christian Inscriptions of Rome and Carthage.* Acta Instituti Romani Finlandiae 2.2. Helsinki: Tilgmann, 1963.

–. "Tacitus on the Slaves." *Arctos* 6 (1970): 43–60.

Kant, Laurence H. "Jewish Inscriptions in Greek and Latin." *ANRW* 2.20.2 (1987): 671–713.

Kehnscherper, Gerhard. *Die Stellung der Bibel und der alten christlichen Kirche zur Sklaverei: Eine biblische und kirchengeschichtliche Untersuchung von den alttestamentlichen Propheten bis zum Ende des römischen Reiches.* Halle (Saale): Max Niemeyer, 1957.

Kent, John Harvey. "The Temple Estates of Delos, Rheneia, and Mykonos." *Hesperia* 17 (1948): 243–338.

Kidd, I. G. *Posidonius.* Vol. 1, *The Fragments*; vol. 2, *The Commentary: (i) Testimonia and Fragments 1–149.* Cambridge: Cambridge University Press, 1971, 1988.

Kiefl, F. X. "Erklärung." *TRev* 15–16 (1917): 469.

—. *Die Theorien des modernen Sozialismus über den Ursprung des Christentums: Zugleich ein Kommentar zu 1 Kor 7,21.* Munich: J. Kösel, 1915.

Klauck, Hans-Josef. *Hausgemeinde und Hauskirche im frühen Christentum.* SBS 103. Stuttgart: Katholisches Bibelwerk, 1981.

Klein, Richard. *Die Sklaverei in der Sicht der Bischöfe Ambrosius und Augustinus.* Forschungen zur antiken Sklaverei 20. Stuttgart: F. Steiner, 1988.

Kless, Hans. *Herren und Sklaven: Die Sklaverei in oikonomischen und politischen Schriften der Griechen in klassischer Zeit.* Forschungen zur antiken Sklaverei 6. Wiesbaden: Franz Steiner, 1975.

Klingenberg, Georg. "Grabrecht (Grabmulta, Grabschändung)." *RAC* 12 (1982): 590–637.

Klostermann, E., and G. C. Hanson, eds. *Eusebius Werke.* Vol. 4, *Gegen Marcell. Über die kirchliche Theologie. Die Fragmente Marcells.* 2d ed. GCS 14. Berlin: Akademie-Verlag, 1972.

Knox, John. *Philemon among the Letters of Paul: A New View of Its Place and Importance.* Rev. ed. Nashville: Abingdon, 1959.

Koester, Helmut. "Writings and the Spirit: Authority and Politics in Ancient Christianity." *HTR* 84 (1991): 353–72.

Kollwitz, J. "Arca." *RAC* 1 (1950): 595–96.

Kornemann, E. "Collegium." *PW* 7 (1900): 379–480.

—. "κοινόν." *PWSup* 4 (1924): 916–41.

Körte, Alfred. "Literarische Texte mit Ausschluss der Christlichen." *APF* 13 (1939): 78–132.

Kraabel, A. Thomas. "The Roman Diaspora: Six Questionable Assumptions." *JJS* 33 (1982): 445–64.

Kraemer, Ross Shepard. *Her Share of the Blessings: Women's Religions among Pagans, Jews, and Christians in the Greco-Roman World.* New York: Oxford University Press, 1992.

—. "Jewish Tuna and Christian Fish: Identifying Religious Affiliation in Epigraphic Sources." *HTR* 84 (1991): 141–62.

—, ed. *Maenads, Martyrs, Matrons, Monastics: A Sourcebook on Women's Religions in the Greco-Roman World.* Philadelphia: Fortress Press, 1988.

Kränzlein, Arnold. "Die attischen Aufzeichnungen über die Einlieferung von φιάλαι ἐξελευθερικαί." In *Symposion 1971: Vorträge zur griechischen und hellenistischen Rechtsgeschichte,* edited by Hans Julius Wolff, 255–64. AGR 1. Cologne: Böhlau, 1975.

Krauss, Samuel. *Griechische und lateinische Lehnwörter in Talmud, Midrasch und Targum.* Pt. 2. 1899. Reprint. Hildesheim: Georg Olms, 1964.

—. "Slaves and Slavery – Freedmen." *The Jewish Encyclopedia,* edited by Isidore Singer, 11: 407–8. New York: Ktav, 1905.

Kudlien, Fridolf. *Sklaven-Mentalität im Spiegel antiker Wahrsagerei.* Forschungen zur antiken Sklaverei 23. Stuttgart: Franz Steiner, 1991.

—. *Die Stellung des Arztes in der römischen Gesellschaft: Freigeborene Römer, Eingebürgerte, Peregrine, Sklaven, Freigelassene als Ärzte.* Forschungen zur antiken Sklaverei 18. Stuttgart: Franz Steiner, 1986.

Kügler, Ulf-Rainer. "Die Paränese an die Sklaven als Modell urchristlicher Sozialethik." Doctoral diss., Erlangen, 1977.

Kühne, H. "Die stadtrömischen Sklaven in den collegia des Clodius." *Helikon* 6 (1966): 95–113.

Kümmel, Werner Georg. *Introduction to the New Testament.* 17th German ed. Translated by Howard Clark Kee. 1975. Reprint. Nashville: Abingdon Press, 1987.

Kyrtatas, Dimitris J. *The Social Structure of the Early Christian Communities.* New York: Verso Press, 1987.

La Piana, George. "Foreign Groups in Rome during the First Centuries of the Empire." *HTR* 20 (1927): 183–403.

Lampe, Peter. *Die stadtrömischen Christen in den ersten beiden Jahrhunderten.* 2d expanded ed. WUNT 18, 2d ser. Tübingen: J. C. B. Mohr (Paul Siebeck), 1989.

Lang, Friedrich. *Die Briefe an die Korinther.* NTD 7. Göttingen: Vandenhoeck & Ruprecht, 1986.

Lappas, Joseph. "Paulus und die Sklavenfrage: Eine exegetische Studie in historischer Schau." Doctoral diss., Vienna, 1954.

Laub, Franz. *Die Begegnung des frühen Christentums mit der antiken Sklaverei.* SBS 107. Stuttgart: Verlag Katholisches Bibelwerk, 1982.

Lauffer, Siegfried. *Die Bergwerkssklaven von Laureion.* 2d ed., rev. Forschungen zur antiken Sklaverei 11. Wiesbaden: F. Steiner, 1979.

Lenox-Conyingham, Andrew. Review of *Die Sklaverei in der Sicht der Bischöfe Ambrosius und Augustinus,* by Richard Klein. *JTS* 43 (1992): 255–58.

Lenschau, T. "Korinthos." PWSup 4 (1924): 991–1036.

Leon, Harry J. *The Jews of Ancient Rome.* The Morris Loeb Series. Philadelphia: Jewish Publication Society, 1960.

Lewis, David M. "Attic Manumissions." *Hesperia* 28 (1959): 208–38.

—. "Dedications of Phialai at Athens." *Hesperia* 37 (1968): 368–80.

—. "The First Greek Jew." *JSS* 2 (1957): 264–66.

Lewis, George. *The Philocalia of Origen: A Compilation of Selected Passages from Origen's Works Made by St. Gregory of Nazianzus and St. Basil of Caesarea.* Edinburgh: T. & T. Clark, 1911.

Lewis, Naphtali, and Meyer Reinhold. *Roman Civilization: Selected Readings.* 2 vols. 3d ed. New York: Columbia University Press, 1990.

Liebenam, W. *Zur Geschichte und Organisation römischen Vereinswesens: Drei Untersuchungen.* Leipzig: B. G. Teubner, 1890.

Lifshitz, Baruch. Prolegomenon to *Corpus of Jewish Inscriptions,* edited by P. Jean-Baptiste Frey, 21–104.

Lightfoot, J. B. *Notes on Epistles of St Paul from Unpublished Commentaries.* London: Macmillan, 1895.

Lindemann, Andreas. *Die Clemensbriefe.* HNT 17, *Die Apostolischen Väter I.* Tübingen: J. C. B. Mohr (Paul Siebeck), 1992.

Linder, Amnon. *The Jews in Roman Imperial Legislation.* Detroit: Wayne State University Press; Jerusalem: The Israel Academy of Sciences and Humanities, 1987.

Littré, É., ed. *Oeuvres complètes d'Hippocrate.* 9 vols. Paris: J.-B. Baillière, 1849.

Llewelyn, S. R. "'If You Can Gain Your Freedom': Manumission and 1 Cor. 7:21." In *New Documents Illustrating Early Christianity,* edited by S. R. Llewelyn et al., 6:63–70. Sydney, Australia: The Ancient History Documentary Research Centre [Macquarie University], 1992.

Locke, John. *Two Treatises of Government.* 2d ed. Revised by Peter Laslett. Cambridge Texts in the History of Political Thought. Cambridge: Cambridge University Press, 1988.

Lohse, Eduard, ed. *Die Texte aus Qumran: Hebräisch und Deutsch.* 4th ed. Munich: Kösel-Verlag, 1986.

Lührmann, Dieter. "Neutestamentliche Haustafeln und antike Ökonomie." *NTS* 27 (1980/81): 83–91.

—. "Wo man nicht mehr Sklave oder Freier ist: Überlegungen zur Struktur frühchristlicher Gemeinden." *WD* 13 (1975): 53–83.

Luppe, Wolfgang. "Zu den neuen Goldblättchen aus Thessalien." *ZPE* 76 (1989): 13–14.

Luther, Martin. *Luther's Works*. Vol. 28, *Commentaries on 1 Corinthians 7. 1 Corinthians 15. Lectures on 1 Timothy*. Translated by Edward Sittler. Saint Louis: Concordia Publishing House, 1973.

Lutz, Cora E. "Musonius Rufus: 'The Roman Socrates.'" *YClS* 10 (1947): 3–147.

MacCary, W. Thomas. "Menander's Slaves: Their Names, Roles, and Masks." *TAPA* 100 (1969): 277–94.

MacDowell, Douglas M. *Spartan Law*. Scottish Classical Studies 1. Edinburgh: Scottish Academic Press, 1986.

MacMullen, Ramsay. *Changes in the Roman Empire: Essays in the Ordinary*. Princeton: Princeton University Press, 1990.

–. *Enemies of the Roman Order: Treason, Unrest, and Alienation in the Empire*. Cambridge: Harvard University Press, 1966.

Mahon, John R. "Liberation from Slavery in Early Christian Experience." Rel.D. diss., Claremont School of Theology, 1974.

Maier, Harry O. *The Social Setting of the Ministry as Reflected in the Writings of Hermas, Clement, and Ignatius*. Dissertations SR 1. Waterloo, Ontario: Wilfrid Laurier University Press, 1991.

Malherbe, Abraham J., ed. *The Cynic Epistles: A Study Edition*. SBLSBS 12. Missoula, Mont.: Scholars Press, 1977.

Manning, C. E. "Stoicism and Slavery in the Roman Empire." *ANRW* 2.36.3 (1989): 1518–43.

Maróti, Egon. "Die Rolle der Seeräuber in der Zeit der Mithradatischen Kriege." In *Ricerche stoiche ed economiche in memoria di Corrado Barbagalla a cura di Luigi de Rose*, 1:481–93. Naples: Edizioni Scientifiche Italiane, 1970.

–. "Der Sklavenmarkt auf Delos und die Piraterie." *Helikon* 9 (1969): 24–42.

Martin, Dale B. "Slavery and the Jewish Family." In *The Jewish Family in Antiquity*, edited by Shaye J. C. Cohen, 113–29. BJS 289. Atlanta: Scholars Press, 1993.

–. *Slavery as Salvation: The Metaphor of Slavery in Pauline Christianity*. New Haven: Yale University Press, 1990.

Martin, Hubert, Jr. "Amatorius (Moralia 748e–771e)." In Betz, *Plutarch's Ethical Writings*, 442–537.

Marx, Karl. *Grundrisse der Kritik der politischen Ökonomie (Rohentwurf) 1857–1858, Anhang 1850–1859*. 2d ed. Berlin (East): Dietz Verlag, 1974.

Mason, Hugh J. *Greek Terms for Roman Institutions: A Lexicon and Analysis*. American Studies in Papyrology 13. Toronto: A. M. Hakkert, 1974.

Mathews, Shailer. *Jesus on Social Institutions*. Edited by Kenneth Cauthen. Lives of Jesus Series. 1928. Reprint. Philadelphia: Fortress Press, 1971.

Mauss, Marcel. *The Gift: Forms and Functions of Exchange in Archaic Societies*. Translated by Ian Cullison. London: Cohen & West, 1954.

McFadyen, John Edgar. *The Epistles to the Corinthians and Galatians*. Interpreter's Commentary on the New Testament 6. New York: A. S. Barnes, 1909.

McKivigan, John R. *The War against Proslavery Religion: Abolitionism and the Northern Churches, 1830–1865*. Ithaca: Cornell University Press, 1984.

Meeks, Wayne A. *The First Urban Christians: The Social World of the Apostle Paul*. New Haven: Yale University Press, 1983.

–. "The Image of the Androgyne: Some Uses of a Symbol in Earliest Christianity." *HR* 13 (1974): 165–208.

–, ed. *The Writings of St. Paul*. Norton Critical Editions. New York: W. W. Norton, 1972.

Meeks, Wayne A., and Robert L. Wilken. *Jews and Christians in Antioch in the First Four Centuries of the Common Era.* SBLSBS 13. Missoula, Mont.: Scholars Press, 1978.

Meiggs, Russell. *Roman Ostia.* 2d ed. Oxford: Clarendon Press, 1973.

Meinhold, Peter. *Studien zu Ignatius von Antiochien.* Veröffentlichungen des Instituts für Europäische Geschichte Mainz 97. Abt. für Abendländ. Religionsgeschichte. Wiesbaden: Franz Steiner, 1979.

Merkelbach, R. "Zwei neue orphisch-dionysische Totenpässe." *ZPE* 76 (1989): 15–16.

Merrill, Elmer T. "The Expulsion of Jews from Rome under Tiberius." *CP* 14 (1919): 365–72.

Metzger, Bruce M. Letter to author, 11 May 1991.

Metzger, Marcel. *Les Constitutions Apostoliques.* Vol. 1. SC 320. Paris: Cerf, 1985.

Meyer, Eduard. *Kleine Schriften.* Vol. 1. 2d ed. Halle (Saale): Max Niemeyer, 1924.

Meyer, Ernst. *Der Emporkömmling: Ein Beitrag zur antiken Ethologie.* Giessen: Otto Kindt, 1913.

Meyer, Heinrich August Wilhelm. *Critical and Exegetical Handbook to the Acts of the Apostles.* 2d ed. Translated by Paton J. Gloag. Translation revised and edited by William P. Dickson. New York: Funk & Wagnalls, 1884.

–. *Critical and Exegetical Handbook to the Epistles to the Corinthians.* Translated by D. Douglas Bannerman. New York: Funk & Wagnalls, 1884.

Millar, Fergus G. B. "Condemnation to Hard Labour in the Roman Empire, Augustus to Constantine." *PBSR* 52 (1984): 124–47.

–. *The Emperor in the Roman World, 31* B.C.–A.D. *337.* London: Duckworth, 1977.

–. "Epictetus and the Imperial Court." *JRS* 55 (1965): 141–48.

–. *The Roman Empire and Its Neighbours.* 2d ed. London: Duckworth, 1981.

–. "The World of the Golden Ass." *JRS* 71 (1981): 63–75.

Miller, Joseph C., ed. *Slavery: A Worldwide Bibliography, 1900–1982.* White Plains, N.Y.: Kraus International, 1985.

–, ed. *Slavery and Slaving in World History: A Bibliography, 1990–1991.* Milford, N.Y.: Kraus International, 1993.

Millett, Paul. *Lending and Borrowing in Ancient Athens.* Cambridge: Cambridge University Press, 1991.

Mitchell, Margaret M. *Paul and the Rhetoric of Reconciliation.* HUTh 28. Tübingen: J. C. B. Mohr (Paul Siebeck), 1991.

Momigliano, Arnaldo. *The Development of Greek Biography.* Expanded ed. Cambridge: Harvard University Press, 1993.

–. "Moses Finley and Slavery: A Personal Note." In Finley, *Classical Slavery,* 1–6.

–. Review of *Libertas as a Political Idea at Rome during the Late Republic and Early Principate,* by C. Wirszubski. *JRS* 41 (1951): 146–53

Mommsen, Theodor. *De collegiis et sodaliciis romanorum.* Kiel: Libraria Schwersiana, 1843.

Montesquieu, M. de Secondat Baron de. *The Spirit of the Laws.* Edited by David Wallace Carrithers. Berkeley and Los Angeles: University of California Press, 1977.

Morgan, J. R., and Richard Stoneman, eds. *Greek Fiction: The Greek Novel in Context.* New York: Routledge, 1994.

Morris, Ian. *Death-Ritual and Social Structure in Classical Antiquity.* Key Themes in Ancient History. Cambridge: Cambridge University Press, 1992.

Morris, Leon. *The First Epistle of Paul to the Corinthians.* Rev. ed. Tyndale New Testament Commentaries. Grand Rapids, Mich.: William B. Eerdmans, 1985.

Morrow, Glenn R. "The Murder of Slaves in Attic Law." *CP* 32 (1937–38): 210–27.

–. *Plato's Law of Slavery in Its Relation to Greek Law.* Illinois Studies in Language and Literature 25.3. Urbana: University of Illinois Press, 1939.

Moule, C. F. D. *An Idiom Book of New Testament Greek*. 2d ed. Cambridge: Cambridge University Press, 1959.

Muller, H. J. *Freedom in the Ancient World*. New York: Harper, 1961.

Müller, Nikolaus. *Die jüdische Katakombe am Monteverde zu Rom, der älteste bisher bekannt gewordene jüdische Friedhof des Abendlandes*. Leipzig: G. Fock, 1912.

Mullin, Gerald W. *Flight and Rebellion: Slave-Resistance in Eighteenth-Century Virginia*. New York: Oxford University Press, 1972.

Mullin, Robert Bruce. "Biblical Critics and the Battle over Slavery." *Journal of Presbyterian History* 61 (1983): 210–26.

Murphy-O'Connor, Jerome. *St. Paul's Corinth: Texts and Archaeology*. GNS 6. Collegeville, Minn.: The Liturgical Press, 1983.

Nadel, Benjamin. "Actes d'affranchissement des esclaves du royaume de Bosphore et les origines de la *manumissio in ecclesia*." In *Symposion 1971: Vorträge zur griechischen und hellenistischen Rechtsgeschichte*, edited by Hans Julius Wolff, 265–91. AGR 1. Cologne: Böhlau, 1975.

–. "Slavery and Related Forms of Labor on the North Shore of the Euxine in Antiquity." In *Actes du colloque 1973 sur l'esclavage*, 195–34. Annales littéraires de l'Université de Besançon 182. Centre de recherches d'histoire ancienne 18. Paris: Les Belles Lettres, 1976.

Nani, T. G. "θρεπτοί." *Epigraphica* 5–6 (1943–44): 45–84.

Nestle, Dieter. "Freiheit." *RAC* 8 (1972): 269–306

Neugebauer, O., and H. B. Van Hoesen. *Greek Horoscopes*. Memoirs of the American Philosophical Society 48. Philadelphia: The Society, 1959.

Neuhäusler, E. "Ruf Gottes und Stand des Christen: Bemerkungen zu 1 Kor 7." *BZ* n.s. 3 (1959): 43–60.

Neyrey, Jerome H. *Paul, in Other Words: A Cultural Reading of His Letters*. Louisville, Ky.: Westminster/John Knox Press, 1990.

Nicholas, Barry. *An Introduction to Roman Law*. 3d ed. Clarendon Law Series. Oxford: Clarendon Press, 1987.

Nieboer, H. J. *Slavery as an Industrial System: Ethnological Researches*. The Hague: Hijhoff, 1910.

Nielsen, Hanne S. "*Alumnus*: A Term of Relation Denoting Quasi-Adoption." *C & M* 38 (1987): 141–88.

Niese, Benedictus, ed. *Flavii Iosephi Opera*. 7 vols. Berlin: Wiedemann, 1885–95.

Nissen, Theodor. "Philologisches zu Act. apost. 6,9." *Philologus* 95 (1942–43): 310–13.

North, J. A. "Religious Toleration in Republican Rome." *PCPhS* n.s. 25 (1979): 85–103.

Oakes, James. *The Ruling Race: A History of American Slaveholders*. New York: Vintage Books, 1983.

Okihiro, Gary Y., ed. *In Resistance: Studies in African, Caribbean, and Afro-American History*. Amherst: University of Massachusetts Press, 1986.

Olivecrona, Karl. "'Corpus' and 'Collegium' in D. 3.4.1." *Iura* 5 (1954): 181–90.

Oliver, James H. "Panachaeans and Panhellenes." *Hesperia* 47 (1978): 185–91.

Omerod, Henry A. *Piracy in the Ancient World*. 1914. Reprint. New York: Doreset Press, 1987.

O'Neil, Edward N. "De cupiditate divitiarum (Moralia 523c –528b)." In Betz, *Plutarch's Ethical Writings*, 289–362.

Onesimus Secundus [pseud.]. *The True Interpretation of the American Civil War and of England's Cotton Difficulty: Slavery, From a Different Point of View, Shewing the Relative Responsibilities of America and Great Britain*. 2d ed. London: Trübner, 1863.

Osiek, Carolyn. "The Genre and Function of the *Shepherd of Hermas.*" In *Early Christian Apocalypticism: Genre and Social Setting,* edited by Adela Yarbro Collins, 113–21. Semeia 36. Decatur, Ga.: Scholars Press, 1986.

—. "The Ransom of Captives: Evolution of a Tradition." *HTR* 74 (1981): 365–86.

Oster, Richard E., Jr. "Use, Misuse and Neglect of Archaeological Evidence in Some Modern Works on 1 Corinthians (1 Cor 7,1–5; 8,10; 11,2–16; 12,14–26)." *ZNW* 83 (1992): 52–73.

Parker, Holt. "Crucially Funny or Tranio on the Couch: The *Servus Callidus* and Jokes about Torture." *TAPA* 119 (1989): 233–46.

Parker, Robert. "Spartan Religion." In *Classical Sparta: Techniques Behind Her Success,* edited by Anton Powell, Oklahoma Series in Classical Culture, 142–72. Norman: University of Oklahoma Press, 1988.

Patterson, Cynthia. "'Not Worth Rearing': The Causes of Infant Exposure in Ancient Greece." *TAPA* 115 (1985): 103–23.

Patterson, Orlando. *Freedom in the Making of Western Culture.* New York: Basic Books, 1991.

—. *Slavery and Social Death: A Comparative Study.* Cambridge: Harvard University Press, 1982.

Penna, Romano. "Les Juifs à Rome au temps de l'Apôtre Paul." *NTS* 28 (1982): 321–47.

Penso, Giuseppe. *La médecine romaine: L'art d'Esculape dans la Rome antique.* Paris: Roger Dacosta, 1984.

Petersen, Norman. *Rediscovering Paul: Philemon and the Sociology of Paul's Narrative World.* Philadelphia: Fortress Press, 1985.

Plassart, A. "Les archers d'Athènes." *REG* 16 (1913): 151–213.

Poland, Franz. *Geschichte des griechischen Vereinswesens.* Leipzig: B. G. Teubner, 1909.

—. "σύνοδος." PWSup 4 (1934): 1415–34.

Pomeroy, Sarah B. "Copronyms and the Exposure of Infants in Egypt." In *Studies in Roman Law in Memory of A. Arthur Schiller,* edited by Roger A. Bagnall and William V. Harris, 147–62. Leiden: E. J. Brill, 1986.

—. *Goddesses, Whores, Wives, and Slaves: Women in Classical Antiquity.* New York: Schocken Books, 1975.

—. "Infanticide in Hellenistic Greece." In *Images of Women in Antiquity,* edited by Averil Cameron and Amélie Kuhrt, 207–22. Detroit: Wayne State University Press, 1983.

Porter, Stanley E. *Verbal Aspect in the Greek of the New Testament with Reference to Tense and Mood.* Studies in Biblical Greek 1. New York: Peter Lang, 1989.

Powell, J. Enoch. "Musonius Rufus Εἰ πάντα τὰ γινόμενα τέκνα θρεπτέον in P. Harr. 1." *APF* 12 (1937): 175–78.

Priest, Josiah. *Bible Defence of Slavery; or, The Origin, History, and Fortunes of the Negro Race.* 6th stereotype ed. 1852. Reprint. Louisville, Ky.: Bradley & Gilbert, n.d. [1864].

Prigent, Pierre. "Thallos, Phlégon et le testimonium flavianum témoins de Jésus?" In *Paganisme, Judaïsme, Christianisme: Influences et affrontements dans le monde antique. Mélanges offerts à Marcel Simon,* 329–34. Paris: Boccard, 1978.

Pringsheim, Fritz. *The Greek Law of Sale.* Weimar: Mermann Böhlaus, 1950.

Purcell, Nicholas. Review of *The Magistrates of the Professional Collegia in Italy from the First to the Third Century A.D.,* by Halsey L. Royden. *CP* 87 (1992): 178–82.

Rabe, Hugo, ed. *Anonymi et Stephani in artem rhetoricam commentaria.* Commentaria in Aristotelem Graeca 19, 21. Berlin: G. Reimer, 1889, 1896.

Radin, Max. "The Exposure of Infants in Roman Law and Practice." *CJ* 20 (1924–25): 337–43.

–. *The Legislation of the Greeks and Romans on Corporations.* New York: Tuttle, Morehouse, & Taylor, 1909.

Rädle, Herbert. "Selbsthilfeorganisationen der Sklaven und Freigelassenen in Delphi." *Gymnasium* 77 (1970): 1–5.

Raffeiner, Hermann. *Sklaven und Freigelassene: Eine soziologische Studie auf der Grundlage des griechischen Grabepigrams.* Commentationes Aenipontanae 23. Philologie und Epigraphik 2. Innsbruck: Wagner, 1977.

Rajak, Tessa. "Inscription and Context: Reading the Jewish Catacombs of Rome." In *Studies in Jewish Epigraphy,* edited by Jan Willem van Henten and Pieter W. van der Horst, 226–41. Arbeiten zur Geschichte des antiken Judentums und des Urchristentums 21. Leiden: E. J. Brill, 1994.

–. "Was There a Roman Charter for the Jews?" *JRS* 74 (1984): 106–23.

Randall, R. H. "The Erechtheum Workmen." *AJA* 57 (1953): 199–210.

Ranft, J. "Depositum." *RAC* 3 (1957): 778–84.

Rawick, George P., ed. *The American Slave: A Composite Autobiography.* Vol. 1, *From Sundown to Sunup: The Making of the Black Community.* Contributions in Afro-American and African Studies 11. Westport, Conn.: Greenwood Publishing, 1972.

Rawson, Beryl. "Children in the Roman *Familia.*" In *The Family in Ancient Rome: New Perspectives,* edited by Rawson, 170–200. Ithaca: Cornell University Press, 1986.

Reardon, B. P. *Collected Ancient Greek Novels.* Berkeley and Los Angeles: University of California Press, 1989.

Redard, G. "Recherches sur ΧΡΗ, ΧΡΗΣΘΑΙ: Étude sémantique." In *Bibliothèque: Sciences historiques et philologiques,* fasc. 303, edited by L'École practique des hautes études, 11–47. Paris: Libraire Ancienne Honoré Champion, 1953.

Rengstorf, K. H. "δοῦλος, κ.τ.λ." *TDNT* 2 (1964): 261–80.

Reynolds, Joyce. "Roman Inscriptions, 1971–75." *JRS* 66 (1976): 174–99.

Rice, Madeleine Hooke. *American Catholic Opinion in the Slavery Controversy.* Studies in History, Economics, and Public Law 508. 1944. Reprint. Gloucester, Mass.: Peter Smith, 1964.

Richardson, Cyril C. "The Church in Ignatius of Antioch." *JR* 17 (1937): 428–43.

Richter, Will. "Seneca und die Sklaven." *Gymnasium* 65 (1958): 196–218.

Rigg, Horace A., Jr. "Thallus: The Samaritan?" *HTR* 34 (1941): 112–19.

Ritter, Adolf Martin. "Zwischen 'Gottesherrschaft' und 'einfachem Leben': Dio Chrysostomus, Johannes Chrysostomus und das Problem einer Humanisierung der Gesellschaft." *JAC* 31 (1988): 127–43.

Robertson, Archibald, and Alfred Plummer. *A Critical and Exegetical Commentary on the First Epistle of St Paul to the Corinthians.* 2d ed. ICC 7. New York: Charles Scribner's Sons, 1925.

Rocca-Serra, G. "Le stoicisme pré-imperial et l'esclavage." *CRDAC* 8 (1976–77): 205–22.

Royden, Halsey L. *The Magistrates of the Professional Collegia in Italy from the First to the Third Century* A.D. Biblioteca di studi antichi 61. Pisa: Giardini, 1988.

Rückert, L. I. *Die Briefe Pauli an die Korinther.* Vol. 1. Leipzig: R. Röhler, 1836.

Ruef, J. S. *Paul's First Letter to Corinth.* Pelican New Testament Commentaries. New York: Penguin Books, 1971.

Russell, D. A. "Caecilius (4)." *OCD* 187.

Russell, Kenneth C. *Slavery as Reality and Metaphor in the Pauline Letters.* Rome: Catholic Book Agency, 1968.

Rutgers, Leonard Victor. "Überlegungen zu den jüdischen Katakomben Roms." *JAC* 33 (1990): 140–57.

St. Hart, H. "Judaea and Rome: The Official Commentary." *JTS* n.s. 3 (1952): 172–204.

Ste. Croix, G. E. M. de. *The Class Struggle in the Ancient Greek World: From the Archaic Age to the Arab Conquest.* 1981. Reprint with corr. Ithaca: Cornell University Press, 1989.

Sakellariou, M. B., and N. Faraklas. *Corinthia–Cleonaea.* Athens: Athens Center of Ekistics, 1971.

Saller, Richard P. "Corporal Punishment, Authority, and Obedience in the Roman Household." In *Marriage, Divorce, and Children in Ancient Rome*, edited by Beryl Rawson, 144–65. Oxford: Clarendon Press, 1991.

—. "*Familia, Domus,* and the Roman Conception of the Family." *Phoenix* 38 (1984): 336–55.

—. "Men's Age at Marriage and Its Consequences in the Roman Family." *CP* 82 (1987): 21–34.

—. *Patriarchy, Property, and Death in the Roman Family.* Cambridge: Cambridge University Press, 1994.

—. *Personal Patronage under the Early Empire.* Cambridge: Cambridge University Press, 1982.

—. "*Pietas,* Obligation, and Authority in the Roman Family." In *Alte Geschichte und Wissenschaftsgeschichte: Festschrift für Karl Christ zum 65. Geburtstag*, edited by Peter Kneissl and Volker Losemann, 393–410. Darmstadt: Wissenschaftliche Buchgesellschaft, 1988.

—. Review of *Roman Corinth*, by Donald Engels. *CP* 86 (1991): 351–57.

—. "Slavery and the Roman Family." In Finley, *Classical Slavery*, 65–87.

Saller, Richard P., and Brent D. Shaw. "Tombstones and Roman Family Relations in the Principate: Civilians, Soldiers, and Slaves." *JRS* 74 (1984): 124–56.

Salmon, J. B. *Wealthy Corinth: A History of the City to 338 B.C.* Oxford: Clarendon Press, 1984.

Samson, Ross. "Rural Slavery, Inscriptions, Archaeology, and Marx: A Response to Ramsay MacMullen's 'Late Roman Slavery.'" *Historia* 38 (1989): 99–110.

Samuel, Alan E. "The Role of *Paramonē* Clauses in Ancient Documents." *JJP* 15 (1965): 256–84.

Schäfer, Klaus. *Gemeinde als "Bruderschaft": Ein Beitrag zum Kirchenverständnis des Paulus.* Europäische Hochschulschriften, 23d ser. 333. Frankfurt: P. Lang, 1989.

Schaff, Philip. *Slavery and the Bible, a Tract for the Times.* Chambersburg, Pa.: M. Kieffer, 1861.

Schenk, Wolfgang. "Der Brief des Paulus an Philemon in der neueren Forschung (1945–1987)." *ANRW* 2.25.4 (1987): 3439–95.

Schenkel, Daniel. *Bibel-Lexikon: Realwörterbuch zum Handgebrauch für Geistliche und Gemeindeglieder.* Vol. 4. Leipzig: Brockaus, 1872.

Schiedel, Walter. "Slavery and the Shackled Mind: On Fortune-telling and Slave Mentality in the Graeco-Roman World." *The Ancient History Bulletin* 7 (1993): 107–14.

Schlaifer, Robert. "Greek Theories of Slavery from Homer to Aristotle." In Finley, *Slavery in Classical Antiquity: Views and Controversies*, 93–132. First published in *HSPh* 47 (1936): 165–204.

Schlatter, A. *Paulus der Bote Jesu: Eine Deutung seiner Briefe an die Korinther.* 4th ed. Stuttgart: Calwer, 1969.

Schlier, H. " ἐλεύθερος, κ.τ.λ." *TDNT* 2 (1964): 487–502.

Schneider, Carl. *Kulturgeschichte des Hellenismus.* 2 vols. Munich: C. H. Beck, 1967, 1969.

Schoedel, William R., ed. *Athenagoras: Legatio and de resurrectione.* OECT. Oxford: Clarendon Press, 1972.

—. "Ignatius and the Archives." *HTR* 71 (1978): 97–106.

—. *Ignatius of Antioch: A Commentary on the Letters of Ignatius of Antioch.* Hermeneia. Philadelphia: Fortress Press, 1985.

Scholl, Reinhold, ed. *Corpus der ptolemäischen Sklaventexte.* 3 vols. Forschungen zur antiken Sklaverei, Beiheft 1. Stuttgart: Franz Steiner, 1990.

Schulz, Siegfried. *Gott ist kein Sklavenhalter: Die Geschichte einer verspäteten Revolution.* Zurich: Flamberg, 1972.

—. "Hat Christus die Sklaven befreit? Sklaverei und Emanzipationsbewegungen im Abendland." *EvK* 5 (1972): 13–17.

Schürer, Emil. *The History of the Jewish People in the Age of Jesus Christ (175 B.C.–A.D. 135).* New ed. Revised by Geza Vermes, Fergus Millar, and Martin Goodman. 3 vols. Edinburgh: T. & T. Clark, 1973–87.

—. "Die Juden im bosporanischen Reiche und die Gnossenschaften der σεβόμενοι θεὸν ὕψιστον." *SPAW* 12–13 (1897): 200–225.

Schütz, John Howard. *Paul and the Anatomy of Apostolic Authority.* SNTSMS 26. Cambridge: Cambridge University Press, 1975.

Scranton, Robert L. *Corinth: Results of Excavations Conducted by the American School of Classical Studies at Athens.* Vol. 1.3, *Monuments in the Lower Agora and North of the Archaic Temple.* Princeton: American School, 1951.

Scullard, H. H. *From the Gracchi to Nero: A History of Rome 133 B.C. to A.D. 68.* 5th ed. London: Methuen, 1982.

—. *A History of the Roman World: 753 to 146 B.C.* 4th ed. New York: Methuen, 1980.

Seccombe, David. "Was There Organized Charity in Jerusalem before the Christians?" *JTS* 29 (1978): 140–43.

Senft, Christophe. *La première épître de Saint Paul aux Corinthiens.* 2d ed., rev. CNT 2d ser. 7. Geneva: Labor et Fides, 1990.

Sereni, E. "Recherche sur le vocabulaire des rapports de dépendance dans le monde antique." In *Actes du colloque 1973 sur l'esclavage,* 11–43. Annales littéraires de l'Université de Besançon 182. Centre de recherches d'histoire ancienne 18. Paris: Les Belles Lettres, 1976.

Sevenster, J. N. *Paul and Seneca.* NovTSup 4. Leiden: E. J. Brill, 1961.

Shaw, Brent D. "The Age of Girls at Marriage: Some Reconsiderations." *JRS* 77 (1987): 30–46.

—. "Bandits." In Giardina, *The Romans,* 300–341.

—. "Bandits in the Roman Empire." *P & P* 105 (1984): 3–52.

—. "The Divine Economy: Stoicism as Ideology." *Latomus* 44 (1985): 16–54.

Shelton, Jo-Ann. *As the Romans Did: A Source Book of Roman Social History.* New York: Oxford University Press, 1988.

Sherwin-White, A. N. *The Letters of Pliny: A Historical and Social Commentary.* 1966. Corr. reprint. Oxford: Clarendon Press, 1985.

—. *Racial Prejudice in Imperial Rome.* Cambridge: Cambridge University Press, 1967.

—. *Roman Foreign Policy in the East, 169 B.C. to A.D. 1.* Norman: University of Oklahoma Press, 1983.

Siegel, Bernard J. "Some Methodological Considerations for a Comparative Study of Slavery." *American Anthropologist* n.s. 47 (1945): 357–92.

Smallwood, E. Mary. *The Jews under Roman Rule: From Pompey to Diocletian.* SJLA 20. Leiden: E. J. Brill, 1976.

—, ed. and trans. *Philonis Alexandrini: Legatio ad Gaium.* 2d ed. Leiden: E. J. Brill, 1970.

Smith, Jonathan Z. *Drudgery Divine: On the Comparison of Early Christianities and the Religions of Late Antiquity.* Chicago Studies in the History of Judaism. Chicago: University of Chicago Press, 1990.

Smith, Nicholas D. "Aristotle's Theory of Natural Slavery." *Phoenix* 37 (1983): 109–22.

Smith, Wesley D., ed. *Hippocrates: Pseudepigraphic Writings.* Studies in Ancient Medicine 2. Leiden: E. J. Brill, 1990.

Smyth, Herbert Weir. *Greek Grammar.* 2d ed. Revised by Gordon M. Messing. Cambridge: Harvard University Press, 1956.

Snell, Bruno. "The Rendel Harris Papyri of Woodbrooke College, Birmingham." *Gnomon* 13 (1937): 577–86.

Snowden, Frank M., Jr. *Before Color Prejudice: The Ancient View of Blacks.* Cambridge: Harvard University Press, 1983.

–. *Blacks in Antiquity: Ethiopians in the Greco-Roman Experience.* Cambridge: Harvard University Press, Belknap Press, 1970.

Sokołowski, Franciszek. *Lois sacrées de l'Asie Mineure.* École Française d'Athènes: Travaux et mémoires, fasc. 9. Paris: Boccard, 1955.

Solin, Heikki. "Juden und Syrer im westlichen Teil der römischen Welt: Eine ethnisch-demographische Studie mit besonderer Berücksichtigung der sprachlichen Zustände." *ANRW* 2.29.2 (1984): 590–789.

–. "Die Namen der orientalischen Sklaven in Rom." In *L'onomastique latine,* edited by Noël Nuval, 205–20. Colloques internationaux de Centre National de la Recherche Scientifique 564. Paris: Centre National de la Recherche Scientifique, 1977.

–. "Onomastica ed epigrafia: Riflessioni sull'esegesi onomastica delle iscrizioni romane." *QUCC* 18 (1974): 105–32.

Sotgiu, Giovanna. "Un collare di schiavo reinvenuto in Sardegna." *ArchClass* 25–26 (1973–74): 688–97.

Souter, Alexander, ed. *Pelagius's Expositions of Thirteen Epistles of St Paul.* Pt. 2, *Text and Apparatus Criticus.* Texts and Studies 9.2. Cambridge: Cambridge University Press, 1929.

Spengel, Leondari, ed. *Rhetores Graeci.* Vol. 2. Leipzig: B. G. Teubner, 1854.

Sperber, Daniel. *A Dictionary of Greek and Latin Legal Terms in Rabbinic Literature.* Dictionaries of Talmud, Midrash, and Targum 1. Jerusalem: Bar-Ilan University Press, 1984.

Spicq, C. *Charité et liberté selon le Nouveau Testament.* 2d ed. Paris: Les Éditions de Cerf, 1964.

–. "La liberté selon le Nouveau Testament." *ScEccl* 12 (1960): 229–40.

Spranger, Peter P. *Historische Untersuchungen zu den Sklavenfiguren des Plautus und Terenz.* Forschungen zur antiken Sklaverei 17. Wiesbaden: Akademie Mainz, 1960.

Staats, Reinhart. "Deposita pietatis – Die Alte Kirche und ihr Geld." *ZTK* 76 (1979): 1–29.

Stace, C. "The Slaves of Plautus." *G & R* 15 (1968): 64–77.

Štaerman, E. M. *Die Blütezeit der Sklavenwirtschaft in der römischen Republik.* Translated by Maria Bräuer-Pospelova. Übersetzungen ausländischer Arbeiten zur antiken Sklaverei 2. Wiesbaden: Franz Steiner, 1969.

–, et al. *Die Sklaverei in den westlichen Provinzen des römischen Reiches im 1.–3. Jahrhundert.* Translated by Jaroslav Kriz. Übersetzungen ausländischer Arbeiten zur antiken Sklaverei 4. Stuttgart: Franz Steiner, 1987.

Stampp, Kenneth M. *The Peculiar Institution: Slavery in the Ante-Bellum South.* New York: Vintage Books, 1956.

Stanton, G. R. "Τέχνον, παῖς, and Related Words in Koine Greek." In *Proceedings of the*

XVIII International Congress of Papyrology, edited by Basil G. Mandilaras, 1:464–80. Athens: Greek Papyrological Society, 1988.

Starr, Chester. "Epictetus the Tyrant." *CP* 44 (1949): 20–29.

Steinmann, Alphons. "Antwort." *TRev* 15–16 (1917): 469–70.

—. *Paulus und die Sklaven zu Korinth: 1. Kor. 7,21 aufs neue untersucht*. Braunsberg: Verlag Hans Grimme, 1911.

—. *Sklavenlos und alte Kirche: Eine historisch-exegetische Studie über die sozial Frage im Urchristentum*. 4th ed. Apologetische Tagesfragen 8. Gladbach: Volksvereins Verlag, 1922.

—. "Zur Geschichte der Auslegung von 1 Kor 7,21." *TRev* 15–16 (1917): 340–48.

Stern, Menachem. *Greek and Latin Authors on Jews and Judaism*. 3 vols. Jerusalem: Israel Academy of Sciences and Humanities, 1974–84.

—. "The Jewish Diaspora." In *The Jewish People in the First Century: Historical Geography, Political History, Social, Cultural and Religious Life and Institutions*, edited by S. Safrai and M. Stern, 1:117–83. CRINT 1.1. Philadelphia: Fortress Press, 1974.

Stoops, Robert F., Jr. "'If I Suffer …': Epistolary Authority in Ignatius of Antioch." *HTR* 80 (1987): 161–78.

Straaten, Modestus van. "Menschliche Freiheit in der stoischen Philosophie." *Gymnasium* 84 (1977): 501–18.

Strasburger, Hermann. "Poseidonius on Problems of the Roman Empire." *JRS* 55 (1965): 40–53.

Stringfellow, Thornton. "A Brief Examination of Scripture Testimony on the Institution of Slavery." In *The Ideology of Slavery: Proslavery Thought in the Antebellum South, 1830–1860*, edited by Drew G. Faust, 136–67. Library of Southern Civilization. Baton Rouge: Louisiana State Press, 1981.

—. *Scriptural and Statistical Views in Favor of Slavery*. 4th ed. Richmond, Va.: J. W. Randolf, 1856.

Struve, V. V., et al., eds. *Corpus Inscriptionum Regni Bosporani*. Moscow and Leningrad: Institute of Archaeology of the Academy of Sciences of the USSR, 1965.

Stuhlmacher, Peter. *Der Brief an Philemon*. 2d ed. EKKNT 18. Zurich: Benziger Verlag; Cologne: Neukirchener Verlag, 1981.

—. Review of *ΜΑΛΛΟΝ ΧΡΗΣΑΙ*, by S. Scott Bartchy. *TLZ* 101 (1976): 837–39.

Sydenham, Edward A. *The Coinage of the Roman Republic*. London: Spink & Son, 1952.

Syme, Ronald. "Marriage Ages for Roman Senators." *Historia* 36 (1987): 318–32.

Synodinou, Ekaterini. "On the Concept of Slavery in Euripides." Ph.D. diss., University of Cincinnati, 1974.

Taubenschlag, Raphael. *The Law of Greco-Roman Egypt in the Light of the Papyri: 332 B.C.–640 A.D.* 2d ed. Warsaw: Państowowe Wydawnictwo Naukowe, 1955.

Taylor, Lily Ross. "Freedmen and Freeborn in the Epitaphs of Imperial Rome." *AJP* 82 (1961): 113–32.

Tcherikover, Victor A., et al., eds. *Corpus Papyrorum Judaicarum*. 3 vols. Jerusalem: Hebrew University Press, Magnes Press, 1957–64.

—. *Hellenistic Civilization and the Jews*. Translated by S. Applebaum. Philadelphia: Jewish Publication Society of America, 1959.

Thébert, Yvon. "The Slave." In Giardina, *The Romans*, 138–74.

Theissen, Gerd. *Social Reality and the Early Christians: Theology, Ethics, and the World of the New Testament*. Translated by Margaret Kohl. Minneapolis: Fortress Press, 1992.

—. *The Social Setting of Pauline Christianity*. Edited, translated, and with an introd. by John H. Schütz. Philadelphia: Fortress Press, 1982.

Thompson, Dorothy J. Review of *Corpus der ptolemäischen Sklaventexte*, edited by Reinhold Scholl. *CR* 42 (1992): 164–66.

Thompson, Wesley E. "Insurance and Banking." In *Civilization of the Ancient Mediterranean: Greece and Rome*, edited by Michael Grant and Rachel Kitzinger, 2:829–36. New York: Charles Scribner's Sons, 1988.

Thrall, Margaret E. *Greek Particles in the New Testament: Linguistic and Exegetical Studies.* NTTS 3. Leiden: E. J. Brill, 1962.

Tise, Larry E. *Proslavery: A History of the Defense of Slavery in America, 1701–1840.* Athens: University of Georgia Press, 1987.

Tod, Marcus N. "Some Unpublished 'Catalogi Paterarum Argentearum.'" *ABSA* 8 (1901–2): 197–230.

Trebilco, Paul R. *Jewish Communities in Asia Minor.* SNTSMS 69. Cambridge: Cambridge University Press, 1991.

Treggiari, Susan. "Jobs in the Household of Livia." *PBSR* 43 (1975): 48–77.

—. *Roman Freedmen during the Late Republic.* Oxford: Clarendon Press, 1969.

—. *Roman Marriage: Iusti Coniuges from the Time of Cicero to the Time of Ulpian.* Oxford: Clarendon Press, 1991.

Trevett, Christine. "Prophecy and Anti-Episcopal Activity: A Third Error Combated by Ignatius?" *JEH* 34 (1983): 1–18.

Trummer, Peter. "Die Chance der Freiheit: Zur Interpretation des μᾶλλον χρῆσαι in 1 Kor 7,21." *Biblica* 56 (1975): 344–68.

Uhlhorn, G. *Christian Charity in the Ancient Church.* Translated by Sophia Taylor. Edinburgh: T. & T. Clark, 1883,

Urbach, Ephraim E. "The Laws Regarding Slavery as a Source for Social History of the Period of the Second Temple, the Mishnah and Talmud." Translated by R. J. Loewe. In *Papers of the Institute of Jewish Studies London*, edited by E. G. Weiss, 1:1–94. 1964. Reprint. Lanham, Md.: University Press of America, 1989.

Ustinovo, Julia. "The *Thiasoi* of Theos Hypsistos in Tanais." *HR* 31 (1991): 150–80.

van den Berghe, Peter L. Review of *Slavery and Social Death*, by Orlando Patterson. *Ethnic and Racial Studies* 7 (1984): 301–5.

Van Hook, La Rue. "The Exposure of Infants at Athens." *TAPA* 51 (1920): 134–45.

Versnel, S. *Inconsistencies in Greek and Roman Religion.* Vol. 1, *Ter Unus: Isis, Dionysos, Hermes. Three Studies in Henotheism.* Studies in Greek and Roman Religion 6. Leiden: E. J. Brill, 1990.

Vettius Valens. *Vettii Valentis anthologiarum libri IX.* Edited by W. Kroll. Berlin: Weidmann, 1908.

—. *Vettii Valentis Antiocheni anthologiarum libri novem.* Edited by David Pingree. Bibliotheca scriptorum Graecorum et Romanorum Teubneriana. Berlin: B. G. Teubner, 1986.

Vidal-Naquet, Pierre. *The Black Hunter: Forms of Thought and Forms of Society in the Greek World.* Translated by Andrew Szegedy-Maszak. Baltimore: Johns Hopkins University Press, 1986.

Vidman, L., ed. *Corpus Inscriptionum Latinarum.* Vol. 6, pt. 6, *Indices*, fasc. 6. Berlin: Walter de Gruyter, 1980.

Vincent, L.-K. "Découverte de la 'synagogue des affranchis' à Jérusalem." *RB* 30 (1921): 258–60.

Vlastos, Gregory. "Does Slavery Exist in Plato's Republic?" *CP* 63 (1968): 291–95.

—. "Slavery in Plato's Thought." In Finley, *Slavery in Classical Antiquity*, 133–49. First published in *Philosophical Review* 50 (1941): 289–304.

Vogt, Hermann J. "Ignatius von Antiochien über den Bischof und seine Gemeinde." *TQ* 158 (1978): 15–27.

Vogt, Joseph. *Ancient Slavery and the Ideal of Man.* Translated by Thomas Wiedemann. New York: Oxford University Press, 1974.

–. "Ecce Ancilla Domini: The Social Aspects of the Virgin Mary in Antiquity." In *Ancient Slavery and the Ideal of Man*, 145–69. First published in *VC* 23 (1969): 241–63.

Vogt, Joseph, and Heinz Bellen, eds. *Bibliographie zur antiken Sklaverei: Im Auftrag der Kommission für Geschichte des Altertums der Akademie der Wissenschaften und der Literatur*. New ed. 2 pts. Revised by E. Herrmann and N. Brockmeyer. Bochum: N. Brockmeyer, 1983.

Vollenweider, Samuel. *Freiheit als neue Schöpfung: Eine Untersuchung zur Eleutheria bei Paulus und in seiner Umwelt*. FRLANT 147. Göttingen: Vandenhoeck & Ruprecht, 1989.

Vondeling, J. *Eranos*. Historische Studies 17. Groningen: J. B. Wolters, 1961.

Vos, M. F. *Scythian Archers in Archaic Attic Vase-Painting*. Archaeologica Traiectina 6. Groningen: J. B. Wolters, 1963.

Waddell, W. G. Review of *The Rendel Harris Papyri*, edited by J. Enoch Powell. *CR* 51 (1937): 70.

Walbank, F. W. *The Hellenistic World*. Cambridge: Harvard University Press, 1982.

Walbank, Mary E. Hoskins. Review of *Roman Corinth*, by Donald Engels. *JRS* 81 (1991): 220–21.

Waldstein, Wolfgang. *Operae Libertorum: Untersuchungen zur Dienstpflicht freigelassener Sklaven*. Forschungen zur antiken Sklaverei 19. Stuttgart: Franz Steiner, 1986.

Wallace-Hadrill, Andrew. "The Social Structure of the Roman House." *PBSR* 56 (1988): 43–97.

Wallon, Henri. *Histoire de l'esclavage dans l'antiquité*. 2d ed. 3 vols. Paris: Hachette, 1879.

Waltzing, Jean-Pierre. *Étude historique sur les corporations professionnelles chez les Romains depuis les origines jusqu'à la chute de l'empire d'occident*. 4 vols. 1895–1900. Reprint. Bologna: Forni, 1968.

Watson, Alan. "Morality, Slavery and the Jurists in the Later Roman Republic." *Tulane Law Review* 42 (1967–68): 289–303.

–. *Roman Slave Law*. Baltimore: Johns Hopkins University Press, 1987.

–. "Roman Slave Law and Romanist Ideology." *Phoenix* 37 (1983): 53–65.

Watts, William. "Seneca on Slavery." *DR* 90 (1972): 183–95.

Wayatt-Brown, Bertram. Review of *Slavery and Social Death*, by Orlando Patterson. *Society* 21.3 (1984): 92–94.

Weaver, P. R. C. "Children of Freedmen (and Freedwomen)." In *Marriage, Divorce, and Children in Ancient Rome*, edited by Beryl Rawson, 166–90. Oxford: Clarendon Press, 1991.

–. "Cognomia Ingenua: A Note." *CQ* 14 (1964): 311–15.

–. *Familia Caesaris: A Social Study of the Emperor's Freedmen and Slaves*. Cambridge: Cambridge University Press, 1972.

–. "Misplaced Officials." *Antichthon* 13 (1979): 70–102.

–. "The Status Nomenclature of Imperial Freedmen." *CQ* 13 (1963): 272–78.

–. "Where Have All the Junian Latins Gone? Nomenclature and Status in the Early Empire." *Chiron* 20 (1990): 275–305.

Weber, Carl W. *Sklaverei im Altertum: Leben im Schatten der Säulen*. Düsseldorf: Econ, 1981.

Weber, Max. *The Agrarian Sociology of Ancient Civilizations*. Translated by R. I. Frank. Foundations of History Library. London: N.L.B., 1976.

Weinreich, Otto. *Stiftung und Kultsatzungen eines Privatheiligtums in Philadelphia in Lydien*. SHAW 1919. Heidelberg: Carl Winter, 1919.

Weiss, Johannes. *Der erste Korintherbrief*. 2d ed. MeyerK 5. Göttingen: Vandenhoeck & Ruprecht, 1910.

Welles, C. Bradford. "Manumission and Adoption." *RIDA* 2d ser. 3 (1949): 507–20.

Wells, Colin. *The Roman Empire*. Stanford: Stanford University Press, 1984.
Wendland, H. D. *Die Briefe an die Korinther*. 12th ed. NTD 7. Göttingen: Vandenhoeck & Ruprecht, 1968.
West, M. L., ed. *Hesiod, Works & Days*. Oxford: Clarendon Press, 1974.
—. *The Orphic Poems*. Oxford: Clarendon Press, 1983.
Westermann, William Linn. "Athenaeus and the Slaves of Athens." In Finley, *Slavery in Classical Antiquity*, 73–92. First published in *HSPh* Suppl. (1941): 451–70.
—. "The *Paramonē* as General Service Contract." *JJP* 2 (1948): 9–50.
—. *The Slave Systems of Greek and Roman Antiquity*. Memoirs of the American Philosophical Society 40. Philadelphia: The Society, 1955.
—. "Slavery and the Elements of Freedom in Ancient Greece." In Finley, *Slavery in Classical Antiquity*, 17–32. First published in *Quarterly Bulletin of the Polish Institute of Arts and Sciences in America* 2 (1943): 1–14.
—. "Two Studies in Athenian Manumissions." *JNES* 5 (1946): 92–104.
—. "Warehousing and Trapezite Banking in Antiquity." *Journal of Economic and Business History* 3 (1930–31): 30–54.
Whedon, D. D., ed. Review of *The Bible and Slavery*, by Charles Elliott. *Methodist Quarterly Review* (New York) 39 (October 1857): 634–44.
White, Kenneth D. "Roman Agricultural Writers I: Varro and His Predecessors." *ANRW* 1.4 (1973): 439–95.
White, L. Michael. "Finding the Ties that Bind: Issues from Social Description." In *Social Networks in the Early Christian Environment: Issues and Methods for Social History*, edited by White, 3–36. Semeia 56. Atlanta: Scholars Press, 1992.
Wicker, Kathleen O'Brien. "Mulierum virtutes (Moralia 242e –263c)." In Betz, *Plutarch's Ethical Writings*, 106–34.
Wieacker, Franz. *Römische Rechtsgeschichte: Quellenkunde, Rechtsbildung, Jurisprudenz und Rechtsliteratur*. Pt. 1, *Rechtsgeschichte des Altertums*. Handbuch der Altertumswissenschaft 3.1. Munich: C. H. Beck, 1988.
Wiedemann, Thomas E. J. "Duties of Freedmen." Review of *Operae Libertorum: Untersuchungen zur Dienstpflicht freigelassener Sklaven*, by Wolfgang Waldstein. *CR* n.s. 38 (1988): 331–33.
—. *Greek and Roman Slavery*. 1981. Reprint. London: Routledge, 1988.
—. "The Regularity of Manumission at Rome." *CQ* n.s. 35 (1985): 162–75.
—. *Slavery*. Greece and Rome: New Surveys in the Classics 19. Oxford: Clarendon Press, 1987.
Wilckens, Ulrich, Alois Kehl, and Karl Hoheisel. "Heuchelei." *RAC* 14 (1988): 1205–31.
Wiles, David. "Greek Theatre and the Legitimation of Slavery." In *Slavery and Other Forms of Unfree Labour*, edited by Léonie J. Archer, 53–67. History Workshop Series. London: Routledge, 1988.
Wilken, Robert L. *The Christians as the Romans Saw Them*. New Haven: Yale University Press, 1984.
Willetts, Ronald F. "Freedmen at Gortyna." *CQ* 4 (1954): 216–19.
—. *The Law Code of Gortyn*. Kadmos Suppl. 1. Berlin: Walter de Gruyer, 1967.
Williams, Charles K., II. "Corinth and the Cult of Aphrodite." In Del Chiaro and Biers, *Corinthiaca*, 12–24.
Wimbush, Vincent L. *Paul, the Worldly Ascetic: Response to the World and Self-Understanding according to 1 Corinthians 7*. Macon, Ga.: Mercer University Press, 1987.
Winter, Sara C. "Methodological Observations on a New Interpretation of Paul's Letter to Philemon." *USQR* 39 (1984): 203–12.

−. "Paul's Letter to Philemon." *NTS* 33 (1987): 1–15.

Wire, Antoinette Clark. *The Corinthian Women Prophets: A Reconstruction through Paul's Rhetoric*. Minneapolis: Fortress Press, 1990.

Wirszubski, C. *Libertas as a Political Idea at Rome during the Late Republic and Early Principate*. 1950. Reprint. Cambridge: Cambridge University Press, 1960.

Wiseman, James. "Corinth and Rome I: 228 B.C.–A.D. 267." *ANRW* 2.7.1 (1979): 438–548.

−. *The Land of the Ancient Corinthians*. Studies in Mediterranean Archaeology 1. Göteborg: Paul Åströms Förlag, 1978.

Wistrand, Erik. *The So-Called Laudatio Turiae: Introduction, Text, Translation, and Commentary*. Studia Graeca et Latina Gothoburgensia 24. Gothenburg: Acta Universitatis Gothoburgensis, 1976.

Witherington, Ben, III. *Women in the Earliest Churches*. SNTSMS 59. Cambridge: Cambridge University Press, 1988.

Wolf, Joseph Georg. *Das Senatusconsultum Silanianum und die Senatsrede des C. Cassius Longinus aus dem Jahre 61 n. Chr.* SHAW 2. Heidelberg: Carl Winter, 1988.

Wood, Ellen M. *Peasant-Citizen and Slave: The Foundations of Athenian Democracy*. London: Verso Press, 1988.

Wood, Neal. *Cicero's Social and Political Thought*. Berkeley and Los Angeles: University of California Press, 1988.

Wuellner, W. "Greek Rhetoric and Pauline Argumentation." In *Early Christian Literature and the Classical Tradition: in honorem Robert M. Grant*, edited by W. R. Schoedel and R. L. Wilken, 177–88. Théologie historique 53. Paris: Beauches, 1979.

Yadin, Y. *The Documents from the Bar Kokhba Period in the Cave of Letters: Greek Papyri*, edited by N. Lewis. *Aramaic and Nabatean Signatures and Subscriptions*, edited by Y. Yadin and J. C. Greenfield. JDS 11. Jerusalem: Israel Exploration Society, 1989.

Yavetz, Zvi. "The Failure of Catiline's Conspiracy." *Historia* 12 (1963): 458–99.

−. *Slaves and Slavery in Ancient Rome*. Translated by Adam Vital. New Brunswick, N.J.: Transaction, 1988.

Zeitlin, Solomon. "Slavery During the Second Commonwealth and the Tannaitic Period." In *Solomon Zeitlin's Studies in the Early History of Judaism*. Vol. 4, *History of Early Talmudic Law*, 225–58. New York: Ktav, 1978. First published in *JQR* 53 (1962–63): 185–218.

Ziebarth, Erich. *Das griechische Vereinswesen*. Leipzig: S. Hirzel, 1896.

Ziegler, Joseph, ed. *Septuaginta, 12/2: Sapienta Iesu Filii Sirach*. Vetus Testamentum Graecum Auctoritate Societas Litterarum Gottingensis editum. Göttingen: Vandenhoeck & Ruprecht, 1965.

Zimmerli, Walther. *Ezekiel 1: A Commentary on the Book of the Prophet Ezekiel, Chapters 1–24*. Translated by Ronald E. Clements. Edited by Frank Moore Cross and Klaus Baltzer with Leonard Jay Greenspoon. Hermeneia. Philadelphia: Fortress Press, 1979.

Zuntz, Günther. *Persephone: Three Essays on Religion and Thought in Magna Graeca*. Oxford: Clarendon Press, 1971.

Indexes

1. Hebrew Bible

3. Hellenistic and Rabbinic Jewish Sources

4. Early Christian Literature

5. Greco-Roman Sources *(including inscriptions and papyri)*

Achilles Tatius

Leucippe et Clitophon
6.19.4.4   165 n. 29

Aelian

VH
2.7   40

Aelius Theon of Alexandria

Progymnasmata
178–182   115–16

Aesop   20

Anonyma in Aristotelis artem
  rhetoricam commentaria

In Aristotelis artem rhetoricam commentarium
(1418a1)   114–15, 116

Anonyma in ethica Nicomachea
  commentaria

Heliodori in Ethica Nicomachea paraphrasis
140.26–29   113

Appian

BC
1.26   89 n. 89, 184 n. 121
1.54   89 n. 89, 184 n. 121
1.58   89 n. 89, 184 n. 121
1.65   89 n. 89, 184 n. 121
1.69   88–89
2.74.308   59 n. 206
4.44   131

Gall.
1.2   32 n. 77

Iber.
68   32 n. 78

Mith.
12.17.117   38 n. 108

Pun.
15   32 n. 78
23   32 n. 78
26   32 n. 78
36   32 n. 78

48   32 n. 78

Apuleius
Met.
9.12   47 n. 160

Aretaeus of Cappadocia
De curatione diuturnorum morborum libri duo
1.3.8.5–9.1   110

Aristides
Or.
2.44–46   165 n. 29
3.119   165 n. 29
3.123   165 n. 29
3.281   165 n. 29
4.387   165 n. 29

Aristophanes

F 354   70

Aristotle   14, 26–27, 45, 46, 52,
               59

Pol.
1.3 (1253b)   97 n. 125
1.4 (1253b)   18
1.1–7 (1252a–56a)   26
1.12–13
  (1259b–60b)   97 n. 125
Rhet.
2.13.13–14
  (1390a.15)   165 n. 29

Arrian (Flavius Arrianus)
          (*see* Epictetus)

Artemidorus   28–29

Aspasius
In ethica Nicomachea commentaria
123.21–23   117

Athenaeus
Deipnosophistai
6.262–73   28 n. 63

6.11665	65
6.12236	65
6.12245	65
6.12333	65
6.12692	65
6.14277	65
6.16302	65
6.16330	65
6.16759	65
6.18520	65
6.19078	65
6.19250	65
6.19521	65
6.19755	65
6.19798	65
6.19873	65
6.20252	65
6.20972	65
6.21145	65
6.21644	65
6.21666	65
6.21867	65
6.22082	65
6.22186	65
6.22272	65
6.22443	65
6.22928	65
6.23226	65
6.23515	65
6.23690	65
6.23859	65
6.24504	65
6.24891	65
6.24918	65
6.25177	65
6.25219	65
6.25339	65
6.25867	65
6.26104	65
6.26153	65
6.26167	65
6.26302	65
6.26361	65
6.26497	65
6.27959	57–60, 65
6.29624	65
6.31183	65
6.33813	58
6.34288	65

6.34434	65
6.34513	65
6.34566	65
6.35103	65
6.35162	65
6.35310	65
6.35669	65
6.36019	65
6.36127	65
6.37487	65
6.37594	65
6.37616	65
6.37761	65
6.37916	65
6.38376	65
6.38965	65
6.371716	65
10.1931	65
10.6675	146 n. 76
11.4771	151 n. 98
13.1954	37 n. 105
13.2056	126 n. 210
13.7070	23
14.2874	151 n. 98
14.2875	151 n. 98
14.2877	151 n. 98
14.2878	151 n. 98
14.3579.23	126 n. 210

Cod. Theod.

9.12.1	96
16.8.6	176 n. 76
16.9.2	176 n. 76

Collection of Ancient Greek
  Inscriptions in the British
  Museum, ed. G. Hirsch-
  feld, 4.1.795   143–44

Columella	28

R.R.

1.8.5	34 n. 86
1.8.19	34 n. 86

Crinagoras

Anthologia Graeca
| 9.284 | 71–72 |

6. Modern Authors

7. Subjects